Memoirs of Aaron Burr

With Miscellaneous Selections from His Correspondence

By

Matthew Livingston Davis

Published by Forgotten Books 2012

Originally Published 1837

PIBN 1000537595

MEMOIRS

OF

AARON BURR.

WITH

MISCELLANEOUS SELECTIONS

FROM

HIS CORRESPONDENCE

BY MATTHEW L. DAVIS.

"I come to bury Cæsar, not to praise him."

IN TWO VOLUMES.

VOL. I.

NEW-YORK:

PUBLISHED BY HARPER & BROTHERS
NO. 82 CLIFF-STREET.

1837.

PREFACE.

DURING a period of forty years I was intimately acquainted with Colonel Burr, and have reason to suppose that I possessed his entire confidence. Some time after his return from Europe in 1812, on different occasions, he suggested casually a wish that I would make notes of his *political* life. When the Memoirs and Correspondence of Mr. Jefferson were published, he was much excited at the statements which were made in his Ana respecting the presidential contest in Congress in 1801.

He procured and sent me a copy of the work, with a request that I would peruse the parts designated by him. From this time forward he evinced an anxiety that I would prepare his Memoirs, offering me the use of all his private papers, and expressing a willingness to explain any doubtful points, and to dictate such parts of his early history as I might require. These propositions led to frequent and full conversations. I soon discovered that Colonel Burr was far more tenacious of his *military*, than of his professional, political, or moral character. His prejudices against General Washington were immoveable. They were formed in the summer of 1776, while he resided at headquarters; and they were confirmed unchangeably by the injustice which he said he had experienced at the hands of the

commander-in-chief immediately after the battle of Long
Island, and the retreat of the American army from the city
of New-York. These grievances he wished to mingle
with his own history; and he was particularly anxious to
examine the military movements of General Washington
on different occasions, but more especially at the battle of
Monmouth, in which battle Colonel Burr commanded a
brigade in Lord Stirling's division. I peremptorily refused
entering upon any such discussion; and, for some time,
all communication on the subject ceased.

Colonel Burr, however, renewed the conversation rela
tive to his Memoirs, and agreed that any thing which might
be written should be confined to himself. With this understanding I frequently visited him, and made notes under
his dictation. I never asked him a question on any subject, or in relation to any man or measure, that he did not
promptly and willingly answer. On his part there was no
desire of concealment; nor did he ever express to me a
wish to suppress an account of any act of his whole life.
So far as I could judge, his only apprehensions were that
"*kind friends*" as he sometimes termed them, by attempts
at explanation, might unintentionally misrepresent acts which
they did not understand.

I devoted the summer of 1835 to an examination of his
letters and papers, of which there is an immense quantity.
The whole of them were placed in my hands, to be used
at my discretion. I was authorized to take from among
them whatever I supposed would aid me in preparing the
contemplated book.

I have undertaken the work, aware of the delicacy and
responsibility of the task. But, if I know myself, it has

been performed with the most scrupulous regard to my own reputation for correctness. I have aimed to state facts, and the fair deductions from them, without the slightest intermixture of personal feeling. I am very desirous that a knowledge of Mr. Burr's character and conduct should be derived from his miscellaneous correspondence, and not from what his biographer might write, unsupported by documentary testimony. With this view many of his private letters are selected for publication.

I entertain a hope that I shall escape the charge of egotism. I have endeavoured to avoid *that* ground of offence, whatever may have been my literary sins in other respects. It is proper for me, however, in this place, and for a single purpose, to depart from the course pursued in the body of the work. It is a matter of perfect notoriety, that among the papers left in my possession by the late Colonel Burr, there was a mass of letters and copies of letters written or received by him, from time to time, during a long life, indicating no very strict morality in some of his female correspondents. These letters contained matter that would have wounded the feelings of families more extensively than could be imagined. Their publication would have had a most injurious tendency, and created heartburnings that nothing but time could have cured.

As soon as they came under my control I mentioned the subject to Colonel Burr; but he prohibited the destruction of any part of them during his lifetime. I separated them, however, from other letters in my possession, and placed them in a situation that made their publication next to impossible, whatever might have been my own fate. As soon as Colonel Burr's decease was known, with my own hands I committed to the fire all such correspondence, and not a vestige of it now remains..

It is with unaffected reluctance that this statement of facts is made; and it never would have been made but for circumstances which have transpired since the decease of Colonel Burr. A mere allusion to these circumstances will, it is trusted, furnish ample justification. No sooner had the newspapers announced the fact that the Memoirs of Colonel Burr were to be written by me, than I received letters from various quarters of the country, inquiring into the nature of the revelations that the book would make, and deprecating the introduction of individual cases. These letters came to hand both anonymously and under known signatures, expressing intense solicitude for suppression.

Under such circumstances, am I not only warranted in these remarks, but imperiously called upon to make them? What other mode remained to set the public mind at ease? I have now stated what must for ever hereafter preclude all possibility for cavil on one part, or anxiety on the other. I *alone* have possessed the private and important papers of Colonel Burr; and I pledge my honour that every one of them, so far as I know and believe, that could have injured the feelings of a female or those of her friends, is destroyed. In order to leave no chance for distrust, I will add, that I never took, or permitted to be taken, a single copy of any of these letters; and, of course, it is quite impossible that any publication hereafter, if any should be made of such papers or letters, can have even the pretence of authenticity.

THE AUTHOR

New-York, November 15th, 1836.

CONTENTS

OF

THE FIRST VOLUME.

CHAPTER IV.

CHAPTER V.

CHAPTER VI.

CHAPTER VII.

CHAPTER X.

CHAPTER XI.

CHAPTER XII.

CHAPTER XIII.

CHAPTER XIV.

CHAPTER XV.

CHAPTER XVIII.

MEMOIRS

OF

AARON BURR

MEMOIRS

OF

AARON BURR.

CHAPTER I.

THE grandfather of Colonel AARON BURR, the subject of these memoirs, was a German by birth, and of noble parentage. Shortly after his arrival in North America, he settled in Fairfield, Connecticut, where he purchased a large tract of land, and reared a numerous family. A part of this landed estate remained in the possession of his lineal descendants until long after the revolutionary war. During Colonel Burr's travels in Germany, in the year 1809, various communications were made to him, orally and in writing, by different branches of the Burr family, some of whom were then filling high and distinguished scientific and literary stations.

His father, the Rev. Aaron Burr, was born in Fairfield, on the 4th day of January, 1715, and was educated at Yale College. In a manuscript journal which he kept, and which has been preserved, he says, "In September, 1736, with many fears and doubts about my qualifications (being under clouds with respect to my spiritual state), I offered myself to trials, and was approved as a candidate for the ministry. My first sermon was preached at Greenfield, and immediately after I came into the Jerseys. I can hardly give any account why I came here. After I had preached for some time at Hanover, I had a call by the people of New

VOL. I.—C

ark; but there was scarce any probability that I should suit their circumstances, being young in standing and trials. I accepted of their invitation, with a reserve, that I did not come with any views of settling. My labours were universally acceptable among them, and they manifested such great regard and love for me, that I consented to accept of the charge of their souls.

"A. D. 1738–39, January the 25th, I was set apart to the work of the ministry, by fasting, prayer, and imposition of hands. God grant that I may ever keep fresh upon my mind the solemn charge that was then given me; and never indulge trifling thoughts of what then appeared to me of such awful importance. The ministers who joined in this solemn transaction were Mr. Dickinson, who gave the charge, and Mr. Pierson, who preached. Mr. Dickinson, who presided at this work, has been of great service to me by his advice and instruction, both before and since my ordination.

"In November, 1739, I made a visit to my friends in New-England, and again in March, 1740. In the following August I was in a declining state of health, and by the advice of my physicians visited Rhode Island. From thence I proceeded to Boston. On the 19th of September I heard Mr. Whitefield preach in Dr. Colman's church. I am more and more pleased with the man. On the 21st, heard him preach in the Commons to about ten thousand people. On Monday, visited him, and had some conversation to my great satisfaction. On the 23d, went to hear him preach in Mr. Webb's church, but the house was crowded before Mr. Whitefield came. The people, especially the women, were put into a fright, under a mistaken notion that the galleries were falling, which caused them to hurry out in such a violent manner, that many were seriously injured and five killed. The same day, Mr. Whitefield preached at Mr. Gee's church. In the evening he preached at Dr. Sewall's church. On Saturday I went to hear him in the Commons; there were about eight thousand hearers. He expounded the parable of the prodigal son in a very moving manner. Many melted into tears. On the 4th of October, being on my return to New-Jersey, I arrived at Fairfield, where I remained two days with my friends."

In the year 1748, Governor Belcher, of New-Jersey, by and with the approbation of his Majesty's Council, granted a charter to the college of New-Jersey, subsequently known as Nassau Hall. This college was opened in Newark, the students living in private families. The Rev. Aaron Burr was appointed the first president. In the year 1754 or 1755, the trustees commenced erecting the college in Princeton; and in 1757 it was so far completed that the students, about seventy in number, were removed to the building.

In June, 1752, President Burr, being then in his 38th year, was married to Esther Edwards, the daughter of Jonathan Edwards, a distinguished metaphysician and divine. He was the second president of Princeton College, being called to that station on the decease of his son-in-law, President Burr. Thus, the father of Colonel Aaron Burr, and the grandfather on his mother's side, were, in succession, at the head of that seminary of learning.

President Burr was alike celebrated for his eloquence and piety ; but, withal, he possessed no inconsiderable degree of eccentricity. His courtship and marriage partook of it. Miss Edwards, after the preliminaries were arranged, was brought to New-Jersey to be married. The occurrence created much conversation, and gave rise to some newspaper commentary. The following is extracted from the New-York Gazette of the 20th of July, 1752.

" A letter to a gentleman from his friend, dated

" July 7th, 1752.

" SIR,

" As you are a known and peculiar votary to the state of celibacy, I judged it would do you no disservice to acquaint you of a late occurrence, which sufficiently evidences, that after the most mature consideration, some of our wisest and best men do prefer the endearment of the nuptial bed.

"About eight days since, the Rev. Aaron Burr, president of the College of New-Jersey, was married to a daughter of the renowned Mr. Jonathan Edwards, late of Northampton. She is a young lady of about twenty-one. Her person may be called agreeable ; her natural genius seems to be sprightly, and, no doubt, is greatly improved by a very virtuous education. In short, she appears to be one every way qualified to make a man of sense and piety happy in the conjugal relation. As to the courtship or marriage, I shall not descend to particulars ; but only observe, in general, that, for some centuries, I suppose there has not been one more in the patriarchal mode.

"I hope, sir, that this instance, both as to matter and form, will have its genuine influence upon you, and as well bear a part in convincing you that wedlock is incomparably preferable to the roving uneasiness of the single state, as to direct you, when you are choosing your mate, that, instead of acting the modern gallant, wisely to imitate this example, and endeavour to restore courtship and marriage to their original simplicity and design.

"PHILOGAMUS."

At different times Colonel Burr received friendly anonymous and other communications, recommending to him the practice of a religious life. It is a remarkable fact, that in almost every such instance he is referred to the letters of his mother. From a communication to him, written by a lady, the following is extracted. If it should meet her eye as it probably will, it is hoped that she will pardon this freedom. Her name is suppressed, and will not be known, unless through her own instrumentality.

" My Dear Sir,

" I trust the purity of the motives by which I am actuated will find an apology in your bosom for the liberty I assume in addressing you on a subject which involves your eternal interest.

" Here, in the wilds of ——, I have found an extract of a letter, written by your inestimable mother nearly sixty years ago, of which you are the principal subject; and a transcript of which I shall enclose for your perusal. Perhaps you will think me a weak, presumptuous being; but permit me, dear sir, to assure you, this does not proceed from a whim of the moment. It is not a mere transient gust of enthusiasm. The subject has long been heavy on my mind. I have more than once resolved to converse with you freely; to tell you how my own feelings were affected relative to your situation; but my faltering tongue refused to obey the impulse of my soul, and I have withdrawn abruptly, to conceal that which I had not confidence to communicate. But meeting (I believe providentially) with this precious relic has determined me. I will write, and transmit it to you. I am too well convinced of the liberality of your sentiments; but I still believe you retain an inherent respect for the religion of your forefathers.

" I have often reflected on your trials, and the fortitude with which you have sustained them, with astonishment. Yours has been no common lot. But you seem to have forgotten the right use of adversity. Afflictions from Heaven 'are angels sent on embassies of love.' We must improve, and not abuse them, to obtain the blessing. They are commissioned to stem the tide of impetuous passion; to check inordinate ambition; to show us the insignificance of earthly greatness; to wean our affections from transitory things, and elevate them to those realities which are ever blooming at the right hand of God. When affliction is thus sanctified, ' the heart at once it humbles and exalts.'

"Was it philosophy that supported you in your trials? There is an hour approaching when philosophy will fail, and all human science will desert you. What then will be your substitute? Tell me, Colonel Burr, or rather answer it to your own heart, when the pale messenger appears, how will you meet him—'undamped by doubts, undarkened by despair?'

"The enclosed is calculated to excite mingled sensations both of a melancholy and pleasing nature. The hand that penned it is now among 'the just made perfect.' Your mother had given you up by faith. Have you ever ratified the vows she made in your behalf? When she bade you a long farewell, she commended you to the protection of Him who had promised to be a father to the fatherless.

"The great Augustine, in his early years, was an infidel in his principles, and a libertine in his conduct, which his pious mother deplored with bitter weeping. But she was told by her friends that 'the child of so many prayers and tears could not be lost;' and it was verified to her happy experience, for he afterward became one of the grand luminaries of the church of Christ. This remark has often been applied to you; and I trust you will yet have the happiness to find that 'the prayers of the righteous' have 'availed much.'

"One favour I would ask : when you have done with this, destroy it, that it may never meet the eye of any third person. In the presence of that God, before whom the inmost recesses of the heart are open, I have written. I consulted him, and him only, respecting the propriety of addressing it to you; and the answer he gave was, freedom in writing, with a feeling of the deepest interest impressed upon my heart.

"Z. Y

"To Col. A. Burr."

"Princeton, Nov. 2, 1757.

. "HONOURED SIR,

" Your most affectionate, comforting letter, by my brother, was exceedingly refreshing to me, although I was some-what damped that I should not see you until spring. But it is my comfort in this disappointment, as well as under all my afflictions, that God knows what is best for me and for his own glory. Perhaps I depended too much on the company and conversation of such a near, and dear, and affectionate father and guide. I cannot doubt but all is for the best, and I am satisfied that God should order the affair of your removal as shall be for his glory, whatever comes of me. Since I wrote my mother's letter, God has carried me through new trials, and given me new supports. My little son* has been sick with the slow fever ever since my brother left us, and has been brought to the brink of the grave. But I hope, in mercy, God is bringing him up again. I was enabled to resign the child (after a severe struggle with nature) with the greatest freedom. God showed me that the child was not my own, but his, and that he had a right to recall what he had lent whenever he thought fit; and I had no reason to complain, or say God dealt hard with me. This silenced me. But how good is God ! He hath not only kept me from complaining, but comforted me, by enabling me to offer up the child by faith. I think, if ever I acted faith, I saw the fulness there was in Christ for little infants, and his willingness to accept of such as were offered to him. ' Suffer little chil-dren to come unto me, and forbid them not, for of such is the kingdom of God,' were comforting words. God also showed me, in such a lively manner, the fulness that was in himself of all spiritual blessings, that I said, Although all

---

* Col. Burr, at that time about twenty months old.

streams were cut off, yet, so long as my God lives, I have enough. He enabled me to say—' Although thou slay me, yet will I trust in thee.' In this time of trial I was led to enter into a renewed and explicit covenant with God, in a more solemn manner than ever before, and with the great est freedom and delight. After much self-examination and prayer, I did give up myself and children to God with my whole heart. Never, until now, had I a sense of the privi lege we are allowed in covenanting with God! This act of my soul left my mind in a quiet and steady trust in God A few days after this, one evening, in talking of the glori ous state my dear departed must be in, my soul was car ried out in such longing desires after this glorious state, that I was forced to retire from the family to conceal my joy. When alone, I was so transported, and my soul car ried out in such eager desires after perfection, and the full enjoyment of God, and to serve him uninterruptedly, that I think my nature would not have borne much more. I think I had that night a foretaste of Heaven. This frame continued, in some good degree, the whole night. I slept but little ; and when I did, my dreams were all of heav- enly and divine things. Frequently since I have felt the same in kind, though not in degree. Thus a kind and gracious God has been with me in six troubles, and in seven. But, oh ! sir, what cause of deep humiliation and abasement of soul have I, on account of remaining corrup- tion which I see working, especially pride ! Oh, how many shapes does pride cloak itself in ! Satan is also busy shooting his darts ; but, blessed be God, those temp- tations of his that used to overthrow me, as yet, have not touched me. Oh to be delivered from the power of Satan as well as sin ! I cannot help hoping the time is near. God is certainly fitting me for himself ; and when I think it will be soon that I shall be called hence, the thought is transporting.

         " Your dutiful and affectionate daughter,

                   " Esther Burr "

Such were the parents of Colonel Aaron Burr. Of the natural guardianship and protection of both he was deprived before he had reached the third year of his age. He was born on the 6th of February, 1756, in Newark, State of New-Jersey. His father died in August, 1757, and his mother the year following, leaving two children, Aaron, and his sister Sarah. She subsequently became the wife of Judge Tappan Reeve, of Connecticut. On the decease of his father, Colonel Burr inherited a handsome estate.

In the year 1760 Aaron was sent to Philadelphia, under the care of an aunt and Dr. Shippen. For the family of the doctor he entertained a high degree of respect. He frequently spoke of them in the kindest terms, and recurred to this early period of his history with emotions of gratitude for their care and protection.

Boswell, in his Life of Johnson, remarks that, " In following so very eminent a man from his cradle to his grave, every minute particular which can throw light on the progress of his mind, is interesting." Johnson himself, in the Life of Sydenham, says " There is no instance of any man, whose history has been minutely related, that did not, in every part of life, discover the same proportion of intellectual vigour."

These high authorities are now quoted in justification of some of the details which will be given in the progress of this work, and which, in themselves, may appear trifling and unimportant. When Aaron was about four years old, he had some misunderstanding with his preceptor, in consequence of which he ran away, and was not found until the third or fourth day after his departure from home; thus indicating, at a tender age, that fearlessness of mind, and determination to rely upon himself, which were characteristics stamped upon every subsequent act of his life.

CHAPTER II.

In 1761 he was removed to Stockbridge, in Massachusetts, and placed in the family of Timothy Edwards, his mother's eldest brother. In 1762 his maternal uncle, Timothy, removed to Elizabethtown, New-Jersey. Aaron and his sister Sarah remained in the family until the former entered college, and the latter became the wife of Judge Reeve. A private tutor was employed for them in the house of Mr. Edwards. For a considerable portion of the time, Judge Reeve was engaged in that capacity.

When about ten years old, Aaron evinced a desire to make a voyage to sea; and, with this object in view, ran away from his uncle Edwards, and came to the city of New-York. He entered on board an outward-bound vessel as cabin-boy. He was, however, pursued by his guardian, and his place of retreat discovered. Young Burr, one day, while busily employed, perceived his uncle coming down the wharf, and immediately ran up the shrouds, and clambered to the topgallant-mast head. Here he remained, and peremptorily refused to come down, or be taken down, until all the preliminaries of a treaty of peace were agreed upon. To the doctrine of unconditional submission he never gave his assent.

In 1769 Burr entered Princeton College; where, owing to his extreme youth and smallness of stature, he was forced to commence with the sophomore, although, upon examination, he was found qualified to enter the junior class. This was a source of extreme mortification to him, and especially as he had been prepared, and was every way qualified, to enter the preceding year. From his infancy Burr was of a slender frame, and appeared to be delicately formed; but exhibited great muscular strength, and was able to endure excessive fatigue of body and mind.

Previous to entering college, young Burr had formed extraordinary notions of the acquirements of collegiates; and felt great apprehension lest he should be found inferior to his classmates. He was therefore, at first, indefatigable as well as systematic in his studies. He soon discovered that he could not pursue them after dinner with the same advantage that he could before. He suspected that this was owing to his eating too abundantly. He made the experiment, and the result convinced him that his apprehensions were well founded. He immediately adopted a system of regimen, to which, in some degree, he adhered through life. So abstemious was he during the greater part of the first year after his entrance into college, that it operated powerfully upon him, and he was supposed to be in bad health. He was in the habit of studying sixteen or eighteen hours of the twenty-four, until the period of examination arrived, when he discovered that the progress he had made was so much beyond his associates, that he formed an opinion as contemptuous as it had been exalted of his college friends. The effect of this was ultimately very injurious upon his habits.

During the last year that he remained in college, he passed a life of idleness, negligence, and, in some measure, of dissipation. He applied himself but little to his studies, and was in the constant pursuit of pleasure. He graduated, however, when only sixteen years of age, with a reputation for talents, and receiving the highest academic honours the faculty could bestow.

In the year 1771–72, there was in the college what was termed, in religious phraseology, " an awakening." A large portion of the collegians became converted. It was only a short time before Burr graduated, and in the midst of his hilarity and amusements. He was frequently appealed to by his associates, and threatened with the most terrific consequences if there was not an inward as well as an outward change. From his infancy Burr's education had been strictly moral; and strong impressions had been made upon his mind as to the existence of a Deity, and the accountability of man. Yet this awakening did not seem to him right in all its parts. He determined, therefore, to have a free and full conversation with Dr. Witherspoon, the then president of the college, on the subject. The result of that conversation in some measure tranquillized young Burr. The Rev. Dr. assured him that it was not true and rational religion, but fanaticism, that was operating upon his friends.

Among the papers preserved by Colonel Burr are the originals of a number of essays or orations, written and read by him, in conformity with the regulations of the college, while yet a student. They are without dates; but, as he graduated in 1772, they must have been composed when he was of an age between thirteen and sixteen. A few of them are here inserted, as exhibiting his manner of writing, and the maturity and tone of his mind. The opinions which he formed, while yet in college, as to public speaking and the selection of language, he appears never to have changed. The style which he then recommended seems ever after to have been his model.

Read in College, by Aaron Burr.—On Style.

" I have often observed, that it is very common for those who are ambitious of excelling in composition, to study swelling words, pompous epithets, and laboured periods This is often practised, especially by young writers. It is, however, generally condemned as a fault, and sometimes too by those who practise it themselves. An elegant simplicity of language is what every one should strive to obtain. Besides the arguments which are usually offered on this head, there is one very important one, which is commonly not much attended to.

" It is the business of every writer to acquire command of

language, in order that he may be able to write with ease
and readiness, and, upon any occasion, to form extempore
discourses. Unless he can do this, he will never shine as a
speaker, nor will he ever make a figure in private conversation. But to do this, it is necessary to study simplicity of
style. There never was a ready speaker, whose language
was not, generally, plain and simple; for it is absolutely impossible to carry the laboured ornaments of language, the
round period, or the studied epithet, into extempore discourses; and, were it possible, it would be ridiculous. We
have learned, indeed, partly from reading poetry, and partly
from reading vicious compositions, to endure, and too often
to admire, such stiff and laboured discourses in writing; but
if it were even possible for a man to speak in the same pompous diction in which Browne has written his vulgar errors,
he would certainly be very disagreeable. This reason,
among others, may be assigned for it; that however such
false ornaments may please for a time, yet, when a long and
steady attention is required, we are tired and disgusted with
every thing which increases our labour, and diverts the attention from the subject before us. A laboured style is a
labour even to the hearer. A simple style, like simple food,
preserves the appetite. But a profusion of ornament, like a
profusion of sweets, palls the appetite and becomes disgusting.
A man might as soon think of filling his stomach with sweetmeats, as going through a long debate filled with pompous
epithets and sounding language. If we have any doubt of
its being ridiculous, let us only suppose a man arguing an
abstruse subject in metaphysics, in the blank verse of Mil-
ton, or the exact rhymes of Pope. The absurdity is the
same, only different in degree. I would not be understood
to cut off an extempore speaker from sublime expressions,
because I do not suppose these to be inconsistent with simplicity of style. I really doubt if there be any such thing
as sublimity of style, strictly speaking. But, indeed, rather
believe that the sublime depends upon the thoughts, which

are the more sublime by being clearly and simply expressed
This, however, is not material at present. It is certainly
impossible for a speaker to carry laboured periods into his
extempore discourses : it is no less certain, that in general,
a simple style is to be preferred, and that he would be ridiculous and disagreeable if he could do it ; and as extempore
speaking is a great object, which we ought to have in view
in the formation of our style, this may be used as one argument why we should study a simple style."

The Passions.

"Amid the variety of literary pieces which have in all
ages been ushered into the world, few, if any, afford greater
satisfaction than those that treat of man. To persons of a
speculative nature and elegant taste, whose bosoms glow
with benevolence, such disquisitions are peculiarly delightful. The reason, indeed, is obvious ; for what more neces
sary to be learned and accurately understood ? what more
near and interesting ? and, therefore, what more proper to
engage the attention ? Well may I say, with our ethic poet,

"'The proper study of mankind is man.'

"If we take a view of the body only, which may be called
the shell or external crust, we shall perceive it to be formed
with amazing nicety and art. How are we lost in wonder
when we behold all its component parts ; when we behold
them, although various and minute, and blended together almost beyond conception, discharging their peculiar functions
without the least confusion. All harmoniously conspiring
to one grand end.

"But when we take a survey of the more sublime parts
of the human frame ; when we behold man's internal make
and structure ; his mental faculties ; his social propensions,
and those active powers which set all in motion—the passions,—what an illustrious display of consummate wisdom is
presented to our admiring view ! What brighter mark—
what stronger evidence need we of a God ? The scanty

limits of a few minutes, to which I am confined, would not permit me, were I equal to the task, to enter into a particular examination of all man's internal powers. I shall therefore throw out a few thoughts on the passions only.

"Man's mental powers, being in their nature sluggish and inactive, cannot put themselves in motion. The grand design then of the passions is, to rouse them to action. These lively and vigorous principles make us eager in the pursuit of those things that are approved by the judgment; keep the mind intent upon proper objects, and at once awake to action all the powers of the soul. The passions give vivacity to all our operations, and render the enjoyments of life pleasing and agreeable. Without them, the scenes of the world would affect us no more than the shadowy pictures of a morning dream.

"Who can view the works of nature, and the productions of art, without the most sublime and rapturous emotions? Who can view the miseries of others, without being dissolved into compassion? Who can read human nature, as represented in the histories of the world, without burning to chastise the perpetrators of tyranny, or glowing to imitate the assertors of freedom? But, were we of a sudden stripped of our passions, we should survey the works of nature and the productions of art with indifference and neglect. We should be unaffected with the calamities of others, deaf to the calls of pity, and dead to all the feelings of humanity. Without generosity, benevolence, or charity, man would be a grovelling, despicable creature. Without the passions, man would hardly rank above the beasts.

"It is a trite truth, that the passions have too much influence over our sentiments and opinions. It is the remark of a late author, that the actions and sentiments of men do as naturally follow the lead of the passions, as the effect does the cause. Hence they are, by some, aptly enough, termed the principles of action. Vicious desires will produce vicious practices; and men, by permitting themselves to think of indulging irregular passions, corrupt the understanding, which is the source of all virtue and morality. The passions, then, if properly regulated, are the gentle gales which keep life from stagnating ; but, if let loose, the tempests which tear every thing before them. Too fatal observation will evince the truth of this.

" Do we not frequently behold men of the most sprightly genius, by giving the reins to their passions, lost to society, and reduced to the lowest ebb of misery and despair ? Do we not frequently behold persons of the most penetrating discernment and happy turn for polite literature, by mingling with the sons of sensuality and riot, blasted in the bloom of life ? Such was the fate of the late celebrated Duke of Wharton, Wilmot, earl of Rochester, and Villers, duke of Buckingham, three noblemen, as eminently distinguished by their wit, taste, and knowledge, as for their extravagance, revelry, and lawless passions. In such cases, the most charming elocution, the finest fancy, the brightest blaze of genius, and the noblest burst of thoughts, call for louder vengeance, and damn them to lasting infamy and shame.

" A greater curse cannot, indeed, befall community, than for princes and men in eminent departments to be under the influence of ill-directed passions. Lo Alexander and Cesar, the fabled heroes of antiquity, to what lengths did passion hurry them ? Ambition, with look sublime, bade them on, bade them grasp at universal dominion, and wade to empire through seas of blood ! But why need I confine myself to these ? Do not provinces, plundered and laid waste with fire and sword ; do not nations, massacred and slaughtered by the bloody hand of war ; do not all these dreadful and astonishing revolutions, recorded in the pages of history, show the fatal effects of lawless passions ?

" If the happiness of others could not, yet surely our own happiness should induce us to keep our passions within the bounds of reason ; for the passions, when unduly elevated, destroy the health, impair the mental faculties, sour the disposition, imbitter life, and make us equally disagreeable to others and uneasy to ourselves. Is it not, then, of moment, that our passions be duly balanced, their sallies confined within proper limits, and in no case suffered to transgress the bounds of reason? Will any one deny the importance of regulating the passions, when he considers how powerful they are, and that his own happiness, and perhaps the happiness of thousands, depends upon it? The regulation of the passions is a matter of moment, and therefore we should be careful to fix them upon right objects, to confine them within proper bounds, and never permit them to exceed the limits assigned by nature. It is the part of reason to sooth the passions, and to keep the soul in a pleasing serenity and calm : if reason rules, all is quiet, composed, and benign : if reason rules, all the passions, like a musical concert, are in unison. In short, our passions, when moderate, are accompanied with a sense of fitness and rectitude ; but, when excessive, inflame the mind, and hurry us on to action without due distinction of objects.

"Among uncivilized nations, the passions do, in general, exceed all rational bounds. Need we a proof of this ? Let us cast our eyes on the different savage tribes in the world, and we shall be immediately convinced that the passions rule without control. Happy it is, that in polished society, the passions, by early discipline, are so moderated as to be made subservient to the most important services. In this respect, seminaries of learning are of the utmost advantage, and attended with the most happy effects. Moreover, the passions are attended with correspondent commotions in animal nature, and, therefore, the real temper will, of course, be discovered by the countenance, the gesture, and the voice. Here I might run into a pleasing enumeration of many instances of this ; but, fearing that I have already trespassed upon your patience, shall desist. Permit me, however unusual, to close with a wish. May none of those unruly passions ever captivate any of my audience." ·

VOL. I.—E   2*

An Attempt to search the Origin of Idolatry.

" It is altogether impossible to fix exactly the period when idolatry took its rise.   Adam, coming immediately from the hands of God, had experienced too many manifestations of his power and goodness to be unacquainted with him, and must have preserved the purest idea of him in his own family, which, most probably, continued in the branch of Seth till the deluge.   The posterity of Cain, on the contrary (the pure idea of God gradually wearing away, and by loose men being connected with sense), fell into idolatry, and every other crime, which brought on the deluge ; a period about which Moses has said but little, and from what he has said we can draw no just conclusion with respect to the idolatry of those times.

" A certain author, being persuaded that idolatry did not take its rise till after the deluge, gives a very singular account of its origin.   According to him, atheism had spread itself over the world.   This disposition of mind, says he, is the capital crime.   Atheists are much more odious to the Divinity than idolaters.   Besides, this principle is much more capable of leading men into that excessive corruption the world fell into before the deluge.   The knowledge of a God, of whatever nature he is conceived, and the worship of a Deity, are apt, of themselves, to be a restraint upon men. So that idolatry was of some use to bear down the corruption of the world.   It is therefore probable, that the horrid vices men were fallen into before the deluge, proceeded only from their not knowing nor serving a God.   I am even of opinion (continues he) that the idolatry and polytheism after the deluge derived their origin from the atheism and impiety that reigned before it.   Such is the temper of men, when they have been severely punished for any crime, they run into the opposite extreme.   I conjecture (concludes the same author) this was the case with men after the deluge.   As they reckoned that this terrible judgment, which carried such indications of Divine wrath, was sent for the punish ment of atheism, they ran into the opposite extreme. They adored whatever seemed to deserve their worship.

" It is true, indeed, that idolatry is capable of furnishing a curb against irregularity of manners; but this author has conjectured, without foundation, that atheism reigned universally before the deluge. He ought, at least, to have excepted the posterity of Seth.

" However idolatry might have reigned before the deluge, it is certain that the knowledge and worship of the true God were again united in the family of Noah; and as long as the children and grandchildren of that patriarch made but one family, in all probability, the worship of the true God was little altered in its purity. Noah being at the head of the people, and Shem, Ham, and Japheth witnesses of God's vengeance on their contemporaries, is it probable that they, living in the midst of their families, would suffer them to depart from the truth? We read of nothing that can incline us to this belief. Various have been the conjectures concerning the authors of idolatry. Some believe it was Serug, the grandfather of Terah, who first introduced idolatry after the deluge. Others maintain it was Nimrod, and that he instituted the worship of fire among his subjects, which continues even to this day in some places in Persia. Others assert that Ham was the author of it, and then his son Canaan; and it is most probable that the unfortunate sons of an accursed father were the first who, following the propensity of their own heart, sought out sensible objects to which they might offer a superstitious worship. As the two sons of Ham, Canaan and Mizraim, settled, the one in Phœnicia, and the other in Egypt, it is probable that these were the first nurseries of idolatry; and the sun, being looked upon as the purest image of the Creator, was the first object of it. It is not probable that men would choose beings like themselves for the first objects of their adoration. Nothing could be more capable of seducing than the beauty and usefulness of the sun, dispensing light and fertility all around. But, to conclude, we must not imagine that all idolatry sprang from the same country. It came by slow degrees, and those who made the first advances towards this impiety, did by no means carry it to that extravagant height to which it afterwards arrived."

CHAPTER III.

IN college, young Burr formed intimacies which ripened into lasting friendship. The attachment between him and Colonel Matthias Ogden, of New-Jersey, was both ardent and mutual; and, it is believed, continued during the life of the latter. Colonel Knapp says, "Samuel Spring, D. D., late of Newburyport, was in college with Colonel Burr, and part of their college life was his chum. The doctor was a student of mature age, and had a provisitorial power over Burr in his daily duties. He has often spoken of his young friend with more than ordinary feeling. He, in fact, prophesied his future genius, from the early proofs he gave of intellectual power in the course of his college life."

At Princeton, Burr enjoyed the counsel and advice of the late William Paterson, subsequently one of the judges of the Supreme Court of the United States. To be thus early in life honoured with the respect and esteem of such a man as Judge Paterson, was highly flattering. Their correspondence commenced in 1772, and continued until the decease of the judge. Extracts from his letters to Colonel Burr will be given occasionally. He says, in a letter dated

."Princeton, January 17th, 1772.

" DEAR BURR,

" I am just ready to take horse, and therefore cannot have the pleasure of waiting on you in person. Be pleased to accept of the enclosed notes on *dancing*. If you pitch upon it as the subject of your next discourse, they may, perhaps, furnish you with a few hints, and enable you to compose with the greater facility and despatch. To do you any little services in my power will afford me great satisfaction, and I hope you will take the liberty (it is nothing more, my dear Burr, than the freedom of a friend) to call upon me whenever you think I can.

"When I shall be here again is uncertain—perhaps not before vacation. Forbear with me while I say *that you cannot speak too slow*. Your good judgment generally leads you to lay the emphasis on the most forcible word in the sentence ; so far you act very right. But the misfortune is, that you lay too great stress upon the emphatical word. Every word should be distinctly pronounced; one should not be so highly sounded as to drown another. To see you shine as a speaker would give great pleasure to your friends in general, and to me in particular. I say nothing of your own honour. The desire of making others happy will, to a generous mind, be the strongest incentive. I am much mistaken if such a desire has not great influence over you. You are certainly capable of making a good speaker. Exert yourself. I am in haste.

"Dear Burr, adieu.

"WM. PATERSON."

Another letter, dated

"Princeton, October 26th, 1772.

"DEAR BURR,

" Our mutual friend, Stewart, with whom I spent part of the evening, informed me you were still in Elizabethtown. You are much fonder of that place than I am, otherwise you would hardly be prevailed upon to make so long a stay. But, perhaps, the reason that I fear it, makes you like it. There is certainly something amorous in its very air. Nor is this a case any way extraordinary or beyond belief. I

have read (and it was in point, too) that a flock of birds, being on the wing, and bending their flight towards a certain
town in Connecticut, dropped down dead just as they were
over it. The people were at first fairly at a loss to account
for this phenomenon in any natural way. However, it was
at length agreed on all hands that it was owing to the noi-
someness of the atmosphere, the smallpox at that time being very rife in the place. I should never have given credit
to the report, had it not come from so good a quarter as that
of New-England. For my part, I always drive through
Elizabethtown as quickly as possible, lest the soft infection
should steal upon me, or I should take it in with the very
air I breathe.

" Yesterday I went to hear Mr. Halsey, and there, too, I
saw his young and blooming wife. The old gentleman
seems very fond of his rib, and, in good sooth, leers very
wistfully at her as she trips along by his side. Some allowance, however, must be made ; he is in the vale of life ;
love is a new thing to him, and the honey-moon is not yet
over.

> ' They are amorous, and fond, and billing,
> Like Philip and Mary on a shilling.'

I have promised to pay him a visit; Stewart, or some of the
tutors, I believe, will accompany me, and I hope you will
too.

" Since commencement I have been at a Dutch wedding,
and expect to be at one or two more very shortly. There
was drinking, and singing, and fiddling, and dancing. I was
pleased extremely. Every one seemed to be in good-humour with himself, and this naturally led them all to be in
good-humour with one another.

" When the itch of scribbling seizes me, I hardly know
when to stop. The fit, indeed, seldom comes upon me;
but when it does, though I sit down with a design to be
short, yet my letter insensibly slides into length, and swells
perhaps into an enormous size. I know not how it hap-

pens, but on such occasions I have a knack of throwing myself out on paper that I cannot readily get the better of.   It
is a sign, however, that I more than barely esteem the person I write to, as I have constantly experienced that my
hand but illy performs its office unless my heart concurs.   I
confess I cannot conceive how I got into so scribbling a vein
at present.   It is now past eleven o'clock at night, and besides being on horse the greater part of the day, I intend
to start early to-morrow for Philadelphia.   There I shall
see the races, and the play, and, what is of more value far
than all, there, too, I shall see Miss ———, you know who.

"The enclosed letter to Spring I commit to your care.   I
should have sent it before, as I wrote it immediately after
you left this place, but I really thought you were in New-
England long ere now.   I know not his address; perhaps
he is at Newport, perhaps he is not.   If, on inquiry, you
find that the letter is wrongly directed, pray give it an en-
velope, and superscribe it anew.   If he is still at Newport,
it would, perhaps, more readily reach him from New-York
than from any part of New-England that you may be at.   I
have said that if I am mistaken in directing the within letter, you should cover it and give it the proper address.   Do,
dear Burr, get somebody who can write at least a passable
hand to back it, for you give your letters such a sharp, slender, and lady-like cast, that almost every one, on seeing
them, would conclude there was a correspondence kept up
between my honest friend Spring and some of the female
tribe, which might, perhaps, affect him extremely in point
of reputation, as many people suppose that nothing of this
kind can be carried on between unmarried persons of the
two sexes without being tinged with love; and the rather
so, since the notion of Platonic love is, at the present day,
pretty generally, and I believe justly too, exploded.   Platonic love is arrant nonsense, and rarely, if ever, takes place
until the parties have at least passed their grand climacteric.
Besides, the New-England people, I am told, are odd, in-

quisitive kind of beings, and, when pricked on by foolish
curiosity, may perhaps open the letter, which I do not
choose should be common to every eye.

"You gave me some hopes that you would see my good
friend Reeve before you returned. If you do, make him my
respectful compliments, and tell him that I fully designed to
write him, but that business prevented, that laziness hinder-
ed, that—in short, tell him any thing, so it does not impeach
my affection, or lead him to think I have entirely forgotten
him. I am,

"Dear Burr yours sincerely,
."WM. PATERSON."

In a letter to Dr. Spring, dated October 5, 1772, speaking
of the commencement, Judge Paterson says :—"The young
gentlemen went through their exercises in a manner passable enough. The speakers were all tolerable—none of them
very bad nor very good. Our young friend Burr made a
graceful appearance ; he was excelled by none, except perhaps by Bradford. Linn, too, was pretty generally approved ; but, for my part, I could not forbear thinking that he
took rant, and rage, and madness for true spirit—a very
common mistake."

For some months after Burr graduated (1772), he remained in college, reviewing his past studies, and devoting his
time to general literature. Possessed of an ample income,
having access to the college library, and continuing, from
time to time, as his correspondence shows, to supply himself with scientific and literary productions, his mind was
greatly. improved during this period. It is true he continued to indulge in amusements and pleasures ; but, sleeping
little, seldom more than six hours, he found ample time for
study. .

In the college there was a literary club, consisting of the
graduates and professors, and still known as *The Clio-So-
phic Society*. Dr. Samuel S. Smith, subsequently presi-

dent of the college, was then (1773) a professor. With him young Burr was no favourite, and their dislike was mutual. The attendance of the professors was expected to be regular. The members of the society in rotation presided over its deliberations. On a particular occasion it was the duty of young Burr to take the chair. At the hour of meeting he took his seat as president. Dr. Smith had not then arrived ; but, shortly after the business commenced, he entered. Burr, leaning on one arm of the chair (for, although now sixteen years of age, he was too small to reach both arms at the same time), began lecturing Professor Smith for his non-attendance at an earlier hour, remarking that a different example to younger members was expected from him, and expressing a hope that it might not again be necessary to recur to the subject. Having finished his lecture, to the great amusement of the society, he requested the professor to resume his seat. The incident, as may well be imagined, long served as a college joke.

FROM TIMOTHY DWIGHT.

New-Haven, March, 1772.

. Dear Aaron,

By a poor candle, with poor eyes and a poorer brain, I sit down to introduce a long wished-for correspondence. You see how solicitous I am to preserve old connexions ; or, rather, to begin new ones. Relationship, by the fashionable notions of those large towns, which usurp a right to lead and govern our opinions, is dwindled to a formal nothing—a mere shell of ceremony. Our ancestors, whose honesty and sim plicity (though different from the wise refinements of mod ern politeness) were perhaps as deserving of imitation as the insincere coldness of the present generation, *cousin'd* it to the tenth degree of kindred. Though this was extending the matter to a pitch of extravagance, yet it was certainly founded upon a natural, rational principle. Who are so naturally our friends as those who are born such ? I defy a

New-Yorker, though callous'd over with city politeness, to be otherwise than pleased with a view of ancient hospitality to relations, when exercised by a person of good-breeding and a genteel education.

Now, say you, what has this to do with the introduction of a correspondence? You shall know directly, sir. The *Edwardses* have been always remarkable for this fondness for their relations. If you have the least inclination to prove yourself a true descendant of that respectable stock, you cannot fail of answering me very soon. This (were I disposed) I could demonstrate by algebra and syllogisms in a twinkling; but hope you will believe me without either. I never asked for many connexions in this way; and was never neglected but once, and that by a Jersey gentleman, to whom I wrote and received no answer. I hope the disease is not epidemical, and that you have not determined against any communication with the rest of the world. It was a mortification, I confess; for I am too proud to be denied a request, though unreasonable, as many of mine are—therefore, I insist upon an answer, at least, and as many more as you can find in your heart to give me; promising, in return, as many by tale, though without a large profit. I shall not warrant their quality.

Your sincere friend,
Timothy Dwight, Junr.

FROM SAMUEL SPRING.

Newport, May 15th, 1772.

Dear Burr,

It is a little strange to me that I have not heard any thing of you since your examination. I don't know but you are dissatisfied, since you are so backward to write; however, I will, if possible, keep such thoughts out of my mind till I hear from you in particular. If you are let down a peg lower, you may tell me of it. If you are permitted to live in college, you may tell me of it; and if you are turned out,

you may tell me of it.   If you passed examination, and have
a syllogism to speak at commencement, *if you are able to
make it,* I suppose you may tell me of that likewise ; or, if
you are first in the class, you may tell me, if you will only
do it softly ; indeed, you may tell me any thing, for I profess to be your friend.   Therefore, since you can trust me
so far, I expect you will now write, and let me know a little
how matters are at present in college.   In particular, let me
know the state of the society (Cliosophic) ; and if I owe any
thing to it, do you pay it, *and charge it to your humble servant.*

I hope you will write the first opportunity, as I trust you
have got some very good news to tell me concerning the
college in general, and yourself in particular.   I have nothing
particular to write.   It is very pleasant to me where I am
at present.

The study of divinity is agreeable ;—far more so than any
other study whatever would be to me.   I hope to see the
time when you will feel it to be your duty to go into the
same study with a desire for the ministry.   Remember, that
was the prayer of your dear father and mother, and is the
prayer of your friends to this time—that you should step
forth into his place, and make it manifest that you are a
friend to Heaven, and that you have a taste for its glory.
But this, you are sensible, can never be the case if you remain in a state of nature.   Therefore, improve the present
and future moments to the best of purposes, as knowing
the time will soon be upon you when you will wish that in
living you had lived right, and acted rationally and like an
immortal.

Your friend,

SAMUEL SPRING.

In 1806–7 great excitement was produced, in consequence
of Colonel Burr writing in cipher to General Wilkinson.   In
this particular he seems to have had peculiar notions.   How-

ever innocent his correspondence, he was, apparently, desirous at all times of casting around it a veil of mystery. The
same trait was conspicuous in his political movements and
intercourse. This has been one of the weak points in Colonel
Burr's character. He was considered a mysterious man;
and what was not understood by the vulgar, was pronounced
selfish or ambitious intrigue. Even his best friends were
often dissatisfied with him on this account. Acting upon
this principle of mystery at every period of his life, he has
corresponded with one or more individuals in cipher. While
yet a student in college, the letters between his sister and
himself are frequently written in cipher. So, also, much
of his correspondence with his most intimate friend, Matthias Ogden, and with others in 1774 and 1775, is in cipher.
Many of these letters, thus written, are now in existence.
To those, therefore, acquainted with the character and pe-
culiarities of Colonel Burr, the fact of his writing a letter in
cipher would not be considered as any thing extraordinary;
because it was a habit which he had adopted and pursued
for more than thirty years preceding the period when this
excitement was thus produced.

Before Burr left Princeton, and while he was indulging
himself in pleasures and amusements, he accidentally visited
a billiard-table. He engaged in play, and, although he had
never before seen the game, he was successful, and won
about half a Joe. On returning home with his gains, he reflected on the incident with great mortification, and determined never again to play; which determination he adhered
to through life. Colonel Burr not only abstained from
playing at billiards, but with equal pertinacity he refused to
play at any game for the purpose of acquiring money.

Although he had been somewhat tranquillized by his conversation with Dr. Witherspoon on the subject of the awakening in college in 1772, yet he was not entirely at ease.
In consequence of which he came to a resolution not to enter
upon the concerns of life until this point was more satis-

factorily settled in his own mind.   He concluded, therefore, to visit and consult the Rev. Joseph Bellamy, a venerable and devoted friend of his late father, and to whom he was known by reputation.

Joseph Bellamy, D. D., was an eminent preacher and theological writer of Connecticut, and intimate friend of Colonel Burr's relative, the famous Jonathan Edwards, with whose particular opinion he fully agreed.   He was celebrated in his days, before the establishment of theological seminaries, as an instructer of young men preparing for the ministry. The late Governor Wolcott used to speak of him with the highest respect for his talent and moderation.   He died in 1790.

In the autumn of 1773, Burr visited him at Bethlehem, in Connecticut, and was received by his aged friend in a most kind and affectionate manner.   His advice, and the use of his library, were promptly tendered.   Burr commenced a course of reading on religious topics, and was thus occupied from sixteen to eighteen hours a day.   His habits were those of great abstinence, and a recluse.   His conversations with the reverend divine were encouraged and indulged in with freedom, and his inquiries answered.   Here he remained until the spring of 1774, when, to use his own language, he " came to the conclusion that the road to Heaven was open to all alike."   He, however, from that time forward, avoided most studiously all disputation on the subject of religion.

An impression has been created that Colonel Burr was placed by his guardian under Dr. Bellamy, for the purpose of studying divinity.   This is an error.   His visit to the Rev. Dr. was not the result of a conference or communication with any person whatever; but the volition of his own mind, and for the purpose already stated.   In fact, after Burr entered college, his studies and his future pursuits in life appear to have been left entirely under his own control. Whether this arose from indolence on the part of his guardian, or from pertinacity in young Burr, is uncertain; per-

haps a little of both, united with the great confidence which
his uncle reposed in his judgment and talents.

In the spring of 1774, while he yet resided at Dr. Bellamy's, he contemplated studying law; but was undecided
whether he should read with Pierpont Edwards, or with his
brother-in-law, Tappan Reeve, and upon this subject he
wrote his guardian, who replies, in a letter dated

" Stockbridge, February 11th, 1774.

" Whether you study law with Mr. Reeve or your uncle
Pierpont is a matter of indifference with me. I would have
you act your pleasure therein. I shall write to your uncle
upon it, but yet treat it as a matter of doubt. Your board I
shall settle with Dr. Bellamy myself. I will send you cash
to pay for your horse very soon. You may expect it in the
forepart of March. If I had known of this want of yours
sooner, I would have paid it before this.

" Your affectionate uncle,

" TIMOTHY EDWARDS."

CHAPTER IV.

IN May, 1774, he left the Rev. Mr. Bellamy's, and went
to the house of his brother-in-law, Tappan Reeve, where
his time was occupied in reading, principally history; but
especially those portions of it which related to wars, and
battles, and sieges, which tended to inflame his natural military ardour. The absorbing topics of taxation and the rights
of the people were agitating the then British colonies from
one extreme to the other. These subjects, therefore, could
not pass unnoticed by a youth of the inquiring mind and
ardent feelings of Burr. Constitutional law, and the relative rights of the crown and the colonists, were examined

with all the acumen which he possessed, and he became a whig from reflection and conviction, as well as from feeling.

At this period, Burr's most intimate and confidential correspondent was Matthias Ogden, of New-Jersey, subsequently Colonel Ogden, a gallant and distinguished revolutionary officer.   He writes to Burr, dated

"Elizabethtown, August 9th, 1774.

"Dear Aaron,

"I received yours by Mr. Beach, dated Sunday.   I am not a little pleased that you have the doctor (Bellamy) so completely under your thumb.   Last Saturday I went a crabbing.   Being in want of a thole-pin, I substituted a large jackknife in its stead, with the blade open and sticking up. It answered the purpose of rowing very well; but it seems that was not the only purpose it had to answer; for, after we had been some time on the flats, running on the mud, as the devil would have it, in getting into the boat I threw my leg directly across the edge of the knife, which left a decent mark of nearly four inches long, and more than one inch deep.   It was then up anchor and away.   Our first port was Dayton's ferry, where Dr. Bennet happened to be, but without his apparatus for sewing, to the no small disadvantage of me, who was to undergo the operation.   Mrs. Dayton, however, furnished him with a large darning-needle, which, as soon as I felt going through my skin, I thought was more like a gimlet boring into me; but, with the help of a glass of wine, I grinned and bore it, until he took a few stitches in the wound.   So much for crabbing.

"I was at New-York about a fortnight since, on my way to Jamaica, Long Island.   The object of this journey you understand.   I stayed at Mr. Willett's three days, and then, went to Colonel Morris's, and spent two days there very agreeably.   Nothing occurred worth relating, unless it be some transactions of the greatest fool I ever knew.

"Mr. Elliot, collector of New-York, Mr. and Mrs. De-

lancey and daughter, dined there on Sunday. Witherspoon* was led in with a large bag tied to his hair, that
reached down to the waistband of his breeches, and a brass
locket hanging from his neck below his stomach. He was
turned round and round by each of the company : was asked
where he got that very neat bag, and the valuable locket?
He readily answered, they were a present from Lady Kitty,
who was violently in love with him, and he expected to
marry her in a short time. He is so credulous that any
child might impose on him. I told him that I came from
Lord Stirling's, and that he might write by me to Lady Kitty.
Accordingly, he wrote a long letter and gave me, which I
opened there, and, by desire of Colonel Morris, answered it,
when I got to New-York, in Lady Kitty's name, informing
him that he must tell Mr. Morris to provide himself with
another tutor, as she intended marrying him without fail the
first of September, which I suppose he will as sincerely believe as he does his existence.

"Yours affectionately,
"MATT. OGDEN."

TO MATTHIAS OGDEN.

Litchfield, August 17th, 1774.

DEAR MATT.,

Before I proceed any further, let me tell you that, a few
days ago, a mob of several hundred persons gathered at
Barrington, and tore down the house of a man who was
suspected of being unfriendly to the liberties of the people ;
broke up the court, then sitting at that place, &c. As
many of the rioters belonged to this colony, and the Superior Court was then sitting at this place, the sheriff was
immediately despatched to apprehend the ringleaders. He
returned yesterday with eight prisoners, who were taken
without resistance. But this minute there is entering the

---

* A relative of President Witherspoon.

town on horseback, with great regularity, about fifty men, armed each with a white club; and I observe others continually dropping in. I shall here leave a blank, to give you (perhaps in heroics) a few sketches of my unexampled valour, should they proceed to hostilities; and, should they not, I can then tell you what I would have done.

The abovementioned *sneaks all gave bonds for their appearance,* to stand a trial at the next court for committing a riot.

Yours affectionately,

A. BURR.

On the 11th of September, 1774, he again writes Ogden :—

I wrote you last Thursday, and enclosed one of the songs you desired, which was all I could then obtain. Miss ——, the fountain of melody, furnished me with it. I knew that she, and no one else, had the notes of the enclosed song. I told her I should be glad to copy them for a most accomplished young gentleman in the Jerseys. She engaged to bring them the first time she came in town, for she lives about two miles from here. I this day received it, precisely as you have it. You may depend upon its being the work of her own hands. If this don't deserve an acrostic, I don't know—sense, beauty, modesty, and music. Matter plenty. .

Pray tell me whether your prayers are heard, and a good old saint, though a little in your way, is yet in Heaven. But remember, Matt., you can never be without plague, and when one gets out of the way, a worse, very often, supplies its place; so, I tell you again, be content, and hope for better times.

I am determined never to have any dealings with your friend Cupid until I know certainly how matters will turn out with you : for should some lucky devil step in between my friend and ——, which kind Heaven grant may never be ; in such a case, I say, I would choose to be untied, and then, you know, the wide world is before us.

Yours sincerely,
A. BURR.

Burr again writes him, dated

Litchfield, February 2d, 1775.

I sent you a packet by N. Hazard, and from that time to this I have not had the most distant prospect of conveying a letter to you. However, I have written a number of scrawls, the substance of which you shall now have.

The times with me are pretty much as usual; not so full of action as I could wish; and I find this propensity to action is very apt to lead me into scrapes. T. B. has been here since I wrote you last; he came very unexpectedly. You will conclude we had some confab about Miss ——. We had but little private chat, and the whole of that little was about her. He would now and then insinuate slyly what a clever circumstance it would be to have such a wife, with her fortune.

T. Burr,* by his kindness to me, has certainly laid me under obligations, which it would be the height of ingratitude in me ever to forget ; but I cannot conceive it my duty to be in the least influenced by these in the present case. Were I to conform to his inclination, it could give him pleasure or pain only as the consequence was good or bad to me. The sequel might be such as would inevitably cause him the most bitter anguish ; and, in all probability, would be such if I should consult his fancy instead of my judgment. And who can be a judge of these consequences but myself ? But even supposing things could be so situated that, by gratifying him, I should certainly be the means of his enjoying some permanent satisfaction, and should subject myself to a bare probability of misery as permanent,

---

* Uncle to Colonel Aaron Burr.

would it not stagger the most generous soul to think of sacrificing a whole life's comfort to the caprice of a friend? But this is a case that can never happen, unless that friend has some mean and selfish motive, such as I know T. Burr has not. I can never believe that too great deference to the judgment of another, in these matters, can arise from any greatness of soul. It appears to me the genuine off-spring of meanness. I suppose you are impatient for my reply to these importunities. I found my tongue and fancy too cramped to say much. However, I rallied my thoughts and set forth, as well as I was able, the inconveniences and uncertainty attending such an affair. I am determined to be very blunt the next time the matter is urged.

I have now and then an affair of petty gallantry, which might entertain you if you were acquainted with the different characters I have to deal with; but, without that, they would be very insipid.

I have lately engaged in a correspondence of a peculiar nature. I write once, and sometimes twice a week, to a lady who knows not that she ever received a line from me. The letters, on both sides, are mostly sentimental. Those of the lady are doubtless written with more sincerity, and less reserve, than if she knew I had any concern with them.

Mr. —— received a letter from Miss ——. He is very little versed in letter-writing, and engaged, or rather permitted, me to answer it, not thinking thereby to embark in a regular correspondence, but supposing the matter would thus end. I have had many scruples of conscience about this affair, though I really entered into it not with any sinister view, but purely to oblige ——. I should be glad to know your opinion of it. You will readily observe the advantage I have over ——. He is of an unsuspicious make, and this gives me an opportunity (if I had any inclination) to insert things which might draw from her secrets she would choose I should be ignorant of. But I would suffer crucifixion rather than be guilty of such an unparalleled meanness. On the contrary, I have carefully avoided saying any thing which might have the least tendency to make her write what she would be unwilling I should see.

Adieu.

A. Burr.

On the 12th of March, 1775, Burr writes Ogden :—

I have received your and Aaron's* letters. I was a little disappointed that you did not send an acrostic; but I still entertain some secret hope that the muse (who, you say, has taken her flight) will shortly return, and, by a new and stricter intimacy, more than repay the pains of this momentary absence.

Your happiness, Matt., is really almost the only present thing I can contemplate with any satisfaction ; though I, like other fools, view futurity with partiality enough to make it very desirable ; but I must first throw reason aside, and leave fancy uncontrolled. In some of these happy freaks I have endeavoured to take as agreeable a sleigh-ride as you had to Goshen ; but I find it impracticable, unless you will make one of the party ; for my imagination, when most romantic, is not lively or delusive enough to paint an object that can, in my eyes, atone for your absence. From this you will conclude that the news you heard of me at Princeton is groundless. It is so far from being true, that scarce two persons can fix on the same lady to tease me with. However, I would not have you think that this diversity of opinion arises from the volatility of my constitution, or that I am in love with every new or pretty face I see. But, I hope, you know me too well to need a caution of this nature.

I am very glad to hear of ——'s downfall. But, with all that fellow's low-lived actions, I don't more sincerely despise him than I do certain other narrow-hearted scoun-

* Subsequently Governor Ogden, of New-Jersey, and brother of Matthias.

drels you have among you.   Mean as he is, he appears to
me to have (or rather to have had) more of something at
bottom that bordered on honour, than some who will pass
through life respected by many.   I say this, not so much
to raise him above the common standard of d   ls, as to
sink them below it.   My idea of a d   l is composed more
of malice than of meanness.

Since I commenced this letter I have passed through a
scene entirely new.   Now, as novelty is the chief and almost only ingredient of happiness here below, you'll fancy
I have had some lucky turn.   I think it quite the reverse, I
assure you.   I have serious thoughts of leaving the matter
here, that you may be on the rack of curiosity for a month
or so.   Would not this be truly satanic ?   What would be
your conjectures in such a case ?   The first, I *guess*, that I
was sadly in love, and had met with some mortifying rebuff.

What would you say if I should tell you that —— had
absolutely professed love for me ?   Now I can see you with
both hands up—eyes and mouth wide open; but don't be
over scrupulous.   Trust me, I tell you the whole truth.   I
cannot at present give you any further particulars about the
matter, than that I felt foolish enough, and gave as cautious
a turn to it as I could, for which I am destined to suffer her
future hostility.

Last week I received a letter from T. Edwards, which I
fear may prove fatal to the dear project of the 15th of April.
He intends to be here about the middle of that month.   Supposing he should come here the 13th of April, what could I
do ?   Run off and leave him ?   Observe the uncertainty of
all sublunary things.   I, who a few months ago was as uncontrolled in my motions as the lawless meteors, am now
(sad reverse !) at the beck of a person forty miles off.   But
all this lamentation, if well considered, is entirely groundless,
for (*between you and me*) I intend to see you at Elizabethtown
this spring.   But even supposing I should fail in this—
where is this sad reverse of fortune ?—this lamentable

change? Is it not a very easy matter to fix on another time, and write you word by T. Edwards?

I have struck up a correspondence with J. Bellamy (son to the famous divine of that name). He has very lately settled in the practice of the law at Norwich, a place about seventy miles S. E. of this. He is one of the cleverest fellows I have to deal with. Sensible, a person of real humour, and is an excellent judge of mankind, though he has not had opportunity of seeing much of the world. Adieu.

A. Burr.

FROM JONATHAN BELLAMY.

Norwich, March 14th, 1775.

To do justice to circumstances, which you know are of the greatest importance in order to form a true estimate of what a person either says or does, it is indispensably necessary for me to tell you that it not only rains very generously, but that it is as dark as it was before light was created. It would be ridiculous to suppose that you need information that nothing but the irresistible desire of writing could possibly keep me at home this evening.

I had received your February favour only just time to laugh at it once, when the melancholy news that Betsy Devotion, of Windham, was very dangerously sick, banished every joyous thought from my heart. This Betsy you may remember to have heard mentioned near the name of Natty Huntington, who died last December; and a very angel she was too, I assure you. You see I speak of her in the *past* sense, for she has left us; and her friends are sure she is not less an angel *now* than she was ten days ago. Very certain I am, that if a natural sweetness of disposition can scale Heaven's walls, she went over like a bird. But I believe we must leave *her* and all the rest of our departed friends to be sentenced by a higher Board.

> " Transports last not in the human heart ;
> But all with transports soon agree to part."

If nature, in spite of us, did not take care of herself, we could not but be perfectly wretched. Philosophy is the emptiest word in the dictionary. And you may observe, wherever you find them, that those persons who profess to place all their reliance upon it, under every affecting circumstance of life, do but make use of the term as a mask for an iron heart. "But" (as the devil said on another occasion) "put forth thine hand, and touch his bone, and his flesh, and he will curse thee to thy face." They have as little fortitude as anybody when sufferings pinch home upon them.

Thus have I relieved a heart that perhaps felt a little too full; and if it *is* at the expense of my *head*, I have nevertheless the consolation that it will be received only as the overflowings of my present feelings.

"When and where shall I see you again?" somebody once asked me. The Lord only knows. Perhaps at the election at Hartford. If we can meet *there*—there will be time for notice. But, happen as it may, be assured that I am your most sincere friend,

JONATHAN BELLAMY.

"Stick my compliments in for him," says Hannah Phelps a jolly girl of fourteen.

.FROM MATTHIAS OGDEN.

Elizabethtown, March 18th, 1775.

Since we last saw each other, the 15th of April has been my mark, but the receipt of yours of the 12th has blotted it from my memory, for which nothing could atone but the expectation of seeing you here nearly as soon.

I read with pleasure your love intrigues; your anonymous correspondence with Miss ——, &c., and, with as much seriousness, the part relative to —— , Thaddeus Burr's' overtures, &c.

Steadily, Aaron. Money is alluring, and there is a pleasure in gratifying a friend; but let not a fortune buy v----

peace, nor sell your happiness. Neither be too much biased
by a friend, or any one's advice, in a matter of so great consequence to yourself. Perhaps she is worthy your love, and, if
I could think she was, I would not say a single thing to discourage you. Be cautious, Aaron; weigh the matter well
Should your generous heart be sold for naught, it would
greatly hurt the peace of mine. Let not her sense, her education, her modesty, her graceful actions, or her wit, betray
you. Has she a soul framed for love? For friendship?
But why need I advise a person of better judgment than
myself? It is not advice, my friend; it is only caution.
You have a difficult part to act. If you reject, she curses:
if you pity, she takes it for encouragement. Matters with
me go on smoothly.

I am now making up a party to go to the Falls, to be
ready against you come. My best regards to Mr. and Mrs.
Reeve. I remain happy in the enjoyment of ——'s love, and
am,   Your unfeigned friend,

.MATT. OGDEN.

After the decease of President Burr, Lyman Hall was
intrusted by the executors with the collection of sundry
debts due to the estate. A removal, and his various avocations, prevented his performing that duty with the necessary
promptitude. In consequence, the heirs were exposed to
loss. A friend of the family, the Rev. James Caldwell, of
New-Jersey, wrote him on the subject, and his answer is
so honourable, that it is deemed only an act of justice to an
upright man to record it here. It is another instance of the
integrity in private life of those patriots that planned and ac
complished the American Revolution. It will be seen that
Mr. Hall was a member of the Congress of 1775 from the
State of Georgia.

Philadelphia, 17th May, 1775.

REV. SIR,

Since I saw you, and afterwards Mr. Ogden, in Georgia, I have written to my attorneys and correspondents in Connecticut, to give me all the information they could obtain respecting the affairs and concerns of the late President Burr, left in my hands; which I had delivered over, before I left that colony in 1759, into the hands of Thaddeus Burr, of Fairfield; but no satisfactory answer can as yet be obtained. One debt, indeed, has been discovered, of about forty pounds New-York currency; but the bond on which it is due is as yet concealed.

On the whole, I find that it is not in my power to rede liver those securities for moneys which I was once in possession of; nor have I received the moneys due on those which were good; but am determined that I will make just satisfaction to the claimant heirs (orphans) of the late President Burr. It is, I know, my indispensable duty, and I have for that purpose brought a quantity of rice to this city, the avails of which, when sold, shall be appropriated to that use. I should be glad that you, or Mr. Ogden, the executor, could be here to transact the business, and, on a settlement, give me a power of attorney, properly authenticated, to recover any part of those moneys I can find due when I shall arrive in Connecticut, to which I propose going as soon as the Congress rises. As I am in Congress, I cannot see you directly; but, if liberty can be obtained, shall wait on you or Mr. Ogden, or both, in my way to New-York, in a few days; but I think Mr. Ogden, the executor, if it will suit, had better come here and settle it. I mention him because I suppose he is the proper person to discharge me, and give me a power of attorney.

I am, reverend sir,

With esteem, yours,

LYMAN HALL.

The Rev. JAS. CALDWELL, *Elizabethtown.*

CHAPTER V.

In his retirement at the house of his brother-in-law (Judge Reeve), Burr was aroused by the shedding of his country-men's blood at Lexington on the 19th of April, 1775. Immediately after that battle, he wrote a letter to his friend Ogden, requesting him to come on to Litchfield and arrange for joining the standard of their country. Ogden wrote for answer that he could not make the necessary arrangements. The battle of Bunker's Hill (on the 16th of June, 1775) followed in rapid succession; whereupon he started for Elizabethtown, New-Jersey, to meet Ogden, and aid him in preparations for the journey to Cambridge, where the American army was encamped.

Burr had been reading those portions of history which detailed the achievements of the greatest military men and tacticians of the age in which they lived. His idea of dis-cipline and subordination was formed accordingly. With the most enthusiastic feelings, and under the influence of such opinions, Burr, in company with his friend Matthias Ogden, left Elizabethtown, in July, 1775, for Cambridge, with the intention of tendering their services in defence of American liberty. He had now entered his twentieth year, but, in appearance, was a mere stripling.

It has been seen that, whatever were Burr's pursuits or studies, his habits were those of intense application. He had already imbibed a military ardour equalled by few—surpassed by none. Panting for glory on the battle-field, information and improvement as a soldier were now the objects that absorbed all his thoughts. On his joining the army, however, he was sadly disappointed in his expectations. The whole was a scene of idleness, confusion, and dissipation. From the want of camp-police, the health of the men was impaired, and many sickened and died. Of the officers, some were ignorant of their duty, while others were fearful of enforcing a rigid discipline, lest it should give offence to those who were unaccustomed to restraint. Deep mortification and disappointment preyed upon the mind of young Burr.

The following original letters are found among the papers of Colonel Burr, and, as casting some light upon the history of those times, are deemed of sufficient interest (and not inapplicable) to be inserted in this work. The patriotic reply of General Montgomery is above all praise.

ROGER SHERMAN TO GENERAL DAVID WOOSTER.

Philadelphia, June 23d, 1775

Dear Sir,

The Congress, having determined it necessary to keep up an army for the defence of America at the charge of the United Colonies, have appointed the following general officers:—George Washington, Esq., commander-in-chief. Major-generals Ward, Lee, Schuyler, and Putnam. Brigadier-generals Pomeroy, Montgomery, yourself, Heath, Spencer, Thomas, Sullivan (of New-Hampshire), and one Green, of Rhode-Island.

I am sensible that, according to your former rank, you were entitled to the place of a major-general; and as one was to be appointed in Connecticut, I heartily recommended you to the Congress. I informed them of the arrangement made by our assembly, which I thought would be satisfactory to have them continue in the same order. But, as General Putnam's fame was spread abroad, and especially his successful enterprise at Noddle's Island, the account of which had just arrived, it gave him a preference in the opinion of the delegates in general, so that his appointment was unanimous among the colonies; but, from your known abilities and firm attachment to the American cause, we were very desirous of your continuance in the army, and hope you will accept of the appointment made by the Congress.

I think the pay of a brigadier is about one hundred and twenty-five dollars per month. I suppose a commission is sent to you by General Washington. We received intelligence yesterday of an engagement at Charlestown, but have not had the particulars. All the Connecticut troops are now taken into the continental army. I hope proper care will be taken to secure the colony against any sudden invasion, which must be at their own expense.

I have nothing further that I am at liberty to acquaint you with of the doings of the Congress but what have been made public. I would not have any thing published in the papers that I write, lest something may inadvertently escape me which ought not to be published. I should be glad if you would write to me every convenient opportunity, and inform me of such occurrences, and other matters, as you may think proper and useful for me to be acquainted with. The general officers were elected in the Congress, not by nomination, but by ballot.

I am, with great esteem,

Your humble servant,

ROGER SHERMAN.

DAVID WOOSTER, Esq.

JAMES DUANE, OF NEW-YORK, TO GENERAL MONTGOMERY.

Philadelphia, July 21st, 1775.

DEAR SIR,

I am directed by the Congress to acquaint you of an arrangement in the Massachusetts department, and the reason which led to it, lest, by misunderstanding it, you might think yourself neglected.

When brigadiers-general were to be appointed, it was agreed that the first in nomination should be one of the Massachusetts generals. The gentlemen from that province recommended General Pomeroy, who was accordingly

Dear Sir

I have been honoured
21.st Ins.tt — my ack
for the attention :
= quess :

I submit with gr
regulation they
judge expedient.
punctilio of the o _
to discharge my
=king myself on _
=ed to the melan
up as said for the

I am ,

James Duane; to face page 61

with your letter of

owledgments are due

hewn me by the Com

at chearfulness to any

n. their prudence shall

laying aside the

ldier, I shall endeavour

duty to society under

as the Citizen more

holy necessity of taking

publick safety —

r &c

[illegible]

fixed upon ; but, before his commission arrived at the camp,
he had retired from the army.   Under these circumstances
the Congress thought it just to fill up the commission designed for Mr. Pomeroy with the name of General Thomas
as first brigadier.   You, consequently, hold the rank to
which you were elected.

I sincerely hope this may not give you any displeasure,
as I am confident no disrespect was intended.

Be pleased to accept my sincere wishes for your honour
and happiness, and particularly in the discharge of the im
portant trust which you have undertaken.

I am, with regard,

Dear sir, your most obedient servant,

JAS. DUANE.

General MONTGOMERY.

GENERAL MONTGOMERY'S ANSWER.

DEAR SIR,

I have been honoured with your letter of the 21st inst.
My acknowledgments are due for the attention shown me
by the Congress.

I submit, with great cheerfulness, to any regulation they,
in their prudence, shall judge expedient.   Laying aside the
punctilio of the *soldier*, I shall endeavour to discharge my
duty to society, considering myself only as the *citizen*, reduced to the melancholy necessity of taking up arms for the
public safety.

I am, &c.,

R. M.

Answer.

The preceding is endorsed, in the handwriting of General
Montgomery, on the back of Mr. Duane's letter.

The laxity of the discipline which pervaded the camp at
Cambridge, the inexperience of the officers, and the con-
tests and petty squabbles about rank, all tended to excite

great jealousy and discontent in the army. As yet, Burr was attached to no particular corps. He mingled indiscriminately with conflicting factions, until, disgusted with the scene which he daily witnessed, he was violently attacked with a nervous fever, by which he was confined to his bed.

One day he heard Ogden and some young men of the army conversing, in an apartment adjoining that in which he was lying, on the subject of an expedition. He called Ogden to his bedside, and inquired what was the nature of the expedition of which they were speaking. Ogden informed him that Colonel Arnold, with a detachment of ten or twelve hundred men, was about to proceed through the wilderness for the purpose of attacking Quebec. Burr instantly raised himself up in the bed, and declared that he would accompany them; and, so pertinacious was he on this point, that he immediately, although much enfeebled, commenced dressing himself. Ogden expostulated, and spoke of his debilitated state—referred to the hardships and privations that he must necessarily endure on such a march, &c. But all was unavailing. Young Burr was determined, and was immoveable. He forthwith selected four or five hale, hearty fellows, to whom he proposed that they should form a mess, and unite their destiny on the expedition through the wilderness. To this arrangement they cheerfully acceded. His friend Ogden, and others of his acquaintance, were conveyed in carriages from Cambridge to Newburyport, distant about sixty miles; but Burr, with his new associates in arms, on the 14th of September, 1775, shouldered their muskets, took their knapsacks upon their backs, and marched to the place of embarcation.

FROM J. BELLAMY.

Litchfield, August 17th, 1775.

My dearest Soldier,

I was infinitely surprised to hear from you in the army I can hardly tell you what sensations I did not feel at the

time. Shall not attempt to describe them, though they de
prived me of a night's sleep. But that was not spent altogether unhappily. My busybody, *Fancy*, led me a most
romantic chase; in which, you may be sure, I visited your
tent; beheld you (unnoticed) musing on your present cir
cumstances, apparently agitated by every emotion which
would naturally fill the heart of one who has come to the
resolution to risk his life for his country's freedom. You
will excuse my mentioning, that from a deep, absent medi
tation, partly expressed by half-pronounced soliloquies, I
beheld you start up, clap your hand upon your sword, and
look so fiercely, that it almost frightened me. The scene,
on your discovering me, immediately changed to something
more tender; but I won't waste paper.

If you should happen to find Dr. James Cogswell, who
is in Colonel Spencer's regiment, please to give my best
love to him, and tell him he is a lazy scoundrel.

It rains, my boy, excessively. Does it not drop through
your tent? Write often to

JONA. BELLAMY.

To A. BURR.

As soon as the guardian and relatives of young Burr
heard of his determination to accompany Arnold in his
expedition against Quebec, they not only remonstrated, but
they induced others, who were friendly to him, to adopt a
similar course. While he remained at Cambridge, he
received numerous letters on the subject. The two follow
ing are selected:—

FROM DR. JAMES COGSWELL.

Camp in Roxbury, 9th September, 1775.

I am extremely sorry to hear that you are determined on
the new expedition to Quebec. I am sorry on my own account, as I promised myself much satisfaction and pleasure
in your company: but I am not altogether selfish; I am

sorry on yours. The expedition in which you are engaged
is a very arduous one; and those who are engaged in it
must unavoidably undergo great hardships. Your constitution (if I am not much mistaken) is very delicate, and not
formed for the fatigues of the camp. The expedition, I am
sensible, is a glorious one, and nothing but a persuasion of
my inability to endure the hardships of it would have de-
terred me from engaging in it. If this excuse was sufficient
for me, I am persuaded it is for you, and ought to influence
you to abandon all thoughts of undertaking it. I have no
friend so dear to me (and I love my friends) but that I am
willing to sacrifice for the good of the grand—the important
cause, in which we are engaged; but, to think of a friend's
sacrificing himself, without any valuable end being answered
by it, is painful beyond expression. *You will die; I know
you will die in the undertaking; it is impossible for you to
endure the fatigue.* I am so exercised about your going,
that I should come and see you if I had not got the Scrip-
tural excuse,—a wife, and cannot come.

My dear friend, you must not go: I cannot bear the
thoughts of it. 'Tis little less melancholy than following
you to your grave.

Your affectionate friend,
JAMES COGSWELL.

FROM PETER COLT.

Watertown, 11th September, 1775.

I cannot retire to rest till I have written you a few lines,
to excuse my casting so many discouragements in the way
of your journey to Quebec. At first I did not think it so
hazardous; but, upon inquiring of those who had more
knowledge of the country, thought it too fatiguing an undertaking for one of your years; and I find it altogether against
the sentiments of your friends. I think you might be fairly
excused, without the risk of being reported as timid, as the
hopes of your family depend in a great degree upon you.

I should have rejoiced to see you relinquish this expedition; but, as you are determined to pursue it, must beg you not to let any thing we have said to you depress your spirits, or damp your resolution, as it may otherwise have a fatal effect. We have held up the dark side of the picture, in order to deter you from going. You must now think only on the bright side, and make the least of every disagreeable circumstance attending your march. Let no difficulty discourage you. The enterprise is glorious, and, if it succeeds, will redound to the honour of those who have planned and executed it.

May God give you health and strength equal to the fatigue of the march, and preserve you safe from every danger you may encounter. Make Quebec a safe retreat to the forces. I hope to have a particular description of Canada from you when you return.

Don't turn Catholic for the sake of the girls. Again I beg you to forget what I have said to discourage you. It proceeded from love to you, and not a desire of rendering you ridiculous. Adieu, my dear friend.

Yours,
PETER COLT.

A day or two after Burr's arrival at Newburyport, he was called upon by a messenger from his guardian, Timothy Edwards, with instructions to bring the young fugitive back. A letter from his uncle (T. Edwards) was delivered to him at the same time. Having read the letter, and heard the messenger's communication, he coolly addressed him, and asked, " How do you expect to take me back, if I should refuse to go? If you were to make any forcible attempt upon me, I would have you hung up in ten minutes." After a short pause the messenger presented a second letter from his guardian, and with it a small remittance in gold. It was couched in the most affectionate and tender language, importuning him to return; and depicting, in the darkest colours, the sufferings he must endure if he survived the at-

tempt to reach Quebec. It affected young Burr very sensibly, insomuch that he shed tears. But his destiny was fixed.
He wrote, however, a respectful letter to his uncle, explanatory of his reasons for accompanying the army, and expressive of his gratitude for the kindness he had experienced.

On or about the 20th of September, 1775, the troops under the command of Arnold embarked at Newburyport.
This detachment was to penetrate Canada about ninety or
one hundred miles below Montreal, proceeding by the Kennebec river, and thence through the wilderness between the
St. Lawrence and the settled parts of Maine. In this route,
precipitous mountains, deep and almost impenetrable swamps
and morasses, were to be passed. Arnold, in a letter to General Washington, dated *Fort Weston*, September 25th, 1775,
says : "I design Chaudiere Pond as a general rendezvous,
and from thence proceed in a body. I believe, from the best
information I can procure, we shall be able to perform the
journey in twenty days ; the distance from this being about
one hundred and eighty miles."

During the march through the wilderness, no regard whatever was paid to order or discipline. Every man was left
to take care of himself, and make the best of his way through
the woods. The sufferings of this detachment from wet,
and cold, and hunger, were excessive. From the latter,
however, Burr suffered less than any of his companions. His
abstemious habits in regard to eating seemed peculiarly calculated for such an expedition. Both Burr and Ogden had
been accustomed, in small boats, to aquatic excursions round
Staten Island and in its vicinity. They were skilful helms-
men, and in this particular, in passing the rapids, were fre
quently useful. Notwithstanding this qualification, how
ever, Burr, with some soldiers in a boat, was carried over a
fall of nearly twenty feet. One man was drowned, and much
of the baggage lost. The weather was cold, and it was with
great difficulty that he reached the shore.

"Arnold, who, at the head of the two first divisions, still

prosecuted his march, was thirty-two days traversing a hideous wilderness, without seeing a house or any thing human. The troops were under the necessity of hauling their bateaux up rapid streams ; of taking them upon their shoulders, with all their provisions, across carrying-places ; and of traversing, and frequently repassing, for the purpose of bringing their baggage, deep morasses, thick woods, and high mountains. These impediments, notwithstanding the zealous and wonderfully persevering exertions of his men, so protracted his march, that, though he had expected certainly to enter Canada about the middle of October, he did not reach the first settlements on the Chaudiere, which empties itself into the St. Lawrence near Quebec, until the third of November.

"On the high grounds which separate the waters of the Kennebec from those of the St. Lawrence, the scanty remnant of provisions was divided among the companies, each of which was directed, without attempting to preserve any connexion with another, to march with the utmost possible celerity into the inhabited country. While those who gained the front were yet thirty miles from the first poor and scattered habitations which composed that frontier of Canada, their last morsel of food was consumed. But, preceded by Arnold, who went forward for the purpose of procuring for them something which might satisfy the first demands of nature, the troops still persevered in their labours, with a vigour unimpaired by the hardships they had encountered, until they once more found themselves in regions frequented by human beings."*

On the arrival of Arnold's detachment at Chaudiere Pond, Burr was despatched with a verbal communication to General Montgomery. He disguised himself as a young Catholic priest. In this order of men he was willing to repose confidence. He knew that the French Catholics were

* Marshall's Life of Washington.

not satisfied with their situation under the provincial government; but especially the priesthood. Feeling no apprehension for his own safety from treachery, he proceeded to a learned and reverend father of the church, to whom he communicated frankly who he was, and what was his object. Burr was master of the Latin language, and had an imperfect knowledge of the French. The priest was an educated man, so that a conversation was held with but little difficulty. He endeavoured to dissuade Burr from the enterprise. Spoke of it as impossible to accomplish. He represented the distance as great, and through an enemy's country. The boyish appearance of Burr induced the reverend divine to consider him a mere child. Discovering, however, the settled purpose of the young adventurer, the priest procured him a confidential guide· and a cabriolet (for the ground was now covered with snow), and, thus prepared, he started on his journey. Without interruption, he was conducted in perfect safety from one religious family to another, until he arrived at Three Rivers. Here the guide became alarmed in consequence of some rumours as to the arrival of Arnold at the Chaudiere, and that he had despatched messengers to Montgomery to announce to him the fact. Under strong apprehensions, the guide refused to proceed any farther, and recommended to Burr to remain a few days until these rumours subsided. To this he was compelled to accede; and, for greater security, he was secreted three days in a convent at that place. At the expiration of this period he again set off, and reached Montgomery without further detention or accident.   ·   · ·   ·

On his arrival at headquarters,.he explained to the general the character of the re-enforcement he was about to receive ; the probable number of effective men, and the time at which their arrival might be anticipated. General Montgomery was so well pleased with the details which had been given him, and the manner in which young Burr had effected his journey after leaving Arnold, that he invited him (Burr) to reside at headquarters, assuring him that he should receive an appointment as one of his aids.   At this time Mont gomery was a brigadier, and not entitled to aids, only in vir tue of his being commander-in-chief of the army.   Previous to his death, however, he was appointed a major-general, but the information did not reach him.

As soon as Burr had joined the family of the general, he entered upon the duties of an aid; but no formal annunciation was made until the army arrived before Quebec, when his appointment was announced in general orders.   Arnold arrived at Point Levi, opposite to Quebec, on the 9th of No vember, 1775.   He paraded for some days on the heights near the town, and sent two flags to demand a surrender, but both were fired upon as rebels with whom no communication was to be held.   The true reason, however, was, that Colonel M'Clean, the British commandant, a vigilant and experienced officer, knowing the weakness of his own garrison, deemed it impolitic, if not unsafe, to receive a flag from Arnold.

The first plan for the attack upon the British works was essentially different from that which was subsequently carried into execution.   Various reasons have been assigned for this change.   Judge Marshall says, " that while the general (Montgomery) was making the necessary preparations for the assault, the garrison received intelligence of his intention from a deserter.   This circumstance induced him to change the plan of his attack, which had been originally to attempt both the upper and lower towns at the same time. The plan now resolved on was to divide the army into four parts; and while two of them, consisting of Canadians under Major Livingston, and a small party under Major Brown, were to distract the attention of the garrison by making two feints against the upper town of St. Johns and Cape Diamond, the other two, led, the one by Montgomery in person,

and the other by Arnold, were to make real attacks on opposite sides of the lower town."[*]

Colonel Burr says, that a change of the plan of attack
was produced, in a great measure, through the advice and
influence of Mr. Antill, a resident in Canada, who had joined
the army; and Mr. Price, a Montreal merchant of property.
and respectability, who had also come out and united his
destiny with the cause of the colonies. Mr. Price, in particular, was strongly impressed with the opinion, that if the
American troops could obtain possession of the lower town,
the merchants and other wealthy inhabitants would have
sufficient influence with the British commander-in-chief to
induce him to surrender rather than jeopard the destruction
of all their property. It was, as Colonel Burr thought, a
most fatal delusion. But it is believed that the opinion was
honestly entertained.

The first plan of the attack was agreed upon in a council, at which young Burr and his friend, Matthias Ogden,
were present. The arrangement was to pass over the highest walls at Cape Diamond. Here there was a bastion.
This was at a distance of about half a mile from any suc-
cour; but being considered, in some measure, impregnable,
the least resistance might be anticipated in that quarter.
Subsequent events tended to prove the soundness of this
opinion. In pursuance of the second plan, Major Livingston, with a detachment under his command, made a feint
upon Cape Diamond; but, for about half an hour, with all
the noise and alarm that he and his men could create, he
was unable to attract the slightest notice from the enemy,
so completely unprepared were they at this point.

While the first was the favourite plan of attack, Burr requested General Montgomery to give him the command of
a small forlorn hope, which request was granted, and forty
men allotted to him. Ladders were prepared, and these

men kept in constant drill, until they could ascend them
(standing almost perpendicular), with their muskets and accoutrements, with nearly the same facility that they could
mount an ordinary staircase.   In the success of this plan
of attack Burr had entire confidence; but, when it was
changed, he entertained strong apprehensions of the result.
He was in the habit, every night, of visiting and reconnoi-
tring the ground about Cape Diamond, until he became
perfectly familiarized with every inch adjacent to, or in the
vicinity of, the intended point of assault.

   When the attack was about to be commenced, Captain
Burr, and other officers near General Montgomery, endeavoured to dissuade him from leading in the advance; remarking that, as commander-in-chief, it was not his place.
But all argument was ineffectual and unavailing.   The
attack was made on the morning of the 31st of December,
1775, before daylight, in the midst of a violent snow-storm.
The New-York troops were commanded by General Montgomery, who advanced along the St. Lawrence, by the way
of Aunce de Mere, under Cape Diamond.   The first barrier to be surmounted was at the Pot Ash.   In front of it
was a block-house and picket, in charge of some Canadians, who, after making a single fire, fled in confusion.   On
advancing to force the barrier, an accidental discharge of a
piece of artillery from the British battery, when the American front was within forty paces of it, killed General
Montgomery, Captain McPherson, one of his aids, Captain
Cheeseman, and every other person in front, except Captain Burr and a French guide.   General Montgomery was
within a few feet of Captain Burr; and Colonel Trumbull,
in a superb painting recently executed by him, descriptive
of the assault upon Quebec, has drawn the general falling in the arms of his surviving aid-de-camp.   Lieutenant Colonel Campbell, being the senior officer on the
ground, assumed the command, and ordered a retreat.

CHAPTER VI.

To evince the high sense entertained by his country for the services of General Montgomery, Congress directed a monument to be erected, with an inscription sacred to his memory. They "*Resolved*, That, to express the venera- tion of the United Colonies for their late general, Richard Montgomery, and the deep sense they entertained of the many signal and important services of that gallant officer, who, after a series of successes, amid the most discouraging difficulties, fell, at length, in a gallant attack upon Quebec, the capital of Canada, and to transmit to future ages, as examples truly worthy of imitation, his patriotism, conduct, boldness of enterprise, insuperable perseverance, and con- tempt of danger and death, a monument be procured from Paris, or other part of France, with an inscription sacred to his memory, and expressive of his amiable character and heroic achievements; and that the continental treasurer be directed to advance a sum, not exceeding three hundred pounds sterling, to Dr. Benjamin Franklin, who is desired to see this resolution properly executed, for defraying the expenses thereof."

This resolve was carried into execution at Paris by that ingenious artist, M. Caffieres, sculptor to Louis XVI., king of France, under the direction of Dr. Benjamin Franklin. The monument is of white marble, of the most beautiful simplicity and inexpressible elegance, with emblematical devices, and the following truly classical inscription, worthy of the modest but great mind of Franklin.

TO THE GLORY OF

RICHARD MONTGOMERY,

MAJOR-GENERAL OF THE ARMIES OF THE

UNITED STATES OF AMERICA,

SLAIN AT THE SIEGE OF QUEBEC,

THE THIRTY-FIRST OF DECEMBER, 1775,

AGED 38 YEARS.

This monument was erected in front of St. Paul's Church, in the city of New-York, in the spring of 1789.

General Arnold temporarily became commander-in-chief of the American army near Quebec, and was accordingly removed to headquarters. Young Burr was now called upon to perform the duties of brigade major. Arnold's plan was, by a close blockade, to starve out the enemy; but, from the weakness of his force, he soon discovered that this was impracticable; and he knew that, on the opening of the spring, he could not retain his present position, but must retreat. He therefore resolved to send in a flag of truce, and demand a surrender. He informed Captain Burr that he was about to send him with a communication to General Carlton, the British commander. Captain Burr required that he should be made acquainted with its contents. Arnold objected; whereupon Burr remarked that, if the general wished it, he would resign; but that he could not consent to be the bearer of the communication without possessing a knowledge of its character. At length, it was exhibited to him. It was demanding a surrender of the fortress, but in terms that Captain Burr considered unbecoming an American officer, and he so stated to the general; adding, that the bearer of such a message, if he were permitted to deliver it, would be treated by the British with contumely and contempt; and therefore declined the mission. Another officer was selected, and met the fate Burr anticipated. Shortly after (April 1st, 1776), General

Wooster arrived from Montreal and took the command. He was succeeded by General Thomas about the 1st of May; and, on the 5th of May, it was determined in council to raise the blockade of Quebec, and that the sick and wounded should be immediately removed, with the artillery and stores, by boats, to Three Rivers, preparatory to a retreat.

Burr's perseverance and zeal during the march through the wilderness with Arnold, his subsequent boldness in joining Montgomery, and his intrepidity at the assault on Quebec, had acquired for him great reputation in the army, and had drawn towards him the attention of some of the most distinguished whigs in the United Provinces. From every quarter he received highly complimentary letters. From a few of them extracts are made. Colonel Antill, a resident of Montreal, who had joined the American army, thus addresses him, five days after the fall of Montgomery:—

"La Chine, 5th January, 1776.

"Dear Burr,

"I have desired Mr. Price to deliver you my pistols, which you will keep until I see you. They are relics from my father's family, and therefore I cannot give them to you. The general (Wooster) has thought proper to send me to the Congress, where I shall have an opportunity of speaking of you as you deserve.

"Yours,

"Edward Antill."

On the 4th of January, General Wooster writes from Montreal to General Arnold:—

"Give my love to Burr, and desire him to remain with Colonel Clinton* for the present. Not only him, but all those brave officers who have so nobly distinguished them-

* James Clinton, afterwards general, brother of Governor George Clinton.

selves, I shall ever remember with gratitude and the highest degree of approbation, and shall not fail to represent them accordingly.

" DAVID WOOSTER."

From a college-chum of great merit, he received a letter, dated

"Philadelphia, January 24th, 1776.

"DEAR BURR,

" I am informed a gentleman is just setting off for Quebec, and snatch the opportunity of at once condoling with you for the loss of your brave general, and congratulating you on the credit you have gained in that action. 'Tis said you behaved well—you behaved gallantly. I never doubted but you would distinguish yourself, and your praise is now in every man's mouth. It has been my theme of late. I will not say I was perfectly disinterested in the encomiums I bestowed. You were a son of Nassau Hall, and reflected honour on the place of *my* education. You were my classmate and friend, and reflected honour on me. I make no doubt but your promotion will be taken care of. The gentlemen of the Congress speak highly of you.

" Your affectionate,
" WILLIAM BRADFORD, Jun."

Judge Tappan Reeve writes—

" Stockbridge, January 27th, 1776.

"DEAR BURR,

" Amid the lamentations of a country for the loss of a brave, enterprising general, your escape from such imminent danger, to which you have been exposed, has afforded us the greatest satisfaction. The news of the unfortunate attack upon Quebec arrived among us on the 13th of this month. I concealed it from your sister until the 18th, when she found it out; but, in less than half an hour, I received letters from Albany, acquainting me that you were m

safety, and had gained great honour by your intrepid conduct. It gave us a kind of happiness that I should be very
loath ever again to enjoy ; for it never can be the case until
you have again been exposed to the like danger, and have
again escaped it, which I hope may never happen. To
know that you were in safety gave great pleasure. It was
heightened by hearing that your conduct was brave. Could
you have been crowned with success, it would have been
complete.

"It was happy for us that we did not know that you were
an aid-de-camp, until we heard of your welfare ; for we
heard that Montgomery and his aid-de-camps were killed,
without knowing who his aid-de-camps were.

"Your sister enjoys a middling state of health. She has
many anxious hours upon your account ; but she tells me
that, as she believes you may serve your country in the
business in which you are now employed, she is contented
that you should remain in the army. It must be an exalted
public spirit that could produce such an effect upon a sister
as affectionate as yours.

"Adieu.

" T. REEVE."

His friend, Jonathan Bellamy, writes,

"Norwich, March 3d, 1776.

"MY VERY DEAR FRIEND,

"Be you yet alive? I have been infinitely distressed for
you ; but I hope it is now as safe with you as glorious.
Doctor Jim Cogswell has left the army. A few days ago I
received a letter from him. 'I doubt not,' he says, 'you
have most sensible pleasure in the applauses bestowed on
our friend Burr ; when I hear of his gallant behaviour, I
feel exquisite delight.'

"Curse on this vile distance between us. I am restless
to tell you every thing ; but uncertainty whether you would
ever hear it bids me be silent, till, in some future happy

meeting, I may hold you to my bosom, and impart to you every emotion of my heart.

"Yours sincerely,

"JONA. BELLAMY."

Immediately after the repulse of the Americans at Quebec, his friend Ogden returned to New-Jersey, but spent much of his time with the army in the city of New-York. He writes to Burr, dated

New-York, 20th March, 1776.

Some weeks have elapsed since I saw Walker and Price. To-day I met with Hopkins at this place. My first inquiry was for letters from you. I mean not to upbraid you. This is the third time of my writing since I left you. I shall continue it, with the hope of giving you some small satisfaction. Miss Dayton is well, and will soon be mine. Barber is appointed major in the third Jersey battalion, of which Dayton is colonel, and Walton White lieutenant-colonel. Hancock was particular in his inquiry after you, and was disappointed in not receiving a line from you. I was kindly received on my arrival at Philadelphia. The Congress have since appointed me lieutenant-colonel in the first Jersey battalion, in the room of Lieutenant-colonel Winds, who has the regiment in the stead of Lord Stirling, who is advanced to a brigadier-general.

Colonel Allen, who hands you this, is much of a gentleman, and worthy your attention. Melcher has hobbled himself. Inquire of Colonel Allen. General Thompson commands. To-morrow my appointment will be announced in general orders, whereupon I shall join my regiment, but shall obtain leave of absence for a week or two. Elizabethtown swarms with girls, among which is Miss Noel. I have not seen Miss Ricketts.

When I was in Philadelphia, Colonel Reed expressed a desire of serving me. He said there was a vacancy in General

Washington's family, and doubted not his recommendation would procure it for me. I declined it, hoping to get a more active office, but desired he would procure it for you. If any thing offers at Quebec, accept it, as it will not hinder your appointment here. Washington is expected in New-York, when I shall have a better chance of bringing it about. The pay and rank are equal to a full major. I shall write you by Price. Miss Dayton is particular in her inquiries after you.

Yours sincerely,
MATT. OGDEN.

In the spring of 1776, the army moved from Montreal to the mouth of the Sorel. Major Burr yet remained with it. While at Montreal, he became disgusted with General Arnold, on account of his meanness and other bad qualities. On the march through the wilderness, he was far from being satisfied with the general. Burr thought he provided too carefully for himself; and that he did not sufficiently share the fatigues and privations of the march in common with the troops. Immediately after arriving at the Sorel, he informed the general of his desire to visit his friends, and to ascertain what was doing, as he wished more active employment. General Arnold objected somewhat petulantly. Burr remarked courteously, but firmly, "Sir, I have a boat in readiness. I have employed four discharged soldiers to row me, and I start to-morrow morning at six o'clock." He then designated the point at which he should embark. Arnold forbade his departure, whereupon Burr reiterated his determination.

The next morning, at the specified hour, he repaired to his boat, and shortly after discovered the general approaching. "Why, Major Burr," says he, "you are not going?"—"I am, sir," replied the major. "But you know, sir, it is contrary to my wish and against my orders."—"I know, sir, that you have the *power* of stopping me, but nothing short of force shall do it." The general then changed his tone and manner, and endeavoured to dissuade ; but, after a few minutes' conversation, Burr wished him great success, then embarked, and took his departure without interruption.

On the Sorel an incident occurred which gave some alarm to the voyagers. Burr had taken into his boat, as a kind of companion, a young merchant. On the borders of the river they suddenly discovered a large brick house, with wings, having loopholes to fire through, and in view, at the door, stood an Indian warrior, in full costume. The oarsmen were for attempting to retreat. Burr said it was too late, as they were within the reach of the Indians' rifles. The passenger was about to stop the men from rowing, when Burr threatened to shoot him if he interfered. The inquiry was then made—"What are we to do ?" The major replied, "Row for the shore and land ; I will go up to the house, and we shall soon learn what they are." By this time several other Indians had made their appearance. On reaching the shore, Burr took his sword and proceeded to meet the red men. An explanation ensued, and it was ascertained that they were friendly. The stores were landed from the boat, and a merrimaking followed.

Major Burr continued his route to Albany. On his arrival, and while there, he was notified verbally that it would be agreeable to the commander-in-chief (General Washington) that he should visit New-York. He forthwith proceeded down the river, and arrived in the city about the 20th of May, 1776. He immediately reported himself to the commander-in-chief, who invited him to join his family at headquarters until he received a satisfactory appointment. The quarters of General Washington were at that time in the house subsequently owned by Colonel Burr, and known as Richmond Hill. This invitation was accepted, and Major Burr occasionally rode out with the general, but very soon became restless and dissatisfied. He wrote to John Hancock, then president of Congress, and who had been an

intimate friend of his father, that he was disgusted, and in
clined to retire from the service. Governor Hancock objected, and asked him whether he would accept the appointment of aid-de-camp to Major-general Putnam, then in command in the city of New-York. Burr consented, and removed from the headquarters of the commander-in-chief to
those of Major-general Putnam. About this period Burr
received a letter from his friend, now Lieutenant-colonel M.
Ogden, who had proceeded to the north with his regiment.
He writes,

Fort George, 5th June, 1776

DEAR BURR, ·

I this evening experienced the greatest disappointment I
have met with since my memory. I yesterday saw Mr
Price ; he informed me that you were on your way, in
company with the commissioners, who, I was this day informed, were coming by the way of Skeenesborough. I
altered my course, and went that way, till I met them on
the road. They informed me you were coming by Lake
George. I then turned about, very much afraid you would
pass me before I came into the lake road. But what necessity for enumerating all these circumstances ? I have missed
you. D—n the luck. I never so much desired, nor had
occasion so much for an interview. I have not received a
single line from you since I left Canada. Perhaps you
have not written, or perhaps they have miscarried. If
they have miscarried, withered be the hand that held them
back. Tell me you omitted through carelessness, neglect,
hurry of business, or any thing, rather than want of friendship.

*General Washington desired me to inform you that he
will provide for you, and that he expects you will come to
him immediately, and stay in his family.* I should have
acquainted you of this by letter, had I not expected to have
seen you. You will now want your horse. I have sold

him, and spent the money, and expect I shall not be able to refund it until my return.

I am, if I ever was,

Yours sincerely,

MATTHIAS OGDEN.

Before the preceding letter was received by Major Burr, he felt piqued at what he supposed the coldness and neglect of his friend Ogden, and, under the influence of such feelings, wrote the following :—

New-York, 18th June, 1776.

DEAR OGDEN,

A correspondence, which I flattered myself in former times was mutually agreeable, has of late somehow strangely found an end. You may remember, when you left Canada, I engaged to answer your first letter immediately, and to continue writing from that time, by every opportunity, as usual. I concluded your letters must have miscarried, and wrote you a line by Mr. Avery. I had no direct intelligence from you, till a verbal message by Mr. Duggan, the beginning of May. A few days after, I received a letter from *Colonel Ogden* by *Colonel Allen.* I should have answered it, but had determined to visit my native colony, and expected, by personal interview, to answer purposes which I scarce hoped the cold medium of ink and paper could effect.

That I unfortunately missed you on my way hither, I need not relate. At Albany I first heard you had passed me. I was upon the point of following you; but the character of troublesome fool struck me in so disagreeable a light, that, in spite of myself, I continued my journey.

There is in man a certain love of novelty; a fondness of variety (useful, indeed, within proper limits), which influences more or less in almost every act of life. New views, new laws, new *friends,* have each their charm. Truly great must be the soul, and firm almost beyond the weakness of humanity, that can withstand the smiles of fortune. Success, promotion, the caresses of the great, and the flatteries of the low, are sometimes fatal to the noblest minds. The volatile become an easy prey. The fickle heart, tiptoe with joy, as from an eminence, views with contempt its former joys, connexions, and pursuits. A new taste contracted, seeks companions suited to itself. But pleasures easiest tasted, though perhaps at first of higher glee, are soonest past, and, the more they are relied upon, leave the severer sting behind. One cloudy day despoils the glow-worm of all its glitter.

Should fortune ever frown upon you, Matt.; should those you now call friends forsake you; should the clouds gather force on every side, and threaten to burst upon you, think then upon the man who never betrayed you; rely on the sincerity you never found to fail; and if my heart, my life, or my fortune can assist you, it is yours.

I go to-morrow to Elizabethtown, where I shall see the best of women—your wife. Whatever letters or commands she may have for you, I shall be careful to forward by the safest hands.

Your friend,

AARON BURR.

In the beginning of July, 1776, Major Burr was appointed aid-de-camp to General Putnam. At this time the headquarters of the general were in the large brick house, yet standing, at the corner of Broadway and the Battery. Burr continued occasionally to correspond with his friends, but was much occupied with his military duties, and those studies which were calculated to render him scientifically master of his profession. During the short period that he remained in the family of General Washington, he was treated with respect and attention; but soon perceived, as he thought, an unwillingness to afford that information, and those technical explanations of great historical military movements, which an inquiring and enlightened mind, like Burr's, sought with avidity and perseverance. He therefore became apprehensive, if he remained with the commander-in-chief, that, instead of becoming a scientific soldier, he should dwindle down into a practical clerk—a species of drudgery to which his pecuniary circumstances did not render it necessary for him to submit, and for which neither his habits, his education, nor his temperament in any degree qualified him. He therefore determined promptly on a change, and was willing to enter the family of Major-general Putnam, because he would there enjoy the opportunities for study, and the duties which he would be required to perform would be strictly military. There is no doubt the short residence of Major Burr with General Washington laid the foundation for those prejudices which, at a future day, ripened into hostile feelings on both sides.

Judge Paterson thus writes him :—

New-Brunswick, July 22d, 1776.

My dear Burr,

I did myself the pleasure of writing you by my brother, who is in General Sullivan's brigade, and who was in expectation of seeing you, as he was destined for the Canada department. Indeed, from the friendship which subsisted between us, I was in expectation of hearing frequently from you, and, to tell the truth, was not a little mortified that I was passed over in silence. Why, Burr, all this negligence? I dare not call it forgetfulness, for I cannot bear the thought of giving up my place in your esteem. I rejoice at your return, and congratulate you on your promotion. I was attending the convention at Burlington when you passed on to Philadelphia, and was full of the pleasing hope of having an interview with you. The Delaware, indeed, ran between us—a mighty obstacle, to be sure! I inquired when you designed to return, that I might plant myself at Bristol, and intercept you on your way. The inquiry was of no avail. I have at times been violently tempted to write you a railing letter, and for that purpose have more than once taken up the pen. But I can hardly tell how, on such occasions, the Genius of Friendship would rise up to view, and soften me down into all the tenderness of affectionate sorrow— perhaps because I counted you as lost. I find I must e'en forgive you—but, remember, you must behave better in future. Do write me now and then. Your letters will give me unfeigned pleasure, and, for your encouragement, I promise to be a faithful correspondent. In the letter-way you used to be extremely careless; you know I am, in that respect, of a different turn.

This will be handed you by Mr. Hugg and Mr. Leaming, members of our convention, whom curiosity partly, and partly business, have impelled to New-York. As men, they are genteel, sensible, and deserving. As politicians, they are worthy of your regard, for they possess the genuine spirit of whiggism. They have no acquaintance in York. They are desirous of seeing the fortifications, and other things in the military line. Pray take them by the hand; and be assured that any kindness shown them will be acknowledged as an additional obligation conferred upon

Your affectionate

WM. PATERSON.

A. Burr replies to this letter :—

New-York, July 26th, 1776.

MY DEAR PATERSON,

I this day received your kind letter. It gave me a pleasure I seldom experience. Can it be that you have still in memory the vagrant Burr? Some fatality has ever attended our endeavours to meet. Why I have not written to you I cannot tell. It has not been for want of friendship, of inclination, or always of opportunity; but some unavoidable accidents prevented so long, that I began to fear a letter from me must be ushered in by some previous introduction, some anecdotes of the writer, which might renew your remembrance, and authorize a freedom of this nature. But your frank and kind epistle precludes fulsome apologies, which, though sometimes necessary, I esteem, at best, but a drug in letters.

I am exceedingly pleased with your friends, Messrs. Hugg and Leaming, but was unfortunate enough to be from home the day they came in town, and had not the pleasure of seeing them till this afternoon. I felt myself so nearly interested in the welfare of the province whose constitution you are now framing, that I did not urge their stay with the warmth my inclination prompted. If any other of our Jersey friends should be coming this way, I should be happy in showing them every civility in my power.

As to promises of writing, I shall make you none, my dear Bill, till those already on hand, and of long standing, are discharged. I am no epistolary politician or newsmonger; and as to sentiments, a variety of novelties and follies has entirely dissipated them. This, however, is only a new apology for an old misfortune. But why this to you, who know me better than I know myself? This epistolary chat, though agreeable, is by no means satisfactory. The sincerity of my long-smothered affections is not to be thus expressed. I must contrive to shake you by the hand. Perhaps I may, ere long, be sent to Elizabethtown or Amboy on business, and will, undoubtedly, take Brunswick in my way. I have, or had once, an agreeable female acquaintance with Miss S. D., now Mrs. S., and with Miss S. was on tolerable terms of intimacy. Could I but reconnoitre a while, and find how the land lay, I might, perhaps, be able to graduate my compliments with some propriety, from cold respects to affectionate regards. I think I must leave you discretionary orders on this head, begging you to

make use of all the policy of war.   There is no knowing of
what importance it may be to

Your affectionate

A. BURR.

CHAPTER VII.

FROM the year 1780 until the year 1795, Mrs. Margaret
Coghlan made no inconsiderable noise in the court and
fashionable circles of Great Britain and France.   She was
the theme of conversation among the lords, and the dukes,
and the M. P.'s.   Having become the victim, in early life,
of licentious, dissolute, and extravagant conduct, alternately
she was revelling in wealth, and then sunken in poverty.
At length, in 1793, she published her own memoirs.   Mrs.
Coghlan was the daughter of Major Moncrieffe, of the
British army.   He was Lord Cornwallis's brigade major.
Her father had three wives.   She was a daughter of the
first wife.   His second wife was Miss L*********, of New-
York, and his third wife Miss J**, of New-York.   Mrs.
Coghlan is introduced here, because her early history is in-
timately connected with the subject of these memoirs.

In July, 1776, she resided in Elizabethtown, New-Jersey.
Her father was with Lord Percy on Staten Island.   In her
memoirs, speaking of herself, she says :—" Thus destitute of
friends, I wrote to General Putnam, who instantly answered
my letter by a very kind invitation to his house, assuring
me that he respected my father, and was only his enemy in
the field of battle ; but that, in private life, he himself, or any
part of his family, might always command his services.   On
the next day he sent Colonel Webb, one of his aid-de-camps,
to conduct me to New-York.   When I arrived in the Broadway (a street so called), where General Putnam resided, I

was received with great tenderness, both by Mrs. Putnam and her daughters, and on the following day I was intro duced by them to General and Mrs. Washington, who like wise made it their study to show me every mark of regard; but I seldom was allowed to be alone, although sometimes, indeed, I found an opportunity to escape to the gallery on the top of the house, where my chief delight was to view, with a telescope, our fleet and army at Staten Island. My amusements were few; the good Mrs. Putnam employed me and her daughters constantly to spin flax for shirts for the American soldiers; indolence, in America, being totally discouraged; and I likewise worked some for General Put- nam, who, though not an accomplished *muscadin*, like our dilletantis of St. James's-street, was certainly one of the best characters in the world; his heart being composed of those noble materials which equally command respect and admiration. * * * * * *

" Not long after this circumstance, a flag of truce arrived from Staten Island, with letters from Major Moncriefle, de- manding me; for he now considered me as a prisoner. Gen- eral Washington would not acquiesce in this demand, saying that I should remain a hostage for my father's good beha- viour. I must here observe, that when General Washington refused to deliver me up, the noble-minded Putnam, as if it were by instinct, laid his hand on his sword, and with a vio- lent oath swore that my father's request should be granted. The commander-in-chief, whose influence governed Con- gress, soon prevailed on them to consider me as a person whose situation required their strict attention; and that I might not escape they ordered me to Kingsbridge, where, in justice I must say, that I was treated with the utmost ten- derness. General Mifflin there commanded. His lady was a most accomplished, beautiful woman; a Quaker," &c.

Mrs. Coghlan then bursts forth in expressions of rapture for a young American officer, with whom she had become enamoured. She does not name him; but that officer was

Major Burr. "May these pages" (she says) "one day meet
the eye of him who subdued my virgin heart. * * * * * To
him I plighted my virgin vow. * * * * * * With this conquer-
or of my soul, how happy should I now have been! What
storms and tempests should I have avoided" (at least I am
pleased to think so) "if I had been allowed to follow the bent
of my inclinations. Ten thousand times happier should I
have been with him in the wildest desert of our native coun
try, the woods affording us our only shelter, and their fruits
our only repast, than under the canopy of costly state, with
all the refinements of courts, with the royal warrior" (the
Duke of York) "who would fain have proved himself the
conqueror of France. *My conqueror* was engaged in another cause; he was ambitious to obtain other laurels. He
fought to liberate, not to enslave nations. He was a colonel in the American army, and high in the estimation of his
country. *His* victories were never accompanied with one
gloomy, relenting thought. They shone as bright as the
cause which achieved them."

The letter from General Putnam of which Mrs. Coghlan
speaks is found among the papers of Colonel Burr, and is
in the following words :—

New-York, July 26th, 1776.

I should have answered your letter sooner, but had it not
in my power to write you any thing satisfactory.

The omission of my title, in Major Moncrieffe's letter, is
a matter I regard not in the least; nor does it in any way
influence my conduct in this affair, as you seem to imagine.
Any political difference alters him not to me in a private
capacity. As an officer, he is my enemy, and obliged to act
as such, be his private sentiments what they will. As a
man, I owe him no enmity; but, far from it, will, with pleasure, do any kind office in my power for him or any of his
connexions.

I have, agreeably to your desire, waited on his excellency

to endeavour to obtain permission for you to go to Staten Island.   He informs me that Lieutenant-colonel Patterson, who came with the last flag, said he was empowered to offer the exchange of —— —— for Governor Skeene.   As the Congress have reserved to themselves the right of exchanging prisoners, the general has sent to know their pleasure, and doubts not they will give their consent.   I am desired to inform you, that if this exchange is made, you will have liberty to pass out with Governor Skeene ; but that no flag will be sent solely for that purpose.

Major William Livingston was lately here, and informed me that you had an inclination to live in this city, and that all the ladies of your acquaintance having left town, and Mrs. Putnam and two daughters being here, proposed your staying with them.   If agreeable to you, be assured, miss, you shall be sincerely welcome.   You will here, I think, be in a more probable way of accomplishing the end you wish—that of seeing your father, and may depend upon every civility from,

Miss,
Your obedient servant,
Israel Putnam.

This letter is in the handwriting of Major Burr, and undoubtedly was prepared by him for the signature of the general.   Miss Moncrieffe was, at this time, in her fourteenth year.   She had travelled, and, for one of her age, had mingled much in the world.   She was accomplished, and was considered handsome.   Major Burr was attracted by her sprightliness and vivacity, and she, according to her own confessions, penned nearly twenty years afterward, had not only become violently in love with, but had acknowledged the fact to him.   Whether the foundation of her future misfortunes was now laid, it is not necessary to inquire.   Her indiscretion was evident, while Major Burr's propensity for intrigue was already well known.

Vol. I.—M

Burr perceived immediately that she was an extraordinary young woman. Eccentric and volatile, but endowed with talents, natural as well as acquired, of a peculiar character. Residing in the family of General Putnam with her, and enjoying the opportunity of a close and intimate intercourse, at all times and on all occasions, he was enabled to judge of her qualifications, and came to the conclusion, notwithstanding her youth, that she was well calculated for a spy, and thought it not improbable that she might be employed in that capacity by the British. Major Burr suggested his suspicions to General Putnam, and recommended that she be conveyed to her friends as soon as might be convenient. She was, in consequence, soon after removed to Kingsbridge, where General Mifflin commanded. This change of situation, in the work which she has published, is ascribed to General Washington, but it originated with Major Burr.

After a short residence at Kingsbridge, leave was granted for her departure to Staten Island. She accordingly set off in a continental barge, under the escort of an American officer, who was ordered to accompany her to the British headquarters. As the boat approached the English fleet, she was met by another, having on board a British officer, and was notified that she could proceed no further, but that the king's officer would take charge of the young lady, and convey her in safety to her father, who was six or eight miles in the country with Lord Percy. She says, in her memoirs, " I then entered the British barge, and bidding an eternal farewell to my dear American friends, *turned my back on liberty.*"

Miss Moncrieffe, before she had reached her fourteenth year, was probably the victim of seduction. The language of her memoirs, when taken in connexion with her deportment soon after her marriage, leaves but little room for doubt Major Burr, while yet at college, had acquired a reputation for gallantry. On this point he was excessively vain, and regardless of all those ties which ought to control an honourable mind. In his intercourse with females he was an unprincipled flatterer, ever prepared to take advantage of their weakness, their credulity, or their confidence. She that confided in him was lost. In referring to this subject, no terms of condemnation would be too strong to apply to Colonel Burr.

It is truly surprising how any individual could have become so eminent as a soldier, as a statesman, and as a professional man, who devoted so much time to the other sex as was devoted by Colonel Burr. For more than half a century of his life they seemed to absorb his whole thoughts. His intrigues were without number. His conduct most licentious. The sacred bonds of friendship were unhesitatingly violated when they operated as barriers to the indulgence of his passions. For a long period of time he seemed to be gathering, and carefully preserving, every line written to him by any female, whether with or without reputation ; and, when obtained, they were cast into one common receptacle,—the profligate and corrupt, by the side of the thoughtless and betrayed victim. All were held as trophies of victory,—all esteemed alike valuable. How shocking to the man of sensibility ! How mortifying and heart-sickening to the intellectual, the artless, the fallen fair !

Among these manuscripts were many the production of highly cultivated minds. They were calculated to excite the sympathy of the brother — the parent — the husband. They were, indeed, testimonials of the weakness of the weaker sex, even where genius and learning would seem to be towering above the arts of the seducer. Why they were thus carefully preserved, is left to conjecture. Can it be true that Moore is correct, when, in his life of Lord Byron, he says, " The allusions which he (Byron) makes to instances of *successful passion* in his career, were not without their influence on the fancies of that sex, whose weakness it is to be most easily won by those who come recommended by the greatest number of triumphs over others?" Some of these productions had been penned more than sixty years. They were all committed to the flames, however, immediately after the decease of Colonel Burr. Of them, it is believed, "not a wreck remains."

The faithful biographer could not pass over in silence this strong and revolting trait in the character of Colonel Burr. It will not again be referred to. From details, the moralist and the good man must shrink with disgust and abhorrence. In this particular, Burr appears to have been unfeeling and heartless. And yet, by a fascinating power almost peculiar to himself, he so managed as to retain the affection, in some instances, the devotion, of his deluded victims. In every other respect he was kind and charitable. No man would go farther to alleviate the sufferings of another. No man was more benevolent. No man would make greater sacrifices to promote the interest or the happiness of a friend. How strange, how inconsistent, how conflicting are these allusions! They are nevertheless strictly true.

Many of the letters to and from Colonel Burr contain hints and opinions as to public men and measures. Thus far, they are links in the chain of history, in relation to the times when they were written. They serve, also, to illustrate the character and the principles of the writers themselves. With these views they are occasionally selected. Theodore Sedgwick is a name recorded in the annals of our country with distinction. He writes to Burr:—

Sheffield, 7th August, 1776.

MY DEAR BURR,

If you remember, some months since, you and I mutually engaged to correspond by letter. I told you then that you were not to expect any thing either entertaining, or in any degree worth the trouble of perusing. What can a reasonable being expect from an inhabitant of such an obscure, remote, and dead place as Sheffield, to amuse, instruct, or even to merit the attention of a young, gay, enterprising, martial genius ? I know you will expect nothing, and I dare pledge my honour, therefore, that you will not, either now or in future, in this respect, be disappointed.

You recollect, perhaps, that when I had the pleasure to see you here, I informed you of a design to visit New-York and the southward. Soon after my business called me to Boston, and, on my return, I was obliged to go with the militia to Peekskill ; from there I should have visited the city and my friends, had not some foolish accidents prevented. I now think, as soon as I can leave home, of making a tour ; but this, like other futurities, is wholly uncertain.

The insignificant figure I make, in my own opinion, in this day of political and martial exertions, is an humbling consideration.· To be stoically indifferent to the great events that are now unfolding, is altogether inconsistent, not only with my inclination, but even with my natural constitution ; and to pursue a line of conduct which indicates such a disposition (I mean my continuance at home), is a mystery for which I will endeavour to account. Remember, I do not intend to libel the colony to which I belong.

Amid the confusion which was at once the cause and consequence of a dissolution of government, men's minds as well as actions became regardless of all legal restraint. All power reverted into the hands of the people, who were determined that every one should be convinced that *the people* were the fountain of all honour. The first thing they did was to withdraw all confidence from every one who had ever any connexion with government. Lawyers were, almost universally, represented as the pests of society. All persons who would pay court to these extravagant and unreasonable prejudices became their idols. Abilities were represented as dangerous, and learning as a crime, or rather, the certain forerunner of all political extravagances. They really demonstrated that they were possessed of creating power; *for, by the word of their power, they created great men out of nothing ;* but I cannot say *that all was very well.*

Observing these violent symptoms, I could not pursue that which was the only road to preferment; and I have never had an offer to go into the army, except the one I accepted; while I have seen, in more than one instance, men honoured with the command of a regiment for heading mobs. Well: with this, I believe, I have troubled you long enough. Pray, say you, what is it to me why you have not been in the army? Why, nothing, my dear friend; but it is something to me. You know, my dear Burr, I love you, or I should not submit such nonsense to your perusal.

If Mr. Swift still lives, give him my best compliments. Pamela desires me to tell you she loves you. Answer this letter, and thereby oblige

Your sincere friend,
THEODORE SEDGWICK.

FROM COLONEL M. OGDEN.

Ticonderoga, July 26th, 1776.

DEAR BURR,

I have been waiting with the greatest impatience to know what is doing in York and Jersey. There are twenty different reports, that contradict each other, relative to Howe and his fleet. It has once been generally believed that a French fleet had arrived at New-York, and blocked up the British army. Independence is well relished in this part of the world. Generalship is now dealt out to the army by our worthy and well-esteemed general, Gates, who is putting the most disordered army that ever bore the name into a state of regularity and defence. If our friends in Canada, commanded by Burgoyne, will wait a few days, we shall give them a very proper reception.

The army are beginning to recruit fast, from the effects of a little fresh meat, and some rum, when on fatigue.

Ten days ago there were not in our regiment eighty men fit for duty. We have now upwards of two hundred and thirty; and, in a few days, they will be all as rugged as New-Jersey is firm.

Colonel Winds is sent home on a fool's errand by the general, that he may be out of the way of doing any more harm to the regiment. The general assures me that I shall not be troubled with him again. I suppose, by that, he has written to have him detained below. A short history of this man will convince you that he ought to be nowhere but on his farm. He, in the first place, is a professed enemy to subordination, and has an utter aversion to discipline. He is positive, and prefers his own opinion to even the general's, because he was in the service last war. He is not possessed of one qualification that distinguishes a gentleman, nor has he genius or education. His whole study is to gain the applause of the private soldiers, at the expense of every officer in the regiment. He is hated by all his own officers except *two*, and despised by every gentleman in the army.

We are in great want of brigadier-generals—three, at least. I mean for the men that are now here. General Arnold will command the water-craft on the lake in person. There are three brigades, commanded by the colonels, Reed, Stark, and St. Clair. The last of these I sincerely wish was appointed a brigadier by Congress. There is no better man; the other two have full enough already.

Please to forward the enclosed, with the letter to Mr. Spencer. My best respects to Generals Putnam, Greene, and Mifflin, and to Colonel Trumbull. Compliments to Webb. I wait, with the greatest impatience, some important news from New-York. Pray write particulars relative to the conduct of the Jerseymen. Should any fall, mention their names.

I am yours sincerely,

MATT. OGDEN.

TO T. EDWARDS.

New-York, 10th of August, 1776.

DEAR UNCLE,

I have received your letters from Stockbridge, with my watch, for which I thank you. Our six galleys which went up the North river attacked the British ships. They beha ved well, but were drove off with the loss of three killed and twelve or thirteen wounded. A second attack is pro posed. Vessels and chevaux-de-frises are sunk in the North river. The channel is said to be effectually stopped. We are endeavouring the same in the East river. The British fleet have been largely re-enforced at different times. They are now said to be upwards of two hundred sail within the Narrows. They have drawn up seven of their heaviest ships in a line, nearly two miles advanced of the rest.

By two Virginia gentlemen who went to England to take the gown, who returned in a packet and landed on Staten Island, where they tarried several days, and were permitted to cross to Elizabethtown on Thursday last, we have some intelligence of the enemy. Clinton has arrived with his shattered fleet and about 3600 men. By this it appears that he has either fallen in with part of Dunmore's fleet, or picked up the remainder of his own, which had been sep- arated, and were not in the action near Charlestown. Of the Hessians only 1300 or 1400 have arrived. The re- mainder, about 9000, are daily expected. They were left near the banks of Newfoundland. Those already here are not much esteemed as soldiers.

The king's land-army is at present about 15 or 16,000 strong. They expect very soon to exceed 25,000. They have taken on board all their heavy cannon from Staten Isl- and, and have called in several of their outposts. Thirty transports have sailed under convoy of three frigates. They are to come through the Sound, and thus invest us by the North and East rivers. They are then to land on both sides of the island, *join their forces, and draw a line across, which will hem us in and totally cut off all communication, after which they will have their own fun.*

These Virginia gentlemen lodged in a house with several king's officers. They hold us in the utmost contempt. Talk of forcing all our lines without firing a gun. The bayonet is their pride. They have forgot Bunker's Hill.

Your nephew,

A. BURR.

FROM COLONEL M. OGDEN.

Ticonderoga, August 11th, 1776.

DEAR BURR,

I yesterday received yours of July 29th and August 2d. The others I made mention of in the letter to Mrs. Ogden that I sent to you unsealed. In my last you had a very particular account of the numbers, force, names, &c., of our navy on the lake. As to our leaving Crownpoint for this place, the field-officers knew nothing of it till it was conclu ded on by the generals, Schuyler, Gates, and Arnold.

General Arnold is taking a very active part, I mean in the command of the fleet. He will sail himself in a few days. He says he will pay a visit to St. Johns. I wish he may be as prudent as he is brave. Well, now have at you for news. Last evening the flag of truce returned, bringing a letter directed to *George Washington, Esq.,* and a truly ridiculous copy of a general order, which you will see at General Washington's by the time you receive this. But there is one part of it in which I think they, in some measure, accuse us justly. I mean that of assassinating, as they term it with too much truth, Brigadier-general Gordon. He was shot by the Whitcomb I mentioned in my last, who had been sent there as a spy. The act, though villanous, was brave, and a peculiar kind of bravery, that, I believe, Whitcomb alone is possessed of. He shot Gordon near by their advanced sentinel; and, notwithstanding a most diligent search was made, he avoided them by mere dint of skulking.

I shall have the honour to command the New-Jersey redoubt, which I am now building with the regiment alone It is situated on the right of the whole, by the water's edge. It is to mount two eighteen-pounders, two twelve, and four nine-pounders. In this I expect to do honour to New-Jersey. I yesterday received a letter from Colonel Dayton, dated the 28th of July, at the German Flats. He informs me that he is to take the command at Fort Stanwix.

Should there be any thing to be had in New-York in the clothing way, should be glad if you will lay some aside, no matter what—either small-clothes, shirts, stockings, or any thing of the kind. My best compliments to General Putnam. If you will let Robert or Sawyer have the perusal of this, they would learn the news of this army. Paper is so scarce, that one letter must serve both, unless something particular.

Yours sincerely,
MATT. OGDEN.

At this time Major-general Greene had the command on Long Island, but his health was so bad that it became necessary for him to resign it. The commander-in-chief ordered General Putnam to assume the command. Major Burr was his aid-de-camp. The landing of the British had been previously effected on the 22d of August, 1776, without opposition, near Utrecht and Gravesend, on the southwest end of the island. The American troops, less than 12,000, were encamped on the north of Brooklyn heights. The British force, including Hessians, was more than 20,000 strong. The armies were separated by a range of hills, at that time covered with wood, called the Heights of Gowannus. Major Burr immediately commenced an inspection of the troops, and made to the general a most unfavourable report, both as to their means of defence and their discipline.

The major proposed, however, several enterprises for beating up the quarters of the enemy. To all which General Putnam replied, that his orders were not to make any attack, but to act on the defensive only.

On the 27th the action was fought. The loss of the Americans, in killed, wounded, and prisoners, was about 1000. That of the British, less than 350. The Americans were driven within the works which they had thrown up. Major Burr, previous to the action, had expressed to General Putnam the opinion that a battle ought not to be risked; and that much was to be gained by placing the troops in a position where the navy of the enemy would not be so serviceable to them.

On the 28th, the British advanced in column to within 500 or 600 yards of the American works. General Robinson, who commanded a portion of the enemy, represents, in his parliamentary examination, that they approached much nearer. The American troops were formed in line to receive them; but gave such indications of alarm, that Major Burr rode to General Putnam, and informed him that he had no hope the men would stand more than a single fire before they retreated. No attack, however, was made. Burr continued to urge upon General Putnam and Mifflin (the latter of whom came over on that day from New-York) the necessity of a retreat. During the night of the 28th, General Mifflin went the rounds, and observed the forwardness of the enemy's batteries, and, on the morning of the 29th, pressed upon General Washington an immediate retreat. A council was held, and the opinion of Mifflin unanimously adopted.

The embarcation of the troops was committed to General M'Dougall. He was at Brooklyn Ferry by eight o'clock. In the early part of the night, the weather was very unfavourable; but about eleven o'clock every thing was propitious. A thick fog ensued, and continued until the whole army, 9000 in number, with all the field artillery, ordnance, &c. were safely landed in New-York. Major Burr was at

Brooklyn. Here General M'Dougall had an opportunity of
noticing his efficiency. His reputation for talents and intrepidity had previously reached the ears of the general. From
this night, the 29th of August, 1776, until Major Burr retired from the army, he possessed the entire confidence and
esteem of General M'Dougall. Subsequent events, as will
hereafter appear, tended to strengthen and confirm the correctness of those prepossessions, thus formed in the hour of
peril, and in the midst of the most appalling dangers.

The situation of General Washington, after retreating from
Long Island, was very distressing. The defeat which the
Americans had experienced produced consternation and
alarm in the ranks of a raw, inexperienced, and undisciplined army. In addition to other discouraging circumstances, within a few days after the retreat, nearly one fourth
of the troops were on the sick-list. Colonel Glover says
that the commander-in-chief divided his army, posting 12,000
at Kingsbridge, 6500 at Harlem, and 4500 in the city of
New-York.

On Sunday, the 15th of September, 1776, General Howe,
as commander-in-chief of the British forces, landed on Manhattan (New-York) Island. General Washington had previously made the necessary arrangements, and given orders
for the troops to evacuate the city and retire to Harlem, distant about seven miles. The descent of the British created
an alarm in the American ranks, and produced no inconsiderable degree of confusion in the retreat. By some unac-
countable mismanagement, General Silliman's brigade was
left in New-York, and conducted by General Knox to a small
fort then in the suburbs, and known as Bunker's Hill. Major
Burr having been despatched, at his own request, with a few
dragoons, by General Putnam, to pick up the stragglers, discovered the error which had been committed, and galloping
up to the fort, inquired who commanded. General Knox
presented himself. Major Burr desired him to retreat immediately, or the whole brigade would be cut off and sacri-

ficed.   General Knox replied, that a retreat, thus in the face
of the enemy, was impracticable, and that he intended to defend the fort.   Burr remarked, that it was not bomb-proof;
that it was destitute of water; and that he could take it with
a single howitzer; and then, addressing himself to the men,
said, that if they remained there, one half of them would be
killed or wounded, and the other half hung, like dogs, before night; but, if they would place themselves under his
command, he would conduct them in safety to Harlem.
Burr's character for intrepidity and military skill was already so well established, that they determined to follow
him.   In the retreat they had some skirmishing, but met
with very little loss in effecting their union with the main
body of the army.   The following documents, furnished by
officers in Silliman's brigade, contain the details.

SAMUEL ROWLAND TO COMMODORE RICHARD V. MORRIS.

Fairfield, (Conn.), 29th January, 1814.

Sir,

In answer to the inquiries relating to the evacuation of
New-York, in 1776, I can only observe, but few persons
who were present, and eyewitnesses of the event, are now
living in this part of the country.   I find, however, the Rev.
Doctor Ripley, a gentleman of eminent respectability, and
Messrs. Wakeman and Jennings, respectable citizens of this
town, now living, who belonged to the brigade of the late
General Silliman, the information of which gentlemen on any
subject can be relied on, and will be no otherwise than correct, however prejudice or other cause might occasion a reluctance in disclosing the information in their power to give;
yet duty impelled their narrative, and the neglecting an opportunity to give evidence of noble acts and unrewarded
worth they consider *ingratitude*.   In preference to communicating to you by way of letter concerning transactions of
so long standing as the year 1776, I desired the enclosed certificates, which the gentlemen freely gave, in order to pre-

vent any misconstruction by passing through a second hand,
by which you will have more correct information than pos
sibly in my power to give.

Very respectfully yours, &c.

SAMUEL ROWLAND.

Certificate of the Rev. Hezekiah Ripley.

On being inquired of by Samuel Rowland, Esq., of Fairfield town and county, in the State of Connecticut, relative
to my knowledge and recollection respecting the merits of
Colonel Aaron Burr as an officer and soldier in the late revolutionary war between the United States and Great Britain, can certify as follows :—

Hezekiah Ripley, of said Fairfield, doth certify, that on or
about the fifteenth day of September, 1776, I was the offi-
ciating chaplain of the brigade then commanded by Gen.
Gold S. Silliman. From mismanagement of the commanding officer, that brigade was unfortunately left in the city of
New-York, and at the time before mentioned. While the
brigade was in front, and myself considerably in the rear, I
was met by the late General Putnam, deceased, who then informed me of the landing of the enemy above us, and that I
must make my escape on the west side of the island.
Whereupon I on foot crossed the lots to the west side of
the island, unmolested excepting by the fire from the ships
of the British, which at that time lay in the North river.
How the brigade escaped, I was not an eyewitness; but
well recollect, from the information I then had from General
Chandler (now deceased), then acting as a colonel in said
brigade, that Mr. Burr's exertions, bravery, and good conduct, was the principal means of saving the whole of that
brigade from falling into the hands of the enemy, and whose
conduct was then by all considered judicious and meritorious.

But, however, I well recollect, before I had the information alluded to from General Chandler, I had seen Mr. Burr,

and inquired of him how the brigade had made their escape,
who then told me the particulars, which were afterwards confirmed by all the officers ; who were all of opinion that, had
it not been for him, they would not have effected their re
treat and escape.

As to my own opinion of the management of the troops
on leaving New-York, I then, and still suppose, as did General Chandler, that Colonel Burr's merits there as a young
officer ought, and did, claim much attention, and whose official duties as an aid-de-camp on that memorable day justly
claimed the thanks of the army and his country.

HEZEKIAH RIPLEY.

Certificate from Isaac Jennings and Andrew Wakeman.

Being requested by Samuel Rowland, Esq., to give information relative to the evacuation of New-York, in the year
1776, by the American army, we, the subscribers, then acting, one in the capacity of a lieutenant, and the other as a private, in the brigade commanded by the late General Silliman, now deceased, do certify, That on the fifteenth day of
September (being on the Lord's day), the British landed on
the east side of the island, about four miles above the city.
The American troops retreated the same day to Harlem
heights. By some misapprehension of the orders, or from
other causes unknown to us, our brigade was left, and was
taken by General Knox to Bunker's Hill,* a small fort (so
called) about a mile from town. The fort was scarcely able
to hold us all. We had but just got into the fort, when
Aaron Burr, then aid-de-camp to General Putnam, rode up
and inquired who commanded there. General Knox presented himself, and Burr (then called Major Burr) asked the
general what he did there ? And why he did not retreat with
the army ? The general replied, that it was impossible to
retreat as the enemy were across the island, and that he

---

* Adjacent to what is now Grand-street.

meant to defend that fort.   Major Burr ridiculed the idea of
defending the place, being, as he said, without provisions, or
water, or bomb-proof; and that, with one mortar, or one
howitzer, the enemy would take the place in.four hours, or
in some very short time, and again urged General Knox to
retreat to Harlem heights; but General Knox said it would
be madness to attempt it.   A smart debate ensued, the general adhering to his opinion.   Burr addressed himself to the
men, and told them that, if they remained there, they would
before night be all prisoners, and crammed into a dungeon,
or hung like dogs.   He engaged to lead them off, and observed that it would be better that one half should be killed
in fighting, than all be sacrificed in that cowardly manner.
The men agreed to follow him, and he led them out; he
and his two attendants riding on the right flank.   About four
miles from town we were fired upon by a party of the enemy.   Burr galloped directly to the spot the firing came from,
hallooing to the men to follow him.   It proved to be only
a guard of about a company of the enemy, who immediately
fled.   Burr and his horsemen pursued and killed several of
them.   While he was thus employed, the head of a column
had taken a wrong road.   Burr came up and hurried us to
the left, into a wood, and rode along the column from front
to rear, encouraging the men, and led us out to the main
army with very small loss.

   The coolness, deliberation, and valour displayed by Major Burr in effecting a safe retreat, without material loss,
and his meritorious services to the army on that day, rendered
him an object of peculiar respect from the troops, and the
particular notice of the officers.

                              ISAAC JENNINGS.
                              ANDREW WAKEMAN.

LETTER FROM NATHANIEL JUDSON TO COMMODORE R. V.
MORRIS.

Albany, 10th February, 1814.

Sir,

I have received your letter, with the preceding statement, respecting our retreat from New-York Island, in September, 1776, and, in compliance with your request, I have to reply, that the relation made by Mr. Wakeman and Mr. Jennings corresponds with my recollection. I was near Colonel Burr when he had the dispute with General Knox, who said it was madness to think of retreating, as we should meet the whole British army. Colonel Burr did not address himself to the men, but to the officers, who had most of them gathered around to hear what passed, as we considered ourselves as lost. But Colonel Burr seemed so confident that he could make good a retreat, and made it clear that we were all lost if we stayed there, that we all agreed to trust to his conduct and courage, though it did appear to us a most desperate undertaking ; and he did not disappoint us, for he effected a retreat with the whole brigade ; and I do not think we lost more than thirty men. We had several brushes with small parties of the enemy. Colonel Burr was foremost and most active where there was danger, and his conduct, without considering his extreme youth, was afterwards a constant subject of praise, and admiration, and gratitude. This affair was much talked of in the army after the surrender of Fort Washington, in which a garrison of about 2500 men was left under circumstances very similar to ours ; this fort having no bomb-proof. That garrison surrendered, as is well known, the very same day our army retreated; and of those 2500 men, not 500 survived the imprisonment they received from the British. I have, since then, heard it repeated hundreds of times by the officers and men of Silliman's brigade, that our fate would have been the same had it not been for Colonel Burr. I was a sergeant-major in Chandler's regiment of Silliman's brigade at the time of the retreat.

I am your very obedient servant,

NATHANIEL JUDSON

CHAPTER VIII.

As early as the 10th of August, Burr, in a letter to his uncle Edwards,* expressed apprehensions that the retreat of the American army from Long Island might be cut off and then that the British "would have their own fun." From that period until the retreat was effected, on the night of the 27th, he continued to entertain the same opinion as to the necessity of retreating. So, also, in relation to the city of New-York. He thought no attempt should be made to hold it. Subsequent events proved his good sense and foresight, as well as his military genius. The city was abandoned on the 15th of September. Ten days after he writes to his aunt Edwards, in reply to a desponding letter he had received from her, his views of the recent movements of the American army.

TO MRS. EDWARDS.

Kingsbridge, 26th September, 1776.

MY DEAR AUNT,

I fear, madam, you give yourself needless anxiety about the situation of public affairs. It has been always held a maxim that our island and seaport towns were at the discretion of the tyrant of Great Britain. Reasons for the retreat from Long Island are well known. The evacuation

* See page 97.

of New-York was a *necessary consequence*. The manner
of conducting these made present advantages but trifling to
the enemy. The loss to us is of still less importance; and,
indeed, some happy consequences resulting from the man-
œuvres appear to me worthy of notice.

We have hitherto opposed them with less than half their
number, and exposed to all their advantages of shipping.
Our force is now more united, theirs more divided. Our
present situation renders their navy of less service to them,
and less formidable to us;—a circumstance of vast importance, and to which I attribute all that has heretofore appeared in their favour. Add to these, besides confirming
our internal union, the effect that every appearance of success on the part of the enemy has upon our leading men.
It arouses them from the lethargy which began to prevail;
convinces them that their measures are unequal to their
grand designs; that the present is the important moment,
and that every nerve must now be exerted.

This is not altogether fanciful. It has been actually the
case. More effectual measures than were ever before
thought of are now taking for levying a new army. A
committee of Congress are on the spot with us to know
all our wants, and report them properly, that they may be
speedily provided for. I do not intend by this, my dear
aunt, to deceive you into an opinion that every thing is
already entirely secure; that we are now actually relieved
from every degree of danger; but to remove your apprehensions concerning the important events which depend on
our military exertions. I hope, madam, you will continue,
with your usual philosophy and resolution, prepared for
the uncertain events of war, not anticipating improbable
calamities. ,

Various have been the reports concerning the barbarities
committed by the Hessians, most of them incredible and
false. They are fonder of plunder than blood, and are

more the engines than the authors of cruelty. But their behaviour has been in some instances savage, and might excuse a fear, if reckoned among usual calamities; but these should be viewed on a larger scale than that of common complaisance. It should be remembered we are engaged in a civil war, and effecting the most important revolution that ever took place. How little of the horrors of either have we known! Fire or the sword have scarce left a trace among us. We may be truly called a favoured people.

I have been not so engaged as common for a short time past, and have liberty of remaining, for three or four days, about two miles from camp, from whence I now write you, a little more at leisure; but I am now within drum-call   -   Your nephew,

A. BURR.

After the abandonment of Manhattan Island by the American army, and some fighting in Westchester, General Washington crossed the North river with a part of the troops, and retreated through New-Jersey. The movements of Lord Cornwallis left no doubt that the object of the British general was Philadelphia. He advanced rapidly from Brunswick upon Princeton, hoping, by forced marches, to get in the rear of the Americans. On the 8th of December, 1776, Washington crossed the Delaware, secured the boats, and broke down the bridges. Great apprehension and alarm for the safety of Philadelphia now existed. Judge Marshall, in his Life of Washington, says,

"In consequence of this state of things, the general advised that lines of defence should be drawn from the Schuylkill, about the heights of Springatsbury, eastward to the Delaware, and General Putnam was ordered to superintend them." Major Burr was now actively engaged as the aid-de-camp of General Putnam, whose esteem and un bounded confidence he continued to enjoy.   He writes Colonel Ogden,

Princeton, 7th March, 1777.

DEAR MATT.,

I this evening received your letter of yesterday's date, by Stockton.   I knew not how to direct to you, nor where to send for the horse, or should have done it sooner.   I do not perfectly recollect the one you mention, but should be glad of any on your recommendation.   Both boots and a saddle I want much, and shall be obliged to you to procure them for me ;—good leather would suit me as well as boots ready made.   I have not had a pair worth sixpence since those I had at Elizabethtown.

As to "expectations of promotion," I have not the least, either in the line or the staff.   You need not express any surprise at it, as I have never made any application, and, as you know me, you know I never shall.   I should have been fond of a berth in a regiment, as we proposed when I last saw you.   But, as I am at present happy in the esteem and entire confidence of my good old general, I shall be piqued at no neglect, unless particularly pointed, or where silence would be want of spirit.   'Tis true, indeed, my former equals, and even inferiors in rank, have left me.   Assurances from those in power I have had unasked, and in abundance ; but of these I shall never remind them.   We are not to judge of our own merit, and I am content to contribute my mite in any station.

I shall probably be at Morris within ten days, on public business.   Write me whether I may expect you there.   With sincere love to Mrs. Ogden,

Yours,

A. BURR.

In the spring of 1777, a new army was to be raised.   For political reasons it was deemed expedient to select, where

it could be done with propriety, for the colonels of regiments, gentlemen supposed to have an influence. Among
those who were thus selected was Colonel Malcolm, formerly a merchant in the city of New-York. He was
highly respectable, and universally esteemed, but was not
a military man. In June, 1777, Burr was appointed lieu
tenant-colonel of his regiment; but he did not receive
official notice of the fact until the 26th of July.

On the 14th of July, 1777, General Putnam's headquarters being then at Peekskill, he issued the following
order :—   .

By the Honourable Major-general Putnam,
          To Major Aaron Burr, Aid-de-camp.
  Sir,   ,

Pursuant to orders received from his excellency General
Washington, you are forthwith to repair to Norwalk, Fairfield, and the places adjacent on the Sound, transmit me
without delay the intelligence you shall from time to time
receive of the movements of the enemy, or any of their
fleets. Request of the committees, or select-men of the
different towns, that they will be very punctual in reporting
to the commanding officer at this post whatever may in
any respect relate to the movements of the army, as both
their safety and the welfare of the country may be promoted
by their diligence in this particular.

On your return, which will be through Litchfield, you
will leave orders for all detachments of any regiments of
General Nixon's brigade to take the most direct route to
Albany, provided they be farther than thirty miles from this
place, as much will be saved, and fatigue avoided by the
observance of this.

Having settled a line of intelligence from the different
towns on the coast, and left the necessary directions for the
detachments of Brigadier-general Nixon's brigade, you will
return with all convenient speed to this place.

Given under my hand, at headquarters, Peekskill, 14th day of July, 1777.

ISRAEL PUTNAM.

This was the last order that Major Burr ever received as the aid-de-camp of his "good old general." On his return to camp he received, in the usual form, a letter from General Washington, announcing to him his appointment as lieutenant-colonel in the Continental Army, to which he replied,

Peekskill, 21st July, 1777.

SIR, -

I was this morning favoured with your excellency's letter of the 29th ult., and my appointment to Colonel Malcolm's regiment. Am truly sensible of the honour done me, and shall be studious that my deportment in that station be such as will ensure your future esteem. I am nevertheless, sir, constrained to observe, that the late date of my appointment subjects me to the command of many who were younger in the service, and junior officers the last campaign.

With submission, and if there is no impropriety in requesting what so nearly concerns me, I would beg to know whether it was any misconduct in me, or any extraordinary merit or services in them, which entitled the gentlemen lately put over me to that preference? Or, if a uniform diligence and attention to duty has marked my conduct since the formation of the army, whether I may not expect to be restored to that rank of which I have been deprived, rather, I flatter myself, by accident than design? I would wish equally to avoid the character of turbulent or passive, and am unhappy to have troubled your excellency with a matter which concerns only myself. But, as a decent regard to rank is both proper and necessary, I hope it will be ex cused in one who regards his honour next to the welfare of his country.

I am not yet acquainted with the state of the regiment.

or the prospect of filling it; but shall immediately repair to rendezvous and receive Colonel Malcolm's directions.

. I have the honour to be, with great respect,
                    Your excellency's obedient servant,
                              A. BURR.

Colonel Malcolm's regiment was at this time stationed at Ramapo, or the Clove, in Orange county, New-York, whither Lieutenant-colonel Burr proceeded. On presenting himself, the colonel was greatly surprised. The youthful appearance of Burr led him to apprehend that he would be wanting in judgment and discretion; but a very short acquaintance removed these impressions. Malcolm retired with his family about twenty miles distant, leaving Burr in command, kindly remarking—" You shall have all the honour of disciplining and fighting the regiment, while I will be its father;" and he kept his word, for it is believed that he never commanded it in battle during the whole war, although it was frequently engaged. This duty devolved upon Colonel Burr.

In September, 1777, the British came out of the city of New-York, on the west side of the Hudson river, about 2000 strong, for the purpose of plundering and devastating the adjacent country, and capturing the public stores. Colonel Burr was with his regiment, distant about thirty miles, when he heard of the enemy, and yet he was in their camp, and captured or destroyed their picket-guards before the next morning. For two days and nights he never slept. His regular force did not exceed three hundred men; but, by surprising the British sentinels, he struck consternation into their ranks, and they fled with precipitation, leaving behind them their plunder and a part of their stores. The following letters afford ample details :—

Statement of Judge George Gardner, dated

Newburgh, 20th December, 1813.

In September, 1777, the regiment called Malcolm's regiment lay at Suffren's, in the Clove, under the command of Lieutenant-colonel Burr Intelligence having been received that the enemy were in Hackensack in great force, and advancing into the country, Colonel Burr immediately marched with the effective men, except a guard to take care of the camp. I understood that while we were on the march, an officer arrived express from Major-general Putnam, who commanded at Peekskill, recommending or ordering Colonel Burr to retire with the public stores to the mountains: to which Colonel Burr replied, that he could not run away from an enemy whom he had not seen, and that he would be answerable for the public stores and for his men.

We arrived at Paramus, a distance of sixteen miles, before sunset. There were considerable bodies of militia, in great alarm and disorder, and doing much mischief to the neighbouring farms. They could give no intelligence of the enemy but from rumour. Supposed them to be within a few miles, and advancing.

Colonel Burr set some of the militia to repair the fences they had destroyed, and arranged them as well as time would permit; and having taken measures to secure the troops from surprise, and also for the protection of the corn-fields, he marched immediately, with about thirty of the most active of the regiment, and a few of the militia, to ascertain the position and numbers of the enemy. About ten o'clock at night, being three miles from Hackensack, we got certain intelligence that we were within a mile of the picket-guards of the enemy. Colonel Burr then led the men into a wood, and ordered them to sleep till he should awake them, of which we had great need, having marched more than thirty miles since noon. Colonel Burr then went alone to discover the position of the enemy. He returned about

VOL. I.—P

half an hour before day and waked us, and told us that he was going to attack the picket of the enemy. That we had only to follow him, and then forbid any man to speak or to fire, on pain of death. He led us between the sentinels in such a way that we were within a few yards of the picket-guard before they suspected our approach. He then gave the word, and we rushed upon them before they had time to take their arms, and the greater part were killed. A few prisoners and some accoutrements were brought off without the loss of one man. Colonel Burr immediately sent off an express to Paramus, to order all the troops to move, and to rally the country. Our little success had so encouraged the inhabitants, that they turned out with great alacrity, and put themselves under the command of Colonel Burr. But the enemy, probably alarmed by these threatening appearances, retreated the next day, leaving behind them the greater part of the cattle and plunder which they had taken. Colonel Burr was prevented from pursuing, by peremptory orders, which were received the day following the action, to join, without delay, the main army, then in Pennsylvania.

I served in this regiment all the time it was under the command of Colonel Burr, being about two years; after which he was called to take a separate command in Westchester. During the whole time he never permitted corporal punishment to be inflicted in a single instance; yet no regiment in the army was under better discipline, and I doubt whether it was equalled by any one.

                                        GEORGE GARDNER.

FROM LIEUTENANT ROBERT HUNTER TO GABRIEL FURMAN,
            ESQ., MEMBER OF ASSEMBLY,

                                New-York, 22d January, 1814.

    SIR,
    I have understood that an application will be made to the legislature by or on behalf of Colonel Burr, for remuneration for his military services during our revolutionary war.

Having had the happiness to serve under him for more than two years, and having retained an unbounded respect for his talents and character, you will pardon me for asking your active support of any thing which may be moved in his favour; for certainly, if any officer of the army deserved recompense, it is Colonel Burr.

He sacrificed his health, and underwent more fatigue and privations than any other officer of whom I had any knowledge. If I thought it could be useful to him or amusing to you, I would enter into details; but the facts are of general notoriety, and his superiority as a military man, as far as my knowledge extends, universally allowed.

I will however detain you while I relate a single incident, because it was the first of which I was a witness. I was attached as a cadet to Colonel Malcolm's regiment, then stationed in the Clove, when Burr joined it as lieutenant-colonel, being in the summer of 1777. Malcolm, seeing that his presence was unnecessary while Burr was there, was with his family about twenty miles distant. Early in September, we heard that the enemy were out in great force. Burr gave orders for the security of the camp and of the public stores, and within one hour after news was received, marched with the choice of the regiment to find the enemy. At Paramus the militia were assembled in considerable force, but in great disorder and terror. No one could tell the force or position of the enemy. Burr assumed the command, to which they submitted cheerfully, as he alone (though but a boy in appearance) seemed to know what he was about. He arranged and encouraged them as well as time would permit, and, taking a few of the most hardy of the men, continued his march towards the enemy. Two or three miles this side Hackensack, we learned that we were near the enemy's advanced guard. Burr chose a convenient place for the men to repose, and went himself to examine the position of the enemy. A little before daylight he returned, waked us, and ordered us to follow him. He

led us silently and undiscovered within a few paces of the
British guard, which we took or killed.   From the prisoners
we learned that the enemy were about two thousand strong.
Without loss of time he sent expresses with orders to the
militia, and to call out the country; and I have no doubt
but he would, within forty-eight hours, have had an army
capable of checking the progress of the enemy, and of pre-
venting or impeding their retreat; but they retreated the day
following, and with every mark of precipitation.   During
these two days and nights the colonel did not lie down or
take a minute's repose.   Thus you perceive, my dear sir,
that Burr, being more than thirty miles distant when he
heard of the enemy, was in their camp the same night.
You will agree with me that things are not done so nowa-
days.

Similar instances of activity and enterprise occurred in
each of the four campaigns he served, and very frequently,
during the winter, he commanded on the lines of Westchester.   I repeat, that it will afford me pleasure to relate
so much of these things as came to my own knowledge, if
it would be of any use.

Malcolm was never a month with the regiment after Burr
joined it; so that it was Burr who formed it, and it was a
model for the whole army in discipline and order.   He
never, in a single instance, permitted any corporal punishment.

His attention and care of the men were such as I never
saw, nor any thing approaching to it, in any other officer,
though I served under many.   It would be a disgrace to
the country if such a man should be denied a liberal compensation, when it is too well known that he stands in need
of it.

I shall consider myself as personally obliged by your exertions in his favour, and hope your colleagues will add
theirs to yours.

Please to show this letter to your colleagues, and to offer them my respects.

I am, very respectfully,

Your obedient servant,

ROBERT HUNTER.

The original order to join the main army in Pennsylvania, to which Judge Gardner refers in the preceding statement, is found among the papers of Colonel Burr, and is as follows :—

Headquarters, Peekskill, 27th September, 1777.

SIR,

I have just received a letter from General Washington, dated *thirty-four miles up Schuylkill,* wherein he informs me that General Howe's army had found means to cross Schuylkill several miles below his army ; upon which he has ordered a further re-enforcement from this post, of which corps you must join. You will therefore, upon the receipt of this, prepare to join General Parsons's brigade, whom I have ordered up from the White Plains. I shall endeavour to send some militia to guard the stores remaining in the Clove Your baggage must go with you.

I am, sir, your very humble servant,

ISRAEL PUTNAM, M. G.

Immediately after Colonel Burr had surprised and captured the British guard, he received various complimentary notes from officers of the army requesting details. A short extract from one is given.

Peekskill, 20th September, 1777.

DEAR SIR,

I congratulate you upon the good fortune you met with in taking off the enemy's picket. We have had various ac

counts about the manner in which you executed the plan
The particulars I should be glad to hear from yourself.,
Yours, &c.
T. YATES.
To Lieutenant-colonel A. BURR.

Colonel Burr, with his accustomed promptitude, as soon
as he received the orders of Major-general Putnam, put his
regiment in motion.   On the second day of his march he
received from General Varnum the following, directed to
Lieutenant-colonel Burr, on his march to Morristown.

Cakeat, October 1st, 1777.

SIR,
I this moment received your favour of this date.   The
enemy have landed at Powler's Hook in great force.   I am
apprehensive they mean attacking Fort Montgomery by the
way of the Clove.   I have sent my baggage and some forces
there.   The enemy must be attended to.   You will therefore halt in the nearest place that is convenient upon the receipt of this.   Keep a good look-out towards Newark, Elizabethtown, &c., or those places from whence they can
march into Pumpton.   Should you be in danger of being interrupted there, throw your party across the river in Pumpton, and defend the bridge, if practicable.   If not, make the
best retreat you can towards Morristown, &c.   But by no
means proceed unless necessity urges, derived from the present object.   In every thing else pursue your best discretion.
I am, sir, your humble servant,
I. VARNUM.

The following note from General Conway tends to prove,
that although Burr was only a lieutenant-colonel in 1777,
yet that he was actually received and treated as the commandant of his regiment, from which he was never absent
Colonel Malcolm, in general, was employed on other duty.

FROM GENERAL CONWAY.

29th October, 1777.

SIR,

I have received a letter from Captain Kearsley respecting the settlement of the rank of the captains and subalterns. I could not give him an immediate answer, because I was then attending a court-martial. I wish this matter was settled as soon as possible to the satisfaction of the officers of your regiment. The general officers being employed in several courts-martial, which, along with the camp-duty, will take up all their time, I think you had best apply to the adjutant-general. Know from him the manner in which the ranks of the Virginia and Pennsylvania officers have been settled, and arrange accordingly, at least pro tempore, the rank of your gentlemen.

I am, sir, your most obedient and humble servant,

T. CONWAY.

The regiment joined the army in November, 1777, at Whitemarsh, in Pennsylvania, twenty miles from Philadelphia. Colonel Burr, in command of it, was stationed about half a mile in advance of the main body. After a few weeks, the army went into winter-quarters at Valley Forge. During the winter, Colonel Burr proposed to General Washington an expedition against Staten Island. He stated to the commander-in-chief that he was personally and well acquainted with many of the inhabitants in the vicinity of the island. That he believed they would join him as volunteers ; and that he only asked two hundred men of his own regiment as a nucleus. General Washington declined granting the request. But subsequently, an unsuccessful attempt was made under the command of Lord Stirling.

Within eight or ten miles of Valley Forge, there was a narrow and important pass, known as the Gulf. A strong body of militia were stationed to defend it. They were in the habit of exciting in the camp false alarms; and the main body, in consequence, was frequently put in motion. When not put in motion, they were greatly disturbed, especially at night. These alarms generally resulted from the want of a rigid discipline. General M'Dougall was at Valley Forge, and exceedingly annoyed. Of Burr, as a disciplinarian and a soldier, he entertained a high opinion; and recommended to Washington that he withdraw from this detachment Burr's seniors, as officers, and give him the command of the post, which was accordingly done Colonel Burr immediately commenced a rigid system of police, visiting every night, and at all hours of the night, the sentinels; changing their position, &c. During the day he kept the troops under a constant drill. The rigour of this service was not adapted to the habits of militia, who had been accustomed to pass, in camp, a life of idleness, and to act as suited their individual whims and caprices. A portion of the most worthless became restless, and were determined to rid themselves of such a commander.

Colonel Burr was notified of the contemplated mutiny, in which he would probably fall a victim. He ordered the detachment to be formed that night (it being a cold, bright moonlight), and secretly directed that all their cartridges should be drawn, so that there should not be a loaded musket on the ground. He provided himself with a good and well-sharpened sabre. He knew all the principal mutineers. He marched along the line, eying the men closely. When he came opposite to one of the most daring of the ringleaders, the soldier advanced a step, and levelled his musket at Colonel Burr, calling out—" Now is your time, my boys." Burr, being well prepared and in readiness, anticipating an assault, with a celerity for which he was remarkable, smote the arm of the mutineer above the elbow, and nearly severed it from his body, ordering him, at the same time, to take and keep his place in the line. In a few minutes the men were dismissed, and the arm of the mutineer was next day amputated. No more was heard of the mutiny; nor were there afterwards, during Colonel Burr's command, any false alarms. This soldier belonged to Wayne's brigade; and some of the officers talked of having Colonel Burr arrested, and tried by a court-martial, for the act; but the threat was never carried into execution.

That Colonel Burr joined the army at White Marsh, and was there in command of his regiment, the following application and order will show:—

Near White Marsh, Nov., 1777.

SIR,

The papers and clothing of the companies which have lately joined Malcolm's regiment are at Bethlem. The papers are now wanted; and several of the officers cannot appear decent until they receive other clothes: for these reasons I would ask your indulgence for leave of absence, for two subalterns, six days. Their presence is not particularly necessary with their companies.

Respectfully your ob't serv't,
A. BURR.

Hon. General CONWAY.

This application General Conway returns, with the following endorsement:—

Colonel Burr is master to send such officers as he thinks requisite, in order to procure the papers wanted, and the clothes for the use of the regiment.

T. CONWAY.

While the army was at Valley Forge, in the winter of 1777–78, the difficulties between General Washington and General Gates, and their respective friends, became, in a great measure, matter of publicity. At this period there were two parties among the officers. Washington had his warm friends and supporters. Lee and Gates had theirs

Colonel Burr was of the latter. The merits of the question will not be discussed; and the subject will only be referred to so far as Burr is concerned.

In the spring of 1776, at the request of the commander-in-chief, Burr joined his military family for a short space of time, but soon became dissatisfied and retired. On the 29th of August, 1776, the American army retreated from Long Island. This retreat Burr had pressed upon Putnam, Mifflin, and others. In his letter to T. Edwards,* dated the 10th of August, nearly *three weeks* before it took place, he says: "They (the British) are to come through the Sound, and thus invest us by the North and East rivers. They are then to land on both sides of the island, join their forces, and draw a line across, *which will hem us in, and totally cut off all communication, after which they will have their own fun.*"

During the night of the retreat, Burr was actively enga-ged aiding M'Dougall in the embarcation of the troops at Brooklyn; and, from a personal knowledge of the localities of it and the adjacent places, he imagined that he had ren-dered some service. It has been shown that, by his intre-pidity and perseverance in the retreat from New-York, he rescued from impending danger the brigade of General Sil-liman. In neither of these cases was his conduct noticed by the commander-in-chief, either in general orders or otherwise. Young, ardent, ambitious, and of a fiery tem-perament, he thought that justice was not done to his efforts, and construed these, with other minor occurrences about the same time, into acts of hostility towards him. In September, 1776, therefore, his prejudices against General Washington became fixed and unchangeable; and to the latest hour of his life he recurred to the retreat from Long Island, and from the city of New-York, with acrimonious feelings towards the commander-in-chief. Whatever may

* See page 96.

be said to the contrary, as early as this period those prejudices were formed and confirmed. That General Washington placed no confidence in Burr, and that, for some
reason, he was exceedingly hostile towards him, is equally
certain. Whether his hostility commenced at this period
is matter of more uncertainty. Events already noticed
demonstrate that the general considered him an intrepid,
efficient, and vigilant officer.

Thus, in 1777, Burr was the friend of Lee and Gates in
opposition to General Washington. In the beginning of
January, 1778, it was reported to Burr that Lord Stirling
had made some remarks respecting the manner in which the
colonel had contributed to arrange the rank of his (Burr's)
subaltern officers. Lord Stirling at this time commanded
the division. It will be recollected that, a few weeks previous, Colonel Burr had proposed to the commander-in-chief
an enterprise against Staten Island, which was rejected;
but, immediately after, it was unsuccessfully attempted by
Lord Stirling. The difficulty, therefore, in fact, between
these gentlemen, grew out of the latter circumstance. On
the 7th of January, 1778, Burr addressed Lord Stirling,
requesting an explanation, which was promptly given in the
following note, and thus the matter terminated.

Camp, January 8th, 1778.

SIR,

The receipt of your letter of yesterday's date not a little
surprised me, for I can assure you that I have never made
use of a word in censure of yourself, or of the court you
mention. I some days ago ordered a return to be brought
in of the names and rank of the officers of the division,
independent of what the two courts were doing, and desired Major Monroe* to direct the brigade-majors to make
them out as soon as possible : from this, I suppose, some

---

* James Monroe, late president of the United States, then aid to Lord Stirling.

mistake has arose, which I will call upon Major Stagg to
explain.   .   I am,
Your most obedient humble servant,
STIRLING.
Lieutenant-colonel BURR.

CHAPTER IX.

COLONEL BURR was a rigid disciplinarian, and in the per
formance of his duty made no difference between those officers who were his friends and those who were not; yet he
never failed to adopt the most delicate and gentlemanly
course, where, in his opinion, rigour became necessary.
There are many documents tending to establish this fact,
such as the following:—

Camp, April 10th, 1778.

MY LORD,
In my weekly returns, your lordship may have observed
that Captain Tom has been returned—*absent without leave.*
As he had been long from the regiment, and no reasons had
been assigned to me for his extraordinary absence, I thought
myself in duty bound to make such report.   Upon his return
to camp, he has accounted for his conduct in a manner more
satisfactory than I feared he could.
Unwilling to deal too severely with a valuable officer, and
conscious of the impropriety of passing any seeming neglect
in entire silence, I refer him to your lordship as the proper
judge of his conduct and excuses.
My lord, you are acquainted with the character of Captain
Tom.   You have often heard me mention him with respect.
Should his absence appear, in any degree, to have arisen
from inattention, I hope your lordship will treat it with all

the delicacy which the conduct of a man of feeling and of spirit can desire.

I have the honour to be,

Your lordship's most obedient servant,

A. BURR.

FROM COLONEL MALCOLM.

Yorktown, June 16th, 1778.

MY DEAR SIR,

I have just now met with Captain Kearsley, which enables me to let you know that I am here, sent by General Gates to Congress on a variety of business.

I have consented to do duty as adjutant-general to the northern army, on conditions of holding my regiment, and that it should come to the northward. The first agreed to; the last according to events.

None of the sixteen additional regiments stand on the new establishment. Of the strongest, if ours comes within that description, it will be one. *As General Washington writes General Gates that he cannot conveniently spare you at this time*, I recommend your sending three or four officers to the State of New-York on the recruiting service. You know who will answer best, and who can be best spared; and to recruit for the regiment at large, I think I can provide you with some men.

As I have not time either to pass through, come, or to write any other of the officers, do tell them how I am circumstanced, and offer them my best respects. I am happy to hear that Major Pawling is better. I shall write from Peekskill very soon, and beg to hear from you.

I ever am, very sincerely, affectionately yours,

W. MALCOLM.

By the preceding letter it appears that "General Washington had written to General Gates that he could not conveniently spare Colonel Burr." The reason is obvious. It

was at the very moment when Sir Henry Clinton was about
to evacuate Philadelphia, and to retreat through New-Jersey.   The commander-in-chief was unwilling at such a crisis to part with an efficient and gallant officer.   On the 18th
of June, Sir Henry Clinton, with his forces, left the city,
proceeded to Gloucester Point, three miles down the river,
and crossed the Delaware into New-Jersey.   That day he
marched as far as Haddonfield.   The Americans crossed
the Delaware at Corriel's Ferry, and halted, after a distressing march from heat and rain, within five miles of Princeton.   During the preceding winter General Lee had been
exchanged, and joined the army at Valley Forge.

The enemy's force was now estimated at between 9000
and 10,000, rank and file.   The Americans at 10,600, exclusive of Maxwell's brigade, about 1200, and about 1200 militia.   On the 24th of June, 1778, the commander-in-chief
propounded to the general officers the question, " Will it be
advisable to hazard a general action?"   The answer was,
" Not advisable ; but a detachment of 1500 to be immediately sent to act, as occasion may serve, on the enemy's left
flank and rear, in conjunction with the other continental
troops and militia already hanging about them, and the main
body to preserve a relative position, to act as circumstances
may require."   Signed by Lee, Stirling, Greene, Fayette,
Steuben, Poor, Paterson, Woodford, Scott, Portail, Knox.

Four days after, viz., the 28th of June, the battle of Monmouth was fought.   It was on this occasion that General
Washington ordered the arrest of General Lee : 1stly, For
disobedience of orders in not attacking the enemy on the
28th of June, agreeably to repeated instructions ; 2dly, For
misbehaviour before the enemy on the same day, by making
an unnecessary, disorderly, and shameful retreat ; 3dly,
For disrespect to the commander-in-chief, in two letters, dated the 20th of June.   On the 12th of August the court-
martial, of which Lord Stirling was president, found Lee
guilty, and sentenced him to be suspended from any com-

mand in the armies of the United States for the term of twelve months. The history of the battle of Monmouth, with all the consequences that followed, has long since been given to the world by the friends and the opponents of the respective parties. It is only necessary to state here, that Colonel Burr, on that occasion, was ranked among the sup porters of Lee, and had himself real or imaginary cause of complaint against the commander-in-chief.

In this action Colonel Burr commanded a brigade in the division of Lord Stirling, composed of his own regiment and some Pennsylvanians, under the immediate command of Lieutenant-colonel Dummer. Gordon, in his History of the American Revolution, says, " The check the British received gave time to make a disposition of the left wing and second line of the main army in the wood, and on the eminence to which he had been directed and was retreating. On this were placed some batteries of cannon by Lord Stirling, who commanded the left wing, which played upon the British with great effect, and, *seconded by parties of infantry detached to oppose them, effectually put a stop to their advance.* The British, finding themselves warmly opposed in front, attempted to turn the American left flank, but were repulsed."

Shortly after the action had become general, Burr discovered a detachment of the enemy coming from the borders of a wood on the southward. He instantly put his brigade in motion for the purpose of checking them. It was necessary to cross a morass, over which a bridge was thrown. He ordered Lieutenant-colonel Dummer to advance with the Pennsylvania detachment, and that he would bring up the rear with his own regiment. After a part of the brigade was over the bridge, Colonel Barber, aid to General Washington, rode up, and said that the orders of the commander-in-chief were that he should halt. Colonel Burr remonstrated. He said his men, in their present position, were exposed to the fire of the enemy, and that his whole brigade must now cross the bridge before they could halt with any safety. Colonel Barber repeated that the orders of General Washington were peremptory that he should halt, which was accordingly done, and the brigade, in their divided state, suffered severely. Lieutenant-colonel Dummer was killed; Colonel Burr's horse was shot under him; and those who had crossed the bridge were compelled to retreat.

The movements and the firing of the armies continued until dark. The Americans remained on the battle-ground, with an intention of renewing the attack in the morning. Burr's uniform practice was, when near an enemy, to be up at night, visiting his own pickets, and taking the necessary precautions for avoiding a surprise. The night preceding the action Colonel Burr was thus engaged, as it was known that the British would move at dawn of day, if not before, and General Washington had given orders to Lee, who was in the advance, to commence the attack as soon as they did move. The weather was intensely hot. Notwithstanding the fatigue which Colonel Burr had undergone during the night of the 27th and the succeeding day, yet he remained up the night of the 28th also. Sir Henry Clinton's troops were employed in removing their wounded, and then marched away in such silence, that, though General Poor lay near them, their retreat was effected without his knowledge.

Exhausted with fatigue, and worn out for the want of repose, on the 29th, Colonel Burr lay down under the shade of some trees and fell asleep. When he awoke, he was exposed, and had been for some time, to the rays of the sun. He found himself unable to walk without great difficulty; and so severely was he afflicted, that he did not recover from its effects for some years afterwards. A stranger to complaints or murmurs when enduring pain, the real state of his health was unknown to even his brother officers. In this situation he was immediately ordered by

General Washington, through Lord Stirling, to repair to Elizabethtown, on highly important and confidential business. The great object of the commander-in-chief was to ascertain, as far as practicable, the future movements of the enemy, Sir Henry Clinton having secured his retreat to the city of New-York. General Washington proceeded to New-Brunswick, at which place Lord Stirling was attending as president of the court-martial for the trial of General Lee. The following notes will explain the character of Burr's mission, and the confidence reposed in him by the commander-in-chief.

FROM LORD STIRLING.

Brunswick, July 4th, 1778.

DEAR SIR,

I have this moment received yours of yesterday's date. On showing it to General Washington, he approves of the progress of your inquiries, and desires they may be continued. But he particularly desires me to *send off this express to you*, to request that you will endeavour to get all the intelligence you possibly can from the city of New-York : What are the preparations of shipping for embarcation of foot or horse ?—what expeditions on hand ?—whether up the North river, Connecticut, or West Indies ? For this purpose you may send one, two, or three trusty persons over to the city, to get the reports, the newspapers, and the truth, if they can. We are just going to exhibit a grand champetre and feu de joie, so must only say that

I am sincerely yours,

STIRLING.

FROM LORD STIRLING.

Brunswick, July 6th, 1778.

DEAR SIR,

I have your letter of yesterday's date. The court-martial, of which I am president, is adjourned to Morristown,

which will oblige me to go there to-morrow. I must therefore desire you will direct your letters, with such intelligence as you may procure, to his excellency General
Washington, who will be on the line of march with the
army. In haste,

Your most obedient servant,

STIRLING.

FROM LORD STIRLING.

Brunswick, July 6, 1778.

General Washington desires me to state that he wishes
you would employ three, four, or more persons, to go to
Bergen heights, Weehawk, Hoebuck, or any other heights
thereabout, convenient to observe the motions of the enemy's shipping, and to give him the earliest intelligence
thereof; whether up the river particularly. In short, every
thing possible that can be obtained.

Yours, &c.,

STIRLING.

FROM TENCH TILGHMAN.

Newark, July 8th, 1778.

DEAR SIR,

His excellency desires me to inquire whether you have
received any information of the enemy's movements, situation, or design? He will leave this place about 4 o'clock
this afternoon, before which he will expect to hear from
you.

I am, dear sir, your most obedient,

TENCH TILGHMAN.

Having completed the business on which he had been
despatched by the commander-in-chief, Colonel Burr proceeded to join his regiment, although his health was very
bad. In a few days he received the following order :—

Camp, near Croton Bridge, 19th July, 1778.

Colonel Malcolm's regiment is ordered to march at two o'clock to-morrow morning, to the fort at West Point, on Hudson river, with the regiment commanded by Lieutenant-colonel Parker, which is to join on the road near Croton bridge. The commander of the two regiments will make all convenient despatch, marching ten miles a day, as water and ground will admit.

The Baron De Kalb.

Early in July, 1778, in consequence of Sir Henry Clinton having arrived in New-York with his army, much excitement and some apprehension existed in the upper part of the state respecting the tories. The legislature had previously adopted rigid measures on the subject, and it became necessary that an intelligent and confidential military officer should be designated to take charge of them. General Washington selected Colonel Burr for this purpose. The trust was one of a delicate character.

FROM ROBERT BENSON.

Camp, White Plains, 2d August, 1778.

Sir,

By an act of the legislature of the State of New-York, the commissioners for detecting and defeating conspiracies, &c., were directed to tender an oath of allegiance, in the said act prescribed, to certain persons, inhabitants of this state, who have affected to observe, during the present war, a dangerous and equivocal neutrality; and on their refusal to take the same, that the said commissioners should cause them to be conveyed within the enemy's lines. In consequence whereof, sundry persons, to whom the said oath hath been tendered, and who have refused to take the same, were by the commissioners directed to rendezvous at Fishkill, on Monday next, in order to embark on board a sloop to be provided at that place for the purpose.

In order that this business might be conducted with as
little danger as possible to the operations of the present
campaign, his excellency Governor Clinton requested his
excellency the commander-in-chief to appoint an officer of
the army for the purpose; and you being assigned to this
business, his excellency Governor Clinton hath directed me,
in his name, to request you to repair to Fishkill on Monday
next, &c.

If by any accident you should not find the commissioners
at Fishkill, his excellency will be much obliged to you if
you would ride up to Poughkeepsie, where the board are
sitting.

I am, with great respect, yours, &c.,

ROBERT BENSON, Secretary.

P. S. Enclosed is the flag; and his excellency the governor desires you will fill the blank with the name of the
sloop, and the names of the persons who may be put on
board by the commissioners.

*At a meeting of the Board of Commissioners for detecting
and defeating Conspiracies, held at Poughkeepsie, August 3d, 1778.*

Present—Mr. Platt, Mr. Harpur, Mr. Cantine, and Mr.
Wynkoop.

The board having received a letter from his excellency
Governor Clinton, dated at camp, White Plains, the second
instant, informing that his excellency General Washington
had appointed Lieutenant-colonel Burr to conduct such
persons as had refused to take the oath of allegiance to this
state, prescribed by an act of the legislature thereof, within
the enemy's lines; therefore,

Resolved, That Colonel Burr be served with a copy of
the proceedings of this board against William Smith and
Cadwallader Colden, Esquires, and Mr. Roeliff J. Eltinge;
and that he is hereby authorized to remove each and every

of them within the enemy's lines, in such way and manner as his excellency General Washington may have already directed, or hereafter shall direct.

Extracts from the minutes, by order,

TEUNIS TAPPAN, Secretary to the Board.

FROM THE COMMISSIONERS TO COLONEL BURR.

Poughkeepsie, August 3d, 1778.

SIR,

The commissioners for conspiracies being informed by his excellency the governor of your appointment to receive at Fishkill such persons as have refused to take the oath prescribed by a law of this state, and who, by virtue of the said law, are to be sent into the enemy's lines, by us appointed to carry the same into execution; in consequence of this, we hereby send you William Smith, Cadwallader Colden, Esquires, and Mr. Roeliff J. Eltinge, who have refused to take the said oath, and thereby have subjected themselves to a removal within the said lines, which removal you will be pleased to take charge of.

The bearer, Cornelius E. Wynkoop, Esquire, is one of the board, to whom we refer you for such particulars as may be necessary to adjust, the more effectually to enable us to convey, in future, such gentlemen as the above over into the enemy's lines.

We are, sir, with respect,

Your most obedient servants,

ZEPHA. PLATT,   ⎱
ROBERT HARPUR,   ⎬ Commissioners.
PETER CANTINE, Jun.,   ⎰

Kinderhook, August 7th, 1778.

My dear Sir,

I write you in haste by Mr. Van Schaack,* who will convey it to you should you be at West Point. This gentleman has, by long acquaintance, manifested such qualities as have much attached me to his interest; but, most unfortunately for his friends, has differed in political opinions from the body of the community in general, and from me in particular, in consequence of which difference (by means of the test act of this state) he is about to be removed to the city of New-York; and has been so obliging as to offer me his assistance in procuring for, and sending to me, a few family necessaries. Should it be in your power, I am very certain it would be an unnecessary request to desire you to lend me any assistance : nor need I desire you to render Mr. Van Schaack's short stay among you as agreeable as his and your circumstances will permit.

I most sincerely congratulate you on the happy prospect of a speedy termination to the war. I believe I shall visit the camp soon, in which case you will have the pleasure to see Mr. Edwards in company. I have, since I saw you, become the father of a second daughter. Pamela has had a most tedious and dangerous illness, but is, thank God, now, for her, very well. You may be sure she will be glad to be affectionately remembered by you.

Yours most sincerely,

THEODORE SEDGWICK.

It has heretofore been stated that Colonel Burr was of the Lee and Gates party in the army. A short note from Lee to Burr will show the poignancy of the general's feel-

---

* There were two families of Van Schaicks in the State of New-York. They spelled their names differently. The family of Colonel *Van Schaick* were revolutionary whigs. The *Van Schaacks* were adherents of the crown.

ings under the sentence of the court-martial, and the mortifi
cation and disappointment he experienced when Congress
refused to reverse that sentence.

FROM GENERAL LEE.

October, 1778.

DEAR SIR,

As you are so kind as to interest yourself so warmly in
my favour, I cannot resist the temptation of writing you a
few lines. Till these two days, I was convinced the Congress would unanimously have rescinded the absurd, shameful sentence of the court-martial; but, within these two
days, I am taught to think that equity is to be put out of
the question, and the decision of the affair to be put entirely
on the strength of party ; and, for my own part, I do not
see how it is possible, if the least decency or regard for
national dignity has place, that it can be called a party
business.

I wish I could send you the trial, and will the moment I
can obtain one. I think myself, and I dare say you will
think on the perusal, that the affair redounds more to
my honour, and the disgrace of my persecutors, than, in
the warmth of indignation, either I or my aid-de-camps
have represented it. As I have no idea that a proper reparation will be made to my injured reputation, it is my
intent, whether the sentence is reversed or not reversed, to
resign my commission, retire to Virginia, and learn to
hoe tobacco, which I find is the best school to form a consummate *general*. This is a discovery I have lately made.
Adieu. Dear sir, believe me to be your most

Sincerely obliged servant,

C. LEE.

After the battle of Monmouth, in June, 1778, Colonel
Burr was constantly employed. His health, from the fatigues of that and the subsequent day, was greatly impaired

Early in October, he found himself, in a measure, unfit for active service. He left West Point, where his regiment was stationed, and repaired to Elizabethtown, in the hope that a few weeks of repose might prove beneficial; but in these hopes he was sorely disappointed. He then determined to ask a furlough, and retire from the army for a few months, provided the furlough was granted without his receiving pay. On this point he was very fastidious. By these feelings he was uniformly governed through a long life. He never sought nor accepted an office for the emolument it afforded. He wrote the commander-in-chief on the subject, as follows :—

TO GENERAL WASHINGTON.

Elizabethtown, 24th October, 1778.

SIR,

The excessive heat and occasional fatigues of the preceding campaign, have so impaired my health and constitution as to render me incapable of immediate service. I have, for three months past, taken every advisable step for my recovery, but have the mortification to find, upon my return to duty, a return of sickness, and that every relapse is more dangerous than the former. I have consulted several physicians ; they all assure me that a few months retirement and attention to my health are the only probable means to restore it. A conviction of this truth, and of my present inability to discharge the duties of my office, induce me to beg your excellency's permission to retire from pay and duty till my health will permit, and the nature of service shall more particularly require my attention, provided such permission can be given without subjecting me to any disadvantage in point of my present rank and command, or any I might acquire during the interval of my absence.

I shall still feel and hold myself liable to be called into service at your excellency's pleasure, precisely as if in full pay, and barely on furlough ; reserving to myself only the privilege of judging of the sufficiency of my health during the present appearance of inactivity. My anxiety to be out of pay arises in no measure from intention or wish to avoid any requisite service. But too great a regard to malicious surmises, and a delicacy perhaps censurable, might otherwise hurry me unnecessarily into service, to the prejudice of my health, and without any advantage to the public, as I have had the misfortune already to experience.

I am encouraged in this proposal by the opinion Lord Stirling has been pleased to express of the justice of my request;—the sense your excellency must entertain of the weak state of the corps in which I have the honour to command, and the present sufficiency of its respective officers. I purpose keeping my quarters at this place until I have the honour of your excellency's answer, which I wait with impatience.

I am, with respect,
Your humble servant,
A. BURR..

His Excellency GEORGE WASHINGTON.

FROM GENERAL WASHINGTON.
Headquarters, Fredericksburgh, 26th October, 1778.

DEAR SIR,

I have your favour of the 24th. You, in my opinion, carry your ideas of delicacy too far when you propose to drop your pay while the recovery of your health necessarily requires your absence from the service. It is not customary, and it would be unjust. You therefore have leave to retire until your health is so far re-established as to enable you to do your duty. Be pleased to give the colonel notice of this, that he may know where to call upon you should any unforeseen exigency require it.

I am your obedient servant,
G. WASHINGTON.

On the receipt of the above letter, Colonel Burr repaired to West Point and joined his regiment, notwithstanding the shattered state of his constitution.   He was unwilling to absent himself from the service, and at the same time receive pay.   Colonel Burr was now in his twenty-third year, and yet so youthful was his appearance, that strangers, on a first introduction, viewed him as a mere boy.   As evidence of the fact, he has often related with great good-humour this anecdote.   While he was commanding at West Point, a countryman had some business to transact with him.   He requested admittance to Colonel Burr.   The orderly sergeant conducted him into headquarters.

" Sir," said the countryman, " I wish to see Colonel Burr, as I have something to say to him."

" You may proceed.   I am Colonel Burr."

" I suppose," rejoined the honest farmer, " you are Colonel Burr's son."

The sentinel at the door heard and repeated the conversation, and Burr was often afterwards designated as Colonel Burr's son.   He remained at West Point until December, when he was removed to Haverstraw by the orders of General M'Dougall, and had the command of a brigade, consisting of Malcolm's regiment, and a portion of Spencer's and Patten's regiments.   He was subsequently ordered to take command on the lines in Westchester county, a most important and not less perilous post.   In December, he received from Mrs. J. Montgomery, the widow of General Montgomery, a letter, as follows :—

FROM MRS. MONTGOMERY.

Rhinebeck, December 25th, 1778.

SIR,

I take the liberty to enclose a list of things Mr. Smith was so kind as to send me from New-York by the return flag. The captain of the flag, of whom I made some inquiries, professed to know nothing of them, and referred me to Col : onel Burr, who might know something of the matter.

I am almost ashamed to take up your attention about so small an affair; but the difficulty that attends obtaining the least article of dress, must, I think, plead my apology. Be sides, having this opportunity, I would wish to assure Col onel Burr of the very great respect I have for those gentle- men whom General Montgomery professed to esteem; among which, sir, I am told you was not the least. To be by him distinguished argues a superior merit, and will ensure you a most sincere welcome at Rhinebeck should it lie in your way.

I am, sir, with esteem, yours, &c.

J. MONTGOMERY.

Colonel BURR.

On taking command of the lines in Westchester, Colonel Burr received from brother officers congratulatory letters, so distinguished was the station considered. Colonel Udney Hay, under date of the 29th of January, 1779, says, "As you have now got the post of honour, accept of my sincere wishes that you may reap the laurels I believe you de- serve."

As soon as Burr arrived at the camp, he commenced a system of reform and discipline. Previous to his arrival, there was exhibited a most disgraceful scene of plunder, and sometimes of murder, along the whole frontier. This he promptly checked; and, in all his efforts to accomplish this end, he was sustained by General M'Dougall.

TO GENERAL M'DOUGALL.

Camp, White Plains, 12th January, 1779.

DEAR SIR,

The enclosed return will show you the deficiency of offi- cers and men at this post. Above the complement for the parties, I wish to have a guard for myself, and a commissary's guard. To detail men for these purposes will interfere with the rotation of duty.

I arrived here on Friday evening. The weather on Saturday was too severe and stormy to permit me to make myself acquainted with the post and disposition of the troops. I improved yesterday for those purposes, and found it necessary to alter the position. I have moved the left three miles forward, and the two centre divisions so as to allign with that and Tarrytown. The posts now possessed by these detachments are,

‸ *First.* Tarrytown.

Second. Isaac Reed's and John Hammond's, near Sawmill river.

Third. Starr's and Moses Miller's, one and a half miles ⁊n front of Young's.

Fourth. Merritt's and neighbouring houses, near Farmer Oakley's.

By this arrangement the extent of my command is contracted three miles, and the distance from my left to the Sound is three miles less than before. The men more compact, and the posts equidistant from the enemy. While I was upon the business above mentioned, Colonel Littlefield and Mr. Thomas visited Colonel Enos and Lieutenant-colonel Holdridge, to enforce the necessity of an immediate junction, to complete the security of the country upon the present plan; but these gentlemen say they have no orders to cross Biram river. They have their quarters in Horseneck, and some troops are north of that place. Thus, notwithstanding my endeavours, the country will be unprotected, and I am insecure.

I enclose you the arrest of a Captain Brown. I am sorry for the necessity of any thing which may have the appearance of severity; but the avowal of behaviour so very unbecoming constrained me to it. The required parties of militia will, I believe, join me this week. I shall write you about iron-bound casks in a few days. There is not a hide, the property of the country, in all this quarter, except fourteen in the hands of the commissary of hides. I shall, as soon as possible, make myself acquainted with the officers of the militia. I have sent to Bedford, but have no answer, about rum, &c.

I send the names of a few of Malcolm's officers, whom I would wish were ordered to join me immediately. Some of them, I believe, are absent. Lieutenant-colonel Littlefield had it in intention to go with most of the men this evening on an expedition to West Farms and Morrisania. Abstracted from your verbal instructions, the plan appeared to me premature. The men here are not half officered; the country by no means sufficiently reconnoitred; the force very inadequate, even for covering parties. As there was a prospect that each of the inconveniences would shortly be removed, I advised to defer it. To convince them that my disapprobation arose from no jealousy of honour, I told Colonel Littlefield that if the enterprise should hereafter be thought more advisable, I would leave to him the execution: if I should think proper to send him on that command, I would act with the covering party. One hundred and fifty continentals and fifty militia was the force proposed for this evening; but as there are a number of volunteers on the spot, I consented to and encouraged an excursion to Frog's Neck, under Colonel Littlefield. I expect little from it, but have not so much to fear.

I hope Mr. Stagg succeeded in his application to Mr. Erskine. A draught of the country would be of great service to me. In your instructions about plunder, you direct that all the fat horses, &c. in the hands of disaffected persons, " lying certain courses," are to be taken, on the supposition that they are designed for, or will fall into the hands of, the enemy. As this mode of determining may be the source of much altercation, I could wish, if you thought proper, the seizable property might be designated by a certain number of miles below our lines, or below the line intended to be

formed from Tarrytown, through White Plains, to Saavpits
or Rye.

The two parties from Paterson's brigade will most of
them want shoes in ten days. It is my opinion that a great
part of those who came last with new shoes, will not, at the
expiration of the time, be able to return for the want of
shoes. Those they now have are of the slightest French
make ; many already worn out. If these men must be
again relieved by others better shod, and they again in a
few days, there will be such an endless marching and coun-
termarching as will harass the troops, and wear out more
shoes than all the duty performed here. Would not these
evils be in some measure remedied by sending me a parcel
of shoes? I will keep an exact account of the regiment
they are delivered to. .   .   '

Your most obedient servant,

'A. BURR.

TO GENERAL M'DOUGALL.

White Plains, January 13th, 1779.

SIR,

All the horsemen were so infatuated with the itch for
scouting, that I had not one to despatch with the letter herewith sent. Colonel Littlefield, with the party, returned this
morning. They brought up one prisoner. I shall send
him up with another grand rascal to-morrow. There are
evidences enough against Merritt to hang a dozen such, but
many of them dare not appear at present.   .

Notwithstanding the cautions I gave, and notwithstanding
Colonel Littlefield's good intentions, I blush to tell you that
the party returned loaded with plunder. Sir, till now, I
never wished for arbitrary power. I could gibbet half a
dozen *good whigs*, with all the venom of an inveterate tory.
The party had not been returned an hour, before I had six
or seven persons from New-Rochelle and Frog's Neck, with
piteous applications for stolen goods and horses. Some of

these persons are of the most friendly families. I am mortified that not an officer on the ground has shown any activity
to detect the plunderers or their spoil. I have got three
horses, and a number of other articles, and have confined
two soldiers who had them in possession. But these are
petty rascals. I feel more pity than indignation towards
them. They were honest men till debauched by this expedition. I believe some officers are concerned. If I can be
assured of that (and I shall spare no labour), you may depend
on seeing them with a file of men. The militia volunteers
excelled in this business. If I detect them I shall treat
them with the same rigour, unless you advise to the contrary. I wish you would give me directions. I have at
least a fortnight's work before me to undo the doings of last
night.

This day I enter on my command. Truly an ominous
commencement. Is this the promised protection? I read
in the face of every child I pass; for the whole *honour*
of the expedition redounds to me. But enough of this;
more perhaps than you will thank me for. Webbers was of
the party, and can give you a history. I now perceive from
whence arose the ardour for scouting. I suppose the sergeants' parties of militia, when they join me, will be subject
to courts of the line.

Your most obedient servant,

A. BURR.

FROM MAJOR PLATT, AID TO GENERAL M'DOUGALL.

Peekskill, January 14th, 1779.

SIR,

The general has received yours, and directs me to inform
you that such assistance will be granted as is necessary for
the protection of the country and your honour.

He desires that no expedition be set on foot till you hear
further from him. He has no objections to Colonel Littlefield's remaining with you till the arrival of more officers.

Handcuffs will be sent you as soon as they can be made. If you have a number of prisoners at any time to send up, let them be fastened right and left hands, and the guard cut the strings of their breeches, and there will be no danger of their making their escape, as they will be obliged to hold them up continually with one hand.

Last evening Josiah Fowler made his escape from the provost; possibly he may fall into the hands of your scouts or patrols. If he does, please to take the best care of him.

The general will write you fully by the captain who will soon re-enforce you. One hundred pair of shoes will be sent you. The map of the country is herewith transmitted, for the purpose of taking a sketch of it. You will please to do it as soon as possible, and send it up by a careful hand. The general does not wish you ever to carry it from your quarters.

Your most obedient servant,
RICHARD PLATT, Aid-de-camp.

FROM GENERAL M'DOUGALL.

Headquarters, Peekskill, January 15th, 1779.

MY DEAR SIR,

Your favours of the 11th and 12th, with their enclosures, came duly to hand.

I am much mortified that Captain Brown should have merited your putting him in an arrest. But you have done your duty, for which accept my thanks.

If an officer commanding an outpost will not be very vigilant, he exposes his party to be butchered, as the unfortunate Colonel Balor lately experienced.

I am very sorry the militia have conducted so disorderly; but I wish you to deal tenderly with them, as they are brave, and are very sore, by the plundering of the tories. But support the honour of our arms and your own, by giving redress to the innocent and defenceless.

As the principal objects of your command are to protect

the good people of these states, and prevent supplies going to the enemy, you will not send out any parties, or make any excursions, but what are necessary for intelligence, and the preservation of your parties, till further orders. Your own ideas on this subject fully meet my approbation. In the meantime, let all the officers and men of your command, who are unacquainted with the ground, traverse it alternately, from flank to flank, and as many miles in front as you may judge necessary. The position of the whole I leave to your own discretion, as circumstances shall arise.

A good captain, and twenty picked men, of Nixon's, with two drums, accompany this, to re-enforce your left, and the orders are despatched to Major Pawling for the officers you wrote for. One hundred pair of *shoes* will be sent to you by this snow.

Send up all Burgoyne's men, with a good corporal and small party of the nine-months men, with the first deserters or prisoners. The sergeants' parties of the militia who are to join you, will, by their engagements, be under the continental articles of war. If any of the militia who may go out on scouts or parties with yours will not submit to the articles of war and your orders, don't suffer them to go with them, nor to appropriate any plunder; but order it to be given to the continental troops, and those who shall submit to those articles.

If any of the militia maraud, send them up to me, with a guard. They must not be suffered to violate civil and military law. The legislature is the proper authority to enable them to make reprisals. For whatever disorders they commit in front of your lines, will be placed by the enemy to your account.

In all doubtful questions which may arise on my orders as to the limits or legality of plunder in your front, *I authorize you to be the sole judge.* In the exercise of this trust, it is my wish you should lean to the honour of our arms.

A surgeon is directed to attend your party; when he

arrives, please to advise me of it, that I may be relieved from all anxiety about you and your corps. If you are not supplied with rum before a quantity of it arrives here, we shall not forget you. If your horsemen are mounted and appointed, as well as your horse-guides, they will receive the same pay. If the oxen at Mr. Hunter's are not in working order, put them in the care of your forage-master till they are.

If you can get the articles taken from the inhabitants in the late expedition restored, let the militia off for that offence. When you get things in train, I flatter myself you will not have any future trouble with them. But the officers of the regular troops must be rigorously dealt with, according to our martial law.

As you and the commissary will be in the rear of the whole, the nine-months men, worse shod than the other troops, may serve till I have more leisure to complete your corps.

Don't omit sending to me all the newspapers you can procure. I am so borne down with correspondence, that I can only add that

I am your affectionate humble servant,

ALEXANDER M'DOUGALL.

P. S. I fear the pickets from your parties are too far advanced from them. The distance ought not to exceed half a mile at night; and the quarters of the pickets should be changed every night after dark. Frequent patrols from each give the best security.

I submit it to your consideration whether it would not be of service to have a quantity of old rags collected at each party and picket, for the patrols to muffle their feet with in frosty weather when there is no snow on the ground. It will prevent their being heard by the enemy, and yours will hear those of the enemy if there are any near them.

A. M'D.

CHAPTER X.

White Plains, 21st January, 1779.

DEAR SIR,

Mr. Benjamin Sands, and three other persons from Long Island, banished for malepractices, wait on you with this. Benjamin Sands, jun. appears to be a man of good understanding. He can give you a detail of their sufferings.

Captain Black and three subalterns of Malcolm's regiment joined me yesterday.

William Burtis goes under guard to you to-morrow. Also a Garret Duyckman, whom I took upon information of Burtis. I knew of Burtis having drove cattle before the receipt of your letter. Of his being a spy I know nothing. Burtis wishes to procure favour by giving information. I enclose his confession to me, that you may compare it with his story to you. He has not told me all he knows, I am convinced. I can secure Elijah Purdy any time if you direct. There is no danger in delaying till I can hear from you. I wish to clear the country of these rascals. It would be of infinite service to hang a few up in this neighbourhood.

The two parties from Nixon's brigade, which came under sergeant's last week, are so distressed for clothes, that I am obliged to send them to their regiments. They came provided but for one week. Lieutenant Wottles marches them up. I wish him to return with the re-enforcement. I have sent the corporal and sixty-nine men to Bedford. I have now about 170 privates. A single company, and twelve from Hammond's regiment, join me to-day. That is his complement.

A commissary of hides at this place can furnish me with

shoes as I want them, if you will give an order for that purpose. He delivers none without a general order. I can purchase rum here at twenty dollars per gallon. There is no commissary of purchases.

There are a number of women here of bad character, who are continually running to New-York and back again. If they were men, I should flog them without mercy.

It was the indolence of the commissary, and not the real scarcity of wheat, which alarmed me. I shall not trouble you again on the score of flour. I send you two papers by the sergeant

Yours respectfully,

A. BURR.

FROM GENERAL M'DOUGALL.

Peekskill, January 22, 1779.

SIR,

There are reasons, which I shall explain to you at a proper time, why —— should not be sought after. Make a great noise about him ; abuse him as the vilest of horse-thieves, and a spy for the enemy ; but send no parties after him. If you are told where he is, turn off the matter by some pretext or other. Don't carry this out on party, or out of your quarters to any unsafe place.

Yours affectionately,

ALEXANDER M'DOUGALL.

FROM WILLIAM PATERSON.

January 27th.

I am at the Hermitage, my dear Burr, and cannot forbear writing you a few lines, although I expected, before this time, to have been favoured with a letter from you. Mrs. Prevost informs me that there is the most flattering prospect of your soon being reinstated in your health. The intelligence gives me real pleasure, and the more so, because, until Mrs. Prevost told me, I had no idea of your disorder being

so rooted and dangerous.   May health soon revisit you, my
good friend; and when it does, may it continue with you for
years.   I am pleased with the hope of seeing you in Jersey
early in the spring.   I shall be this way again in March,
when perhaps I shall meet you at this place.   I write this
standing in the midst of company.   I am called off to
court, and therefore, for this time, adieu.

WILLIAM PATERSON.

.FROM MAJOR PLATT, AID TO GENERAL M'DOUGALL.

Peekskill, January 28th, 1779.

SIR,

Captain Wiley, of Learned's brigade, will hand you this.
He brings with him forty men, I believe as good as any in
the army.   'Tis the general's intention that Nixon's, Paterson's, and the late Learned's brigades, shall each furnish
a party of sixty.   You will please, after selecting the best
men for your parties, to order all the rest (save your own
and commissary's guard) to join their corps, as they complain the duty is hard above.   Either Captain Williams or
Spur must leave you, as Captain Wiley will command the
party from Learned's.   If there are three subs for each party
exclusive of those from your own regiment, you can detain
the whole of the subs of other brigades or not, as you like.

Kearsley has not yet joined.   The general will review
all your letters in a day or two, and give them full answers

I am your most obedient servant,

RICHARD PLATT, Aid-de-camp

TO GENERAL M'DOUGALL.

White Plains, January 29th, 1779.

DEAR SIR,

I had this day the favour of yours by Lieutenant Rost
The same gentleman brought me a re-enforcement of
thirty-nine privates, and a proportion of officers.   This en
ables me to send to camp a few of the worst provided of

the nine-months men. The returning party takes up the prisoners mentioned in my last, and a deserter. Two more of Malcolm's officers have joined me.

I enclose you a copy of a letter from Colonel Holdridge. The enterprise appears to me something romantic; but I have acquainted Colonel Holdridge of the steps I shall take should it prove serious, and have appointed a place near this to meet him, if he thinks it necessary. The number, disposition, and apparent intentions of the enemy will point out our duty. I am this evening told, by good authority, that Emerick is re-enforced, either by volunteer or enlisted refugees, to the amount of 4 or 500, and that there are strong symptoms of an excursion. I shall pay due atten tion to these reports and authorities.

These two days past I have taken a particular view of the country and roads from White Plains to Mamaroneck, Rye, and Sawpits. I find it much easier protected, and more secure, than the western part of this county. From the Bronx to Mamaroneck river, through White Plains, is three miles. There are very few fords or bridges on either of those rivers. Might it not be of service to draw a line, if but for a few days, from Bronx to Rye, or Mamaro- neck? The Purchase would be certainly a ridiculous post.

The map is herewith sent. Lieutenant Chatburn, who has business at West Point, will deliver this.

                              Yours respectfully,
                                        A. BURR.

FROM GENERAL M DOUGALL.
Headquarters, Peekskill. 6th February, 1779.

MY DEAR SIR,

I have devoted part of this night to review your letters, and to give them some kind of answers. I can only men tion ideas. I leave you to dilate them.

The bearer is one of the sentries who was partly tho occasion of the late misfortune. I have reproved them severely, which I hope will have the desired effect. For the future, order the sentry who does not fire the alarm one hundred lashes, and the like number to any who shall part with his arms without its being wrested from him by the enemy ; and a reward of twenty dollars to any non-commissioned officer or soldier who shall bring in such arms. Publish this in orders.

I am fully sensible of your embarrassments and difficulties, for want of vigilant officers and discipline. Be it your honour to surmount them. Accept of my thanks for your attention to the service. Order one pound and a half of flour or bread, and the like quantity of meat, to each man, till the first of April. The duty is hard, and exercise increases the appetite. Will it not advance the service to send you down some biscuit ? Give Commissary Leake no rest without vegetables. His guard will be relieved by a militia one. How many sergeants' parties have you ? Your guard and that of the commissary will be taken from the brigades, as 120 from Paterson's is to 60 from the others. In returns, designate the strength from each brigade. The regiments whose men have no bayonets, some means will be devised to furnish them. Heavy packs should not be at the stated quarters. Fix a day beforehand when you will hear the complaints of the disaffected. If any come on other days, give them thirty-nine lashes first ; wait the effects of this discipline.

The oath of allegiance is no criterion of characters, nor the want of a certificate thereof an evidence of a person's being disaffected. Uniform character is the best rule to judge. Send up under guard all women who stroll to New-York without leave. But cause them to be well searched by matrons for papers *immediately* when they are taken ; hair, caps, stays, and its lining, should be well examined. Do the like to those going down. Send up the evidences against Bettice. I approve your manner of treating Captain Williams. I did not yet intend the hard money taken by him should be distributed. But, if it is done, let it remain so. In future, no hard money should be distributed. You will see the use I intend it for in a few days. I am sure it will divert you. I hope soon to make up another party of sixty. If Lieutenant Freeman is not returned to you, I shall send for him. Are the wagons you mentioned some time ago returned? What is become of the rifles? I want them much for the servants who go out with me on horseback. All returning parties should march together till they arrive at the cantonment of the first corps, then with their respective officers. This will prevent disorders.

After rain or snow, I wish you to inspect the arms, and order them, in your presence, to discharge them at a mark. The few cartridges spent in this way will be well disposed of. Colonel Putnam is marched to the mouth of Croton. Greaton's, in two or three days, moves near Pine's bridge on that river. I think the present scarcity of bread will prevent a movement of the enemy with regular troops. Major-general Putnam is right in having the militia of Fairfield ready, if it has not the effect on them, like that of the boy and the wolf in the fable. If Ensign Lecland is still on the lines, send him up as an evidence against Captain Brown.

A sea-captain, who, with three others, made their escape from New-York the night of the 4th instant, says fourteen sail of the Cork fleet had arrived last Sunday.

I am your affectionate

ALEXANDER M'DOUGALL.

FROM GENERAL M'DOUGALL.

Headquarters, Peekskill, 7th February, 1779.

MY DEAR SIR,

I directed Major Platt, some days since, to inform you, no provision of any kind should be suffered to go below you till further orders. Please to announce this to the justices. You have herewith a flag; fill up the blank. On its return, desire the officer to call at Colonel Phillips's for any papers or catalogues of books which may be left there for me. The letter to Mr. Delancey to be left with the enemy's officer on his advanced post. Cast your mind on the best means of sweeping Westchester and West Farms of the tories when it is good sledding, supposing two regiments to cover you. But this under the rose.

Gonsalez Manuel, the bearer of this, brings with him John Broughton, a prisoner of war, who is exchanged. You will please to order him kept at a convenient distance in the rear till the flag goes in, when he is to be sent and delivered to the commanding officer of the advanced post. A receipt must be taken for him and transmitted to me.

Affectionately,

ALEXANDER M'DOUGALL.

FROM MAJOR PLATT.

Peekskill, February 23d, 1779.

DEAR BURR,

In yours of yesterday you requested particular care of the enclosed, but there was none. Malcolm left this yesterday for Haverstraw. He intends, with Major Pawling, to pay you a visit by water, and perhaps it will be to-day. I think there is some probability of his relieving you. At any rate, you will be relieved by the time you wish.

As the general writes fully by this conveyance, I shall not be so particular as I otherwise would. Cammell will be down shortly to pay off accounts. One dollar per day is allowed for a saddle-horse. Your certificates to the Van Warts will entitle them to their pay, be it what it may.

The general has ordered Williams and Wattles to return the hard money to him. It will be put in your hands. Love to Roger, when he comes. Compliments to Malcolm's lads and Benson.

With singular affection,

R. PLATT.

FROM GENERAL M'DOUGALL

Headquarters, 23d February, 1779.

My dear Sir,

Your several favours have been handed to me. I have not time now to answer them fully. It will, however, be done by Major Hull, who is ordered down to assist you. All your wishes will be gratified. One hundred and twenty picked men, with bayonets, will reach you to-morrow. Send your commissary up for rum. Let him call on me.

I am yours,

ALEXANDER M'DOUGALL.

FROM GENERAL M'DOUGALL.

Headquarters, 15th February, 1779.

Sir,

Your favour of the 12th came to hand with the prisoners. I have long known Ackerly was up, and his business, but did not think his present situation of sufficient importance to have him taken by K. Mr. Platt will inform you how I intend to supply you with bayonets. He reached you, I suppose, yesterday evening. I intend to send down the remains of Colonel Poor's regiment for a few days, to cover a forage making by Mr. Hayes near Mamaroneck; and shall send by them public arms, with bayonets, to be exchanged for yours which want them. No good officer or man now below with you must be relieved till further orders. Give the officers of Poor's all the advice and assistance you can. The money taken from Ketor will be divided among the officers and men in such manner as you think proper. I shall send them down six for one when I can raise cash. Greaton's is at Pine bridge. Nixon moves in two days to support Putnam. The stated express is on this side Croton, at his own house. His name is John Cross, a refugee from New-York. Give me the earliest advice of any appearance of a movement of the enemy on the river.   Mrs. Pollock was detained with the late bad weather two nights.   She left this at eight this morning.

I am, sir, yours, &c.,

ALEXANDER M'DOUGALL.

FROM MAJOR PLATT, AID TO GENERAL M'DOUGALL.

Headquarters, 25th February, 1779.

SIR,

The general wishes you to detain the best officers and men, for five complete parties of sixty : and, as soon as Major Hull can be made acquainted with your posts, and the nature of your command, he desires you will ride up to headquarters if there is no probability of a movement from below, and he will concert with you such measures as shall be thought expedient.

The combustible balls are not yet come to hand.   Five or six boxes of ammunition will be sent down to Tarrytown by water the first opportunity.   'Tis necessary that Dr Eustis, if not at the Plains, should be sent for.

I am your obedient servant,

RICHARD PLATT, Aid-de-camp.

P. S.—Please to inform the general whether Colonel Poor's men have accomplished the business they were sent upon or not.

FROM GENERAL M'DOUGALL.

Headquarters, Peekskill, 26th February, 1779.

SIR,

I received your letter of this day.   Colonel Putnam is ordered to march and join you, and to act as circumstances shall cast up.   Five boxes of ammunition are ordered to be carried to you immediately from King's ferry, by water. Leave a small party to receive it, and a cart to carry it where you shall order it.   As the strength of the enemy is not mentioned, I can give no other orders.

Yours, &c.,

ALEXANDER M'DOUGALL.

FROM GENERAL M'DOUGALL.

                                    Headquarters, 27th February, 1779.

My dear Sir,

Your favour of yesterday reached me at 8 P. M. It was immediately answered. Colonel Putnam was ordered to march and join you; he has taken Nixon's regiment with him. Greaton's was put in motion at the same time, to join the brigade, if the enemy did not continue to advance in Connecticut. At half past ten of the same evening, five boxes of ammunition was sent to you from King's ferry, by water, with orders to keep close in shore, for fear of accidents. I hope it has reached you. Your letter of this day, at 7 A. M., came to hand an hour ago. From the reputed strength of the enemy, I am pleased with your position. I think it promises success and laurels. I hope Bearmore will smart for his temerity. You are all too remote from me to render orders expedient. Circumstances must direct your movements. If the enemy *move*, or appear in *force* on the river, or a movement on it in force should *apparently* be intended, send up all Paterson's detachments by *forced* marches. I commit you and your corps to the Lord of Hosts. Greaton has four boxes of spare ammunition. He will be on the North Castle road to the Plains. .

                    Yours affectionately,

                              ALEXANDER M'DOUGALL.

FROM GENERAL M'DOUGALL.

                          Headquarters, Peekskill, 6th March, 1779.

Sir,

This will be delivered to you by Mr. John Pine, who acted last campaign as a horse-guide. He is a true friend to the country. Whenever he shall get properly mounted, and reports himself to you for service, give him a certificate of the day, and employ him.

Enclosed you have a list of horse-thieves and others who

act very prejudicial to our cause. I wish to have them taken and sent up here. Perhaps it will be most eligible to make the attempt on all at the same time. But I do not wish to retard the forage on your left, as those posts are in great want of that article.

I am, sir, your humble servant,
ALEXANDER M'DOUGALL.

FROM GENERAL PUTNAM.

Camp, Horse Neck, 9th March, 1779.

SIR,

I have received a letter from Colonel Emerick (British), informing me that one Butler, who has been a prisoner in New-York, being unable to travel on foot, obtained of Colonel Emerick a dragoon and two horses to conduct him some part of his way in the country. That Butler made the dragoon drunk, then brought him off, together with the horses. The whole of which he, in his letter, makes a demand to be returned.

Colonel Emerick has been misinformed as to Butler's acting so faithless. The truth of the matter is, that Butler wanted the dragoon to return with the horses, but that he (the dragoon) refused to do, and swore he would never return. I would advise you by all means to send the dragoon to Colonel Emerick in irons, together with the horses, as a refusal would be contrary to all public faith.

I am, with the greatest respect,
ISRAEL PUTNAM

FROM GENERAL M'DOUGALL.

Headquarters, Peekskill, 11th March, 1779.

SIR,

Yours of the 9th has reached me. If the militia of Colonel Drake's are good men, arm them of General Paterson's, and I will replace them to him. Take the receipts of every man who shall be armed by the public, and send them to me.

The old general is not a civilian.   Send Colonel Emerick
the enclosed copy of the horseman's deposition.   Stop no
provisions, when small quantities answer for the purpose
of   .   The plunderers will be punished on the lines, but
tried here.   The names of the witnesses are wanting.
What you wrote for, to answer certain purposes, shall be
collected as soon as possible.

Give me the true history of the facts relative to the mare
sold by Wattles.   He quibbles.   Did he know the printed
orders ?—was she sold conformable ?   The paymasters will
be ordered down, and soap shall be sent.

In haste, yours, &c.,

ALEXANDER M'DOUGALL.

The preceding correspondence is evidence of the military
character of Colonel Burr, and his standing with General
M'Dougall.   Although his rank was only that of a lieutenant-
colonel, yet he was constantly in the actual command of a
regiment, and frequently of a brigade.   His seniors were
withdrawn from the post (which was generally a post of
danger) where he was stationed ; or detachments were
taken from different regiments so as to make up for him a
separate and independent command.   No man had a better
opportunity than Samuel Young, Esq., of knowing Colonel
Burr's habits and conduct while stationed in Westchester.
Mr. Young was at one time a member of the state legislature, and for many years surrogate of the county.   The
following letter contains some interesting details.

SAMUEL YOUNG TO COMMODORE VALENTINE MORRIS.

Mount Pleasant (Westchester), 25th January, 1814.

DEAR SIR,

Your letter of the 30th ultimo, asking for some account
of the campaign in which I served, under the command of
Colonel Burr, during the revolutionary war, was received
some days ago, and has been constantly in my mind.   I

will reply to it with pleasure, but the compass of a letter will not admit of much detail.

I resided in the lines from the commencement of the revolution until the winter of the year 1780, when my father's house was burnt, by order of the British general. The county of Westchester, very soon after the commencement of hostilities, became, on account of its exposed situation, a scene of deepest distress. From the Croton to Kingsbridge, every species of rapine and lawless violence prevailed. No man went to his bed but under the apprehension of having his house plundered or burnt, or himself or family massacred, before morning. Some, under the character of whigs, plundered the tories; while others, of the latter description, plundered the whigs. Parties of marauders, assuming either character or none, as suited their convenience, indiscriminately assailed both whigs and tories. So little vigilance was used on our part, that emissaries and spies of the enemy passed and repassed without interruption.

These calamities continued undiminished until the arrival of Colonel Burr, in the autumn of the year 1778. He took command of the same troops which his predecessor, Colonel Littlefield, commanded. At the moment of Colonel Burr's arrival, Colonel Littlefield* had returned from a plundering expedition (for to plunder those called tories was then deemed lawful), and had brought up horses, cattle, bedding, clothing, and other articles of easy transportation, which he had proposed to distribute among the party the next day. Colonel Burr's first act of authority was to seize and secure all this plunder; and he immediately took measures for restoring it to the owners. This gave us much trouble, but it was abundantly repaid by the confidence it inspired.

He then made known his determination to suppress plun-

* See page 142.

dering. The same day he visited all the guards; changed their position; dismissed some of the officers, whom he found totally incompetent; gave new instructions. On the same day, also, he commenced a register of the names and characters of all who resided near and below his guards. Distinguished by secret marks the whig, the timid whig, the tory, the horse-thief, and those concerned in, or suspected of, giving information to the enemy. He also began a map of the country, in the vicinity of the fort; of the roads, by-roads, paths, creeks, morasses, &c., which might become hiding-places for the disaffected or for marauding parties. This map was made by Colonel Burr himself, from such materials as he could collect on the spot, but principally from his own observation.

He raised and established a corps of horsemen from among the respectable farmers and young men of the country, of tried patriotism, fidelity, and courage. These also served as aids and confidential persons for the transmission of orders. To this corps I attached myself as a volunteer, but did not receive pay. He employed discreet and faithful persons, living near the enemy's lines, to watch their motions, and give him immediate intelligence. He employed mounted videttes for the same purpose, directing two of them to proceed together, so that one might be despatched, if necessary, with information to the colonel, while the other might watch the enemy's movement. He established signals throughout the lines, so that, whether by night or by day, instant notice could be had of an attack or movement of the enemy. He enforced various regulations for concealing his positions and force from the enemy.

The laxity of discipline which had before prevailed enabled the enemy frequently to employ their emissaries to come within the lines, and to learn the precise state of our forces, supplies, &c. Colonel Burr soon put an end to these dangerous intrusions, by prohibiting all persons residing below the lines, except a few whom he selected, such as Parson Bartow, Jacob Smith, and others, whose integrity was unimpeachable, from approaching the outposts, without special permission for the purpose. If any one had a complaint or request to make of the colonel, he procured one or more of the persons he had selected to come to his quarters on his behalf. This measure prevented frivolous and vexatious applications, and the still more dangerous approach of enemies in disguise. All these measures were entirely new; and, within eight or ten days, the whole system appeared to be in complete operation, and the face of things was totally changed.

A few days after the colonel's arrival, the house of one Gedney was plundered in the night, and the family abused and terrified. Gedney sent his son to make a representation of it to the colonel. The young man, not regarding the orders which had been issued, came to the colonel's quarters, undiscovered by the sentinels, having taken a secret path through the fields for the purpose. For this violation of orders the young man was punished. The colonel immediately took measures for the detection of the plunderers; and though they were all disguised, and wholly unknown to Gedney, yet Colonel Burr, by means which were never yet disclosed, discovered the plunderers, and had them all secured within twenty-four hours. Gedney's family, on reference to his register, appeared to be tories; but Burr had promised that every quiet man should be protected.

He caused the robbers to be conveyed to Gedney's house, under the charge of Captain Benson, there to restore the booty they had taken, to make reparation in money for such articles as were lost or damaged, and for the alarm and abuse, the amount of which the colonel assessed, to be flogged ten lashes, and to ask pardon of the old man; all which was faithfully and immediately executed.

These measures gave universal satisfaction, and the terror they inspired effectually prevented a repetition of similar depredations. From this day plundering ceased. No further instance occurred during the time of Colonel Burr's command, for it was universally believed that Colonel Burr could tell a robber by looking in his face, or that he had supernatural means of discovering crime. Indeed, I was myself inclined to these opinions. This belief was confirmed by another circumstance which had previously occurred. On the day of his arrival, after our return from visiting the posts, conversing with several of his attendants, and, among others, Lieutenant Drake, whom Burr had brought with him from his own regiment, he said, " Drake, that post on the North river will be attacked before morning; neither officers nor men know any thing of their duty ; you must go and take charge of it ; keep your eyes open, or you will have your throat cut." Drake went. The post was attacked that night by a company of horse. They were repulsed with loss. Drake returned in the morning with trophies of war, and told his story. We stared, and asked one another —How could Burr know that ? He had not then established any means of intelligence.

The measures immediately adopted by him were such that it was impossible for the enemy to have passed their own lines without his having immediate knowledge ; and it was these very measures which saved Major Hull, on whom the command devolved for a short time, when the state of Colonel Burr's health compelled him to retire.

These measures, together with the deportment of Colonel Burr, gained him the love and veneration of all devoted to the common cause, and conciliated even its bitterest foes. His habits were a subject of admiration. His diet was simple and spare in the extreme. Seldom sleeping more than an hour at a time, and without taking off his clothes, or even his boots.

Between midnight and two o'clock in the morning, accompanied by two or three of his corps of horsemen, he visited the quarters of all his captains, and their picket-guards, changing his route from time to time to prevent notice of his approach. You may judge of the severity of this duty, when I assure you that the distance which he thus rode every night must have been from *sixteen* to *twenty-four* miles; and that, with the exception of two nights only, in which he was otherwise engaged, he never omitted these excursions, even in the severest and most stormy weather; and, except the short time necessarily consumed in hearing and answering complaints and petitions from persons both above and below the lines, Colonel Burr was constantly with the troops.

He attended to the minutest article of their comfort; to their lodgings; to their diet: for those off duty he invented sports, all tending to some useful end. During two or three weeks after the colonel's arrival, we had many sharp conflicts with the robbers and horse-thieves, who were hunted down with unceasing industry. In many instances we encountered great superiority of numbers, but always with success. Many of them were killed, and many were taken.

The strictest discipline prevailed, and the army felt the fullest confidence in their commander and in themselves, and by these means became really formidable to the enemy. During the same winter, Governor Tryon planned an expedition to Horse Neck, for the purpose of destroying the salt-works erected there, and marched with about 2000 men. Colonel Burr received early information of their movements, and sent word to General Putnam to hold the enemy at bay for a few hours, and he (Colonel Burr) would be in their rear and be answerable for them. By a messenger from him, Colonel Burr was informed by that general that he had been obliged to retreat, and that the enemy were advancing into Connecticut. This information, which unfortunately was not correct, altered Colonel Burr's route towards Mamaroneck, which enabled Tryon to get the start of him. Colonel Burr then endeavoured to interrupt him in Eastchester, according to his first plan, and actually got within cannon-shot of him; but Tryon ran too fast, and in his haste left most or all of his cattle and plunder behind him, and many stragglers who were picked up.

I will mention another enterprise, which proved more successful, though equally hazardous. Soon after Tryon's re treat, Colonel Delancey, who commanded the British refugees, in order to secure themselves against surprise, erected a block-house on a rising ground below Delancey's bridge This Colonel Burr resolved to destroy. I was in that expe dition, and recollect the circumstances.

He procured a number of hand-grenades, also rolls of port-fire, and canteens filled with inflammable materials, with contrivances to attach them to the side of the block-house. He set out with his troops early in the evening, and arrived within a mile of the block-house by two o'clock in the morning. The colonel gave Captain Black the command of about forty volunteers, who were first to approach. Twenty of them were to carry the port-fires, &c., &c. Those who had hand-grenades had short ladders to enable them to reach the port-holes, the exact height of which Colonel Burr had ascertained. Colonel Burr gave Captain Black his instructions, in the hearing of his company, assuring him of his protection if they were attacked by superior numbers; for it was expected that the enemy, who had several thousand men at and near Kingsbridge, would endeavour to cut us off, as we were several miles below them. Burr directed those who carried the combustibles to march in front as silently as possible. That, on being hailed, they should light the hand-grenades, &c., with a slow match provided for the purpose, and throw them into the port-holes. I was one of the party that advanced. The sentinel hailed and fired. We rushed on. The first hand-grenade that was thrown in drove the enemy from the upper story, and before they could take any measure to defend it, the block-house was on fire in several places. Some few escaped, and the rest surrendered without our having lost a single man. Though many shot were fired at us, we did not fire a gun.

During the period of Colonel Burr's command, but two attempts were made by the enemy to surprise our guards, in both of which they were defeated.

After Colonel Burr left this command, Colonel Thompson, a man of approved bravery, assumed it, and the enemy, in open day, advanced to his headquarters, took Colonel Thompson, and took or killed all his men, with the exception of about thirty.

My father's house, with all his outhouses, were burnt. After these disasters our troops never made an effort to protect that part of the country. The American lines were afterwards changed, and extended from Bedford to Croton bridge, and from there, following the course of that river, to the Hudson. All the intermediate country was abandoned and unprotected, being about twenty miles in the rear of the ground which Colonel Burr had maintained.

The year after the defeat of Colonel Thompson, Colonel Green, a brave, and in many respects a valuable officer, took the command, making his headquarters at Danford's, about a mile above the Croton. This position was well chosen. But Colonel Green omitted to inform himself of the movements of the enemy, and consequently was surprised. Himself, Major Flagg, and other officers were killed, and a great part of the men were either killed or taken prisoners: yet these officers had the full benefit of Colonel Burr's system.

Having perused what I have written, it does not appear to me that I have conveyed any adequate idea of Burr's military character. It may be aided a little by reviewing the effects he produced. The troops of which he took command were, at the time he took the command, undisciplined, negligent, and discontented. Desertions were frequent. In a few days these very men were transformed into brave and honest defenders; orderly, contented, and cheerful; confident in their own courage, and loving to adoration their commander, whom every man considered as his personal friend. It was thought a severe punishment, as well as disgrace, to be sent up to the camp, where they had nothing to do but to lounge and eat their rations.

During the whole of this command there was not a single desertion. Not a single death by sickness. Not one made prisoner by the enemy; for Burr had taught us that a soldier with arms in his hand ought never, under any circumstances, to surrender; no matter if he was opposed to thousands, it was his duty to fight.

After the first ten days there was not a single instance of robbery. The whole country, under his command, enjoyed security. The inhabitants, to express their gratitude, frequently brought presents of such articles as the country afforded; but Colonel Burr would accept no present. He fixed reasonable prices, and paid in cash for every thing that was received, and sometimes, I know, that these payments were made with his own money. Whether these advances were repaid, I know not.

Colonel Simcoe, one of the most daring and active partisans in the British army, was, with Colonels Emerick and Delancey, opposed to Burr on the lines, yet they were completely held in check.

But perhaps the highest eulogy on Colonel Burr is, that no man could be found capable of executing his plans, though the example was before them.

When Burr left the lines a sadness overspread the country, and the most gloomy forebodings were too soon fulfilled, as you have seen above.

The period of Colonel Burr's command was so full of activity and of incident, that every day afforded some new lesson of instruction. But you will expect only a general outline, and this faint one is the best in my power to give.

With esteem, yours,
SAMUEL YOUNG.

CHAPTER XI.

THE military career of Colonel Burr was now drawing to a close. The state of his health became alarming. His constitution was shattered. His medical and other friends were of the opinion that he was incapable of enduring the fatigues of another campaign. In the judgment and talents of Dr. Eustis he reposed great confidence. That gentleman pressed upon him, in a manner the most affectionate, the necessity for his retiring. The sacrifice required of Burr was inconceivably great. All his views and feelings were military. He seemed as though he was born a soldier. He was ambitious of fame in his profession. He had acquired a character for vigilance and intrepidity unrivalled in the army. He was more than respected by his brother officers, and idolized by the troops. As a man and a citizen, he was exceedingly disliked by General Washington. Causes, unnecessary to examine at this late period of time, had created between these gentlemen feelings of hostility that were unconquerable, and were never softened or mollified. Yet even General Washington, while he considered Burr destitute of morals and of principle, respected him as a soldier, and gave repeated evidence of entire confidence in his gallantry, his persevering industry, his judgment, and his discretion. At length, however, protracted disease compelled him to abandon all those hopes of glory, nobly won in the battle-field, which had inflamed his ardent and youthful mind; and on the 10th of March, 1779, he tendered to the commander-in-chief his resignation.

TO GENERAL WASHINGTON.

Phillipsburgh, 10th March, 1779.

SIR,

The reasons I did myself the honour to mention to your excellency in a letter of September last still exist, and determine me to resign my rank and command in the army. The polite indulgence you favoured me with at that time restored temporarily my health. At the instance of General M'Dougall, I accepted the command of these posts; but I find my health unequal to the undertaking, and have acquainted him of my intentions to retire. He has ordered an officer to relieve me before the 15th of March, on which day I purpose to leave this command and the army.

Very respectfully,

A. BURR.

FROM GENERAL WASHINGTON.

Middlebrook, 3d April, 1779.

SIR,

I have to acknowledge your favour of the 10th ultimo. Perfectly satisfied that no consideration save a desire to reestablish your health could induce you to leave the service, I cannot therefore withhold my consent. But, in giving permission to your retiring from the army, I am not only to regret the loss of a good officer, but the cause which makes his resignation necessary. When it is convenient to transmit the settlement of your public accounts, it will receive my final acceptance.

I am, &c.,

GEORGE WASHINGTON.

A few days previous to Colonel Burr's resignation of his commission, he received from the widow of General Montgomery the following letter :—

FROM MRS. J. MONTGOMERY.

Rhinebeck, 7th March, 1779.

SIR,

I should before this have answered your obliging letter, had not the marriage of my eldest sister entirely taken up my time. I now return you, sir, many thanks for your kind offers of service. The sincerity with which they were made would have allowed me to accept them, without fears of giving you trouble, had I not determined to run no more risks, as I have been very unfortunate in my ventures that way.

You have awakened all my sensibility by the praises you bestow on my unfortunate general. He was, indeed, an angel sent us for a moment. Alas! for me, that this world was not more worthy of him—then had I still been the happiest of women, *and his friends in stations more equal to their own merits.* Reflections like these imbitter continually each day as it passes. But I trust in the same merciful Hand which has held me from sinking in my extreme calamity, that he will still support and make me worthy of a blessed meeting hereafter. Can you excuse, sir, the overflowing of a heart that knows not where to stop when on a subject so interesting?

Mr. Tutard tells me you mean to quit the service. Whenever that happens, you will doubtless have leisure to pay us a visit, which I wish you to believe will give real pleasure to,

Sir, your obliged

J. MONTGOMERY.

FROM WILLIAM PATERSON.

The Ponds, 18th March, 1779.

MY DEAR BURR,

I came to this place yesterday in the afternoon, and regret extremely that I did not arrive earlier in the day, as I should have received your letter. My stay here will be un-

certain. At home I must be by the beginning of April. I
should be happy in seeing you before my return, but how to
effect it is the question. If I could possibly disengage myself from business, I would take a ride to Paramus. My
best respects await on Mrs. Prevost; and every thing you
think proper to the mistress of your affections.

I am married, Burr, and happy. May you be equally so.
I cannot form a higher or a better wish. You know I should
rejoice to meet you. Tell Mrs. Prevost that I shall take it
unkindly if she does not call upon me whenever she thinks
I can be of any service to her. To oblige her will give me
pleasure for her own sake, and double pleasure for yours.
This is a strange, unconnected scroll; you have it as it
comes.

I congratulate you on your return to civil life, for which
(I cannot forbear the thought) we must thank a certain lady
not far from Paramus. May I have occasion soon to thank
her on another account; and may I congratulate you both
in the course of the next moon for being in my line: I
mean the married. Adieu.

I am most sincerely yours,

WILLIAM PATERSON.

Headquarters, Peekskill, 20th March, 1779.

SIR,

My late intelligence from New-York and headquarters
clearly mark the enemy's intention to make a movement very
soon. Whether it is intended against the grand army, these
posts, or New-London, time only can determine. It is,
however, our duty to be prepared. As a few days will open
up his views, *I imagine you do not think of quitting the
ground when business is to be done.* Should the enemy
move up the river in force, his thieves will be very busy
below. Colonel Hammond's regiment, on such an event, is
to remain there ; and one hundred rank and file of continental

troops *only* are to keep them in countenance. The rest, under charge of officers, to be sent up to join their corps.

You know the state of forage at this post. I wish you would make an exertion to your left in front, to secure all you can for us ; as much as will consist with the safety of your party, and covering to the rebels at Tarrytown. Send for Haynes and his assistant, and keep them on the ground till they secure all that is practicable to be got from your left. The weather has been so stormy and uncertain, the are not yet sent for. To-morrow morning it will be done. Please to attend to the enclosed order respecting provisions. Late Learned's is moved to West Point.

Major Hull's, of the 19th, is this moment received, and will be attended to. I wish Captain Kearsley, Lieutenants Hunter and Lawrence, to be sent to their regiments when Colonel Burr has finished what he intends. They are much wanted. Note the contents of the enclosed resolve.

Yours, very respectfully,

ALEXANDER M'DOUGALL.

It has been seen that Colonel Burr, while he commanded at White Plains, on the frontier, not only kept the adjacent country in a state of security, but that he kept the enemy in complete check. He was succeeded in his command by Colonel Littlefield, who was soon captured, and the post abandoned. Major Hull, in a letter to Colonel Burr, dated the 29th of May, 1779, says, " *The ground you so long defended is now left to the depredations of the enemy, and our friends in distressing circumstances.*"

In the beginning of June, Sir Henry Clinton captured the forts at Stony Point and Verplanck's Point, and threatened West Point. His force in this direction was upwards of six thousand rank and file. The communication between General Washington, who was in New-Jersey, and General M'Dougall, who was at Newburgh, was greatly embarrassed Bandits were placed by the British in or near the passes through the chains of mountains leading to Sussex, for the purpose of capturing the expresses charged with despatches. At this critical moment Colonel Burr was on a visit to M'Dougall, who informed him that he had made various unsuccessful attempts to communicate with Washington, and that his expresses had either been captured or had deserted. After apologizing to Burr, who was no longer in active service, the general stated the importance of the commander-in-chief's knowing the position and movements of the enemy, as well as the state of the American army. He then very courteously requested Burr to be the bearer of a verbal communication to Washington on the subject. To this, notwithstanding his ill health and the danger of the enterprise, he assented. The mission was undertaken and succeeded. He was also charged at the same time with *verbal orders* from General St. Clair, of a confidential character, to officers commanding at different posts.

To whom it may concern :—
Colonel Burr, being on urgent public business, is to be put across the ferry to New-Windsor without delay. Given this second day of June, 1779.
    ALEXANDER M'DOUGALL, Major-general.

To whom it may concern :—
Colonel Burr, being on very pressing public business, every magistrate will assist him in changing horses, and all friends of the country will also assist him. June 2d, 1779.
    ALEXANDER M'DOUGALL, Major-general.

To whom it may concern :—
Colonel Burr, being on urgent public business, must be put across the ferry to Fishkill landing without a moment's delay. Given at Pompton, 3d June, 1779.
    ARTHUR ST. CLAIR, Major-general.

To whom it may concern :—

The quartermaster and commissary, at Newburgh or New-Windsor, will receive and observe, as my orders, the verbal directions given by Colonel Burr. Given at Pompton, 3d June, 1779.

ARTHUR ST. CLAIR, Major-general.

On this enterprise a most amusing incident occurred. Colonel Burr arrived at the iron-works of the elder Townsend, in Orange county, with a tired and worn-out horse. No other could be obtained ; but, after some detention, a half-broken mule, named *Independence*, was procured, and the colonel mounted. But *Independence* refused to obey orders, and a battle ensued. The mule ran off with his rider, and ascended a high bank, on the side of which stood a coal-house, filled with coal through an aperture in the top. At length, *Independence*, in the hope of clearing himself of his encumbrance, entered the coal-house at full speed, the colonel firmly keeping his seat, and both came down an inclined plane of coal, not less than thirty feet in height. On reaching the ground without injury, Burr hired a man to lead the animal a mile or two, and then again mounted him and pursued his journey. This scene was exhibited on a hot day in the month of June, amid a cloud of coal-dust. The anecdote Burr occasionally repeated to his friends, and some of the younger branches of the Townsend family.

About the first of July, 1779, Colonel Burr, then in feeble health, visited his friends in Connecticut. He was at New-Haven when, on the 5th of July, the British landed, with 2600 men, in two divisions ; one under Governor Tryon, at East Haven, and the other under Garth, at West Haven. At East Haven, where Tryon commanded, great excesses were committed, and the town set on fire. Colonel Burr was at this moment confined to his bed ; but, on hearing that the enemy were advancing, rose and proceeded to a part of the town where a number of persons had collected. He volunteered to take command of the militia, and made an unsuccessful attempt to rally them. At this moment he was informed that the students had organized themselves, and were drawn up in the college-yard. He immediately galloped to the ground, and addressed them; appealing, in a few words, to their patriotism and love of country; imploring them to set the example, and march out in the defence of those rights which would, at a future day, become their inheritance. All he asked was, that they would receive and follow him as their leader.

The military character of Colonel Burr was known to the students. They confided in his intrepidity, experience, and judgment. In their ranks there was no faltering. They promptly obeyed the summons, and volunteered. Some skirmishing soon ensued, and portions of the militia united with them. The British, ignorant of the force that might be presented, retired; but shortly returned, with several pieces of artillery, when a cannonading commenced, and the boys retreated in good order. An American historian says,—"The British entered the town after being much galled and harassed." The slight check which they thus received afforded an opportunity for the removal of some valuables, and many of the women and children.

Trifling and unimportant as this skirmishing appears to have been, Colonel Burr never referred to the incident but with exultation and pride. Perhaps no event in his military life has he more frequently mentioned. The confidence evinced by these young men he considered complimentary to himself as a soldier; and usually alluded to the circumstance as evidence of the effect which the character of an officer would ever have upon undisciplined men, when called to command them upon trying occasions.

The following letter, written by Colonel Platt, will close all that is intended to be said of Colonel Burr as a soldier. More space has been occupied with an account of his military character than would have been thus occupied, if it was not known that he felt proud of his own career as an officer. For history Mr. Burr entertained a great contempt. He confided but little in its details. These prejudices were probably strengthened by the consideration that justice, in his opinion, had not been done to himself.

COLONEL RICHARD PLATT TO COMMODORE VALENTINE MORRIS.

New-York, January 27th, 1814.

DEAR SIR,

In reply to yours of the 20th of November last, requesting to be informed what was the reputation and services of Colonel Burr during the revolutionary war? I give you the following detail of facts, which you may rely on. No man was better acquainted with him, and his military operations, than your humble servant, who served in that war from the 28th of June, 1775, till the evacuation of our capital on the memorable 25th of November, 1783; having passed through the grades of lieutenant, captain, major, major of brigade, aid-de-camp, deputy adjutant-general, and deputy quartermaster-general; the last of which by selection and recommendation of Generals Greene, M'Dougall, and Knox, in the most trying crisis of the revolution, viz., the year 1780, when the continental money ceased to pass, and there was no other fiscal resources during that campaign but what resulted from the creative genius of Timothy Pickering, at that crisis appointed successor to General Greene, the second officer of the American army, who resigned the department because there was no money in the national coffers to carry it through the campaign, declaring that he could not, and would not attempt it, without adequate resources, such as he abounded in during the term of nearly three years antecedently as quartermaster-general.

In addition to the foregoing, by way of elucidation, it is

to be understood by you, that so early as from the latter part of the year 1776, I was always attached to a commanding general; and, in consequence, my knowledge of the officers and their merits was more general than that of almost any other in service. My operations were upon the extended scale, from the remotest parts of Canada, wherever the American standard had waved, to the splendid theatre of Yorktown, when and where I was adjutant-general to the chosen troops of the northern army.

At the commencement of the revolution, Colonel Burr, then about eighteen years of age, at the first sound of the trump of war (as if bred in the camp of the great Frederick, whose maxim was "to hold his army always in readiness to break a lance with, or throw a dart against, any assailant"), quit his professional studies, and rushed to the camp of General Washington, at Cambridge, as a volunteer; from which he went with Colonel Arnold on his daring enterprise against Quebec, through the wilds of Canada (which vied with Hannibal's march over the Alps), during which toilsome and hazardous march he attracted the attention and admiration of his commander so much, that he (Arnold) sent him alone to meet and hurry down General Montgomery's army from Montreal to his assistance; and recommended him to that general, who appointed him an aid-de-camp, in which capacity he acted during the winter, till the fatal assault on Quebec, in which that gallant general, his aid McPherson, and Captain Cheeseman, commanding the forlorn hope, fell. He afterwards continued as aid to Arnold, the surviver in command.   .

Here I must begin to draw some of the outlines of his genius and valour, which, like those of the British immortal, Wolf, who, at the age of twenty-four, and only major of the 20th regiment, serving on the continent, gave such specimens of genius and talents as to evince his being destined for command.

· At the perilous moment of Montgomery's death, when dis-

may and consternation universally prevailed, and the column
halted, he animated the troops, and made many efforts to lead
them on ; and stimulated them to enter the lower town ; and
might have succeeded, but for the positive orders of Colonel
Donald Campbell, the commanding officer, for the troops to
retreat. Had his plan been carried into effect, it might
have saved Arnold's division from capture, which had, after
our retreat, to contend with all the British force instead of a
part. On this occasion I commanded the first company in
the first New-York regiment, at the head of Montgomery's
column, so that I speak from ocular demonstration.

The next campaign, 1776, Colonel Burr was appointed
aid-de-camp to Major-general Putnam, second in command
under General Washington at New-York; and from my
knowledge of that general's qualities and the colonel's, I am
very certain that the latter directed all the movements and
operations of the former.

In January, 1777, the continental establishment for the
war commenced. Then Colonel Burr was appointed by
General Washington a lieutenant-colonel in Malcolm's regi
ment, in which he continued to serve until April, 1779,
when the ill state of his health obliged him to retire from
active service, to the regret of General M'Dougall, commanding the department, and that of the commander-in-
chief, who offered to give him a furlough for any length of
time, and to get permission from the British general in
New-York for him to go to Bermuda for his health. This
item will show his value in the estimation of Generals
Washington and M'Dougall.

During the campaign of 1777, Malcolm's regiment was
with the main army, and commanded by Lieutenant-colonel
Burr. For discipline, order, and system, it was not surpassed by any in the service ; and could his (the lieutenant-
colonel's) and Wolfe's orderly-books be produced, they
would be very similar in point of military policy and instructions, and fit models for all regiments.

This regiment was also hutted at the Valley Forge in 1777 and winter of 1778, under General Washington, and com posed part of his army at the battle of Monmouth on the 28th of June, 1778, and continued with it till the close of the campaign of that year, at which time it was placed in garrison at West Point by General Gates; but, upon General M'Dougall's assuming the command of the posts in the highlands in December, Malcolm's, Spencer's, and Patten's regiments were together ordered to Haverstraw. The three colonels were permitted to go home for the winter on furlough, and Lieutenant-colonel Burr had the command of the whole brigade, at a very important advanced post.

At this period General M'Dougall ordered a detachment of about three hundred troops, under the command of Lieutenant-colonel Littlefield, of the Massachusetts line, to guard the lines in Westchester county, then extending from Tarrytown to White Plains, and from thence to Mamaroneck or Sawpits, which last extension was guarded by Connecticut troops from Major-general Putnam's division.

In this situation of affairs a very singular occurrence presented, viz., that neither Lieutenant-colonel Littlefield, nor any other of his grade, in the two entire brigades of Massachusetts troops composing the garrison of West Point, from which the lines were to be relieved, was competent, in the general's estimation, to give security to the army above and the lines of those below; and, in consequence, he was compelled to call Colonel Burr from his station at Haverstraw to the more important command of the lines in Westchester, in which measure, unprecedented as it was, the officers acquiesced without a murmur, from a conviction of its expediency. At this time I was doing the duty of adjutant-general to General M'Dougall.

It was on this new and interesting theatre of war that the confidence and affections of the officers and soldiers (who now became permanent on the lines, instead of being relieved every two or three weeks as before), as well as of

the inhabitants, all before unknown to Colonel Burr, were
inspired with confidence by a system of consummate skill,
astonishing vigilance, and extreme activity, which, in like
manner, made such an impression on the enemy, that after
an unsuccessful attack on one of his advanced posts, he
never made any other attack on our lines during the winter.

His humanity, and constant regard to the security of the
property and persons of the inhabitants from injury and insult, were not less conspicuous than his military skill, &c.
No man was insulted or disturbed. The health of the
troops was perfect. Not a desertion during the whole
period of his command, nor a man made prisoner, although
the colonel was constantly making prisoners.

A country, which for three years before had been a scene
of robbery, cruelty, and murder, became at once the abode
of security and peace. Though his powers were despotic,
they were exercised only for the peace, the security, and
the protection of the surrounding country and its inhabitants.

In the winter of 1779, the latter part of it, Major Hull, an
excellent officer, then in the Massachusetts line, was sent
down as second to Colonel Burr, who, after having become
familiarized to his system, succeeded him for a short time
in command, about the last of April, at which time Colonel
Burr's health would not permit him to continue in command;
but the major was soon compelled to fall back many miles,
so as to be within supporting distance of the army at the
highlands.

The severity of the service, and the ardent and increasing
activity with which he had devoted himself to his country's
cause, for more than four years, having materially impaired
his health, he was compelled to leave the post and retire from
active service. It was two years before he regained his
health.

Major Hull has ever since borne uniformly the most
honourable testimony of the exalted talents of his commander, by declaring his gratitude for being placed under

an officer whose system of duty was different from that of all other commanders under whom he had served. ·

Having thus exhibited the colonel's line of march, and his operations in service, I must now present him in contrast with his equals in rank, and his superiors in command.

In September, 1777, the enemy came out on both sides of the Hudson simultaneously, in considerable force, say from 2 to 3000 men. On the east side (at Peekskill) was a major-general of our army, with an effective force of about 2000 men. The enemy advanced, and our general retired without engaging them. Our barracks and storehouses, and the whole village of Peekskill, were sacked and burnt, and the country pillaged.

On the west side, at the mouth of the Clove, near Suffren's, was Colonel Burr, commanding Malcolm's regiment, about three hundred and fifty men. On the first alarm he marched to find the enemy, and on the same night attacked and took their picket-guard, rallied the country, and made such show of war, that the enemy retreated the next morning, leaving behind him the cattle, horses, and sheep he had plundered.

The year following, Lieutenant-colonel Thompson was sent to command on the same lines in Westchester by General Heath, and he was surprised at nine or ten o'clock in the day, and made prisoner, with a great part of his detachment.

Again, in the succeeding winter, Colonel Greene, of the Rhode Island line, with his own and another Rhode Island regiment, who was a very distinguished officer, and had with these two regiments, in the year 1777, defeated the Hessian grenadiers under Count Donop, at Red Banks, on the Delaware, who was mortally wounded and taken prisoner, commanded on the lines in Westchester; there receded to Pine's bridge, and in this position Colonel Greene's troops were also surprised after breakfast and dispersed, the colonel himself and Major Flagg killed, and many soldiers made prisoners, besides killed and wounded.

On the west side of the Hudson, in the year 1780, General Wayne, the hero of Stony Point, with a large command and field artillery, made an attack on a block-house nearly opposite to Dobbs's ferry, defended by cowboys, and was repulsed with loss; whereas Colonel Burr burnt and destroyed one of a similar kind, in the winter of 1779, near Delancey's mills, with a very few men, and without any loss on his part, besides capturing the garrison.

Here, my good friend commodore, I must drop the curtain till I see you in Albany, which will be on the first week in February, where I can and will convince you that he is the only man in America (that is, the United States) who is fit to be a lieutenant-general; and let you and I, and all the American people, look out for Mr. Madison's lieutenant-general in contrast.

I am your friend,
RICHARD PLATT.

CHAPTER XII.

On retiring from the army, Colonel Burr visited his friends in New-Jersey and Connecticut. He had previously determined, as soon as his health would permit, to commence the study of law. During the four years he was in public service, his patrimony was greatly impaired. Towards his brethren in arms he had acted with liberality. Naturally of an improvident character, he adopted no means to preserve the property which he inherited. The cardinal vices of gaming and drinking he avoided. But he was licentious in the extreme, and regardless of consequences in the grati fication of his desires. His extravagance was unrestrained when, in his opinion, necessary to the enjoyment of his pleasures. From the arms of his nurse until he had numbered fourscore years, he was perpetually the dupe of the artful and the selfish.

Colonel Burr was about five feet six inches in height. He was well formed, and erect in his attitude. In all his movements there was a military air. Although of small stature, yet there was about him a loftiness of mien that could not pass unnoticed by a stranger. His deportment was polished and courtly. His features were regular, and generally considered handsome. His eye was jet black, with a brilliancy never surpassed. The appropriate civilities of the drawing-room were performed with a grace almost peculiar to himself. His whole manner was inconceivably fascinating. As a gentleman, this was his great theatre. He acted upon the principle that the female was the weaker sex, and that they were all susceptible of flattery. His great art consisted in adopting it to the grade of intellect he addressed. In this respect he was singularly fortunate as well as adroit. In matters of gallantry he was excessively vain. This vanity sometimes rendered him ridiculous in the eyes of his best friends, and often enabled the most worthless and unprincipled to take advantage of his credulity.

Such traits of character would appear to be incompatible with an elevated and towering mind ; yet they usually influenced, and frequently controlled, one of the greatest and most extraordinary men of the age. A volume of anecdotes might be related as evidence of Colonel Burr's quickness of perception and tact at reply, when an ill-judged or thoughtless expression was addressed by him to a lady. One is sufficient for illustration.

After his return from Europe, in 1812, he met a maiden lady in Broadway somewhat advanced in life. He had not seen her for many years. As she passed him, she exclaimed to a gentleman on whose arm she was resting, " Colonel

Burr !"   Hearing his name mentioned, he suddenly stopped
and looked her in the face.   " Colonel," said she, " you do
not recollect me."

" I do not, madam," was the reply.

" It is Miss K., sir."

" What !" said he, " Miss K. *yet !*"

The lady, somewhat piqued, reiterated, " Yes, sir, Miss
K. *yet !*"

Feeling the delicacy of his situation, and the unfortunate
error he had committed, he gently took her hand, and em-
phatically remarked, " Well, madam, then I venture to assert *that it is not the fault of my sex.*"

On Burr's being appointed, in 1777, a lieutenant-colonel
in the army, he joined his regiment, then stationed at Rama-
poa, in New-Jersey.   At Paramus, not far distant, resided
Mrs. Prevost, the wife of Colonel Prevost, of the British
army.   She was an accomplished and intelligent lady.   Her
husband was with his regiment. in the West Indies, where
he died early in the revolutionary war.   She had a sister residing with her.   It was her son, the Hon. John B. Prevost, who in 1802 was recorder of the city of New-York,
and subsequently district judge of the United States Court
for the district of Louisiana.   The house of Mrs. Prevost
was the resort of the most accomplished officers in the
American army when they were in the vicinity of it.   She
was highly respected by her neighbours, and visited by the
most genteel people of the surrounding country.   Her situation was one of great delicacy and constant apprehension.

The wife of a British officer, and connected with the adherents of the crown, naturally became an object of political
suspicion, notwithstanding great circumspection on her part
Under such circumstances, a strong sympathy was excited
in her behalf.   Yet there were those among the whigs who
were inclined to enforce the laws of the state against her,
whereby she would be compelled to withdraw within the

lines of the enemy. In this family Colonel Burr became
intimate in 1777, and in 1782 married the widow Prevost.

JAMES MONROE* TO MRS. PREVOST.

Philadelphia, November 8th, 1778.

A young lady who either is, or pretends to be, in love, is,
you know, my dear Mrs. Prevost, the most unreasonable
creature in existence. If she looks a smile or a frown, which
does not immediately give or deprive you of happiness (at
least to appearance), your company soon becomes very insipid. Each feature has its beauty, and each attitude the
graces, or you have no judgment. But if you are so stu-
pidly insensible of her charms as to deprive your tongue and
eyes of every expression of admiration, and not only to be
silent respecting her, but devote them to an absent object,
she cannot receive a higher insult; nor would she, if not
restrained by politeness, refrain from open resentment.

Upon this principle I think I stand excused for not wri
ting from B. Ridge. I proposed it, however; and, after meeting with opposition in ——, to obtain her point, she promised to visit the little " Hermitage,"† and make my excuse herself. I took occasion to turn the conversation to a
different object, and plead for permission to go to France. I
gave up in one instance, and she certainly ought in the other.
But writing a letter and going to France are very different,
you will perhaps say. She objected to it, and all the arguments which a fond, delicate, unmarried lady could use, she
did not fail to produce against it. I plead the advantage I
should derive from it. The personal improvement, the
connexions I should make. I told her she was not the only
one on whom fortune did not smile in every instance. I
produced examples from her own acquaintance, and represented their situation in terms which sensibly affected both
herself and Lady C   . I painted a lady full of affection

---

* Late President of the United States.
† The residence of Mrs. Prevost.

of tenderness, and sensibility, separated from her husband, for a series of time, by the cruelty of the war—her uncertainty respecting his health; the pain and anxiety which must naturally arise from it. I represented, in the most pathetic terms, the disquietudes which, from the nature of her connexion, might possibly intrude on her domestic retreat. I then raised to her view fortitude under distress; cheerfulness, life, and gayety, in the midst of affliction.

I hope you will forgive me, my dear little friend, if I produced you to give life to the image. The instance, she owned, was applicable. She felt for you from her heart, and she has a heart capable of feeling. She wished not a misfortune similar to yours; but, if I was resolved to make it so, she would strive to imitate your example. I have now permission to go where I please, but you must not forget her. She and Lady C—— promise to come to the Hermitage to spend a week or two. Encourage her, and represent the advantage I shall gain from travel. But why should I desire you to do what I know your own heart will dictate? for a heart so capable of friendship feels its own pain alleviated by alleviating that of another.

But do not suppose that my attention is only taken up with my own affairs. I am too much attached ever to forget the Hermitage. Mrs. Duvall, I hope, is recovering; and Kitty's indisposition is that of my nearest relation. Mrs. de Visme has delicate nerves. Tell me her children are well, and I know she has a flow of spirits, for her health depends entirely on theirs.

I was unfortunate in not being able to meet with the governor. He was neither at Elizabethtown, B. Ridge, Princeton, nor Trenton. I have consulted with several members of Congress on the occasion. They own the injustice, but cannot interfere. The laws of each state must govern itself. They cannot conceive the possibility of its taking place. General Lee says it must not take place; and if he

VOL I.—A a

was an absolute monarch, he would issue an order to pre·
vent it.

I am introduced to the gentleman I wished by General
Lee in a very particular manner. I cannot determine with
certainty what I shall do till my arrival in Virginia. ·

Make my compliments to Mrs. and Miss De Visme, and
believe me, with the sincerest friendship,

·· Yours, ·

JAMES MONROE

Mr. Peter De Visme, the brother of Mrs. Prevost, was
captured at sea, and made prisoner of war. As she was
personally acquainted with General Washington, she solicited his influence to promote his exchange, to which the
general replied :—

Headquarters, Middlebrook, 19th May, 1779

MADAM,

It is much to be regretted that the pleasure of obeying
the first emotions in favour of misfortune is not always in
our power. I should be happy could I consider myself at
liberty to comply with your request in the case of your
brother, Mr. Peter De Visme. But, as I have heretofore
taken no direction in the disposal of marine prisoners, I cannot, with propriety, interfere on the present occasion, however great the satisfaction I should feel in obliging where
you are interested. Your good sense will perceive this, and
find a sufficient excuse in the delicacy of my situation.

I have the honour to be, madam,

Your obedient servant,

GEORGE WASHINGTON.

.FROM WILLIAM PATERSON.

Morristown, 29th September, 1779.

DEAR BURR, ·

About four weeks ago I received a letter from you of the
8th of August, and, a week after, another of the 23d. They

came by the way of Moorestown, from which to Rariton, where I reside. The conveyance is easy and safe. I cannot point out any mode of sending your letters better than that which you have adopted.

I was pleased extremely to hear from you, and, indeed, was quite disappointed in not hearing from you sooner. I was for a time in expectation that you would return into Jersey, as the scene of military operations was directed to your part of the world, and would unavoidably drive you from your study and repose. Military operations are so fluctuating and uncertain as to render it exceedingly difficult to fix upon a retreat which may not be broken in upon in the course of a campaign. New-Haven bid fair to be the seat of calmness and serenity, of course well suited for a studious and contemplative mind, and therefore made choice of as the place of your abode. New-Haven, however, partook of the common calamity; and, in the evolution of human events, from a place of safety and repose, was turned into a place of confusion and war.

You are not contented, my dear Burr, and why are you not? You sigh for New-Jersey, and why do you not return? It is true we are continually broken in upon by the sons of tumult and war. Our situation is such that the one army or the other is almost constantly with us, and yet we rub along with tolerable order, spirit, and content. Oh! that the days of peace would once more return, that we might follow what business, partake of what amusements, and think and live as we please. As to myself, I am, my dear Burr, one of the happiest of men. The office I hold calls me too frequently, and detains me too long, from home, otherwise I should enjoy happiness as full and high as this world can afford. It is, as you express it, "serene, rural, and sentimental;" and such, one day, you will *feel*.

"You see no company—you partake of no amusements— you are always grave." Such, too, has been the life that I have lived for months and years. I cannot say that it is an unpleasing one.   I avoided company; indeed, I do so still, unless it be the company of chosen friends.   I have been ever fond of my fireside and study—ever fond of calling up some absent friend, and of living over, in idea, past times of sentimental pleasure.   Fancy steps in to my aid, colours the picture, and makes it delightful indeed.   You are in the very frame of mind I wish you to be; may it continue.

I cannot tell you what has become of Mrs. Prevost's affairs.   About two months ago I received a very polite letter from her.   She was apprehensive that the commissioners would proceed.   It seems they threatened to go on.   I wrote them on the subject, but I have not heard the event. I am at this place, on my way to a superior court in Bergen.   If possible, I shall wait on the good gentlewoman. At Bergen I shall inquire into the state of the matter.   It will, indeed, turn up of course.   You shall soon hear from me again.   Adieu.   May health and happiness await you

WILLIAM PATERSON.

The precarious and unsettled state of Colonel Burr's health, in the autumn of 1779 and the beginning of 1780, was such that he was unable to adopt and adhere to any regular system of study.   Among his most intimate personal friends was Colonel Robert Troup.   He, too, had determined to retire from public service, and was anxious to study in the same office with Burr.   His letters cast much light on their pursuits at the time they were written.

FROM COLONEL TROUP.

Philadelphia, 16th January, 1780.

MY DEAR FRIEND,

Watkins was kind enough to deliver me yours of the 8th of December, written, I presume, at Paramus.   I almost envy you the happiness you have enjoyed.   From the first moment of my acquaintance with Mrs. Prevost and her sister, I conceived an admiration for them both, which is much increased by the opinion you entertain of them. How, then, am I flattered by their polite manner of mentioning my name. To whom am I indebted but to you, my friend, for this unmerited favour? Surely these ladies saw nothing in me at Governor Livingston's which was worthy of remembrance, unless a terrible noise, which some people call laughter, could be worth remembering. With the best intention, therefore, to serve me, you have done me an injury, Aaron. I shall be afraid to see our favourites in the spring, because I shall fall infinitely short of their ideas of cleverness. Pray, do you recollect the opinion which Judge Candour solemnly pronounced upon us both, in a court of reason held at the Indian King? Why, then, will you expose my weakness by ascribing to me imaginary excellences? If you persist in such cruel conduct, sir, I will make you feel the weight of my resentment, by publishing to the world the purity of my esteem for your public and private character.

I am happy to find our plan of studying together appears more and more rational to you. It really does to me, and I hope we shall follow it. Since you left Philadelphia, some circumstances have turned up which render my office so disagreeable to me that I am determined to resign. *Vous pouvez compter sur moi.* Besides the disgust I have taken, I am led to it by ambition, which has a small share of influence over me as well as you.

But I am desirous of a change in our plan, which I request you to think of seriously. I am inclined to believe it would be best for us to study the law with Mr. Stockton, at Princeton. This, I know, will surprise you; but your surprise will be lessened when you hear my reasons.

The practice of Connecticut differs so materially from the practice of New-York and New-Jersey, that we should' lose time by being with Mr. Osmer. For, after being eighteen months or two years with him, it would be necessary to continue nearly the same time in another office, to get a!

competent knowledge of the practice. This is a matter of consequence, especially as it is my object to qualify myself for practice as soon as possible.

I have the highest opinion of Mr. Osmer, and, did I intend to follow the law in Connecticut, there is no man I would sooner study with. I believe he would ground us well in the knowledge of the dead-letter of the law ; but I wish to have the practice and the theory accompanying each other. Mr. Stockton has been polite enough to make me an offer, and has promised to spare no pains to instruct me. He would be glad to instruct you likewise ; for I have heard him express himself of you in the most friendly manner. I propose to lodge at some substantial farmer's house, about a mile from the main road, and have made a solemn league and covenant with my own mind to seclude myself from the pleasures of the world. This I know I can do. And have you not as much philosophy as I have ?

It is true, Mr. Stockton has unmarried daughters, and there is a number of genteel families in and near Princeton. But why should we connect ourselves with any of them, so as to interrupt our studies ? They will be entitled to a civil bow from us whenever we meet them; and, if they expect more, they will be disappointed. Indeed, I shall take care to inform them of my intentions, and if they afterwards complain of my want of politeness in not visiting them, it will give me little uneasiness.

I entreat you, my dearest and best friend, to reflect on this matter, and favour me with your answer without a moment's loss of time. My happiness, and my improvement in the law, depend entirely upon pursuing my studies with you. The change I now propose is conformable to the sentiments and wishes of all my friends, particularly of Chancellor Livingston, who is certainly a judge.

I forgot to mention that Mr. Stockton is universally allowed to be one of the best speakers we ever had in this part of the continent, and it will therefore be in his power to teach us the eloquence of the bar, which may be considered as a capital advantage.

I have communicated my sentiments on this subject more fully to our mutual friend, Colonel Wadsworth, who will deliver you this letter, than I have to you in writing He will explain them to you, and, I am sure, will give you his own with the utmost candour and sincerity.

I have left several messages at the house Dr. ——— lodges when he is in town; but cannot get an answer, and see little prospect of getting your money unless you write him a dunning letter. I shall leave one for him to-morrow, and will endeavour to have the affair settled this week.

I write this at my lodgings, where I have not a single newspaper. Colonel Wadsworth will leave town in the course of an hour; and, if I can find time, I will go to the office and collect all I can find. There have been none, however, since you left town, which are worth reading. Wadsworth will tell you all the news I have, which is, that old Roger Sherman is metamorphosed, by some strange magical power, into a *very honest man.*

God bless you, and may Dom. Tetard soon have the pleasure of drinking a glass of wine with us both, in his house at Kingsbridge. I mean, after the British gentry have left it. I should have written to you before, but I have been waiting these three weeks past for Colonel Wadsworth to leave Philadelphia. He will inform you of the cursed slavish life I lead at the treasury office. I am obliged to attend it even on Saturday nights, which places me below the level of a negro in point of liberty. Pray present my best respects to Tetard, and assure him of my wishes to serve him at all times, and on all occasions.

Yours,

ROBERT TROUP.

FROM COLONEL TROUP.
Philadelphia, February 14th, 1780.

My dear Burr,

I have resigned my office, and am now preparing to leave Philadelphia to go to Princeton, agreeable to the plan in my letter by Colonel Wadsworth. This week I expect to finish a little private business I have on hand, and, by the lat ter end of the next, to be settled in a regular course of study with Mr. Stockton. What think you of this alteration in the plan we settled? Can you leave Mr. Osmer without injury? I assure you, the only motive I have to prefer Stockton is a desire to qualify myself for practice as soon as possible. All my friends are against my studying in Connecticut, for the reason mentioned in my last; and they all recommend Stockton to me. I am therefore deter- mined to study with him.

I am very much afraid that Princeton will be disagree able to you on many accounts, and particularly on account of the number of acquaintances you have in and near it. This is a misfortune, to be sure; but do as I shall, *neglect them all;* it is matter of perfect indifference to me whether I affront them or not. My object is to study with the closest attention. I must do it. I have no other resource.

Permit me to declare, like a sincere friend, that my hap- piness is so intimately connected with yours, that I shall be chagrined to an extreme if you find it inconvenient to join me. We could be useful to each other. Besides facilita- ting each other's progress in the law, we could improve our- selves in writing and speaking. In one word—I am con fident I should acquire as much knowledge in three years with you as in six years without you. I never was more serious. Come, therefore, immediately, and bring Mr. Tetard with you to perfect us in the French language, which I have paid little attention to since I wrote you, and indeed since you left me.

Pray why have you neglected to answer my letter by Colonel Wadsworth? I suspect something extraordinary is the matter with you. Or are you so angry as not to think I merit an answer? Whatever your reason was, let me request you to favour me with an answer to this by the first opportunity. If it is sent under cover to Mr. Stockton, it will perhaps reach me sooner.

It is reported, and pretty generally believed, that Sir Henry Clinton, with the fleet that came from New-York about six weeks ago, has touched at Georgia; taken Prevost's troops with him, and gone either to St. Augustine or the Havannah. This is very important news, if true; but it seems to wait confirmation.

· Your unalterable friend,

ROBERT TROUP

TO WILLIAM PATERSON.

Middletown, February 16th, 1780.

Your friendly letter of September has at length found its way to me. I am once more a recluse. It accords with my feelings. I should doubtless be happier if I enjoyed perfect health and the society of a friend like you; but why do I say *like you?* No likeness could compensate for the absence of the original.

I am something at a loss how to regulate my motions for the coming summer. The prospect of peace is still distant. It is an object of importance with me to be not only secure from alarms, but remote from the noise of war. My present situation promises at least those advantages. Perhaps yours does equally. Events only can determine.

My health, which was till of late very promising, seems to decline a little. This circumstance will oblige me to alter my course of life. I shall be in your state in May or June, perhaps sooner. If you have a prospect of tranquillity, I shall have no thought of returning. Colonel Troup, a worthy, sensible young fellow, and a particular friend of

mine, wishes to know where I shall prosecute my studies,
and is determined, he says, to be my companion. A gentleman who has been long eminent at your bar, and whom
we both know perfectly well, had made Troup some polite
offers of his service as an instructer. He was pleased with
the scheme, and as he knew the gentleman was professedly
my friend, urged me to put myself also under his tuition. I
mentioned to him in a late letter the objections which had been
decisive with me, and I fancy he will view them in the same
light. He is the companion I would wish in my studies.
He is a better antidote for the spleen than a ton of drugs.
I am often a little inclined to *hypo.*

My best respects attend Mrs. Paterson. Speak of her in
your letters. I would not feel indifferent to one so near to
you, even if no personal acquaintance had confirmed my
esteem. You would have heard from me sooner, but no
post has rode this fortnight. I have been pursuing the
track you marked out for me, though not with the ardour I
could wish. My health will bear no imposition. I am
obliged to eat, drink, sleep, and study, as it directs. No
such restraint interrupts your bliss. May you feel no bonds
but those of love and friendship—no rules but those that
lead to happiness. Adieu.

Yours sincerely,

A. BURR.

FROM COLONEL TROUP.

Philadelphia, 29th February, 1780.

MY DEAR BURR, ...

Your favours of the 1st and 5th inst. came to hand last
night, and are both before me. I am very much indebted
to you for your candour in stating the objections which are
against Princeton, as well as Mr. Stockton. I had anticipated them all. They are far from being groundless. But
my situation was peculiar when I determined to live with
Mr. Stockton. In my last a principle of delicacy induced

me to be more reserved than is consistent with·the sincerity of our affection for each other. Forgive my criminal reserve. I will be plain with you now.

By a strange kind of contracted system, which pervades all the civil establishments of Congress, I was reduced to the necessity of resigning my office at least six weeks sooner than I expected. Though I laboured both day and night, with as much drudgery as a negro on a plantation in the West Indies, the board of treasury did not think themselves authorized to report a warrant in my favour for money to answer the common demands of living. They confined me to my salary of *ten thousand dollars** per annum. Finding that I had not the most distant prospect of getting a decent support while I continued in office, and that I was obliged to pay four or five thousand dollars out of my own private purse for *necessaries, I cursed and quit them* the beginning of this month.

Being thus out of office, I thought it would be prudent to settle myself at the law without a moment's delay, both on account of the heavy expense of living in this city, and the loss of time, which is of the greatest consequence to me. I did not forget Mr. Paterson when I gave the preference to Mr. Stockton. The private character of the former is infinitely superior to that of the latter, and so is his public. But he is immersed in such an ocean of business, that I imagined it would be out of his power to bestow all the time and pains on our improvement we would wish. Besides, I was afraid of being more confined to the drudgery of copying in his office than I ought. This is inseparable from an office in which there is a good deal done, however well disposed a lawyer may be to promote the interest of his clerk. You observe that his present office expires next summer. I grant it. Yet he may be chosen attorney-general again ; and this I believe will be the case, for there is

---

* Continental paper dollars—equal in value to *sixty* for one *silver dollar.*

not a man of sufficient abilities in the state, except him and Morris, to whom the people would give the office. Morris, I fancy, will not accept it if offered to him, as he has lately resigned his seat on the bench; and I will venture to predict that Paterson will be continued, though against his inclination.

Upon the whole, then, I feel extreme regret in telling you that I must go and sit down at Princeton the latter end of this week at farthest. The die is cast. My honour forbids me to act contrary to the engagement I have entered into with Mr. Stockton. Had I received your kind letter before my *absolute determination*, I should certainly have followed your advice. Our plan, therefore, will be frustrated. Painful the reflection! You would hurt me exceedingly if you came to live at Princeton, and subjected yourself to the inconveniences you mention, merely to please me.

I am glad to hear your health is mending, and should be still more happy if it was unnecessary to make use of the mineral springs in the Clove. I have always suspected that the law would disagree with your delicate constitution. It requires the most intense study. Your ambition to excel will stimulate you to the closest application, and I dread the effects it may produce. You should therefore be cautious. Health is a source of more substantial pleasure than the most cultivated understanding.

A few days ago Dr. Edwards left a bundle of bills, amounting, as he says, to one thousand pounds, at Dr. Rush's for me, to be sent to you. I have not yet counted it, but I suppose it is right. To-day or to-morrow I shall leave a receipt for it at Dr. Rush's.. I believe I shall presume so far upon your friendship as to borrow a part of it for my own use for about a fortnight. I am much disappointed in receiving a small sum to pay my debts in town. I sold two thousand dollars in certificates to Mr. Duer just before he left town, and he gave me an order upon a lady for the money. I find she will not be able to pay it for some time hence, and I am so pressed for cash that I have written to Duer, at Baskenridge, for the certificates or money immediately. I expect an answer every moment; and, till I receive it, shall consider part of yours as my own. The remainder I shall transmit you by the first safe conveyance. I think it would be wrong to trust the post with it.

I thank you sincerely for your offer of a horse. The present state of my finances is such that I cannot afford to keep one. If I could it might detach me from my studies. Beware of temptation, saith the Scripture, and so saith my interest.

I suppose you have read the king's speech. He makes no mention of his rebellious subjects in America, or of any allies, and is resolved to prosecute the war. The debates in the House of Lords, as well as Commons, on the motion for an address of thanks, were very warm. Lord North, in one of his speeches, makes no scruple of declaring that they have no allies to assist them. That they can get none. That the combined fleets have a *decided superiority*, and that it would have been highly dangerous for the English fleet to have fought them last fall. The bills on Spain and Holland sell very fast. They will all be disposed of in a very short time. There are large arrivals in Virginia and Maryland; and there are several vessels below, waiting for the river to be cleared of ice, which will be in three or four days. Poor *continental* is still going down hill. *Fifty-eight* was refused yesterday; and I have no doubt it will be *seventy* for *one* before ten days hence. Adieu. As long as you are Aaron Burr, I will be

ROBERT TROUP.

FROM MAJOR R. ALDEN.

I intended to have wrote you a letter in answer to your last, but neither head or heart will enable me at present. Although I am answerable for my conduct, yet I cannot govern the animal fluids. I am so much of a *lunatic thermometer*, that both *moon* and *atmosphere* very much influence my *aerial* constitution. My brain is subject to such changes, and so much affected by *external* objects, that I may be properly compared to a *windmill.* You may make the similitudes as you please. I have not a single sentiment in my head, or feeling in my heart, that would pay for expressing. At any rate, my mill will not grind. What is all this says my friend Aaron? The pleasure I enjoyed yesterday in feasting in good company, and in a variety of other agreeables, at the nuptial anniversary of our dear and happy friends, Mr. and Mrs. Thaddeus Burr, has deprived me of that common share of sensibility which is generally distributed through the days of the year, and rather destroyed the equilibrium. I set out for camp the last of this week; may I expect letters from my friend? Be assured of my warmest friendship, and make me happy by the like assurance, as it will afford the sincerest pleasure to,

Yours, with affection,

R. ALDEN.

FROM WILLIAM PATERSON.

Rariton, April 14th, 1780.

MY DEAR BURR,

I take the earliest opportunity of acknowledging the receipt of your *dateless* letter, and returning you my best thanks for it. Mr. and Mrs. Reeve* have been so kind as to tarry a night with me. We endeavoured to prevail upon them to pass a few days with us, and should have been happy if we could have succeeded. This letter goes with them. That circumstance cannot fail of making it still more welcome to your honest and benevolent heart.

I wrote you the latter end of January from the Hermit-

* Judge Tappan Reeve, whose lady was the sister of Colonel Burr.

age, and intrusted the letter to Mrs. Prevost. It was a mere
scrawl. This is of the same cast. However, I promise, the
very first leisure hour, to devote it entirely to you in the letter way. Although I do not write frequently to you, yet, believe me, I think frequently of you. Oh, Burr! may you
enjoy health, and be completely happy; as much so as I am
—more I cannot wish you. Nor will you be able to attain
high felicity until you experience such a union as I do. Mrs.
Paterson is in tolerable health, and gives you her best respects. I wish her safely through the month of May, and
then I shall be still more happy.

When you come to Jersey I shall certainly see you. If
I do not, it will be treason against our friendship.

Peace is distant. There is no prospect of it in the present year. Nor do I think that Britain will come to terms
while she fancies herself superior on the ocean. The war,
however, goes southward, and there is some hope that we
shall be more in quiet this year than we have been since
the commencement of hostilities. On the opening of the
campaign we shall be able to judge better. Adieu.

                                        WILLIAM PATERSON.

                    FROM COLONEL TROUP.

                                        Princeton, April 27th, 1780.

My DEAR BURR,

I wrote to you yesterday, and happened to put the letter
into the postoffice a little after the post had gone. In that
letter I requested you to come here as soon as possible, for
it was highly probable that I should leave Princeton entirely, and determine to follow our original plan. The event
has confirmed my conjecture. I came here from General
Morris's yesterday, and exerted all the influence I was master of to get new lodgings, but could not, without lodging in
the town, which would be disagreeable to me on many accounts. I have now given over all thoughts of staying here,
and, having an excellent pretext for changing my ground, I

shall write to Mr. Stockton, who is still in Philadelphia, and acquaint him with my intentions of going away. Nothing is therefore wanting but yourself, with a horse and chair, to make me completely happy. I wish to God I could push off eastward immediately, but I cannot. I have no horse, neither is it practicable to borrow or hire one. I must, then, wait for you; and I request you, in the most pressing terms, to lose not a moment's time in coming for me at General Morris's, about six miles from this, near Colonel Van Dyke's mill, on the road to Somerset, where I shall wait impatiently for you.

I am extremely uneasy lest this letter should reach you after you have left home, and begun your journey north ward. In that case I shall be very unfortunate; and, to pro vent too great a delay, I write to Mr. Reeves at Litchfield, and enclose him a letter for you, and desire him to forward it to you, wherever you are, with all expedition. I shall likewise enclose another for you to Mrs. Prevost, who will be kind enough to give it to you the moment you arrive there.

If we once get together, I hope we shall not be soon parted. It would afford me the greatest satisfaction to live with you during life. God grant our meeting may be soon. You have my best and fervent wishes for the recovery of your health, and every other happiness. Adieu.

ROBERT TROUP.

TO COLONEL TROUP.

Fairfield, 15th May, 1780.

MY DEAR BOB,

I wrote you from this place the 12th inst. This follows close upon it, that I may rest assured of your having heard from me.

I go to-morrow to Middletown, from whence I shall hasten my departure as much as possible. No trifling concerns should command me a moment; but business of im-

portance, and some embarrassments too serious to be laughed
out of the way, will, I fear, detain me this month. But the
month is already gone before you can receive this. I hope
your philosophy will not have forsaken you. Far from you
be gloom and despondency. Attune your organs to the genuine ha! ha! 'Tis to me the music of the spheres; the sov-
ereign specific that shall disgrace the physician's art, and
baffle the virulence of malady. Hold yourself aloof from
all engagements, even of the *heart*. We will deliberate unbiased, that we may decide with wisdom. I form no decision on the subject of our studies till I see you.

I write from the house of our friend Thaddeus, in a
world of company, who are constantly interrupting me with
impertinent questions. Your summons came unexpected,
and found me unprepared. Nevertheless, my assiduity shall
convince you that you may command

                                          A. BURR.

At General Morris's, near Princeton, 16th May, 1780.

MY DEAR BURR,

I wrote you, about three weeks ago, a very pressing letter, and requested you to come for me here as soon as
possible. My anxiety to see you is extreme, and, lest my
letter should have miscarried, I cannot help troubling you
with another. Every thing, my dear Burr, has succeeded
to my wishes. I have left Mr. Stockton upon the most
friendly terms imaginable, and I am still at General Morris's to avoid expense, but am so situated that I cannot
study. I assure you, my future prosperity and happiness in
life depends, in a greater measure than you may imagine,
on my living and studying with you; and the sooner we get
seated in some retired place, where we may live cheaply
and study without interruption, the better. I know myself
—I think I know you perfectly. I am more deceived than
ever I was if we do not live happily together, and improve

beyond our most sanguine expectations. Delay not, therefore, a single moment, my dear Burr, but come for me yourself. A horse or a chair without you will be unwelcome.
I want to consult you about several matters of importance
to me before I leave this state. I say leave this state, for
our original plan of studying with Mr. Osmer appears the
most rational to me on many accounts.

I am so much attached to you, my dear Burr, and feel
myself so much interested in every thing which concerns
you, that I believe, and hope sincerely, it will be many years
before we separate if we can once sit down together. As
long as my slender fortune will permit me to live without
business, we will, if you find it agreeable, enjoy the pleasures of retirement. . And when we enter on the theatre of
the world, why not act our parts together? Heaven grant
that we may. I repeat it again, my dearest friend, lose not
a moment's time in coming for me. It is painful to trespass
so long upon General Morris's bounty, though he be my
friend, and I have not any means of stirring an inch from
him unless I walk. For fear you should not be at Middletown, I shall enclose a copy of this letter to Mr. Reeves,
and request him to forward it to you immediately if you
should not be with him.

With what pleasure did I receive yours of the 24th ult.,
at Princeton, the other day, when I went to pay Mr. Stockton a visit after his return from Philadelphia. I cordially
congratulate you on the improvement of your health by rash
experiments. May it be as well established as my own,
which is perfectly capable of the closest application. But
I was not a little mortified to find you say nothing about
your intention to ride to Jersey. Let me entreat you once
more to set off as soon as possible. Every moment is precious, and ought to be employed to advantage. I shall wait
for you with the greatest impatience; and, in the meantime,
I am, what I always wish to be,

     Your affectionate and sincere friend,

                              ROBERT TROUP.

Society-Hall, General Morris's, 23d May, 1780.

MY DEAR AARON, . .

My patience is almost exhausted. I have been waiting
for you this month past. Here I am, a pensioner upon the
bounty of my good friend General Morris, and am likely to
continue so, unless you are kind enough to come and carry
me away. This is the fifth or sixth letter I have written
you on the subject. What can be the reason of the great
delay in forwarding letters by the post? Your last was
above a fortnight old before it got to Princeton; and, upon
inquiry, Daddy Plumb informs me the riders are ordered to
ride *forty miles* a day during the season. Must I attribute
it to the fatality which has already separated us, and, I fear,
is determined to put an eternal bar to our junction? Such
an event would blast all my hopes of future happiness.

My dear Aaron, I want words to express my pleasure in
anticipating the satisfaction of retiring from the cares of the
world with you, and living in all the simple elegance of ancient philosophers. We should make a rapid improvement
in every branch of useful literature; and when we came to
act our parts on the theatre of the world, we might excite
admiration, and, what would be infinitely more pleasing to
us, we should be better men and better citizens.

After Mr. Stockton returned from Philadelphia, I communicated to him my situation and my intentions. He approved of my determination to go away, and gave me some advice, which you shall know when you see me. Thus I
have left Mr. Stockton without causing the least uneasiness,
and I am now ready to enter upon our old plan, which appears the most consistent with our present views. As I
said in all my letters to you on the subject, I am here from
a principle of economy; but it is disagreeable to stay so
long as a visiter, and I am therefore obliged to request you
to alter your intention about coming here, and set off the

moment you receive this. I have no horse, and depend entirely upon you. Besides the time we lose by postponing
our settlement, I have a matter of great importance to us
both to communicate to you, that has no connexion with our
studying, and which makes it necessary for me to see you
immediately.

Poor Mr. Stockton is incurable. He cannot survive the
summer.   Yours,

ROBERT TROUP.

FROM COLONEL TROUP.

Baskenridge, June 27th, 1780.

MY DEAR AARON,

After a very disagreeable ride indeed, I came here the day
before yesterday in the afternoon; and yesterday morning,
just as I was going to mount my horse, I was seized with a
violent fever, which lasted till sunset. This morning I feel
much better, though I am exceedingly weak. In a few
minutes I shall take an emetic; after which I suppose the
bark will be necessary. The fever seems to be of the inter-
mittent kind, and, I think, is occasioned principally by riding
in the hot sun. I am so agreeably situated here, that I shall
stay till I recover, which I hope will be in three or four days.
The family are very polite and attentive to me, and Dr. Cutting, who quarters in the neighbourhood, is both my physician and apothecary.

The Miss Livingstons have inquired in a very friendly
manner about you, and expect you will wait upon them
when you pass this way. Since I have been here, I have
had an opportunity of removing entirely the suspicion they
had of your courting Miss De Visme.* They believe
nothing of it now, and attribute your visits at Paramus to
motives of friendship for Mrs. Prevost and the family.

* The sister of Mrs. Prevost.

Wherever I am, and can with propriety, you may be assured I shall represent this matter in its true light.

I have obtained a few particulars of ——, which I was before unacquainted with, and which I cannot forbear communicating. He is the son of the vice-president of Pennsylvania, who I always understood in Philadelphia was a respectable merchant, and I believe is worth a moderate fortune, though I am not certain. His family was not ranked in the genteeler class before the war; but at present may be called fashionable, or *a la mode*. The girls here think him handsome, genteel, and sensible, and say positively he is no longer engaged to Miss Shippen. He has frequently spoken to them in raptures, latterly of Miss De Visme, and once declared he was half in love with her. I have taken care to touch this string with the greatest delicacy.

How is your health? Better or worse? Pray neglect no opportunity of writing to me. Present my most respectful compliments to Mrs. Prevost and the family, and also the ladies on the hill.

Miss Susan Governor Livingston desires her compliments to you and the two families. So do Susan and Eliza Baskenridge.

Yours affectionately, .
ROBERT TROUP.

FROM PETER COLT.* .

• Weathersfield, 7th July, 1780.

MY DEAR SIR,

Will you allow me that appellation, who have so long neglected to inform you of the situation of your affairs left in my hands? But figure to yourself the thousand embarrassments that have attended me in conducting my public concerns *towards a close*, and you will be led to put a more

* Deputy quartermaster-general; subsequently commissary for the French army, and treasurer of the State of Connecticut.

favourable construction on my conduct than I should otherwise expect.

My last informed you of the loss of the *Hawk*, being
chased on shore the back side of Long Island. It was a few
days after she went out on her last cruise, and before she
had any success. Of course, about £20,000, the amount of
her last outfits, were thrown away. I fear this will make
her die in debt. Though all her goods are either sold or
divided, yet her accounts are not settled. I wish I could
see a tolerable prospect of their being speedily closed: But
the agents are embarrassed. As soon as I can get her accounts, will inform you of the state of this unlucky adventure.
There is on hand some clothing, some duck, and rigging, out
of which I hope to raise hard money. What shall I do with
the other articles, a small parcel of glassware and rum,
and the money arising from the sales of the vessel's
sea-coat, &c. ? I am advised to sell every thing for continental money, at the present going prices, and exchange it
for hard. What is the exchange with you ? With us it
is from sixty to seventy for one. Let me know what I am
to do with your money when I get it into my hands. I have
not settled any of your accounts but Stanley's.

Your friends are generally well, and wish to hear from
you. Miss H ⁚ has been quite unwell since you left us,
as she tells me she hears you are. You will not be vain
when I add, she has more than once lamented *your ill state
of health*, and expressed some fears that it was not growing
better. The Sallys beg me to make their best wishes for
your health and happiness acceptable to you. Shall I add,
their love also ?

Friend Wadsworth has engaged in the supplies for the
French navy and troops. I think it will keep him employed,
and much to his advantage.

                    Yours sincerely,
                                PETER COLT.

Weathersfield, July 16th, 1780.

DEAR SIR,

I have to acknowledge the receipt of your polite and friendly letter of the 1st inst. My little family would have been too much elated with your attention to them had you not dashed the pleasure with the account of your ill state of health. Pray be more attentive to the recovery of it, even should it interfere with your study of the law. Let your diet and exercise be simple and regular; directed by experience. The former not too low. It is a good old maxim—be religious, but not superstitious. So respecting health, be exactly attentive, but not whimsical. Excuse the term, for invalids are but too apt to be governed by whim rather than reason and experience.

Enclosed you have an account current with the agents of the Hawk.· Indeed, take it altogether, it is but a poor adventure. I shall endeavour the settlement of your account with Friend ——, and remit you. In the meantime, it will not be amiss to send me an account of money advanced to him.

As to news, must refer you to the newspapers, where you will get a large supply. I wish *our printers* did not deal so much in the marvellous. It is in vain for them to attempt copying Rivington.* They had better stick to the truth.

Yours, &c.,

PETER COLT.

FROM COLONEL TROUP.

Rariton, July 18th, 1780.

MY DEAR BURR,

Mr. Paterson went to Brunswick court this morning. The few lines by Dr. Brown are the first I have had from

* Printer to the king, in the city of New-York.

you since I left Paramus; where the other letters you refer
to stay, I know not.' .   .   .   .

I am charmed with my present situation in every respect. It could not be more agreeable to my wishes. I
shall have reason to thank you, as long as I live, for my
change   The man I lodge with is an able farmer—has a
large house—is fond of me, and is possessed of every thing
a reasonable person could expect or wish for. I study
attentively, and have no interruption whatever. There is
an agreeable neighbourhood in this part of the country,
and, when I choose, I can unbend myself in very genteel
company.

I am reading. Wood at present. I have almost done
with his 4th chapter, and am looking over his chapter on
courts. I confine my whole attention to the practice, for
reasons I will tell you when we meet. I am translating
Burlamaqui's Politic Law. Reading Robertson's Charles
V., Dalrymple on Feudal Property, and Swift's. Works.
The morning I devote to the law. I am up 'sometimes
before, generally at sunrise. From two to half after three
in the afternoon, and from nine to eleven in the evening, I
apply to other matters. I am in a fair way, if public affairs
will suffer me, to be retired.

Paterson is the very man we want. He is sensible,
friendly, and, as far as I am capable of judging, profound
in the law. He is to examine me on Saturday or Monday
on what I have read, and I am preparing accordingly. I
have heard him examine Noel yesterday on the practice,
and I find his examinations are critical. In a couple of
months I expect to be as far advanced in the practice as
Noel. I cannot bear that he should be before me. It
must not, it shall not be. .

My health is perfectly restored, and I am now as well as
ever I was. I am happy to hear you grow better. May
you soon be well enough to join me. The weather is so

intensely hot, and I am so closely engaged in study, that I cannot determine when I shall pay you a visit.

Yours, &c.,

ROBERT TROUP.

FROM COLONEL TROUP.

On the Rariton, 21st August, 1780.

MY DEAR BURR,

The account I have given of my situation is far from a fiction. You will find it a pleasing reality when you come here, which I suppose you will postpone till you see me, as I have no doubt at present that the second division of the French fleet has arrived, with a re-enforcement of 4000 troops. This event will render it necessary for me to be ready to move at a moment's warning; and, presuming there will be no delay in commencing our operations, I think, in the course of a fortnight, or three weeks at most, I shall be at Paramus.

Will your health permit you to join the army? I fear not. Fatigue and bad weather may ruin it. I confess I am much disappointed in my opinion of the mineral waters. From your letters, I conclude the stock of health you have gained since I left you is scarcely perceptible. Something else must be tried. Life is precious, and demands every exertion and sacrifice to preserve it. Mr. Paterson and I have often spoken together on this subject, and we both agree that a ride to the southward next winter, and a trip to the West Indies in the spring, would be of infinite service to you. This might be done with ease in five or six months.

Mrs. Paterson is perfectly recovered, and her little girl grows finely, and promises to be handsome. Mrs. Paterson often asks about you, and seems anxious to have you among us. When you come, remember to bring with you the book you took with you on our way to Paramus. I believe it is an essay on health. Mrs. Paterson wants it.

VOL. I.—D d

The idea you gave me of her is just. She is easy, polite,· sensible, and friendly. Paterson is rather deficient in the graces, but he possesses every virtue that enters into the composition of an amiable character.

I can hardly go out anywhere without being asked a number of questions about you. You seem to be universally known and esteemed. Mr. Morris's family are exceedingly particular in their inquiries concerning your health. It would be easier for you to conceive, than for me to tell you, how much they like you. They insist upon our paying them a visit as soon as you are settled here, which I have promised, on your part as well as my own.

Let me entreat you to avoid engaging any of your French books in Connecticut, especially Chambaud's Exercises, to any person whatever. I, and perhaps you, will stand in need of them all.

I am greatly indebted to the good family for their favourable sentiments, which, as I said once before, must proceed more from affection to you than what they find meritorious in me. I am certain, however, that their esteem for me cannot exceed mine for them, and this you will be kind enough to hint to them when you present my respectful compliments. Assure Dom. Tetard of my friendship for him, and fixed determination to use all endeavours to metamorphose him into a Crassus after the war is ended. Adieu

ROBERT TROUP.

CHAPTER XIII.

FROM WILLIAM PATERSON.

Morristown, 27th August, 1780.

MY DEAR BURR,

I was not at Rariton when the doctor, who was the bearer of your letter, passed that way. It would have given me pleasure to have shown him every mark of attention and esteem in my power.

I dare say you count it an age since I have written you; and, indeed, I must confess that the time has been long. Your good-nature, however, will induce you to forgive me, although I cannot expect it from your justice. I hope the water you drink will prove medicinal, and soon restore you to health; although I am more disposed to think that it will take time, and be effected gradually. Persons indisposed (I speak from experience) are generally impatient to become well, and that very impatience has a natural tendency to prevent it. Do not be restless, my dear Burr; nor think that, because you do not get well in a month, or in a season, you will not get well at all. The heat of this summer has been intense, nor is it as yet much abated. Perhaps that too may have had some effect upon you. The hale and hearty could scarcely bear up under it. May health soon visit you, my good friend. ·

Mrs. Paterson is well. Our little pledge, a girl, *Burr* * has been much indisposed, but is at present on the mending hand. I am from home as usual. My official duty obliges me to be so. I grow quite uneasy under it, and I find ease and retirement necessary for the sake of my constitution, which has been somewhat broken in upon by unceasing at-

* The lady of the Hon. Stephen Van Rensselaer.

tention to business. The business has been too much for me. I have always been fond of solitude, and, as it were, of *stealing* along through life. I am now sufficiently fond of domestic life. I have every reason to be so. Indeed, I know no happiness but at home. Such one day will be your situation.

My compliments to the family at the Hermitage. I shall write you before I leave this place.

Yours, &c.

WILLIAM PATERSON.

FROM WILLIAM PATERSON.

Morristown, 31st August, 1780.

MY DEAR BURR,

It is now near the midnight hour, and yet, late as it is, I could not acquit myself to my conscience if I had not again written you before I left this place, which will be early to-morrow. My life is quite in the militant style—one continued scene of warfare. From this place I go down to the Supreme Court at Trenton, which will be on Tuesday next, and the Tuesday after that I shall return once more to Morristown, and when I shall leave it will be uncertain. I rejoice when the hour of rest comes up, and sicken at the approach of day. Business fairly bears me down. The truth is, that I am tired of writing, tired of reading, tired of bustling in a crowd, and, by fits, heartily tired of myself.

I hope you go on gaining strength, and that you will in a little while get the better of your disorder. The mind and the body affect each other extremely. To a person in your state, hilarity, cheerfulness, a serene flow of spirits, are better than all the drugs in a doctor's shop. Gentle exercise is of infinite service. I hope you are not wanting in any of these. If you are, I cannot easily pardon you, because they are all within your power.

Make my compliments acceptable to the family at the Hermitage. I have a high regard for them, and sincerely

wish their happiness. I really pity and admire Mrs. Prevost. Her situation demands a tear ; her conduct and de-
meanour the warmest applause. Tell Mrs. Prevost that she
must remember me among her friends ; and that I shall be
happy to render her all the service in my power

Since I have been at this place I have had a letter from
Mrs. Paterson, who is well. Our little girl, who was indisposed when I left home, is not worse. I flatter myself I
shall find her better when I return. Alas, that I cannot be
more at home. A husband and a parent have a thousand
tendernesses that you know nothing of. Adieu, my dear
Burr ; live and be happy. . .

WILLIAM PATERSON.

FROM COLONEL TROUP.

Morristown, October 23d, 1780.

MY DEAREST FRIEND,

I want words to express the pleasure I feel at the receipt
of yours of the 22d, by the boy who came for your horse. It
relieved me from a burden which had sunk my spirits lower
than I recollect them to have been by any calamity I have
met with during the war. My imagination had crowded
my mind with a thousand melancholy reflections from the
moment I got your letter by Dr. Cutting, who, like a
modern well-bred gentleman, left it at my lodgings only
three days ago. Some evil genius certainly interrupts our
correspondence. I write letters without number, and yet
you seldom hear from me, and when you do, the letter is as
old as if.it had come from the other side of the Atlantic. It
is exactly the case with yours.

Mr. Paterson has been more unfortunate than I. He has
often complained of your neglect, as he thought it ; but I
informed him of the fate my letters shared, and he was
easy. However, he desired me last night to give you a hint,
that he had lately written you several long letters without
receiving an answer to either. He is now at Princeton, at-

tending court. . I shall forward your letter that accompanied mine to him by a safe conveyance. Paterson really loves you with the tenderest affection, and can scarcely speak of your state of health without shedding a friendly tear. As God is my judge, I could not forbear shedding several when I read yours by Dr.. Cutting, which is the first I have had from you in near five weeks. I was afraid all farther attempts to recover your health, so as to qualify you to execute our plan, would be fruitless. In short, I thought you on the brink of eternity, ready to take your final farewell of this wrangling world. The critical situation of your sister increased my distress, and extinguished every hope. How much more happy should I be if your sister's health took the same fortunate turn. Your ride to Litchfield must be doubly agreeable, as it will tend to establish your health and better hers.

I must now communicate to you a disagreeable piece of news respecting myself. It shows how rare it is to find a man of real disinterested benevolence. Sears and Broome, I understand by Mr. Noel, who returned from Philadelphia a few days ago, have protested the bill I drew upon them last summer. Colonel Palfrey bought it, and has it returned to him, for what reasons I cannot say positively, but I suspect they are determined not to assist me, although they were lavish of their offers when they supposed I never would be reduced to the necessity of accepting them. Such conduct is characteristic of excessive meanness of spirit, and I confess I am deceived in my opinion of them most egregiously. True it is, that instances of this kind of behaviour often occur in our intercourse with mankind; but, from the fortunes these men have made since the war, and the frequent reports of their generosity, I was led to imagine there was something more than mere idle compliment and ostentatious parade in their offers. I was deceived, and I hope it will be the last time. This affair has wounded my pride so sensibly, that I shall be extremely cautious in future. I must and will endeavour to adopt some mode of drawing supplies from my certificates, which will be three years old next spring, and therefore ought to be taken up by Congress By the table of depreciation published by Congress to regulate the payment of the principal of their certificates, I am entitled to three hundred and fifty pounds, at the very low est calculation, and this sum in specie.

When you come here you must exert all your abilities in finance, to make me no longer dependant upon the bounty of friends; or rather, I should say, your bounty, for you are the only person I have borrowed money of. Till that time, my dear friend, can you keep me above water, and do justice to yourself? Will you be able to extricate me from the difficulties attending this bill? In plain terms, can you spare me the amount of it? My reputation suffers by having the bill protested, and I must, in a short time, send the money to Colonel Palfrey, for I am persuaded I have no farther ground to expect the least assistance from Sears and Broome. Fail not, by any means, to write me on this subject before you leave Paramus, and be careful how you send the letter.

There is nothing but your health and my poverty that retards my progress in study. They are fruitful sources of disquietude. When I lay me down to sleep, they often prevent me from closing my eyes. When I look into a book, they present a variety of melancholy images to my imagination, and unfit me for improvement. In all other respects I am situated to my wishes. Paterson treats me as a bosom friend. He has gone so far as to press me in the warmest terms to command his purse. How I shall be able to requite your friendship is a matter beyond my penetration. I declare, before the Searcher of all hearts, that I consider your happiness and welfare as inseparable from my own, and that no vicissitudes of fortune, however prosperous or calamitous they may be, will ever tear you from my heart. Circumstanced as I now am, words are the only proofs I can give you of my gratitude and affection. Time will prove whether they are the cant of hypocrisy or the language of esteem.

I lent your horse to Mrs. Paterson about a week ago, to carry her to Elizabethtown to see her brother, who was to meet her there from New-York; and disappointments in not seeing him, from day to day, have detained her much longer than was expected, and it is probable that she will not return until Thursday next; I have therefore sent the boy down to Elizabethtown, or, more properly, shall send him in the morning, with Mr. Noel's horse, which will answer full as well in the wagon. This change will produce no inconvenience at all, and is better than to detain the boy till Mrs. Paterson returns. She was exceedingly well when she left home, and so was her little girl, which is handsome, good-tempered, fat, and hearty. I am very particular in presenting *her* your respects, and *she* is as particular in inquiring about you.

Bring all the French books you can from Connecticut, particularly Chambaud's Exercises, and all the other elementary books you have. I should be fond of having the perusal of Rousseau's Social Compact, if you can borrow it of Mrs. Prevost for me. I am quite rusty in the French, for I have neglected it totally for two or three months. The business of the office has engrossed so much of my attention, that I have not lately read any other book but Blackstone. I am still in the third volume. I digest thoroughly as I advance. I have unravelled all the difficulties of the practice, and can do common business with tolerable dexterity.

The horse will be delivered to you without a saddle. Gales, a young fellow who was studying with Mr. Paterson, requested me to lend it to him to ride as far as Newark last August, and he ran off to New-York, and I never could get the saddle again. This piece of villany I could not foresee, and it surprised almost as much as Arnold's. The grass has been very short, and I fancy the horse will be leaner than you expect. He is a most excellent saddle-horse.

I am extremely sorry to hear Mrs. Prevost and her sister are unwell. Remember me to them in the most friendly manner. Give my compliments also to Dr. Latimer, and all friends in the army near you. Don't forget Mrs. De Visme, the children, Dom. Tetard, and the family on the hill, although I hear they are strongly prejudiced against me. Mrs. Judith Watkins, as you well know, has spoken maliciously. She is far from being your friend. Every thing that passed one day at dinner in confidence respecting our reception at her house, has been told to her and her husband, with no small exaggerations, by some person of the company. Governor Bill Livingston related some particulars that astonished me, and added, that he and Mr. and Mrs. Watkins thought it cruel in you to put such an unfair construction upon Watkins's behaviour to us. All this talk is beneath our notice. What I said to Bill was sufficient to erase any unfavourable impression from a candid mind. If it has not produced that effect, any further attempt to refute the calumny will only serve to confirm it.

Mrs. P. Livingston is here, and desires her respects to you. She was glad to hear of the prospect you have of growing hearty. She is an amiable woman, and loves you.

Your friend,

ROBERT TROUP.

The preceding correspondence contains in itself a tolerable history of Colonel Burr's situation and employment from the summer of 1779 until the autumn of 1780. After retiring from the army, he suffered most severely from ill health—that ill health was, in a great degree, produced by the fatigues and exposure on the 27th and 28th of June, 1779, at the battle of Monmouth. His constitution was feeble, and had been shattered by his unparalleled vigilance

in the winter of 1778–79, while commanding the advanced
post in Westchester. But the battle of Monmouth seemed
to have given it the finishing stroke.

The letters of Judge Paterson and Colonel Troup afford
the best evidence of his ill health, and of their affectionate
devotion to him as friends. They are given at some length,
because they present rare and extraordinary examples of
fidelity in friendship. Both these gentlemen preceded
Colonel Burr to the tomb. Both continued to respect, to
esteem, and to love him, to their last hour. Their character
requires no panegyric. Colonel Troup lived until the year
1832. In manhood, for more than half a century, he ven-
erated Colonel Burr for his genius, his talents, his chivalry,
his intrepidity of character, his disinterestedness, his generosity. He deplored his weaknesses, and abhorred his
vices. But when he viewed the whole man, from youth to
more than threescore and ten years, he loved and respected him. Both these distinguished citizens, as politicians,
were opposed to Colonel Burr from the year 1788 until the
close of their lives.   ·   ·

In the autumn of 1780, Colonel Burr commenced the
study of law with Judge Paterson, who resided at that
time on the Rariton, about twenty miles from Brunswick,
in New-Jersey. Here he remained till the spring of 1781.
The judge was a man governed by fixed and settled rules.
In the application of these rules Colonel Burr found that
his study of the law would require much more time to prepare him for an examination than he was willing to devote.
He concluded that there must be a shorter mode to get at
the mechanical or practical part ; and, having determined to
make the experiment, he left the office of Judge Paterson.

From New-Jersey, in the spring of 1781, he removed to
Haverstraw, then in Orange county, State of New-York.
Residing at this place was Thomas Smith, Esq., formerly
of the city of New-York, and brother to William Smith, the
king's attorney-general. Thomas Smith had a good law

library, which had been removed from the city into the Highlands for safety. With Smith, Colonel Burr made an arrangement to study on a plan of his own. By the contract, for a specified sum to be paid, Smith was to devote certain portions of his time to Burr. At these interviews, he was to answer such questions as Burr propounded. The answers were taken down in writing, and formed the basis of additional interrogatories ; while, at the same time, they aided in directing his attention to those legal points or authorities which were necessary for him to examine or read. During the time he remained at Haverstraw, he studied from sixteen to twenty hours a day. ·

In the summer of 1780, Major Andre, of the British army, was in correspondence with Mrs. Arnold (the wife of General Arnold), under a pretext of supplying her, from the city of New-York, with millinery and other trifling articles of dress. On the 23d of September, 1780, Major Andre was captured, and the treason of the general discovered. When this news reached West Point, Mrs. Arnold became, apparently, almost frantic. Her situation excited the sympathy of some of the most distinguished officers in the American army. Mrs. Arnold, having obtained from General Washington a passport, and permission to join her husband in the city of New-York, left West Point, and on her way stopped at the house of Mrs. Prevost, in Paramus, where she stayed one night. On her arrival at Paramus the frantic scenes of West Point were renewed, and continued so long as strangers were present. Mrs. Prevost was known as the wife of a British officer, and connected with the royalists. In her, therefore, Mrs. Arnold could confide.

As soon as they were left alone Mrs. Arnold became tranquillized, and assured Mrs. Prevost that she was heartily sick of the theatrics she was exhibiting. She stated that she had corresponded with the British commander—that she was disgusted with the American cause and those who had the management of public affairs—and that, through great persuasion and unceasing perseverance, she had ultimately brought the general into an arrangement to surrender West Point to the British. Mrs. Arnold was a gay, accomplished, artful, and extravagant woman. There is no doubt, therefore, that, for the purpose of acquiring the means of gratifying an inordinate vanity, she contributed greatly to the utter ruin of her husband, and thus doomed to everlasting infamy and disgrace all the fame he had acquired as a gallant soldier at the sacrifice of his blood. Mrs. Prevost subsequently became the wife of Colonel Burr, and repeated to him these confessions of Mrs. Arnold.

The preceding statement is confirmed by the following anecdote. Mrs. Arnold was the daughter of Chief-justice Shippen, of Pennsylvania. She was personally acquainted with Major Andre, and, it is believed, corresponded with him previous to her marriage. In the year 1779–80, Colonel Robert Morris resided at Springatsbury, in the vicinity of Philadelphia, adjoining Bush Hill. Some time previous to Arnold's taking command of West Point, he was an applicant for the post. On a particular occasion Mrs. Arnold was dining at the house of Colonel Morris. After dinner, a friend of the family came in, and congratulated Mrs. Arnold on a report that her husband was appointed to a different, but more honourable command. The information affected her so much as to produce hysteric fits. Efforts were made to convince her that the general had been selected for a preferable station. These explanations, however, to the astonishment of all present, produced no effect. But, after the treason of Arnold was discovered, the family of Colonel Morris entertained no doubt that Mrs. Arnold was privy to, if not the negotiator for, a surrender of West Point to the British, even before the general had charge of the post.

In the autumn of 1781 Colonel Burr left Haverstraw and went to Albany, with a determination to make an effort to be admitted to the bar. He continued his studies with the most untiring industry. He had his own apartments and his own library, sleeping, when he did sleep, in a blanket on the floor.

Colonel Burr's liberality in pecuniary matters had tended to impair his private fortune. No man possessed a more benevolent heart. The following letter presents one case out of many which might be enumerated, evincing his generosity, and the delicate manner in which he could confer a favour. Major Alden had become embarrassed in his circumstances, and was greatly at a loss for a profession, at the approaching close of the war, by which he might acquire a decent support. These reflections rendered him gloomy and desponding. At length he unbosomed himself to Colonel Burr, who thus replies to his letter :—

TO MAJOR R. ALDEN.

Rariton, February 15th, 1781.

DEAR SIR,

If it will solace your woes to know there is a heart that feels them as its own, that heart is mine. The thwarts of delicacy, which you would exclude from the catalogues of distress, are certainly the keenest humanity can feel. I know their force. I have felt them in all their pungency.

A want of uniformity in the mode and object of my pursuit has been long my misfortune, and has, I fear, been yours. There is a persevering firmness that will conquer embarrassment, and, aided with the secret smile of an approving conscience, cannot fail to put us above the power of adversity. Thus " we shall shun misfortunes, or shall learn to bear them."

I have ever found the moment of indecision to be the moment of completest anguish. When our resolutions are taken with determined firmness, they engross the mind and close the void of misery. Yes, my friend, save the pang of sympathy, I am happy. These are my halcyon days. Let us taste them together. We shall mutually heighten their relish. Let us rescue some moments of rational enjoyment from the wreck of impetuous time. Friendship shall smooth the rugged path of science, and virtue cheer the way.

If law is your object, this situation is favourable to the pursuit. You shall have access to the library and office, without the customary expense. Your *ostensible reason* for coming here shall be to pursue your studies with me, under my friend Mr. Paterson. The two boys* I wish you to instruct are of the sweetest tempers and the softest hearts. A frown is the severest punishment they ever need. Four hours a day will, I think, be fully sufficient for their instruction. There are hours enough left for study—as many as any one can improve to advantage; and these four will be fully made up to you by the assistance you will derive from such of us as have already made some small progress.

If it is possible, we live together. At any rate, you shall live near me; we shall at least meet every day, or oftener, if we please. Nothing will interrupt us. We will regulate our own amusements and pursuits. Here are no expensive diversions of any kind. Your salary shall be a genteel maintenance in such a situation. You shall have sixty pounds, New-York currency, which is more than I expend here. You will find it impossible to spend a farthing except board and clothing. If, from this short sketch, you think the situation adapted to your views, of which I feel a pleasing assurance, acquaint me immediately, that I may prepare for your reception.

I purpose bringing the boys here the beginning of April. Be here by that time, if possible. Get Mr. Thaddeus Burr to enclose your letter to Loudon the printer, who will be careful to forward it to me. How could I write to you How divine your residence? Never again harbour, for a moment, a surmise that derogates from my sincerity.

---

* The sons of Mrs. Prevost, Frederick and John B. The latter was Judge Prevost, of Louisiana. Mrs. Prevost was unable to expend such a sum on these young gentlemen. It was a means adopted by Colonel Burr delicately to assist, from his own purse, a desponding son of science. Similar instances of his liberality, in the course of his life, were numerous.

My health is nearly established. I have not enough to despise the blessing, but enough to relish every enjoyment of life. Adieu, my friend; may that cheerfulness of which you have been robbed return, and be as permanent as your merit or my affection.

A. BURR. ·

FROM THOMAS SMITH.

Haverstraw, 1st March, 1781.

DEAR SIR,

The preparations at New-York look this way, and that inclines me to seek an asylum in New-Jersey, any part of which I believe will be safe, if Hudson's river is the object of the enemy. If I could get Mrs. De Visme's place, it would be most agreeable to Mrs. Smith. A few weeks will determine me, and then I shall be in a situation to give you and Colonel Troup every assistance in my power. As it is your object to fit yourselves as soon as possible for admission to the bar, without submitting to the drudgery of an attorney's office, in which the advancement of the student is but too often a secondary consideration, I should cheerfully devote a sufficient part of my time to lead you through the practice of the law in all its parts; and make no doubt, with close application on your part, I should be able in a short time to introduce you to the bar, well qualified to discharge the duties of the profession, with honour to yourselves, and safety to your clients.

My library is now in a situation to be removed. Two boxes are missing, and I fear have fallen a sacrifice to the liberty of the times. I only wait till the roads will permit me to remove the remainder down, as I think my books by no means safe where they now are, if the forts should be attacked.

Your obedient servant, ·

THOMAS SMITH.

At this period Colonel Burr was closely engaged in his studies. His constitution was somewhat renovated. His correspondence now became limited, and was principally confined to Mrs. Prevost. Here again the peculiarity already referred to was in full operation. The greater part of this correspondence is in cipher. But portions of it that are not thus written are highly interesting, and give evidence that Mrs. Prevost possessed a cultivated mind. Her health was very feeble, and continued so, after she became the wife of Colonel Burr, until her decease. Some extracts from her letters will be given.

FROM MRS. PREVOST.

Litchfield, February 12th, 1781

I am happy that there is a post established for the winter. I shall expect to hear from you every week. My ill health will not permit me to return your punctuality. You must be contented with hearing once a fortnight.

Your opinion of Voltaire pleases me, as it proves your judgment above being biased by the prejudices of others. The English, from national jealousy and enmity to the French, detract him. Divines, with more justice, as he exposes himself to their censure. It is even their duty to contemn his tenets; but, without being his disciple, we may do justice to his merit, and admire him as a judicious, ingenious author.

I will not say the same of your system of education. Rousseau has completed his work. The indulgence you applaud in Chesterfield is the only part of his writings I think reprehensible. Such lessons from so able a pen are dangerous to a young mind, and ought never to be read till the judgment and heart are established in virtue. If Rousseau's ghost can reach this quarter of the globe, he will certainly haunt you for this scheme—'tis striking at the root of his design, and destroying the main purport of his admirable production. Les foiblesses de l'humanite, is an easy apology; or rather, a license to practise intemperance; and is particularly agreeable and flattering to such practitioners, as it brings the most virtuous on a level with the vicious. But I am fully of opinion that it is a much greater chimera than the world are willing to acknowledge. Virtue, like religion, degenerates to nothing, because it is convenient to neglect her precepts. You have, undoubtedly, a mind superior to the contagion.

When all the world turn envoys, Chesterfield will be their proper guide. Morality and virtue are not necessary qualifications—those only are to be attended to that tend to the public weal. But when parents have no ambitious views, or rather, when they are of the more exalted kind, when they wish to form a happy, respectable member of society—a firm, pleasing support to their declining life, Emilius shall be the model. A man so formed must be approved by his Creator, and· more useful to mankind than ten thousand modern beaux.

If the person whose kind partiality you mention is Paterson, I confess myself exceedingly flattered, as I entertain the highest opinion of the perspicuity of his judgment. Say all the civil things you please for his solicitous attention to my health. But if it should be Troup, which I think more probable, assure him of my most permanent gratitude.

Affectionately,

THEODOSIA PREVOST.

FROM MRS. THEODOSIA PREVOST.

Litchfield, 6th March, 1781.

——-Where can —— be? Poor suffering soul; worthy a better fate. Heaven preserve him for his own sake; for his distressed mother's. I pity her from my heart, and lament my inability to alleviate her sorrows. I invoke a better aid. May her "afflicted spirit find the only solace of its woes"—Religion, Heaven's greatest boon to man; the

VOL. I.—F f   10*

only distinction he ought to boast. In this, he is lord of the creation; without it, the most pitiable of all created things.

How strangely we pass through life ! All acknowledge themselves mortal and immortal ; and yet prefer the trifles of to-day to the treasures of eternity. Piety teaches resignation. ·Resignation without piety loses its beauty, and sinks into insensibility. Your beautiful quotation is worth more than all I can write in a twelvemonth. Continue writing on the subject. It is both pleasing and improving. The better I am acquainted with it, the more charms I find. Worlds should not purchase the little I possess. I promise myself many happy hours dedicated at the shrine of religion.

Yours, affectionately,

THEODOSIA PREVOST.

FROM MRS. THEODOSIA PREVOST.
Litchfield, May, 1781.

Our being the subject of much inquiry, conjecture, and calumny, is no more than we ought to expect. My attention to you was ever pointed enough to attract the observation of those who visited the house. Your esteem more than compensated for the worst they could say. When I am sensible I can make you and myself happy, I will readily join you to suppress their malice. But, till I am confident of *this*, I cannot think of our union. Till then I shall take shelter under the roof of my dear mother, where, by joining stock, we shall have sufficient to stem the torrent of adversity.

You speak of my spirits as if they were at my command, or depressed only from perverseness of temper. In these you mistake. Believe me, you cannot wish their return more ardently than I do. I would this moment consent to become a public mendicant, could I be restored to the same tranquillity of mind I enjoyed this time twelvemonth.

The influence my letters may have on your studies is

imaginary. The idea is so trite that I was in hopes it was worn from your mind. My last year's trials are vouchers. I was always writing with a view to please you, and as often failed in the attempt. If a desire for my own happiness cannot restore me to myself, pecuniary motives never can. I wish you to study for your own sake; to ensure yourself respect and independence; to ensure us the comforts of life, when Providence deigns to fit our hearts for the enjoyment. I shall never look forward with confidence till your pride extends to that. I had vainly flattered myself that pride was inseparable to true love. In yours I find my error; but cannot renounce my idea of its being a necessary support *to,* and the only security *for,* permanent affection.

You see by the enclosed how ready my friends are to receive you, and promote your interest. I wish you may be fortunate in executing aunt Clark's business. My health and spirits are neither better nor worse than when you left me. I thank you for your attention to Bird's prescription.   Adieu,

THEODOSIA PREVOST.

FROM MRS. THEODOSIA PREVOST.

Sharon, September 11th, 1781.

My friend and neighbour, Mr. Livingston, will have the pleasure of presenting you this. You will find him quite the gentleman, and worthy your attention.

Enclosed is a letter to my sister, which must be delivered by yourself. You know my reasons too well to infer from my caution that I entertain the least doubt of Mr. Livingston's punctuality.

Monsieur Tetard is gone to the manor, summoned by Mrs. Montgomery, on pretence of his being the only surviving witness to the general's will. The business that was to have detained him but a few days has kept him these six weeks   I cannot account for his delay, unless his extrava-

gant encomiums on the progress of a friend of yours has
proved a stimulation to those of superior talents. He ex-
aggerates exceedingly in extolling his pupils. Those whose
expectations are raised from his description must prepare
themselves for disappointment.

Mr. and Mrs. Reeve were well a few days ago. She
rides every morning to visit the boy, and returns before
breakfast. I fear they will disappoint me in the promised
visit.

We were obliged to Dr. Cutting for the most pleasing account of your health and spirits. Also, of your great progress in law. Judge Hobart expects Colonels Burr and
Troup will make his suite to the October court, where he
hopes to usher them, with all the eclat due to their merit.
He counts the·weeks, which he has now reduced to five.
While the warmth of friendship animates his countenance,
his heart swells with pride at the honour of patronising two
such characters. He must not be disappointed; this must
be the route, or he will believe himself slighted. I am
obliged to his zeal, as it will procure us the pleasure of seeing you. The sight of an old acquaintance is quite a phenomenon. I am not surprised that genuine hospitality is
fled to cottages. You will find it a la rustique chez votre
amie.

THEODOSIA PREVOST.

FROM MAJOR R. ALDEN.

Fairfield, 28th February, 1781.

DEAR BURR,

Your letter of the 15th inst. pleases me. You have a
heart that feels : a heart susceptible of tender friendship.
Life has not a single charm to compare with such sensations. You know too well how to excite such emotions.
Happy for us. These expel the keenest pangs. There is
no such thing as real happiness. At best, it is but a delu-

sion. We make our own pleasures as we do our troubles. Friendship will heighten the one and moderate the other.

I have been tortured with the anxiety of suspense. It has given me the most poignant distress. It disordered my mind; at times, almost drove me to despair. Some of my friends saw the effect, but could not conjecture the cause. You alone could penetrate the feelings of my heart; you alone are in possession of that evidence which will convict me of my weakness; my want of fortitude. I dare intrust you. I feel the influence of your friendship. To a heart like yours, this will prove the sincerity and affection of mine.

I bid adieu to camp, having completed my business, with my thanks to our worthy commander-in-chief for his attention to my character. The discharge he gave me equalled my wishes and exceeded my expectations. I have enjoyed the most rational satisfaction for three days past. I have commenced student. Dr. Johnson has given me my plan of studies, and free access to his library. My ambition is not great, nor my views unbounded. I shall proportion the means to the object. If I persevere with attention, I have something more than wishes to build upon. Nothing within the compass of my abilities, that is justifiable, will be left untried, to gratify my reasonable desires.

I know that your request proceeded entirely from your friendship for me, and that you felt happy that it was in your power to oblige me. I feel the force of your kindness, but must deny myself the pleasure of spending some months with my friend. My time is short; age presses upon me. Four years have been devoted to my country, for which I have received no compensation.

It gives me pleasure to hear that your health is such that you can be thankful for the blessing, and are in a situation to enjoy yourself in the pursuit of your studies. My heart is sincerely interested in your happiness. Let me know your feelings, that I may know how to refine mine. Your friendship and letters add a continual charm

to my life, and will always please the heart and secure the
affection of, yours,

With sincerity,

R. ALDEN.

TO MRS. PREVOST.

Albany, 5th June, 1781.

I was absent when yours of the 10th ultimo came, and
therefore did not receive it till the first inst. You may be
assured ―― will one day repent his insolence. Uniformity
of conduct and great appearance of moderation are all that
can be put in practice immediately. The maxim of a man
whom neither of us esteem very highly is excellent on this
occasion—" *Suaviter in modo, fortiter in re.*" See, my
dear Theodosia, what you bring upon yourself by having
once piddled at Latin. The maxim, however, would bear
sheets of comment and days of reflection. I second the
just pride of ――, in being averse to crouch to a villain.
Your letter to E. would have every influence that mine
possibly could.

These crosses are of that class which, though they may
perplex for a moment (a moment is too much), yet cannot
affect our real happiness. That mind is truly great which
can bear with equanimity the trifling and unavoidable vexations of life, and be affected only by those events which
determine our substantial bliss. Every period, and every
situation, has a portion of these trifling crosses; and those
who expect to avoid them all, or conquer them all, must be
wretched without respite. Witness ――. I am half vexed
at the manner in which you speak of what you term " the
sorrows of ――." They are just of this trifling kind. Say
and think no more of them. Their impression was momentary, and is long past.

G.'s uniformity of conduct for some time has established
his character, and crushed the malice of his enemies. He
has, however, mingled some address in his deportment—

has made visits, and some acts of civility, to his avowed enemies, by which means he has gained some and silenced others. His whole conduct, his language, and even his thoughts, seem to have in view the happiness of ——. I believe this idea is impressed on him every hour of his life.

Yours,

. A. BURR.

TO CHIEF-JUSTICE MORRIS.

Albany, 21st October, 1781.

SIR,

I do myself the honour to enclose you several letters, which were intended, I believe, to introduce me to your acquaintance, perhaps to your friendship. I am particularly unfortunate to see neither Mr. Hobart nor yourself on the present occasion; the more so, as I find a rule of unexpected rigour, which, if strictly adhered to, must effectually exclude me from this bar. Mr. Judge Yates gives me reason to hope this rule may be enlarged. If it should be deemed unadvisable to make one of such latitude as may include me within a general description, perhaps my particular situation may be thought to claim particular indulgence.

Before the revolution, and long before the existence of the present rule, I had served some time with an attorney of another state. At that period I could have availed myself of this service ; and, surely, no rule could be intended to have such retrospect as to injure one *whose only misfortune is having sacrificed his time, his constitution, and his fortune, to his country.*

It would give me sensible regret were my admission to establish a precedent which might give umbrage to the bar; but, should your opinion accord with my wishes, with respect to the indulgence due to my particular case, the expression of it, to any gentleman of the profession, would doubtless remove the possibility of discontent.

Perhaps I assume a freedom which personal acquaintance only could warrant. I beg, sir, you will ascribe it to
the reliance I am taught to place on your goodness, and
the confidence with which your character inspires even
those who have no other title to your notice.

Whatever may be the success of my present designs, I
shall do myself the honour of waiting on you, and assuring
you, in person, of the respect and esteem with which
I am your obedient servant,

A. BURR.

Colonel Burr frequently impressed upon those with whom
he was in the habit of a regular correspondence, the advantage of committing to paper daily, in the form of a journal,
such thoughts or ideas as occurred and were deemed desirable to repeat. He adopted this form in his communications
with Mrs. Prevost. The following is a specimen :—

Albany, Thursday, December 3d, 1781.

I am at length arrived at my destined haven, and, .what is
·very unusual for me, have been successful in several trivial
circumstances, such as getting over the ferry (which is diffi
cult at this season), finding temporary quarters for my che
vaux without difficulty or delay. I cannot help regarding
these as harbingers of good luck. I am, however, not fortunate in finding Judge Yates. He is from home. G. civil,
but unwell. The room promised me is not fitted; must
therefore seek other lodgings.· Bon soir. Visit me in my
slumbers.

Friday night, December 4th.

Till sunset I was in doubt whether I should not be obliged to leave Albany for want of quarters. Have at length
found tolerable. No price yet fixed. Probably not less
than trois piasters the week. A day completely lost, and I,
of course, in ill humour with every thing but thee. ·

Saturday, December 5th.

A sick headache this whole day. I earned it by eating
last night a hearty supper of Dutch sausages, and going to
bed immediately after. I am surprised it did not operate in
the way of my disorder, which was formerly the certain
consequence of every error in diet; but no symptom of that,
though I was very restless.

I took the true Indian cure for the headache. Made a
light breakfast of tea, stretched myself on a blanket before
the fire, fasted till evening, and then tea again. I thought,
through the whole day, that if you could sit by me, and
stroke my head with your little hand, it would be well; and
that, when we are formally united, far from deeming a return
of this disorder un malheur, I should esteem it a fortunate
apology for a day of luxurious indulgence, which I should
not otherwise allow myself or you.

Most unexpectedly, Lewis called upon me this evening,
civilly offered me his house, and asked me to dine. I was
wrong, I think, to accept his invitation, but this did not strike
me till I had engaged. Must dine there to-morrow.

Sunday, 6th December.

This is the third day in town, and no business done.
These two days past I have been studying the second volume of Rousseau. G. is returned. He never appeared more
unlike himself. I was somehow uncommonly stupid, and,
would you believe it, even awkward. Said very little, and
that little with hesitation. You know there are days when
every thing goes against one. Paid little attention to anybody (that little, somehow, ill timed), and received still less
from them.

How could we forget Latimer? He has sung Theodosia's praise among the southern army in terms with which
her best friends must be pleased. He has also established

VOL. I.—G g

the character of A. Burr. Quackenbush is determined to be civil. Says his visits will be frequent.

Yates is returned. More of him to-morrow. An old, weather-beaten lady, Miss Depeyster, has given the whole history of Burr, and much of Theo., but nothing unfavourable. In a place where Burr thought himself a stranger, there is scarce any age or sex that does not, either from information or acquaintance, know something of him.

I am surprised I forgot to advise you to get a Franklin fireplace. They have not the inconvenience of stoves, are warm, save wood, and never smoke. The cost will not be, probably, more than ten or fifteen dollars, which will be twice saved this winter in wood and *comfort*, and they may be moved anywhere. If you have fears about *brat* * I have none. He will never burn himself but once ; and, by way of preventive, I would advise you to do that for him. It will be put up in a few hours by anybody. I am in doubt whether it will be best to have it in the common room or one of the back rooms. The latter will have many advantages. You may then have a place sacred to love, reflection, and books. This, however, as you find best; but that you have one I am determined, unless you can give some better reason against it than I at present know of. Indeed, I would wish you had two. You will get them with no trouble from the Salisbury furnace. It is of the first importance that you suffer as little as possible the present winter. It may, in a great measure, determine your health ever after. I confess I have still some transient distrusts that you set too little value on your own life and comfort. Remember, it is not yours alone ; but your letters shall convince me. I waive the subject.

I am not certain I shall be regularly punctual in writing you in this manner every day when I get at business; but I shall, if possible, devote one quarter of an hour a day to

* Mrs. Prevost's youngest child.

you. In return, 1 demand one half of an hour every day from you; more I forbid, unless on special occasions. This half hour is to be *mine*, to be invariably at the same time, and, for that purpose, fixed at an hour least liable to interruption, and as you shall find most convenient. Mine cannot be so regular, as I only indulge myself in it when I am fatigued with business. The children will have each their sheet, and, at the given hour, write, if but a single word Burr, at this half hour is to be a kind of watchword.

Monday, 7th December.

I keep always a memorandum for you, on which, when I think of any thing at any time of day that I wish to write, I make a short note in a manner which no other person would understand. When I sit down to write I have noth ing to do but look at my memorandum. I would recommend the same to you, unless you rather choose to write at the moment when you think of any thing.

I have continually felt some apprehensions about the success of Troup with the court. The Springs are but twenty eight miles from Albany; I will meet you there.

Phil. Van Rensselaer, whom I have never before seen, has been to introduce himself, and tender his services of every kind. He is of the most respectable and richest inhabitants.

Tuesday, 8th December.

No place yet; but, that time need not be lost, I have been looking over Rousseau's 4th volume. I imagine —— gathered thence his sentiments on the subject of jealousy. If so, he has grossly mistaken the ideas of Rousseau. Do you discover a symptom of it? Far otherwise. You see only confidence and love. That jealousy for which you are an advocate, he condemns as appertaining to brutes and sensualists Discard, I beseech you, ideas so degrading to true love. I am mortified with the reflection that they were ever yours.

I think —— must have taken pains to have overlooked the following paragraph, when, in enumerating the duties of a woman towards a lover or husband, he makes it principally to consist " in respecting themselves, in order to acquire respect. How delightful are these privileges ! How respectable are they ! how cordially do men prize them, when a woman knows how to render them estimable." I fear —— will be convinced of this but too late. I am glad to find, however, that the idea so often urged (in vain) by me, is not a mere vagary of my own brain, but is supported by so good authority.

Wednesday, 9th December.

.I have this day made a feint at law. But, were my life at stake, it could not command my attention.

Thursday, 10th December.

We have about twelve or fourteen inches of snow. When you read my letters I wish you would make minutes at the time of such facts as require an answer; for, if you trust your memory till the time of writing, you will omit half you would otherwise say.

Friday, 11th December.

I really wish much to know the conduct of ——. It is, however, more curiosity than anxiety. It would be childish to build any part of one's happiness on a basis so unstable.

The Van Rensselaer before mentioned, and henceforth to be designated by Ll., proves to be a phenomenon of goodness and (can you believe it) even tenderness. Tenderness, I hear you cry, in a Hollandois ! But hold your injustice ; the character and fine heart of Van Rensselaer will, I think, in future, remove your prejudice, especially when you add to this his marked attention and civility.

Saturday, 12th December.

Van Rensselaer finds fault with my quarters, which, in deed, are far removed from elegance, and, in some respects, from convenience. He insists that I suffer him to provide me better.

I have not hitherto had an hour of Yates. His reasons, however, have been good. On Monday we are to mangle law.

Sunday, 13th December.

Van Rensselaer has succeeded perfectly to my wish. I am with two maidens, aunts of his, obliging and (incredi · ble ! !) good-natured. The very paragon of neatness. Not an article of furniture, even to a teakettle, that would soil a muslin handkerchief. I have two upper rooms. I was interrupted at the line above, and cannot now, for my life, recollect what I was intending to write. I leave it, however to plague you as it has done me.

Monday, 14th December.

I really fear Yates is playing the fool with me. Still evasive, though plausibly so. I have just had an interview. To-morrow I must and will come to a positive eclaircisse-ment.

I am determined, in future, when doubt arises in my mind whether I shall write a thing or not, invariably to write it. You recollect ——'s advising that Carlos* should learn the violin. G. was unkind enough to remind him that he was formerly opposed to that opinion. There was a degree of insult in this reproach of which I did not think G. capable. I truly believe he did not reflect on the tendency of it. I do not remember that he is apt to take such unfair advantage of his friends. Happy they who can make improvement of each other's errors. The necessary, but dear-bought knowl-

* A negro boy belonging to Colonel Burr.

edge of experience, is earned at double cost by those who reap alone.

Since I left you, I have not taken pen in hand without intending to write you. I am happy in having done it, for I now feel perfectly relieved.

Tuesday, 15th December.

Yesterday was partly a day of business. The evening wholly and advantageously so. This day has been rather a feint. Yates engaged. I beg ten thousand pardons of Miss Depeyster; she is our warm friend and advocate. One Bogart, at Tappan, is the scoundrel.

Wednesday, 16th December.

I perceive this letter-writing will not answer; though I write very little, it is still half my business; for, whenever I find myself either at a loss what to do, or any how discomposed or dull, I fly to these sheets, and even if I do not write, I ponder upon it, and in this way sacrifice many hours without reflecting that time passes away. Yates still backward, but the day tolerably spent.

I have also been busy in fixing a Franklin fireplace for myself. I shall have it completed to-morrow. I am resolved you shall have one or two of them. You have no idea of their convenience, and you can at any time remove them.

I expect to despatch Carlos to-morrow. I think I have already mentioned that I wrote you from Kinderhook, and also this week by Colonel Lewis, enclosed to our friend at Sharon.

An engagement of business to-day and this evening with Yates, prevents me preparing for Carlos as I expected.

A. BURR.

CHAPTER XIV.

IN the autumn of 1781, as may be seen by the preceding correspondence, Colonel Burr was in Albany, preparing himself for admission to the bar. Judge Yates rendered him essential service on the occasion. His friendship and kindness were appreciated, and gratefully recollected. At that time Chief-justice Richard Morris, Robert Yates, and John Sloss Hobart composed the bench of the Supreme Court of the State of New-York. All these gentlemen were friendly to Burr, and treated him with the utmost courtesy; but for Judge Yates he entertained, during the continuance of his life, the most profound respect and veneration.

By the rules of the court it was required that candidates for admission should have pursued a course of legal studies not less than three years previous to presenting themselves for examination. Colonel Burr applied to the court to dispense with this rule in his case. The application was opposed with great zeal by all the members of the bar; and, as no counsellor would make the necessary motion on the subject, Burr was not only compelled to do it himself, but to argue the question with the ablest of the profession.

After hearing the argument, the court determined that, as he had been employed in the service of his country, when he might, under other circumstances, have been a law-student, they would dispense with the rigour of the rule so far as it applied to the period of study; but that no indulgence would be granted in reference to the necessary qualifications. In pursuance of this decision he underwent a severe and critical examination by some of the most eminent members of the bar, who were anxious for his rejec tion. The examination, however, resulted in a triumphant admission that the candidate was duly qualified to practise ; and he .was accordingly licensed as an attorney, on the 19th day of January, 1782. And at " a supreme court of judicature, held for the State of New-York, at the City Hall of the city of Albany, on the 17th day of April, 1782, Aaron Burr having, on examination, been found of competent ability and learning to practise as counsellor," it was ordered that he be accordingly admitted.

Soon after Colonel Burr commenced the practice of law in the city of Albany, he invited his friend and brother soldier, Major W. Popham, to join him, and pursue a course of legal studies. This invitation was given with his accustomed kindness. About the period of Burr's marriage, Major Popham replies.

FROM MAJOR W. POPHAM.*

Fishkill, August 16th, 1782

Yesterday I was accidentally favoured with your friendly letter of the 3d of May, from Litchfield, which was peculiarly agreeable, as it contained the first official accounts I have had of you since my leaving Albany, and dispelled a train of gloomy reflections which your supposed long silence had suggested.

The approbation you have given of my conduct, in an affair in which you have so generously interested yourself, is very flattering. A detail of the circumstances which rendered it necessary to postpone the prosecution of my intended plan, would be too prolix for the subject of a letter. They would not present one pleasing reflection; and I love you too well to give you pain. Suspend, therefore, your curiosity and your opinion, until the duties of the field permit me to see you, when you shall be satisfied.

---

* Major Popham, fifty-four years after the date of this letter, attended as a pall-bearer the funeral of Colonel Burr, the friend of his youth.

I hope the alterations you have made in your plan of life may equal your most sanguine wishes. I am pleased that you have taken a house in Albany, and sincerely congratulate you on an event that promises you so much happiness. May you long enjoy all the blessings which can flow from that happy state, for which Heaven has so remarkably designed you.

But why am I requested to "*say nothing about obligations,*" while you continue to load me with new ones ? Or, why should I be denied the common privilege of every liberal mind, that of acknowledging the obligation which I have not the power of cancelling ? Yes, my friend, your generous offer claims my warmest thanks; but the very principle which excites my gratitude forbids me to accept it

Dr. L informs me you have written twice to me. One of the letters is lost. Will you speedily supply the deficiency ? If you can spare an hour from business, retirement, or love, let me entreat you to devote it to your friend. I cannot tell you how much I long to hear from you. Adieu.

Yours sincerely,

W. POPHAM.

TO MRS. PREVOST.

Albany, December 23d, 1781.

My dear Theodosia is now happy by the arrival of Carlos. This was not wishing you a happy Christmas, but actually making it so. Let all our compliments be henceforth practical. The language of the world sounds fulsome to tastes refined by the sweets of affection.

I see mingle in the transports of the evening the frantic little Bartow.* Too eager to embrace the bliss he has in prospect; frustrating his own purposes by inconsiderate haste ; misplacing every thing, and undoing what he meant

---

* Mrs. Prevost's son.

to do. It will only confuse you. Nothing better can be done than to tie him, in order to expedite his own business.

That you might not be cheerful alone, I have obeyed the orders of your heart (for you cannot, even at this distance, conceal them) by a determination to take a social, friendly supper with Van Rensselaer.

You wrote me too much by Dom. I hope it was not from a fear that I should be dissatisfied with less. It is, I confess, rather singular to find fault with the quantity, when matter and manner are so delightful. You must, however, deal less in sentiments and more in ideas. Indeed, in the letter in answer to my last, you will need to be particularly attentive to this injunction. I think constantly of the approaching change in our affairs, and what it demands. Do not let us, like children, be so taken with the prospect as to lose sight of the means.

Remember to write me facts and ideas, and don't torment me with compliments, or yourself with sentiments to which I am already no stranger. Write but little, and very little at once. I do not know for what reason, Theodosia, but I cannot feel my usual anxiety about your health, though I know you to be ill, and dangerously so. One reason is, that I have more belief in your attention to yourself.   · \   ·

Your idea about the water was most delightful. It kept me awake a whole night, and led to a train of thoughts and sensations which cannot be described. Indeed, the whole of your letter was marked with a degree of confidence and reliance which augurs every thing that is good. The French letter was truly elegant, as also that enclosed in compliance with my request.

If Reeves has received the money upon the order I gave him, he may send me by Carlos about twenty-five guineas, if he can spare so much of it. I am in no present want.

Pardon me for not answering your last. My mind is so engrossed by new views and expectations, that I cannot disengage it. I have not, these five days past, slept more than *two hours* a night, and yet feel refreshed and well. Your presentiments of my illness on a certain evening were wide from truth: believe me, you have no talent that way. Leave it to others.

I think, if you keep Carlos two nights, it will serve; but keep him longer rather than fatigue yourself. Adieu.

A. Burr.

On the 2d of July, 1782, Colonel Burr was married to Mrs. Theodosia Prevost. In April preceding he had entered into the practice of the law in the city of Albany. His attention to business was unremitted. In consequence, he soon found himself crowded with clients from every quarter of the state. During his residence in Albany, his mind was exclusively engrossed with his profession and his family. In the education of Mrs. Burr's children by her first husband he took a deep interest. Neither labour nor expense was regarded. It was his wish that they should be accomplished, as well as educated men.

The preliminary treaty of peace having been signed, Colonel Burr resolved to remove his family to the city of New-York so soon as the British should evacuate it. Here he anticipated (and in this he was not disappointed) an extensive practice. On the 20th of November, 1781, the legislature of the State of New-York passed an act disqualifying from practice, in the courts of the state, all " attorneys, solicitors, and counsellors at law," who could not produce satisfactory certificates, showing their attachment and devotion to the whig cause during the then pending war with Great Britain. This act was in full force at the peace of 1783, and remained so, without any attempt to modify it, until March, 1785, when a bill was introduced into the legislature to repeal certain sections of it, so far as they operated upon individuals therein named. The bill was lost. But, on the 4th of April, 1786, the restriction thus imposed on the tory lawyers was removed by an act of the legislature. The law of 1781, previous to its repeal, had operated most favourably for the whig lawyers. Those of talents and standing, such as Colonel Burr and others, had obtained a run of business which enabled them to compete with the most profound of their tory rivals.

It was supposed that the British troops would evacuate the city of New-York in the spring or early in the summer of 1783 ; but they remained until the 25th of November of that year. Colonel Burr applied to his friend, Thomas Bartow, to procure him a house for the accommodation of his family, which he accordingly did.

FROM MR. BARTOW.

New-York, April 16th, 1783.

Dear Sir,

I received your agreeable favour a few days ago, and am happy to congratulate you on the establishment of a peace : hope I shall soon have the pleasure of seeing you in town. I have procured you a good house in Maiden-lane, at the rate of two hundred pounds a year. The rent to commence when the troops leave the city. Doctor Brown can inform you more particulars about it, as he went with me to view it. Before I engaged this house, I consulted Mrs. Clark She proposed her house in Broadway, but could not get the tenant out, so that she gave her consent to this.

Very respectfully yours,

Thomas Bartow.

FROM MRS. BURR.

Albany, 25th March, 1783.

Some think absence tends to increase affection ; the greater part that it wears it away. I believe neither, but that it only tends to prove how far the heart is capable of loving; or rather, whether it is real or imaginary. When the latter, every object that amuses, blots out the idea of the absent, we find that they are not so necessary to our happiness as we had fancied. But when that love is real, what can amuse, what engage the mind, to banish, for a single instant, the object of its delight? It hates every necessity that wrests it an instant from the contemplation of its beauties; its virtues are ever presenting themselves to increase our regret, and suggest innumerable fears for its safety. Such have been the occupations of this day. I tremble at every noise : new apprehensions are ever alarming me. Every tender sensation is awake to thee.

26th March.

My extreme anxiety operated severely upon my health. I have not had so ill a turn in some months. The remedies of S. prove but little more efficacious than those of G. I do without either. Various are the conjectures respecting your errand. All think me of the party. My spirits need, my heart grows impatient for your return. Every countenance speaks for you, while Theodosia grieves.

27th March.

My health is rather better. I have just this moment heard of General Schuyler's going; have only time to tell you I rejoice at the enclosed. It will save your hurry and anxiety   Popham has written and engaged for your attendance

THEODOSIA BURR

When the British were about to evacuate the city of New-York, and it was ascertained that Colonel Burr had made the necessary arrangements to settle there, his whig friends became anxious that he should receive an appointment. Among those who urged this measure was Judge Hobart, who had ever entertained an exalted opinion of his talents and business habits. As soon as Colonel Burr was informed of the friendly views entertained by the judge, he wrote him,

expressing his unwillingness to be considered a competitor
with any gentleman for an appointment. To this he received an answer.

FROM JUDGE HOBART.

June 17th, 1783.

Sir,

Your favour has been received. However pure your
views may be, I fear you must be contented with the character of a private gentleman so long as you determine to
avoid a competition ; for I am told there are long lists of
applicants for all the offices in the city and county of New-
York.

With great respect, yours,

JOHN SLOSS HOBART.

FROM MRS. BURR.

Albany, August 14th, 1783.

How unfortunate, my dearest Aaron, is our present separa-
tion. I never shall have resolution to consent to another.
We must not be guided by others. We are certainly formed
of different materials ; and our undertakings must coincide
with them.

A few hours after I wrote you by Colonel Lewis, our
sweet infant* was taken ill, very ill. My mind and spirits
have been on the rack from that moment to this. When
she sleeps, I watch anxiously ; when she wakes, anxious
fears accompany every motion. I talked of my love towards
her, but I knew it not till put to this unhappy test. I know
not whether to give her medicine or withhold it : doubt and
terror are the only sensations of which I am sensible. She
has slept better last night, and appears more lively this
morning, than since her illness. This has induced me to
postpone an express to you, which I have had in readiness

---

* The unfortunate Mrs. Alston, of whom much will be said hereafter.

since yesterday. If this meets you, I need not dwell upon my wish.

I will only put an injunction on your riding so fast, or in the heat, or dew. Remember your presence is to support, to console your Theo., perhaps to rejoice with her at the restoration of our much-loved child. Let us encourage this hope; encourage it, at least, till you see me, which I flatter myself will be before this can reach you. Some kind spirit will whisper to my Aaron how much his tender attention is wanted to support his Theo. : how much his love is necessary to give her that fortitude, that resolution, which nature has denied her but through his medium. Adieu.

THEODOSIA.

FROM MRS. BURR.

New-York, March 22d, 1784.

My Aaron had scarce quitted the door when I regretted my passiveness. Why did I consent to his departure? Can interest repay the sacrifice? can aught on earth compensate for his presence? Why did I hesitate to decide? Ten thousand fears await me. What thought suggested my assent? The anxiety he might suffer were he to meet with obstacles to raising the sum required; should his views be frustrated for want of the precaution this journey might secure; his mortification; mine, at not having the power to relieve him, were arguments that silenced my longing wish to hold him near me; near me for ever. My Aaron, dark is the hour that separates my soul from itself.

Thus pensive, surrounded with gloom, thy Theo. sat, bewailing thy departure. Every breath of wind whistled terror; every noise at the door was mingled with hope of thy return, and fear of thy perseverance, when Brown arrived with the word—*embarked*—the wind high, the water rough. Heaven protect my Aaron; preserve him, restore him to his adoring mistress. A tedious hour elapsed, when our son was the joyful messenger of thy safe landing at Paulus Hook.

Stiff with cold, how must his papa have fared? Yet, grateful for his safety, I blessed my God. I envied the ground which bore my pilgrim. I pursued each footstep. Love engrossed his mind; his last adieu to Bartow was the most persuasive token—" Wait till I reach the opposite shore, that you may bear the glad tidings to your trembling mother." O, Aaron, how I thank thee! Love in all its delirium hovers about me; like opium, it lulls me to soft repose! Sweet serenity speaks, 'tis my Aaron's spirit presides. Surrounding objects check my visionary charm. I fly to my room and give the day to thee.

THEODOSIA.

TO MRS. BURR.

Albany, October 29th, 1784.

Mr. Watts this instant acquaints me that he is just setting off for New-York. I run from court to waft you a memorandum of affection. I have been remarkably well; was fortunate in my journey. The trial of Livingston and Hoffman is now arguing. It began on Thursday of last week, and will not conclude till to-night. No other business has been or will be done this term. All this cursed long absence for nothing.

I cannot leave this till Sunday or Monday. Then to Westchester Court. The return to joy and Theo. cannot be till Thursday or Friday, and that depending on my business in Westchester. Miss Yates is on her passage to New-York to spend eight or ten days.

I read your memorandum ten times a day, and observed it as religiously as ever monk did his devotion. Yesterday I burnt it. To me it seemed like sacrilege.

I fear I did not caution you enough against sleeping in the new house. For Heaven's sake (or rather for my sake), don't think of it till I come and judge. I left you an immensity of trouble, which I fear has not promoted your health. Kiss our dear little flock for me. Adieu.

A. BURR.

Late in the autumn of 1783 Colonel Burr removed from Albany into the city of New-York. In the spring of 1784 he was elected a member of the state legislature. At that early period political parties had not assumed either form or shape. The simple and intelligible terms of whig and tory were universally used. Colonel Burr's mind was occupied with his professional business. The legislature met in the city of New-York. He attended two sessions as a member. The first commenced on the 12th of October, 1784. He was in the house only a small portion of the time, and never interfered in what might be considered the ordinary business of the day. On great questions he took an active and decided part. His character for sagacity, discrimination, and firmness, was well established; and he would, therefore, have possessed great influence, if such had been his object; but his ambition, at this time, was not political; or, if it was, he had determined to smother it "until a more convenient season."

The second session while he was a member commenced on the 27th of January, 1785. During this he was more attentive than at the preceding session, but governed by the same system of policy, acting only when great and important questions were under consideration. On the 14th of February a joint committee of the two houses was appointed to revise the laws of the state. Colonel Burr was chairman of the committee on the part of the house. He introduced, on leave granted him, several important bills. One in relation to the public lands, another relative to the titles to real estate, &c. On the 25th of February a bill was pending for the gradual abolition of slavery within the State of New-York. It provided that all born after its passage should be born free. Burr moved to amend, and proposed to insert a provision, that slavery should be entirely abolished after a day specified. His amendment being lost, he voted for the bill as reported. He was a member of the

legislature, and supported the law in 1799, by which, ultimately, slavery within the state was abolished.

The question upon which he took the most prominent
part related to an application of some tradesmen and mechanics in the city of New-York for an act of incorporation.
The advocates of this bill had united their interest with
certain land speculators, and by these means it was supposed both bills might be carried through the legislature.
Both, however, failed. Colonel Burr was the only member
from the city of New-York that opposed what was termed
the Mechanics' Bill. His opposition produced so much feeling and excitement, that a man of less firmness would have
been driven from his course. Riots were threatened, and
by many it was supposed his house would be assaulted.
His friends volunteered their services to protect him, but he
declined receiving their aid, averring that he had no fears of
any violation of the laws by men who had made such sacrifices as the whigs had made for the right of self-govern-
ment, and that he could and would protect himself, if, contrary to his expectations, it should become necessary. That
he was prepared to resist any attack was universally known,
but none was attempted, and perhaps for that reason.

The Mechanics' Bill passed the legislature late in February, and was sent to the Council of Revision. At that time
the chancellor and the judges of the Supreme Court formed
a Council of Revision, and had a qualified negative on all
bills. If they considered a bill unconstitutional, they returned it to the house in which it originated, with their objections ; after which, if it received the vote of two thirds
of both houses, it became a law. This bill was returned on
the 9th of March by the council, with their objections, and,
two thirds not voting in favour, it was lost. These objections, in substance, were precisely what had been urged
against it by Colonel Burr on the floor of the assembly.

The petitioners were forty-three in number. The bill
gave them unlimited powers in some particulars. It did not

incorporate their successors, only so far as they pleased to admit them. They might hold landed estate in perpetuity to an unlimited amount, provided their *income* did exceed fifteen hundred pounds beyond their *outgoings.* Their by-laws were to be approved by the city corporation ; thus, by rendering the one dependant on the other, either the mechanics would influence the magistrates, and the powers of the corporation of the city and county of New-York be made, at some future day, instruments of monopoly and oppression ; or, which was more probable, the corporation of the city and county of New-York obtain a controlling power over the mechanics, and thus add to the extensive influence which that corporation already enjoyed, thereby rendering it dangerous to the political freedom of the people. Such were some of the objections entertained and urged by Colonel Burr against this bill. The great body of the community were prepared to sustain him ; and, before the succeeding session of the legislature, the intelligent among the mechanics were so well satisfied with the correctness of his views, that a similar application was never afterward made.

From the year 1785 until the year 1788, Colonel Burr was unknown as a politician. His practice was extensive and lucrative. His domestic relations seemed to occupy all his leisure time. His family was large, and to direct the education of his children was to him the most delightful employment. His zeal for their improvement is evinced in some of the preceding letters. His own health was precarious, while that of Mrs. Burr caused him constant alarm and apprehension. He had but one child, a daughter ; but the children of his wife by her first husband (Colonel Prevost) he reared as his own, and with all the tenderness of an affectionate father. The subjoined letters present Mrs. Burr in a most estimable point of view, while they cast some light upon Colonel Burr's character as a parent and a husband. They cannot be read, it is believed, by even the giddy and the thoughtless without feeling an interest in the destiny of their writers.

In the office of Colonel Burr, as students, were his two stepsons, Frederick and John Bartow. When absent from home on professional or other business, one of them frequently accompanied him as an amanuensis. On these occasions all his instructions in relation to lawsuits in which he was employed as counsel, or papers connected therewith, were communicated to the attorney or clerk in the office through Mrs. Burr. She appeared to be held responsible for the punctual and prompt performance of any duty required of them. To him she was indeed a helpmate; for she not only had charge of his domestic concerns, but was counselled with, and intimately associated in, all his business transactions.

TO MRS. BURR.

Princeton, April, 1785.

I had just embarked in the stage at Paulus Hook when I learned that it went no further than Newark ; so that, after being three hours close packed with rabble, I trudged an hour more to find a conveyance to Elizabethtown, where I arrived at eight o'clock, chilled, fatigued, and with a surly headache. A comfortable bed and tea made amends.

We arrived here at six o'clock this evening. I am fortunate in company, and find the travelling much less fatiguing than I imagined. Remind Frederick of the business with Platt. Write me by the next post, and by every stage. If I should even have left Philadelphia, I shall meet the letters. Speak of Harriet, and sur tout des trois Theo's. Adieu.

A. BURR.

TO MRS. BURR.

Philadelphia, April, Saturday, 1785.

I did not write you on Friday, as promised in my letter from Princeton, for which I will apologize when we meet.

I arrived here in good plight on Friday evening. Augus tine came down about noon on Saturday. We have made some satisfactory progress in our business. Seeing the great men of other countries puts me in more conceit of those of my own.

I shall be released on Tuesday evening, which will per mit me to see thee on Thursday morning. Mr. Colt will inform you about every thing. Unfortunately, a gentleman with whom part of our business is has left town. If he should return to-morrow morning, I shall be the happiest of swains on Wednesday morning. I am very minute in these calculations, because I make them very often. Does Theodosia employ herself ever in the same way ?

I have been to twenty places to find something to please you, but can see nothing that answers my wishes ; you will therefore, I fear, only receive

Your affectionate

A. BURR.

FROM MRS. BURR.

New-York, April, Saturday, 1785.

I persuade myself this is the last day you spend in Phil- adelphia. That to-morrow's stage will bring you to Eliz- abethtown ; that Tuesday morning you will breakfast with those who pass the tedious hours regretting your absence, and counting time till you return. Even little Theo. gives up her place on mamma's lap to tell dear papa—" come home." Tell Augustine he does not know how much he owes me. 'Tis a sacrifice I would not make to any human being but himself, nor even to him again. It is the last time of my life I submit to your absence, except from ne- cessity to the calls of your profession. All is well at home. Ireson gone on his intended journey. Morris very little here. The boys very attentive and industrious ; much more so for being alone. Not a loud word spoken by the

servants. All, in silent expectation, await the return of
their much-loved lord; but *all faintly* when compared to thy

THEE.

TO MRS. BURR.

Since writing to you last evening, every thing has con-
spired to harass and delay me. I was really in hopes of
surprising you on Wednesday morning; but am now most
unfortunately and cruelly detained here till to-morrow evening; shall therefore, with the usual luck of stages, embrace you on Thursday morning.

I have been walking, in the course of this day, hunting
offices, records, &c., &c., above eight hours, and am not
fatigued. I must really be very robust. Thine,

A. BURR.

TO MRS. BURR.

Albany, April, 1785.

1 arrived here on Tuesday evening very late, though little fatigued. Wednesday afternoon I went with Sill to
Bethlehem (Nichols), drank tea, supped, and breakfasted.
I am pleased with our friend's choice, of which more next
Tuesday evening. I am vexed you were not of my party
here—that we did not charter a sloop. I have planned a
circuit with you to Long Island, with a number of pleasant
&c.s, which are also reserved to a happier moment.

I shall succeed in all Mrs. Clarke's business except that
of the lands, in which I hope little.

I feel impatient, and almost angry, that I have received
no letter from you, though I really do not know of any opportunity by which you could have written; but it seems
an endless while to wait till Saturday night before I can
hear from you. How convenient would a little of the
phlegm of *this region* be upon such occasions as these! I
fear very much for our dear petite. I tell every one who
asks me that both she and you are well, because I abhor

the cold, uninterested inquiries, which I know would be made if I should answer otherwise. Do you want the pity of such? Those you thought your very good friends here have forgotten you.

Mademoiselle Y. is very civil. Are the Wadsworths with you? Have you not been tormented with some embarrassments which I wickedly left you to struggle with? I hope you don't believe the epithet. But why these questions, to which I can receive no answer but in person? I nevertheless fondly persuade myself that I shall receive answers to them all, and many more about yourself, which I have in mind, notwithstanding you will not have seen this. There is such a sympathy in our ideas and feelings, that you can't but know what will most interest me.

Give Johnstone the enclosed memorandum; or, if he has gone home, to Bartow; the business is of importance, an' admits of no delay.

Affectionately adieu,
A. BURR.

TO MRS. BURR.

Chester, Friday, May, 1785.

I arrived here about eleven o'clock this forenoon, with little fatigue, my horse being an excellent one. Appearances are hostile; they talk of twenty or twenty-five days at least. I believe I shall not hold out so long. The commissioners are met, but not all the parties, so that the business is not yet begun. The gentlemen from Albany are not yet arrived or heard of. We shall probably do nothing till they come. I have comfortable clean quarters.

Tell one of the boys to send me some supreme court seals; about six. I forgot them. Write me what calls are made at the office for me. Distribute my love. Let each of the children write me what they do. You may certainly find some opportunity. Adieu.

A. BURR.

Chester, May, 1785.

I strayed this morning for an hour or two in the woods, where I lay on a rock to enjoy the wild retreat. The cheerfulness of all around me led me to ask why all animated nature enjoyed its being but man? Why man alone is discontented, anxious—sacrificing the present to idle expectations;—expectations which, if answered, are in like manner sacrificed. Never enjoying, always hoping? Answer, *tu mihi magna Apollo.* I would moralize, but time —and my companions are coming in. Let me hear of your health. Avoid all fatigue. Judge Yates proposes to come down with me. Quoi faire?

My good landlady is out of tea, and begs me to send for a pound. Put it up very well. I am in better health than spirits. Adieu.

A. BURR

FROM MRS. BURR.

New-York, May, 1785.

I am vexed that I did not inquire your route more particularly. I cannot trace you in imagination, nor find your spirit when at rest; nor dare I count the hours to your return. They are still too numerous, and add to my impatience. I expect my reward in the health you acquire. If it should prove otherwise, how I shall hate my acquiescence to your departure. I anticipate good or evil as my spirits rise or fall; but I know no medium; my mind cannot reach that stage of indifference. I fancy all my actions directed by you; this tends to spur my industry, and give calm to my leisure.

The family as you left it. Bartow never quits the office, and is perfectly obliging. Your dear little daughter seeks you twenty times a day; calls you to your meals, and will not suffer your chair to be filled by any of the family.

Judge Hobart called here yesterday ; says you are absent for a month. I do not admit that among possibilities, and therefore am not alarmed. I feel obliged to Mr. Wickham for his delay, though I dare not give scope to my pen ; my heart dictates too freely. O, my Aaron ! how many tender, grateful things rush to my mind in this moment ; how much fortitude do I summon to suppress them ! You will do justice to their silence ; to the inexpressible affection of your *plus tendre amie.*

Bartow has been to the surveyor-general ; he cannot inform him the boundaries of those lots for J. W. There is no map of them but one in Albany.

THEODOSIA.

TO MRS. BURR.

Chester, May, 1785.

I joined the commissioners and parties in the woods, near this place, on Wednesday noon ; found the weather severe, and roads bad. Have, since my arrival, been following the commissioners in their surveys. Nothing transpires from which we can conjecture their intentions.

This morning came your kind, your affectionate, your truly welcome letter of Monday evening. Where did it loiter so long ? Nothing in my absence is so flattering to me as your health and cheerfulness. I then contemplate nothing so eagerly as my return ; amuse myself with ideas of my own happiness, and dwell on the sweet domestic joys which I fancy prepared for me.

Nothing is so unfriendly to every species of enjoyment as melancholy. Gloom, however dressed, however caused, is incompatible with friendship. They cannot have place in the mind at the same time. It is the secret, the malignant foe of sentiment and love. Adieu.

A. BURR.

New-York, May, 1785.

Your dear letter was handed me this day, at a moment which, if possible, increased its value. I have a little fever hanging about me, which tends to depress my spirits for the time. Your moralizing changed my dulness to a pleasing melancholy. I am mortified at the interruption it met, and impatient to renew the theme; to renew it in a more pleas ing manner than even your letters afford. When my health is ill, I find your absence insupportable; every evil haunts me. It is the last that must take place till term; *that* I must submit to. I am pleased with your account of your health and spirits; they are both as I wish.

When you write again, speak of your return. The uncertainty makes it more irksome. The company you speak of will be as welcome as any at this juncture; but my health and mind seem to require the calm recreation of friendly sympathy; the heart that has long been united to mine by the tenderest esteem and confidence, who has made every little anxiety its own, to whom I can speak without reserve every imaginary wo, and whose kind consolation shall appease those miseries nature has imposed. But whatever present inconveniences may arise, I submit to them with perfect resignation, rather than, even in idea, to expect the one mentioned by you when last at home. My mind is impressed with a perfect dread of all of that kind. We never can have one to give us so little trouble as E. W., and yet we found it great. We must avoid all such invitations, for the sacrifice on my part is too great.

Friday morning.

I have passed a most tedious night. I went to bed much indisposed. M. absent; mamma also. Ten thousand anxieties surrounded me till three, when I fell asleep; waked at six, much refreshed, and in better health than I could possibly have expected. I flatter myself your task will end sooner than you expected. Mr. Marvin calls for my letter this morning, which will be delivered with a pound of green tea I have purchased for your landlady at two dollars. He has called. I am hurried. Ten thousand loves

Toujours la votre.

THEODOSIA.

TO MRS. BURR.

Jane's in the Mountains, May, 1785.

I wrote my dear Theodosia a long letter of business and nonsense last evening from Chester. I am now about twelve miles nearer to you, and shall sleep to-night within thirty-five miles (only six hours' ride), and shall to-morrow return surlily to Chester.

Our cavalcade is most fortunately composed. Some who abhor fatigue, others who admire good fare, by which combination we ride slow and live well. We have halted here half an hour to lounge and take a luncheon. Of the last, I partook reasonably. The time which others devote to the former, I devote (of right) to you, and thus lounge with peculiar glee. .

By return of Mr. Smith (who is obliging enough to deliver this), I expect much longer letters from our lazy flock. By the next opportunity I determine not to write you, but some others who deserve more attention than I fear they will think I mean to give them.

The girls must give me a history of their time, from rising to night. The boys any thing which interests them, and which, of course, will interest me. Are there any, or very pressing calls at the office? The word is given to mount. I shall have time to seal this and overtake them. Kiss for me those who love me.

A. BURR.

FROM MRS. BURR.

New-York, April, 1785.

Mrs. Wickham just called to tell me of an opportunity to Chester. How joyfully I embrace it. I had a most insupportable impatience to communicate to you my gratitude and thanks for your last visit. It was a cordial to my health and spirits; a balm to my soul. My mind is flushed with pleasing hopes. Ten thousand tender thoughts rush to my pen; but the bearer may prove faithless. I will suppress them to a happier moment, and anticipate the dear indulgence.

The family as you left it. Thy Theodosia's health and spirits increase daily. Bartow's industry and utility are striking to the family and strangers. Johnstone returned yesterday. Your letter was as eagerly read as though I had not seen you. Write when you have leisure; if it does not reach me immediately, it will serve to divert some tedious moment in a future absence; even when you are at home, engrossed by business, I frequently find a singular pleasure in perusing those testimonies of affection.

I find I am continually speaking of myself. I can only account for it from my Aaron having persuaded me 'tis his favourite subject, and the extreme desire I have to please him induces me to pursue it. I take no walks but up one stairs and down the other. The situation of my house will not admit of my seeing many visiters. I hope some arrangement will be accomplished by the next week.

A packet from Sill. He writes like a happy man—not the happy man of a day, or I am much deceived in him. She is certainly to be ranked among the fortunate. I wish she may be sensible of her lot.

I have fixed the time of seeing you. Till Saturday I will hope the best. I cannot extend my calculations beyond it; four days of your absence is an age to come. My compliments to your chum, and who else you please. *Pense avec tendresse de la votre.*

THEODOSIA

TO MRS. BURR.

Chester, May 12, 1785.

Nothing could be more welcome than your affectionate letters by Mr. Wickham. They met me on Tuesday evening, on our return from a tour through the mountains. I was for some hours transported home, to partake of that domestic tranquillity which you so feelingly paint. Continue to write if opportunity presents. They will cheer me in these rustic regions. If not, they will not be lost.

This being a rainy day, we have kept within doors. To-morrow, if fair, we resume the business of climbing mountains, which will probably be our employment till about the middle of next week. After which a week more (at most) will finish the controversy.

Pay Moore nothing till I return, unless you see cause. Let him rough-cast, if he is confident of succeeding; but tell him I will not pay him till I am convinced it will bear weather, and last. .

If the sheriff of Bergen (Dey) calls for his money, I enclose a note with a blank for the name. You must speak to either Malcom or Lente for their assistance, unless you can think of something more convenient, putting the matter in such light as your address shall think proper. If for any reasons you should prefer to make use of Popham's name, do it. The person whose name is put in the note must endorse it, and the note be dated. Let one of the boys go over to Mrs. Baldwin for the certificate of the balance of the account, which, if obtained, a deduction must be made accordingly. Perhaps, by paying three or four hundred pounds, Mr. Morris will consent to wait my return. Perhaps, at your instance, he will wait that time without any payment. All which is humbly submitted. I enclose two notes, that you may take your choice.

Mr. Watrous's business respecting the land is not very material. If it should have failed, you may inform him that I have long since filed a caveat which will cover his claim.

I bear the fatigues of our business to admiration. Have great appetite, and sleep sound about ten hours a night. I am already as black as a Shawanese. You will scarce know me if I continue this business a few days longer. Thank our dear children for their kind letters. But they are so afraid of tiring either me or themselves (I suspect the latter), that they tell me few, very few, of those interesting trifles which I want to know.

Let T. give them any new steps he pleases, but not one before the others. If any one is behind or less apt, more pains must be taken to keep them on a par. This I give in charge to you.

I fear you flatter me with respect to your health. You seem a little studied on that score, which is not very natural to you when speaking truth. But, if it is not true, it is surely your own fault. Go to bed early, and do not fatigue yourself with running about house. And upon no account any long walks, of which you are so fond, and for which you are so unfit. Simple diet will suit you best. Restrain all gout for intemperance till some future time not very distant.

I do not *nor can* promise myself all you promise me with respect to the children. I have been too much mortified on that subject to remove it at once.

This is the last expedition of the kind I shall ever undertake ; and ever since I have been here I have been planning ways to extricate myself from it, but am defeated, and shall be absolutely detained prisoner till the business is concluded. Johnstone can give you an account of my quarters and mode of life. You haunt me daily more and more. I really fear I shall do little justice to the business which brought me here.

The children must pardon my not writing. I have a number of memorandums of business to make out for

Johnstone. Thank them again for their letters, and beg
them not to be so churlish.

Let one of the boys haunt Moore. But you surely can
do it without letting him vex you, even supposing he does
nothing. I had much rather that should be the case than
that you should be one minute out of humour with him.

The girls must go on with Tetard in his own way till I
come, when I will set all right.

It is already late. I must be up at sunrise. Bon soir,
ma chere amie.

A. BURR.

TO MRS. BURR.

Chester, 19th May, 2 o'clock P. M., 1785.

We have this day begun the examination of witnesses,
which, together with the arguments, will keep us the greater
part, and probably the whole, of next week. I find myself
gaining strength exceedingly since my return from New-
York, though perfectly out of humour with the business, the
distance, and the delay.

My trip to New-York has quite ruined me for business.
I cannot confine my mind to it. I am literally homesick,
and think of nothing else. A witness attending in court informs me of his going to New-York as soon as his testimony is finished. I desert a moment to tell you that I am
wholly yours.

6 o'clock P. M., 19th May.

Since I wrote you at two o'clock our court is adjourned
till nine to-morrow. We go on briskly and in great good-
nature. If you were half as punctual or as fortunate (which
shall I call it?), I should absolutely fancy myself talking
with you. It would be some indemnification for the distance and vexation. Make up in thinking of me, and taking
care of yourself, what you omit in writing. Thine at all
moments.

9 o'clock at night, 19th May.

A thousand thanks for your dear affectionate letter of Tuesday evening. I was just sitting pensively and half complaining of your remissness, when your letter is received and dispels every gloomy thought. I write this from the impulse of my feelings, and in obedience to your injunctions, having no opportunity in view.

The letters of our dear children are a feast. Every part of them is pleasing and interesting. Le Jeune is not expected to be in New-York for some weeks at least. I avoid the subject. I shudder at the idea of suffering any thing to mar the happiness I promise myself.

There is no possibility of my return till the middle of next week. In one of my letters I put it to the last of next week, but we have this day made unexpected progress. If we are equally fortunate and equally good-natured, we may finish Wednesday night; but this is conjecture, and perhaps my impatience makes me too sanguine.

I broke off at the bottom of the other page to pay some attention to those who deserve much from me (our dear children). To hear that they are employed, that no time is absolutely wasted, is the most flattering of any thing that can be told me of them. It ensures their affection, or is the best evidence of it. It ensures, in its consequences, every thing I am ambitious of in them. Endeavour to preserve regularity of hours; it conduces exceedingly to industry.

I have just heard of a Mr. Brown who goes down by water. As I may not have another opportunity, I hazard it by him. He promises to leave it at old Mr. Rutherford's.

Our business goes on very moderately this morning. Witnesses all tardy. We have adjourned for want of something to do. Melancholy and vexatious. It has given me a headache. We shall be holden, I fear, all next week. Adieu.

A. BURR.

To MRS. BURR.

Chester, 8 o'clock, 20th May, 1785.

Worse and worse. During the whole day we have not been five hours at business. Our witnesses are so aged, and many so remote, that they will not be in till Monday, so that, at this rate, we shall eke out the whole of next week. I have at no time been so completely out of patience ; just now particularly, being a little churlish with my headache, which, though not very severe, unfits me for any thing but writing to you.

I wrote you and the whole flock last evening, and added a line to you this morning, and sent off the packet by a Mr. Brown, who goes by water, and promised to deliver it himself. He has business at old Mr. Rutherford's. If he is punctual, don't forget him in thinking of the letters. Do say something that will make me a little more content with this vexatious delay and imprisonment.

I am prompted to write a hundred things, which I dare not, for fear I shall not find a safe conveyance : that was particularly the case last evening and this morning. It is perhaps fortunate, or I should spend too much time with you in this way. I believe I do as it is. Adieu, a little while. I am just going to prepare some hot punch.

Ten o'clock.

I have been till this minute making and sipping punch, and with great success. It has thrown me into a perspiration, which obliges me to go to bed. I am very illy reconciled to leave you and bid you good-night, but so says my hard lot.

Saturday morning, 8 o'clock.

I lay awake till after three o'clock this morning; then got up and took a large dose of medicine. It was composed of laudanum, nitre, and other savoury drugs, which procured me sleep till now : have no headache ; must eat breakfast, and away to court as fast as possible.

Saturday Evening.

Every thing almost stands still. I begin to despair of getting away. I am sure the whole of next week will not finish our business at the present rate. To make it more tedious and disagreeable, some of us are less good-humoured than at first. Not a line from you since that I have mentioned. I can find no opportunity for this. I am too vexed to utter one sentiment.

Sunday, 22d May.

No opportunity for this scrawl yet. I begin to be tired of seeing it, and wish it gone for this reason ; and also, because I try to persuade myself you would be glad to receive it.

To-day we have fine scope to reflect how much better we might have employed it, had we been active in our business last week. I find the whole might have been finished by yesterday (if the witnesses on both sides had been ready) as well as a month hence.

My room is a kind of rendezvous for our side : have seldom, therefore, time either to think or write, unless at night or early in the morning. Judge Yates concludes to give us a few days of his company, and to accept of a room with us. The coming of Le Jeune uncertain; not probably till fall. You will receive a pail of butter, perhaps, with this. I have been contracting for the year.

Have you done running up and down stairs ? How do you live, sleep, and amuse yourself? I wish, if you have leisure (or, if you have not, make it), you would read the Abbe Mably's little book on the Constitution of the United States. St. John has it in French, which is much better than a translation. This, you see, will save me the trouble of reading it; and I shall receive it with much more em-

phasis par la bouche d'amour. Adieu. I seal this instantly,
lest I be tempted to write more. Again adieu.

A. BURR.

New-York, May 22d, 1785.

Your letter by Mr. Bayard was brought me on Saturday,
and the first I had received since the one by Mr. Marvin
till to-day. Mr. Brown very punctually and civilly came with
your welcome packet of Thursday, nine o'clock. It was
just before dinner; the children were dispersed at different
employments. I furnished the mantelpiece with the contents of the packet. When dinner was served up they were
called. You know the usual eagerness on this occasion.
They were all seated but Bartow, when he espied the letters; the surprise, the joy, the exclamations exceed description. The greatest stoic would have forgot himself. A
silent tear betrayed me no *philosopher*. A most joyous repast succeeded. We talked of our happiness, of our first
of blessings, our best of papas. I enjoyed, my Aaron, the
only happiness that could accrue from your absence. It
was a momentary compensation; the only one I ever experienced.

Your letters always afford me a singular satisfaction;—
a sensation entirely my own; this was peculiarly so. It
wrought strangely on my mind and spirits. My Aaron, it
was replete with tenderness! with the most lively affection.
I read and re-read, till afraid I should get it by rote, and
mingle it with common ideas; profane the sacred pledge.
No; it shall not be. I will economize the boon. I will
limit the recreation to those moments of retirement devoted
to thee. Of a sudden I found myself unusually fatigued. I
reflected on the cause, and soon found I had mounted the
stairs much oftener than I could possibly have done on any
other occasion.

I am vexed with my last letter to you; 'tis impossible for

me to disguise a single feeling or thought when I am writing or conversing with the friend of my heart. I hope you
have attended only to the last paragraph, and avoided all
unnecessary anxiety for her who wishes to be a constant
source of pleasure to thee. I have been in good health since
Saturday morning. Since yesterday, unusually gay and
happy; anticipating a thousand pleasures, studying every
little arrangement that can contribute to thy comfort. This
wet weather is a bar to any essential progress. The walls
are still too damp to admit of either paint or paper. I have
a bed ready for the judge ; *ne vous genez pas la-dessus.* I
am afraid some foolish reflections in my last will embarrass
you. Your affection and tenderness has put them to flight.
" Let nothing mar the promised bliss." Thy Theo. waits
with inexpressible impatience to welcome the return of her
truly beloved. Every domestic joy shall decorate his man-
sion. When Aaron smiles, shall Theo. frown? Forbid it
every guardian power.

Le Jeune perplexes me no longor. I am provoked with
myself for having repeated it to you. Your dear little
Theo. grows the most engaging child you ever saw. She
frequently talks of, and calls on, her dear papa. It is impossible to see her with indifference. All moves as you
wish it. All count the passing hours till thy return. Remember, I am in good health and spirits ; that I expect the
same account of yours. To think of me affectionately is
my first command ; to write me so, the second. Hasten
to share the happiness of thy much loved and much loving

THEODOSIA.

FROM MRS. BURR.

New-York, August 28th, 1785.

The enclosed was to have gone yesterday, but the intended bearer disappointed me. Young —— and his companions have just left us ; at tasting your Madeira he pronounced you a d   d clever fellow. Your merit increased

with the number of glasses; they went away in good-humour with themselves and the hostess. O! my love, how earnestly I pray that our children may never be driven from your paternal direction   Had you been at home to-day, you would have felt as fervent in this prayer as your Theo.   Our children were impressed with utter contempt for their guest.   This gave me real satisfaction.

I really believe, my dear, few parents can boast of children whose minds are so prone to virtue.   I see the reward of our assiduity with inexpressible delight, with a gratitude few experience.   My Aaron, they have grateful hearts; some circumstances prove it, which I shall relate to you with singular pleasure at your return.   I pity A. C. from my heart.   She will feel the folly of an over zeal to accumulate.   Bartow's assiduity and faithfulness is beyond description.   My health is not worse.   I have been disappointed in a horse; shall have Pharaoh to-morrow.   Frederick is particularly attentive to my health; indeed, none of them are deficient in tenderness.   All truly anxious for papa's return; we fix Tuesday, beyond a doubt, but hope impossibilities.

I had a thousand things to write, but the idea of seeing you banishes every other thought.   I fear much the violent exertions you are obliged to make will injure your health.   Remember how dear, how important it is to the repose, to the life of

THEODOSIA.

FROM MRS. BURR.

New-York, August 29th, 1785.

As soon as Tuesday evening came, I sent repeated messages to Cape's, who persevered in the answer of there being no letter.   I slept ill; found my health much worse in the morning; rode out; in spite of exercise, continued ill till your dear letter was handed me.   I immediately called for refreshment, and imagined I had recovered my health;

my sensations still tell me so.   Ten thousand thanks for the
best prescription that ever physician invented.   I ride daily ;
breakfasted with Clem.   Clarke this morning, who has
scarce a trait of himself. ' He neither knows nor cares for
anybody but his son, who is three years and a half old, fair
hair, but not handsome ; much humoured ; is introduced as
a pet of the first value.   Aunt more in temper than was
expected.   He dines here to-morrow with the two Blakes.
I felt no other compulse to notice them than your wish.

Our little daughter's health has improved beyond my expectations.   Your dear Theodosia cannot hear you spoken
of without an apparent melancholy ; insomuch that her
nurse is obliged to exert her invention to divert her, and
myself avoid to mention you in her presence.   She was
one whole day indifferent to every thing but your name.
Her attachment is not of a common nature ; though this
was my opinion, I avoided the remark, when Mr. Grant
observed it to me as a singular instance.   .

You see I have followed your example in speaking first
of myself.   I esteemed it a real trait of your affection, a
sympathy in the feelings, the anxiety of your Theo., who
had every fear for your health ; more than you would allow
her to express.   .

The garden wall is begun.   I fear the front pavement
will not answer your intention.   I write you again to-mor
row.   Much love awaits thee.   Thine, unchangeably,   '

THEODOSIA BURR.

FROM MRS. BURR.

New-York, 25th September, 1785.

Your dear letter of Saturday morning has just reached
me.   I was relieved, delighted, till the recollection of the
storm you have since weathered took place.   How have you
borne it ?   Ten thousand fears alarm me.   I pursued thee
yesterday, through wind and rain, till eve, when, fatigued,
exhausted, shivering, thou didst reach thy haven, surround-

ed with inattention, thy Theo. from thee. Thus agitated,
I laid my head upon a restless pillow, turning from side to
side, when thy kindred spirit found its mate. I beheld my
much-loved Aaron, his tender eyes fixed kindly on me;
they spake a body wearied, wishing repose, but not sick.
This soothed my troubled spirit : I slept tolerably, but dare
not trust too confidently. I hasten to my friend to realize
the delightful vision ; naught but thy voice can tranquillize
my mind. Thou art the constant subject of love, hope, and
fear. The girls bewail the sufferings of their dear papa ;
the boys wish themselves in his place ; Frederick frets at
the badness of the horse ; wishes money could put him in
thy stead. The unaffected warmth of his heart delights
me. If aught can alleviate thy absence, 'tis these testimo
nies of gratitude and affection from the young and guile
less to the best of parents. They feel the hand that bles
ses them, and love because they are blessed.

Thy orders shall be attended to. Mamma joins in the
warmest assurances of sincere affection. Theodosia and
Sally in perfect health. Beyond expression,

Yours,

THEODOSIA BURR.

FROM MRS. BURR.

New-York, 27th September, 1785.

I have counted the hours till evening; since that, the minutes, and am still on the watch ; the stage not arrived : it is
a cruel delay. Your health, your tender frame, how are
they supported! Anxiety obliterates every other idea; every noise stops my pen; my heart flutters with hope and
fear ; the pavement from this to Cape's* is kept warm by
the family; every eye and ear engrossed by expectation;
my mind is in too much trepidation to write.

I resume my pen after another messenger, in vain. I will

* Stagehouse.

try to tell you that those you love are well; that the boys are very diligent; Ireson gone to Westchester. My new medicine will, I flatter myself, prove a lucky one. Sally amazingly increased. Fream at work at the roof. He thinks it too flat to be secured. The back walls of the house struck through with the late rain. M. Y. still at Miss W. You must not expect to find dancing on Thursday night. I should think it a degree of presumption to make the necessary preparations without knowing the state of your health. Should this account prove favourable, I still think it best to delay it, as the stage is very irregular in its return. That of Saturday did not arrive till Sunday morning; it brought an unfavourable account of the roads. Thus you probably would not partake, nor would I wish spectators to check my vigilance, or divide that attention which is ever insufficient when thou art the object. O, my Aaron, how impatient I am to welcome thy return; to anticipate thy will, and receive thy loved commands.

The clock strikes eleven. No stage. My letter must go. I have been three hours writing, or attempting to write, this imperfect scrawl. The children desire me to speak their affection. Mamma will not be forgot; she especially shares my anxiousness. Adieu.

THEODOSIA BURR

TO MRS. BURR.

Albany, October 30th, 1785.

I have received your two affectionate letters. The enclosed was intended to have been sent by the stage which I met on my way up; but, by untoward accidents (needless to detail), yet lies by me. My disorder has left me almost since I left the city.

The person with whom I had business had gone from this place before my arrival, so that I should have been, ere this, on my return, but that I have suffered myself to be engaged in two land causes (Van Hoesen and Van Rensse laer), which begin to-morrow, and will probably last the whole week. I am retained for Van Hoesen, together with J. Bay and P. W. Yates. Such able coadjutors will relieve me of the principal burden. You may judge with what reluctance I engaged in a business which will detain me so long from all that is dear and lovely. I dare not think on the period I have yet to be absent. I feel it in some sort a judgment for the letters written by the girls to N. W.

Your account of your health is very suspicious; you are not particular enough; you say nothing of the means you use to restore yourself; whether you take exercise, or how you employ your time.

I shall probably leave this on Sunday next; my horse will not take me home in three days. I fear I shall not see you till Wednesday morning of next week; perhaps not even then, for I am engaged to attend the court at Bedford on Tuesday of next week. You shall hear again by the stage.

Will not these continued rains deprive us of the pleasure of the promised visit of the W.s ? How is it possible you can write me such short letters, having so much leisure, and surrounded with all that can interest me ? Adieu.

                                        A. BURR.

TO MRS. BURR.

Albany, 2d November, 1785.

I have lived these three days upon the letters I expected this evening, and behold the stage without a line! I have been through the rain, and dark, and mud, hunting up every passenger to catechise them for letters, and can scarce yet believe that I am so totally forgotten.

Our trial, of which I wrote you on Sunday, goes on moderately. It will certainly last till twelve o'clock on Saturday night; longer it cannot, that being the last hour of court. Of course, I leave this on Sunday ; shall be detained

at Westchester till about Thursday noon, and be home on
Friday. This is my present prospect; a gloomy one, I
confess; rendered more so by your unpardonable silence. I
have a thousand questions to ask, but why ask of the dumb?

I am quite recovered. The trial in which I am engaged
is a fatiguing one, and in some respects vexatious. But it
puts me in better humour to reflect that you have just received my letter of Sunday, and are saying or thinking
some good-natured things of me. Determining to write any
thing that can amuse and interest me; every thing that can
atone for the late silence, or compensate for the hard fate
that divides us.

Since being here I have resolved that you in future accompany me on such excursions, and I am provoked to have
yielded to your idle fears on this occasion. I have told
here frequently, within a day or two, that I was never so
long from home before, till, upon counting days, I find I
have been frequently longer. I am so constantly anticipating the duration of this absence, that when I speak of it I
realize the whole of it.

Let me find that you have done justice to yourself and
me. I shall forgive none the smallest omission on this
head. Do not write by the Monday stage, or rather, do
not send the letter you write, as it is possible I shall leave
the stage-road in my way to Bedford.

Affectionately adieu,

A. BURR.

CHAPTER XV.

FROM MRS. BURR

New-York, August, 1786.

Your letter was faithfully handed us by the boy from Hall's. Bartow has enclosed the papers. Those you mentioned to me on the night of your departure I cannot forward, as I have forgot the names of the parties, and they cannot guess them in the office from my description. I hope the disappointment will not be irreparable.

If you finish your causes before court is over, cannot you look at us, even should you return to the manor? The two girls followed you to the stagehouse, saw you seated and drive off. Frederick's tooth prevented his attendance. My heart is full of affection, my head too barren to express it. I am impatient for evening; for the receipt of your dear letter; for those delightful sensations which your expressions of tenderness alone can excite. Dejected, distracted without them ; elated, giddy even to folly with them ; my mind, never at medium, claims every thing from your partiality.

I have just determined to take a room at aunt Clarke's till Sally recovers her appetite ; by the advice of the physician, we have changed her food from vegetable to animal. A change of air may be equally beneficial. You shall have a faithful account. I leave town at six this evening. All good angels attend thee. The children speak their love. Theodosia has written to you, and is anxious lest I should omit sending it. Toujours la votre,

THEODOSIA.

TO MRS. BURR.

Albany, August, 1786.

Your letter of Thursday evening was stuffed into one of the office papers, so that I did not find it for half an hour after I received the packet, during all which time I had the pleasure of abusing you stoutly. But I had only prepared myself for the most delightful surprise. I apologized with great submission.

Why are you so cautiously silent as to our little Sally? You do not say that she is better or worse; from which I conclude she is worse. I am not wholly pleased with your plan of meat diet. It is recommended upon the idea that she has no disorder but a general debility. All the disorders of this season are apt to be attended with fevers, in which case animal diet is unfriendly. I beg you to watch the effects of this whim with great attention. So essential a change will certainly have visible effects. Remember, I do not absolutely condemn, because I do not know the principles, but am fearful.

Every minute of my time is engrossed to repair the loss of my little book. Thank the boys for their attention to the business I left them in charge. I wish either of them had given me a history of what is doing in the office, and you of what is doing in the family. The girls I know to be incorrigibly lazy, and therefore expect nothing from them. The time was—but I have no leisure to reflect.

Thine,

A. BURR.

TO MRS. BURR.

Albany, August, eleven o'clock at night, 1786.

I have this day your letter by my express. I am sorry that you and others perplex yourselves with that office nonsense. Am too fatigued and too busy to say more of it. We began our Catskill causes this morning, and have this minute adjourned to meet at seven in the morning. We shall be engaged at the same disagreeable rate till Saturday evening. I think our title stands favourably ; but the jury are such that the verdict will be in some measure hazardous.

I have judgment for Maunsel against Brown, after a laboured argument. Inform him, with my regards.

Since writing thus far, I have your affectionate letter by the stage, which revives me. I shall not go to the manor. But, if I succeed in our causes, shall be obliged to go to Catskill to settle with the tenants, make sales, &c. Of this you cannot know till Tuesday evening.

I am wrong to say that I shall not go to the manor. I am obliged to attend a Court of Chancery there. The chancellor had gone hence before my arrival. I cannot be home till Thursday evening. I hope your next will be of the tenour of the last. Your want of cheerfulness is the least acceptable of any token of affection you can give me. Good angels guard and preserve you.

A. BURR.

FROM MRS. BURR.

New-York, November, 1787.

What language can express the joy, the gratitude of Theodosia? Stage after stage without a line. Thy usual punctuality gave room for every fear; various conjectures filled every breast. One of our sons was to have departed tomorrow in quest of the best of friends and fathers. This morning we waited the stage with impatience. Shrouder went frequently before it arrived ; at length returned—*no letter.* We were struck dumb with disappointment. Bartow set out to inquire who were the passengers ; in a very few minutes returned exulting,—a packet worth the treasures of the universe. Joy brightened every face ; all expressed their past anxieties ; their present happiness. To enjoy was the first result. Each made choice of what they could best relish. Porter, sweet wine, chocolate, and sweetmeats made the most delightful repast that could be shared without thee. The servants were made to feel *their lord was well*, are at this instant toasting his health and bounty ; while the boys are obeying thy dear commands, thy Theodosia flies to speak her heartfelt joys :—her Aaron safe, mistress of the heart she adores ; can she ask more ? has Heaven more to grant ? " *Plus que jamais a vous*," dost thou recollect it ? Do I read right ? I can't mistake ; I read it everywhere ; 'tis stamped on the blank paper ; I sully the impression with reluctance ; I know not what I write. You talk of long absence. I stoop not to dull calculations ; thou hast judged it best ; thy breast breathes purest flame. What greater blessing can await me ? Every latent spark is kindled in my soul. My imagination is crowded with ideas ; they leave me no time for utterance ; *plus que jamais ;* but for Sally, I should set out to-morrow to meet you. I must dress and visit to-morrow. I have heard nothing of the W.s.

Our two dear pledges have an instinctive knowledge of their mother's bliss. They have been awake all the evening. I have the youngest in my arms. Our sweet prattler exclaims at every noise, There's dear papa, and runs to meet him. I pursue the medicine I began when you left us, and believe it efficacious. Exercise costs me a crown a day ; our own horse disabled by the nail which penetrated the joint. I have grown less, and better pleased with myself; feel confident of your approbation. W. hastens the first assembly. F. feigns herself lame, that she may not accompany M., who submits to every little meanness, and bears all hints with insensibility. Has called here once. Clement sailed on Monday.   ˙

Your remark on the shortness of my letters is flattering. This is the last you shall complain of. My spirits and nerves coincide in asking repose. Your daughter commands it. Our dear children join in the strongest assurances of honest love. Mamma will not be forgotten. Sweet sleep attend thee. Thy Theo.'s spirit shall preside

I wish you may find this scrawl as short at reading as I
have at writing. I am surprised to find myself obliged to
enclose it. Adieu.

THEODOSIA BURR.

FROM MRS. BURR.

New-York, Wednesday, November, 1787.

My health is better. As I fondly believe this the most
interesting intelligence I can give thee, I make it my preamble. What would I not give to have but those four
small words from thee? Though I had but little hope, I
found myself involuntarily counting the passing hours. My
messenger met the stage at the door. I need not relate
his success. I fancy many ills from the situation of your
health when you left home, and pray ardently they may
prove merely fanciful. I have still three tedious days to
the next stage, when a line of affection shall repay all my
anxieties. Ireson returned to-day. The poor boys have
really been models of industry. They write all day and
evening, and sometimes all night, nor allow themselves
time to powder.

I feel as though my guardian angel had forsaken me. I
fear every thing but ghosts. Tell me, Aaron, why do I
grow every day more tenacious of thy regard? Is it possible my affection can increase? Is it because each revolv-
ing day proves thee more deserving? Surely, thy Theo.
needed no proof of thy goodness. Heaven preserve the
patron of my flock; preserve the husband of my heart:
teach me to cherish his love, and to deserve the boon.

THEODOSIA BURR.

TO MRS. BURR.

Poughkeepsie, 28th June, 1788.

This afternoon the stage will pass through this place.
Your letters will not come to me till the morning, so that I
can only thank you for them, and the kind things they con-

tain, by anticipation.   I have already read them in the same
way, and therefore do thank you for them, *de plein cœur.*

I have a convenient room for my business in one house,
board at a different house, and bad lodgings at a third
house. This is, indeed, not so convenient an arrangement
as might be wished; but I could not procure these different
accommodations at less than three houses in this metropo-
lis and seat of government.

As the boys will wish to know something of the progress
of business here, tell them that the cause of Freer and Van
Vleeck has been this day put off by the defendants, on payment of costs, on an affidavit of the want of papers. In
Noxon's cause I have a verdict for thirty-four pounds.
The evidence clearly entitled Mr. Livingston to three or
four hundred pounds, and so was the charge of the judge ;
but landlords are not popular or favoured in this county.
I am now going to court to defend an action of trespass,
in which I have been employed here ; and shall try Mr.
Lansing's cause to-morrow, which will close my business
here. With how much regret I shall go further from
home. Kiss our dear children.

                                      A. BURR.

TO MRS. BURR.
Poughkeepsie, 29th June, 1788.

I have sat an hour at the door watching the arrival of
the stage. At length it comes, and your dear packet is
handed to me just in season to be acknowledged by Mr.
Johnstone. He will tell you of the further progress of my
business and my intended movements. I go this evening
to Rhinebeck. How wishfully I look homeward. I like
your industry, and will certainly reward it as you shall
direct.

My time is much engrossed. My health perfectly good.
You say nothing of yours ; but your industry is a good
omen. You can write to me by Monday's stage, directed

to be forwarded to me from Rhinebeck. I shall be then at Kingston. Much love to the smiling little girl. I received her letter, but not the pretty things. I continually plan my return with childish impatience, and fancy a thousand incidents which render it more interesting. Reserve your health and spirits, and I shall not be deceived. .

Affectionately,
A. BURR.

TO MRS. BURR.

Albany, August 7th, 1788.

Oh Theo.! there is the most delightful grove—so darkened with *weeping willows*, that at noonday a *susceptible* fancy like yours would mistake it for a bewitching moonlight evening. These sympathizing willows, too, exclude even the prying eye of curiosity. Here no rude noise interrupts the softest whisper. . Here no harsher sound is heard than the wild cooings of the gentle dove, the gay thresher's animated warbles, and the soft murmurs of the passing brook. Really, Theo., it is *charming*.

I should have told you that I am speaking of Fort Johnson, where I have spent a day. From this *amiable* bower you ascend a gentle declivity, by a winding path, to a cluster of lofty oaks and locusts. Here nature assumes a more august appearance. The gentle brook, which murmured soft below, here bursts a cataract. Here you behold the stately Mohawk roll his majestic wave along the lofty Apalachians. Here the mind assumes a nobler tone, and is occupied by sublimer objects. What *there* was tenderness, *here* swells to rapture. It is truly *charming*.

The windings of this enchanting brook form a lovely island, variegated by the most sportive hand of nature. This shall be yours. We will plant it with jessamines and woodbine, and call it Cyprus. It seems formed for the residence of the loves and the graces, and is therefore yours by the best of titles. It is indeed most *charming*.

But I could fill sheets in description of the beauties of this romantic place. We will reserve it for the subject of many an amusing hour. And besides being little in the habit of the sublime or poetical, I grow already out of breath, and begin to falter, as you perceive. I cannot, however, omit the most interesting and important circumstance ; one which I had rather communicate to you in this way than face to face. I know that you was opposed to this journey to Fort Johnson. It is therefore with the greater regret that I communicate the event; and you are not unacquainted with my inducements to it.

In many things I am indeed unhappy in possessing a singularity of taste ; particularly unhappy when that taste differs in any thing from yours. But we cannot control necessity, though we often persuade ourselves that certain things are our choice, when in truth we have been unavoidably impelled to them. In the instance I am going to relate, I shall not examine whether I have been governed by mere fancy, or by motives of expediency, or by caprice ; you will probably say the latter.

My dear Theo., arm yourself with all your fortitude. I know you have much of it, and I hope that upon this occasion you will not fail to exercise it. I abhor preface and preamble, and don't know why I have now used it so freely But I am well aware that what I am going to relate needs much apology *from* me, and will need much *to* you. If I am the unwilling, the unfortunate instrument of depriving you of any part of your promised gayety or pleasure, I hope you are too generous to aggravate the misfortune by upbraiding me with it. Be assured (I hope the assurance is needless), that whatever diminishes your happiness equally impairs mine. In short, then, for I grow tedious both to you and myself ; and to procrastinate the relation of disagreeable events only gives them poignancy ; in short, then, my dear Theo., the beauty of this same Fort Johnson, the fertility of the soil, the commodiousness and elegance of the buildings, the great value of the mills, and the very inconsiderable price which was asked for the whole, have *not* induced me to purchase it, and probably never will: in the confidence, however, of meeting your forgiveness,

Affectionately yours,

A. BURR.

TO MRS. BURR.

Albany, 26th October, 1788.

I wrote you a few hours ago, and put the letter into the postoffice. Little did I then imagine how much pleasure was near at hand for me. Judge Hobart has this minute arrived, and handed me your letter of Monday. I cannot thank you sufficiently for all the affection it contains. Be assured it has every welcome which congenial affection can give.

The headache with which I left New-York grew so extreme, that finding it impossible to proceed in the stage, the view of a vessel off Tarrytown, under full sail before the wind, tempted me to go on board. We reached West Point that night, and lay there at anchor near three days. After a variety of changes from sloop to wagon, from wagon to canoe, and from canoe to sloop again, I reached this place last evening. I was able, however, to land at Rhinebeck on Thursday evening, and there wrote you a letter which I suppose reached you on Saturday last.

My business in court will detain me till Saturday of this week, when I propose to take passage in sloop. I have just drunk tea with Mrs. Fairlie, and her daughter, five days old. Thank Bartow for the papers by Judge Hobart. When I wrote him this evening I had not received them.

Yours,

A. BURR.

TO MRS. BURR.

Albany, November, 1788.

I received your affectionate letter just as I was going into court, and under the auspices of it have tried with success two causes. The bearer of this was my client in one of them, and is happy beyond measure at his success. Business has increased upon my hands since I came here. My return seems daily more distant, but not to be regretted from any views but those of the heart.

I hope you persevere in the regular mode of life which I pointed out to you. I shall be seriously angry if you do not. I think you had best take less wine and more exercise. A walk twice round the garden before breakfast, and a ride in the afternoon, will do for the present, and this will be necessary to fit you for the journey to Long Island.

A Captain Randolph will call with Mr. Mersereau : *c'est un soldat et honnete homme, donnez eux à boire.* They will answer all your questions.

　　　　　　　　.　. Yours truly,

　　　　　　　　　　　　A. BURR.

TO MRS. BURR.

Albany, 23d November, 1788.

I thank you for your obliging letter of the 19th. It is not, indeed, so long as I had hoped, but your reason for being concise is too ingenious not to be admitted. I have, however, a persuasion that you are at this moment employed in the same manner that I am ; and in the hope that your good intentions will not be checked by either want of health or want of spirits, I venture to expect a much longer letter by the coming post. .

Your account of the progress of the measles is alarming. I am pleased to find that you yet keep your ground. It persuades me that, notwithstanding what you have written, you do not think the hazard very great. That disorder hath found its way to this city, but with no unfavourable symptoms. It is not spoken of as a thing to be either feared or avoided.

I have no prospect of being able to leave this place before this day week, probably not so soon. You must, by return of post, assure me that I shall find you in good health and spirits. This will enable me to despatch business and hasten my return. Kiss those who love me.

A. BURR

/

TO MRS. BURR.

Albany, 26th November, 1788.

The unusual delay of the post deprives me of the pleasure of hearing from you this evening. This I regret the more, as your last makes me particularly anxious for that which I expected by this post.

I am wearied out with the most tedious cause I was ever engaged in. To-morrow will be the eighth day since we began it, and it may probably last the whole of this week. Write me whether any thing calls particularly for my return so as to prevent my concluding my business here. I am at a loss what to write until I have your answer to my letters, for which I am very impatient.

Yours affectionately,

A. BURR.

From the commencement of the year 1785 until the year 1788, Colonel Burr took but little part in the political discussions of the day. In the year 1787 the opinion had become universal that the states could not be kept together under the existing articles of confederation. On the second Monday in May, 1787, a convention met in Philadelphia for the avowed purpose of *"revising the Articles of Confederation,"* &c. On the 28th of September following, that convention, having agreed upon a *" new constitution,"* ordered that the same be transmitted to the several legislatures

for the purpose of being submitted to a convention of delegates, chosen in each state, for its adoption or rejection.

In January, 1788, the legislature of New-York met, and
warm discussions ensued on the subject of the new constitution. These discussions arose on the question of calling a
state convention. Parties had now become organized. The
friends of the new constitution styled themselves *federalists*. Its opponents were designated *anti-federalists*. The
latter denied the right of the general convention to form a
" new constitution," and contended that they were limited in
their powers to "revising and amending the Articles of Confederation." The former asserted that the general convention had not transcended its powers.

Colonel Burr, on this point, appears to have assumed a
neutral stand ; but, in other respects, connected himself with
what was termed the anti-federal party. He wished amendments to the constitution, and had received, in common with
many others, an impression that the powers of the federal
government, unless more distinctly defined, would be so exercised as to divest the states of every attribute of sover-
eignty, and that on their ruins ultimately there would be
erected a splendid *national* instead of a *federal* government.

In April, 1788, Colonel Burr was nominated by the anti-
federalists of the city of New-York as a candidate for the
assembly. The feelings of that day may be judged of by
the manner in which the ticket was headed. It was published in the newspapers and in handbills as follows :—

" The sons of liberty, who are again called upon to con
tend with the *sheltered aliens*, who have, by the courtesy of
our country, been permitted to remain among us, will give
their support to the following ticket :—

" *William Deming, Melancton Smith, Marinus Willet,
and Aaron Burr* "

The federalists prevailed by an overwhelming majority.
The strength of the contending parties was in the ratio of
about seven federalists (or tories) for one anti-federalist (or

whig). Such were the political cognomens of the day.
The federalists styled their opponents *anti-federalists*.
The anti-federalists designated their opponents *tories.*··

In April, 1789, there was an election for governor of the
State of New-York. The anti-federal party nominated
George Clinton. A meeting of citizens, principally federalists, was held in the city of New-York, and Judge Robert Yates was nominated in opposition to Mr. Clinton. Mr.
Yates was a firm and decided anti-federalist. He was
known to be the personal and political friend of Colonel
Burr. At this meeting a committee of correspondence was
appointed. Colonel Hamilton and Colonel Burr were both
members of this committee. ··

In their address recommending Judge Yates they state,
that Chief-justice Morris or Lieutenant-governor Van Courtlandt were the favourite candidates of the federal party;
but, for the sake of harmonizing conflicting interests, a gentleman (Mr. Yates), known as an anti-federalist, had been selected, and they respectfully recommend to Mr. Morris and
Mr. Van Courtlandt to withdraw their names, and to unite
in the support of Mr. Yates. This address was signed by
Alexander Hamilton as chairman. Mr. Clinton, however,
was re-elected.

This support of Judge Yates did not diminish Governor
Clinton's confidence in the political integrity, or lessen his
respect for the talents, of Colonel Burr. A few months
after the election the governor tendered to him the office of
attorney-general of the state. At first he hesitated about
accepting the appointment; but, on the 25th of September
1789, addressed his excellency as follows :—   ·   ·

TO GOVERNOR GEORGE CLINTON.

SIR,   .

In case the office you were pleased to propose should be
offered to me, I have, upon reflection, determined to accept
it ; at least until it shall be known upon what establish-

ment it will be placed. My hesitation arose not from any
dislike to the office, but from the circumstances which I took
the liberty to suggest in our conversation on this subject.

    I have the honour to be

        Your excellency's obedient servant,

                    A. BURR.

    On the receipt of the above note, Governor Clinton nom-
inated Colonel Burr to the council of appointment as attor-
.ey-general of the state, and the nomination was confirmed.
This office was rather professional than political. It was,
however, at the time, highly important, and imposed the most
arduous duties upon the incumbent. Under the new constitution of the United States, after the organization of the government, many intricate questions arose. To discriminate
between the claims upon the respective states and those
upon the federal government, often required close investigation and no inconsiderable degree of legal astuteness. The
claims of individuals who had been in the service of the
state during the war of the revolution, or who had otherwise
become creditors, were now presented for adjustment.
There were no principles settled by which their justice or
legality could be tested. All was chaos ; and the legislature
was about to be overwhelmed with petitions from every
quarter for debts due, or for injuries alleged to have been
sustained by individuals who had been compelled to receive
depreciated money, or whose private property had been
taken for public use. In this dilemma the legislature passed
an act authorizing the appointment of commissioners to report on the subject. The commissioners were Gerard
Bancker, treasurer, Peter T. Curtenius, state auditor, and
Aaron Burr, attorney-general.

    During the period that Colonel Burr was attorney-gen-
eral, the seat of government was in the city of New-York.
His official duties, therefore, seldom required his absence
from home, when his private business, as a professional

man, would not have rendered that absence necessary. His correspondence, although more limited, lost none of its interest, and miscellaneous selections from it are therefore continued.

TO MRS. BURR.

Albany, 21st October, 1789.

MY DEAREST THEODOSIA,

I have this moment received your letter of Sunday evening, containing the account of your alarming accident and most fortunate rescue and escape. I thank Heaven for your preservation, and thank you a thousand times for your particular and interesting account of it.

I left my sloop at Kinderhook on Monday morning, and came here that day in a wagon. I wrote you on the passage, and attempted to leave the letter at Poughkeepsie, but the wind not permitting us to stop, I went on board a Rhinebeck sloop, and there found Mrs. Peter R. Livingston, who offered to take charge of my letter.

I am relieved from much anxiety by your management of certain arrangements ; I am glad M. W. is content. Mrs. Witbeck met with an accident a little similar to yours ; but she lost only her cap and hair.

I am delighted to find that you anticipate as a pleasure that by this post you may write as much as you please. If you set no other bound to your pen than my gratification, you will write me the history every day, not of your actions only (the least of which will be interesting), but of your thoughts. I shall watch with eagerness and impatience the coming of every stage. Let me not be disappointed ; you have raised and given confidence to these hopes. We lodge at a neat, quiet widow's, near the Recorder Gansevoort's. Sill invited us very friendly.

Affectionately,

A. BURR.

Albany, 24th October, 1789.

With what pleasure have I feasted for three days past upon the letters I was to receive this evening. I was engaged in court when the stage passed. Upon the sound of it I left court and ran to the postoffice ; judge of my mortification to find not a line from your hand. Surely, in the course of three days, you might have found half an hour to have devoted to me. You well knew how much I relied on it ; you knew the pleasure it would have given me, and the disappointment and chagrin I should feel from the neglect. I cannot, will not believe that these considerations have no weight with you. But a truce to complaints. I will hope that you have written, and that some accident has detained the letter.

Your misfortunes so engrossed me, that I forgot to in quire about Augustine's horses ; and to give a caution, which I believe is needless, about the blank checks. Do not part with one till you see it filled up with sum and date. T. P. is apt to make mistakes, and once lost a check which was by accident detected before it was presented for payment.

This is my fourth letter. Perhaps I write too much, and you wish to give me an example of moderation.   ·

Yours affectionately,

A. BURR·

TO MRS. BURR.
‒   ·   Albany, 28th October, 1789.

The history of your sufferings, this moment received, is truly unexpected and affecting. My sympathy was wholly with your unfortunate left hand. The distressing circumstances respecting your face must certainly be owing to something more than the mere misfortune of your burn. I cannot help feeling a resentment which must not be in this way expressed. I am sure your sufferings might have been pre-

vented. I had promised myself that they were at an end
many days ago.

Forgive my splenetic letter by the last post. I cannot
tell you how much I regret it. When I was complaining
and accusing you of neglect, you were suffering the most ex-
cruciating pain ; but I could not have imagined this unfortunate reverse. Impute my impatience to my anxiety to hear
from you. I am pleased at the gayety of your letter. Do
not think a moment of the consequences which you apprehend from the wound. Let me only hear that you are relieved from pain, and I am happy. This is my fifth letter.
Frederick is the laziest dog in the world for not having
written me of your situation.

Yours, truly and affectionately,

A. BURR.

TO MRS. BURR.

Claverack, 27th June, 1791.

I have just arrived here, and find Mr. B. Livingston
about to return to New-York. He informs me that he left
home on Saturday, and sent you word that he was to meet
me here. It was kind in him. I cannot say as much of
the improvement you made of his goodness.

It is surprising that you tell me nothing of Theo. I
would by no means have her writing and arithmetic neglected. It is the part of her education which is of the
most present importance. If Shepherd will not attend her
in the house, another must be had ; but I had rather pay
him double than employ another. Is Chevalier still punctual ? Let me know whether you are yet suited with horses,
and how ?

In your letters, speak of Brooks and Ireson's attendance.
I wish you would often step into the office, and see as
many as you can of the people who come on business.
Does young Mr. Broome attend ? Other and more interesting questions have been made and repeated in my for-

mer letters; I will therefore, at present, fatigue with no more interrogatories. Adieu.

A. BURR.

New-York, 30th June, 1791.

My letter missed the post yesterday not from my neglect. It waited for Brooks's packet, which was not ready till the mail was gone. Mr. B. Livingston just handed me the one you intrusted to him. I was the more pleased with it, as he accompanied it with the most favourable account of your health I have received since your absence, and promises to forward this in the afternoon.

The Edwardses dine with me; they had taken lodgings previous to their arrival, in consequence of a report made them by the little Bodowins (who were at Mrs. Moore's last winter), that my house was too small and inconvenient to admit of a spare bed. I esteem it a lucky escape. It would have been impossible for me to have borne the fatigue. Charlotte is worn out with sleepless nights, laborious days, and an anxious mind. Hannah constantly drunk. Except William, who is a mere waiter, I have no servant.

My guests are come to dinner. I have solicited them, and shall again, to stay here; but, if they positively decline it, I will go to Frederick. I will steal a moment after din ner to add another page.

July 2d.

The person Mr. Livingston expected to forward my letter by did not go, nor could I hear of an opportunity, till, this moment, Mr. Williams offered to take charge of this. I had arranged every thing to set out for Frederick this morning, when a mortification was found to have taken place on Charlotte's child, and she could not be moved. As I had carted every thing on board, which I assure you was no small piece of business, I sent Natie with the three younger children, and kept Louise and Theo. to go with me, whenever this disagreeable event is past.

Theo. never can or will make the progress we would wish her while she has so many avocations. I kept her home a week in hopes Shepherd would consent to attend her at home, but he absolutely declined it, as his partners thought it derogatory to their dignity. I was therefore obliged to submit, and permit her to go as usual. She begins to cipher. Mr. Chevalier attends regularly, and I take care she never omits learning her French lesson. I believe she makes most progress in this. Mr. St. Aivre never comes; he can get no fiddler, and I am told his furniture, &c. have been seized by the sheriff. I don't think the dancing lessons do much good while the weather is so warm; they fatigue too soon. I have a dozen and four tickets on hand, which I think will double in value at my return. As to the music, upon the footing it now is she can never make progress, though she sacrifices two thirds of her time to it. 'Tis a serious check to her other acquirements. She must either have a forte-piano at home, or renounce learning it. For these reasons I am impatient to go in the country. Her education is not on an advantageous footing at present. Besides, the playfellows she has at home makes it the most favourable moment for her to be at liberty a few weeks, to range and gain in health a good foundation for more application at our return, when I hope to have her alone; nay, I will have her alone. I cannot live so great a slave, and she shall not suffer. My time shall not be an unwilling sacrifice to others; it shall be hers. She shall have it, but I will not use severity; and without it, at present, I can obtain nothing; 'tis a bad habit, which she never deserves when I have her to myself. The moment we are alone she tries to amuse me with her improvement, which the little jade knows will always command my attention; but these moments are short and seldom. I have so many trifling interruptions, that my head feels as if I had been a twelvemonth at sea. I scarcely know what I speak, and much less what I write.

What a provoking thing that I, who never go out, who never dress beyond a decent style at home, should not have a leisure moment to read a newspaper. It is a recreation I have not had since you left home, nor could I get an opportunity by water to send them to you. Albany will be a more favourable situation for every conveyance. But I don't understand why your lordship can't pay your obeisance at home in this four week vacation. I think I am entitled to a reason.

Brooks attends regularly. Ireson from six to twelve, and from two to six, as punctual as possible. I should have made the office more my business had I known it would have been agreeable to you. I shall be attentive for the future. Bartow is here every morning. Most people either choose to wait for him, or call at some appointed hour when he can be here. Mr. Broome is here every day.

God knows the quality of this epistle; but the quantity I am certain you won't complain of. 'Tis like throwing the dice—a mere game at hazard; like all gamblers, I am always in hopes the last will prove a lucky cast. Pray, in what consists the pleasure of a familiar correspondence? In writing without form or reflection your ideas and feelings of the moment, trusting to the partiality of your friend every imperfect thought, and to his candour every ill-turned phrase. Such are the letters I love, and such I request of those I love. It must be a very depraved mind from whom such letters are not acceptable.

Neither the packet you left at Kingston, nor the money and greatcoat by Colonel Gausbeck, have yet reached me. I wish you could have passed that leisure four weeks with me at Frederick's. How pleasant such a party would have been. How much quiet we should have enjoyed.

July 3d.

I was interrupted yesterday by the death of Charlotte's child. Though a long expected event, still the scene is painful. The mother's tears were almost too much for me. I hope nothing new will occur to impede my journey. I set off to-morrow morning. ·

I am not so sick as when I wrote you last, nor so well as when you left me. I confess I have neglected the use of those medicines I found relief from. The situation of my family has obliged me to neglect myself, nor can I possibly use them at Frederick's. We shall be too crowded. I will nevertheless take them with me. I live chiefly on ale. I buy very good for one dollar per dozen. I have had twenty-one dozen of your pipe of wine bottled. I think it very good.

I thank you for your remembrance per post of 30th June. It was acceptable, though short. How is it possible you had nothing more to write? I know the head may be exhausted, but I was in hopes the heart never could. I am surprised at your not getting my letters. I fear several have either gone to Albany or are lost. I shall, from this day, keep the dates. I wrote you last Sunday—so did Ireson.

You can have no idea how comfortable the house seems since the small tribe have left it. A few weeks' quiet would restore my head. It really wants rest. You can't know how weak it is. I cannot guide a single thought. Those very trifling cares were ever more toilsome to me than important matters; they destroy the mind. But I am beginning another sheet; I am sure you must be tired of this unconnected medley. I will bid you adieu.

Theo. has begun to write several letters, but never finished one. The only time she has to write is also the hour of general leisure, and, when once she is interrupted, there is no making her return to work. I have nothing more to write, except that I am yours affectionately,

THEO. BURR.

TO MRS. BURR.

Albany, 17th July, 1791.

I returned yesterday from Johnstown, worn down with heat, fatigue, and bad fare. It is some small consolation that these tedious journeys are not wholly unproductive.

At Johnstown I was very unexpectedly and agreeably surprised by your letter of the 21st June, which was addressed to me at Kingston. It had been intrusted to an Irishman, whom I at length met pretty much by accident. It informs me of the villany of Frederick's servants, and of his wanting a rib. The latter I have equally at heart with you, and never lose sight of it; but, really, the big mother will not do; the father is not much better—rêputable and rich, but coarse and disgusting.

On my return to this place I found your letter of Wednesday morning. I fear the bad road near Pelham will discourage you from riding. As you are likely to make considerable use of it, would it not be worth while to have a few days' work done on it? About an hour after the receipt of the last-mentioned letter, I was made happy by the receipt of that of the 10th instant, which came by sloop. You seem fatigued and worried, your head wild and scarcely able to write, but do not name the cause. Whatever it may have been, I am persuaded that nothing will so speedily and effectually remove such sensations as gentle exercise (or even if it is not gentle) in the open air. The extreme heat of the weather, and the uncommon continuance of it, have, I fear, interrupted your good intentions on this head, especially as you are no friend to riding early. I wish you would alter this part (if it is any part) of your system. Walking early is bad on account of the dew; but riding can, I think, in such weather, be only practised with advantage early in the morning. The freshness of the air, and the sprightliness of all animated nature, are circumstances of no trifling consequence.

I have no letter from you by the last post, which put me almost out of humour, notwithstanding the receipt of the three above mentioned within forty-eight hours, of which, however, the latest is a week old.

I hope Theo. will learn to ride on horseback. Two or three hours a day at French and arithmetic will not injure her. Be careful of green apples, &c.

I have been persuaded to undertake a laborious piece of business, which will employ me diligently for about ten days. The eloquence which wrought upon me was principally money. I am now at wages. What sacrifices of time and pleasure do I make to this paltry object—contemptible indeed in itself, but truly important and attractive as the means of gratifying those I love. No other consideration could induce me to spend another day of my life in objects in themselves uninteresting, and which afford neither instruction nor amusement. They become daily more disgusting to me; in some degree, perhaps, owing to my state of health, which is much as when I left New-York. The least fatigue brings a slight return of fever.

Your exercise, your medicine, and your reading are three subjects upon which you have hitherto dwelt only in prospect. They must be all, in some degree, within your power. I have a partiality for the little study as your bedroom. Say a word of each of these matters in your next.

Continue and multiply your letters to me. They are all my solace in this irksome and laborious confinement. The six last are constantly within my reach. I read them once a day at least. Write me of all I have requested, and a hundred things which I have not. You best know how to please and interest.

Your affectionate

A. BURR.

Pelham, 23d July, 1791.

I have just now received your welcome letter of the 17th inst. The pleasure imparted by so flattering a testimony of your good-will, was tempered with a large portion of alloy in the confession of your ill health. I was apprehensive travelling in the heat and bad accommodations would check your recovery. Do return home as soon as possible; or, rather, come to Pelham; try quiet, and the good air, and the attention and friendship of those who love you. You may command Bartow's attendance here whenever it suits you, and you have a faithful envoy in Frederick, who will go post with your commands as often as you wish. It is, indeed, of serious consequence to you, to establish your health *before you commence politician:* when once you get engaged, your industry will exceed your strength; your pride cause you to forget yourself. But remember, you are not your own; there are those who have stronger claims than ambition ought to have, or the public can have.

Why did you undertake that very laborious task you mention? 'Tis certain I have a great pleasure in spending money, but not when it is accompanied with the unpleasant reflection of sacrificing your health to the pursuit.

Theo. is much better; she writes and ciphers from five in the morning to eight, and also the same hours in the evening. This prevents our riding at those hours, except Saturday and Sunday, otherwise I should cheerfully follow your directions, as I rise at five or six every day. Theo. makes amazing progress at figures. Though Louisa has worked at them all winter, and appeared quite an adept at first, yet Theo. is now before her, and assists her to make her sums. You will really be surprised at her improvement. I think her time so well spent that I shall not wish to return to town sooner than I am obliged. She does not ride on horseback, though Frederick has a very pretty riding horse he keeps for her; but were she to attempt it now, there would be so much jealousy, and so many would wish to take their turn, that it would really be impracticable. But we have the best substitute imaginable. As you gave me leave to dispose of the old wheels as I pleased, I gave them as my part towards a wagon; we have a good plain Dutch wagon, that I prefer to a carriage when at Pelham, as the exercise is much better. We ride in numbers and are well jolted, and without dread. 'Tis the most powerful exercise I know. No spring seats; but, like so many pigs, we bundle together on straw. Four miles are equal to twenty. It is really an acquisition. I hope you will see our little girl rosy cheeked and plump as a partridge.

I rejoice with you at the poor major's return. I grow lazy, and love leisure; and, above all, the privilege of dis posing of my own time with quiet and retirement when it suits me. I have also made choice of the little study for my own apartment; but with so large a family, and so few conveniences, there can be no place of retirement. The vacation hours of school, and Sunday, there is a constant hurlyburly, and every kind of noise, though it is really much better than I feared. I take all things as philosophically as I know how; provided I have no real evil to struggle with, I pass on with the tumult. I am now writing in the midst of it. The variety of sounds almost dim my sight; but I write on, and trust to good luck more than reflection. I find so much to say that I need not hesitate for matter, though I might for propriety of speaking. My spirits are better: as to industry, it is of a very flighty kind, and so variegated that it will not bear description. It required some attention to get matters *en train:* it was like moving. My disorder I have not, nor am not able to attend to; 'tis attended with so many disagreeable circumstances that it is not practicable at present; but my general health is greatly improved, and my head much relieved.

The hint you give respecting a rib for Frederick is more

elating than I can express. You say nothing of B. That part of my petition was not less interesting. I humbly pray your honour may take into consideration the equity and propriety of my prayer, and grant me not only a hearing, but deign to give due consideration to the prayer of your humble petitioner, being confident she will find grace and mercy from your tribunal, with a full grant of all your endeavours to reinstate her in that desired tranquillity whose source is in your breast, to that happiness which is suspended on your will,

The heat and drought exceed all recollection. The town is extremely unhealthy. It is fortunate we are here. There is always air—never heat enough to incommode one. I am certain the child would have suffered in town ; she was much reduced ; her voice and breast were weak. Adieu. I think you must be tired before this. Attend to yourself. If you love us, you will. You will for your

THEODOSIA BURR.

FROM MRS. BURR.

Pelham, 27th July, 1791.

I have lost some of your letters, and I make no doubt some of mine have met the same fate ; for this reason I am discouraged trusting any more to the stage. I am obliged to wait with all the patience I can command till the boat returns from town. I have no prospect at present of forwarding this. I write to repeat my thanks for yours of the 17th. It is the last I have received. I read it frequently, and always with new pleasure. I was disappointed at not having a line from you by the Saturday's mail. It is not fair to stand on punctilio, when you know the disadvantages attending my situation here. You ought to be doubly attentive *pour me soulager.* It is not so practicable to send some miles from home twice a week as you imagine.

Poor Dr. Wright had his house two days ago burnt to the ground, and all the furniture, with every article of clothing both of themselves and the children. She is very disconsolate, and much to be pitied. We certainly see the old proverb very often verified. "That misfortunes never come singly," that poor little woman is a proof.

They talk of a general war in Europe; in that case *le moulin* will be an object. We wait your return to determine all things. The Emperess of Russia is as successful as I wish her. What a glorious figure will she make on the historical page! Can you form an idea of a more happy mortal than she will be when seated on the throne of Constantinople? How her ambition will be gratified; the opposition and threats of Great Britain, &c. will increase her triumph. I wish I had wit and importance enough to write her a congratulatory letter. The ladies should deify her, and consecrate a temple to her praise. It is a diverting thought, that the mighty Emperor of the Turks should be subdued by a woman. How enviable that she alone should be the avenger of her sex's wrongs for so many ages past. She seems to have awakened Justice, who appears to be a sleepy dame in the cause of injured innocence.

Am I dreaming, or do you leave home again before you go to Philadelphia? Tell all your intentions; I love to plan and arrange. Our blind state here is one of our most vexatious evils; that state of uncertainty damps every view, and converts our most pleasing hopes into the most disappointing reflections.

Hy! ho! for the major.* I am tired to death of living in a nursery. It is very well to be amused with children at an idle hour; but their interruption at all times is insupportable to a person of common reflection. My nerves will not admit of it. You judge right as to the roads on the Neck.

Theodosia is quite recovered, and makes great progress at ciphering. I cannot say so much in favour of her wri-

---

* Major Prevost, who was a widower, and whose children were left in the care of Mrs. Burr while he made a voyage to England.

ting. I really think she lost the last month she went to Shepherd. She has not improved since last spring. She is sensible of it, is the reason she is not very desirous to give you a specimen. We now keep her chiefly at figures, which she finds very difficult, particularly to proportion them, and place them straight under each other.

I will conclude my scrawl in the hope that Frederick will be able to forward it for me. Adieu. Remember to answer all my questions, and to take all my prayers in serious consideration. Be attentive to your health, and you will add to the happiness of your ·

THEODOSIA.

TO MRS. BURR.

Albany, 31st July, 1791.

At length expectation is gratified, and my hopes—even my wishes, fulfilled. Your letters of the 16th and 23d came both by the last post. Their ease, their elegance, and, above all, the affection they contain, are truly engaging and amiable. Be assured that petitions so clothed and attended are *irresistible*.

I anticipate with increasing impatience the hour of leaving this place, and am making every possible exertion to advance it. The delay of two days at Red Hook is indispensable, but will cost me much regret.

I finished on Monday last, tolerably to my own satisfaction, and I believe entirely to that of my employers, the business so often mentioned to you. I received in reward for my labour many thanks, twenty half joes, and promises of more of both of these articles. ·

The last post is the only one I have missed since I left Esopus. I was in court upon a trial which gave me not a moment's intermission till ten o'clock that evening. Though I do not pay you in quality and manner (for yours are, without flattery, inimitable), I believe I am nothing in arrear in number or quantity. The present is indeed a poor return for your two last; but though you miss of the recompense in this sheet, you will find it in the heart of your

A. BURR.

TO MRS. BURR.

Philadelphia, 27th October, 1791.

I have this day received your letter dated Sunday morning. It came, not by Mr. Sedgwick, but by the post, and was not put into the postoffice until Tuesday. It was therefore wicked of you not to add a line of that date.

I am surprised to find that you had not received my letter from Brunswick. The illness I then wrote you of increased the next day, so that I did not arrive in town until Sunday. I am still at Miss Roberts's, and unsettled, but hope to be to-morrow in tolerable winter-quarters. I have had some trouble on that head, as well because I am difficult to please, as because good accommodations are difficult to find.

I receive many attentions and civilities. Many invitations to dine, &c. All of which I have declined, and have not eaten a meal except at my own quarters. You see, therefore, how little amusement you are to expect. I called at Mrs. L.'s (the elder), but have not seen either her, or as yet called to see her daughter. I have no news of Brooks, and am distressed by his delay, having scarcely decent clothes. I prudently brought a coat, but nothing to wear with it, and the expectation of Brooks has prevented me from getting any thing here. Send me a waistcoat, white and brown, such as you designed. You know I am never pleased except with your taste.

I wrote you the day after my arrival here, but it being past the post hour, kept it till Tuesday; made a small addition, and gave it to Mat. to carry to the office. He put it into his coat-pocket (I suppose with his pocket-handkerchief, which you know he has occasion to flourish along street). On the day following, with a face of wo, he told me he had lost the letter, but had concealed it from me in hopes to have found it. I hope it may fall into good-natured hands, and so get eventually into the postoffice. It was short and stupid; unusually so, which perhaps vexed me the more for the loss. Be assured you have nothing to regret.

This letter can have nothing to recommend it but goodwill and length, though the latter, without some other merit, ought to condemn it; and it would, I am sure, with any but you, who will give the best construction to any thing from your

A. BURR.

TO MRS. BURR.

Philadelphia, 30th October, 1791.

I am at length settled in winter-quarters. The house stands about twenty yards back from the street, and is inhabited by two widows. The mother about seventy, and the daughter about fifty. The latter, however, has her home in the country, and comes to town occasionally. The old lady is deaf, and upon my first coming to take possession of my lodgings, she with great civility requested that I would never attempt to speak to her, for fear of injuring my lungs without being able to make her hear. I shall faithfully obey this injunction. The house is remarkably quiet, orderly, and is well furnished. They have never before taken a person to board, and will take no other.

The honour which I have always done to your taste, and which indeed it merits, ought to have assured you that your advice requires no apology. I shall adopt your ideas about the wheels. If at the same time you had caused the commission to be executed, you would have added civility to good intentions.

Theodosia must not attempt music in the way she was taught last spring. For the present, let it be wholly omitted. Neither would I have her renew her dancing till the family are arranged. She can proceed in her French, and get some teacher to attend her in the house for writing and arithmetic. She has made no progress in the latter, and is even ignorant of the rudiments. She was hurried through different rules without having been able to do a single sum with accuracy. I would wish her to be also taught geography. if a proper master can be found; but suspend this till the arrival of the major.

It is remarkable that you should find yourself so soon discouraged from writing, because you had written one letter before you had received one. I had written you two before the receipt of your first. But I shall in future expect two or three for one, as the labour of business will prevent my writing frequently,.

Remember the note to be put in the bank on Wednesday. If Bartow should not arrive, send Strong for Willet. Adieu.

Yours,
A. BURR.

TO MRS. BURR.

Philadelphia, 14th November, 1791.

I recollect nothing of the letter I wrote to you, and which is referred to in yours of the 9th. You have no forgiveness to ask or to receive of me. If it was necessary, you had it even at the moment I read your letter. You mistake the nature of my emotions. They had nothing of asperity; but it is useless to explain them. I did it partially in a letter I wrote soon after that which I sent you in answer to yours. It was not such a letter as I ought to have written, or you would have wished to receive ; I therefore retained it.

In what way, or to what degree, I am affected by your letter of the 9th, will not be told until we meet. Be assured, however, that I look forward to that time with impatience and anticipate it with pleasure. It rests wholly with you, and your conduct on this occasion will be a better in dex to your heart than any thing you can write.

VOL. I.—Q q

I enclose you a newspaper of this evening, containing a report by Mr. Jefferson about vacant lands. When you have perused it, send it to Melancton Smith. Take care, however, to get it back and preserve it, as it is one of Freneau's. I send you also three of Freneau's papers, which, with that sent this morning, are all he has published. . I wish them to be preserved. If you find them amusing, you may command them regularly. Adieu.

A. BURR.

TO MRS. BURR.

Philadelphia, 14th November, 1791.

I am to-day in much better heart than at any time since I left New-York. John Watts took me yesterday a long walk, and, though fatigued, I was not exhausted. He takes every occasion to show me friendship and attention. I see no reason for your delaying to make a visit here. The roads are good and the season fine. If you do not choose to come directly to my lodgings, which are commodious and retired, I will meet you either at Dr. Edwards's, two miles from the Red Lion, or at the Red Lion, which is twelve miles from this city. Your first stage will be to Brunswick, your second Trenton, and your third here.

I expressed myself ill if I led you to believe that I wished any evidence or criterion of Theodosia's understanding. I desire only to promote its growth by its application and exercise. Her present employments have no such tendency, unless arithmetic engages a part of her attention. Than this, nothing can be more useful, or better advance the object I have in view. Other studies, promising similar advantages, must, perhaps, for the reasons you mention, be for the present postponed.

I hope this weather will relieve you from the most depressing of all diseases, the influenza. Exercise will not cure, but will prevent the return of it. I prescribe, however, what I do not practice. You have often wished for opportunities to read; you now have, and, I hope, improve them. I should be glad to know how your attention is directed. Of the success I have no doubt.

To the subject of politics, which composes a part of your letter, I can at present make no reply. The *mode* of communication would not permit, did no other reasons oppose it.

I have no voice, but could undoubtedly have some influence in the appointment you speak of. For the man, you know I have always entertained much esteem; but it is here said that he drinks. The effect of the belief, even of the suspicion of this, could not be controverted by any exertion or influence of his friends. I had not, before the receipt of your letter, heard of his wishes on the subject you mention. The slander, if slander it be, I had heard often and with pain.

Sincerely yours,

A. BURR.

TO MISS THEODOSIA BURR.*

Philadelphia, 1st December, 1791.

Enclosed in Bartow's last letter came one which, from the handwriting, I supposed to be from that great fat fellow, Colonel Troup. Judge of my pleasure and surprise when I opened and found it was from my dear little girl. You improve much in your writing. Let your next be in small hand.

Why do you neither acknowledge nor answer my last letter? That is not kind—it is scarcely civil. I beg you will not take a fortnight to answer this, as you did the other, and did not answer it at last; for I love to hear from you, and still more to receive your letters. Read my last letter again, and answer it particularly.

Your affectionate

A. BURR.

* In the ninth year of her age.

TO MRS. BURR.

Philadelphia, 4th December, 1791.

I fear I have for the present deprived you of the pleasure of reading Gibbon. If you cannot procure the loan of
a London edition, I will send you that which I have here.
In truth, I bought it for you, which is almost confessing a
robbery. Edward Livingston and Richard Harrison have
each a good set, and either would cheerfully oblige you.

To render any reading really amusing or in any degree
instructive, you should never pass a word you do not understand, or the name of a person or place of which you have
not some knowledge. You will say that attention to such
matters is too great an interruption. If so, do but note them
down on paper, and devote an hour particularly to them
when you have finished a chapter or come to a proper
pause. After an experiment of this mode, you will never
abandon it. Lempriere's Dictionary is that of which I spoke
to you. Purchase also Macbeau's; this last is appropriated
to ancient theocracy, fiction, and geography; both of them
will be useful in reading Gibbon, and still more so in reading ancient authors, or of any period of ancient history.

If you have never read Plutarch's Lives (or even if you
have), you will read them with much pleasure. They are
in the City Library, and probably in many private ones. Be-
loe's Herodotus will amuse you. Bartow has it. You had
better read the text without the notes; they are diffuse, and
tend to distract the attention. Now and then they contain
some useful explanation. After you have read the author,
you will, I think, with more pleasure read the notes and remarks in course by themselves.

You expressed a curiosity to peruse Paley's Philosophy
of Natural History. Judge Hobart has it. If you read it,
be sure to make yourself mistress of all the terms. But,
if you continue your Gibbon, it will find you in employment for some days. When you are weary of soaring

with him, and wish to descend into common life, read the
Comedies of Plautus. There is a tolerable translation in
the City Library. Such books give the most lively and
amusing, perhaps much the most just picture, of the manners and ·degree of refinement of the age in which they
were written. I have agreed with Popham for his share in
the City Library.

The reading of one book will invite you to another. I
cannot, I fear, at this distance, advise you successfully;
much less can I hope to assist you in your reading. You
bid me be silent as to my expectations; for the present I
obey. Your complaint of your memory, even if founded
in fact, contains nothing discouraging or alarming. I would
not wish you to possess that kind of memory which retains
with accuracy and certainty all names and dates. I never
knew it to accompany much invention or fancy. It is
almost the exclusive blessing of dulness. The mind which
perceives clearly adopts and appropriates an idea, and is
thus enlarged and invigorated. It is of little moment
whether the book, the time, or the occasion be recollected.

I am inclined to dilate on these topics, and upon the
effects of reading and study on the mind; but this would
require an essay, and I have not time to write a letter. I am also much prompted to convince you, by undeniable proof, that the ground of your complaint does not
exist except in your own apprehensions, but this I reserve
for an interview. When I am informed of your progress,
and of the direction of your taste, I may have something
further to recommend.

There is no probability of an adjournment of Congress
during the holydays, or for any longer time than one day.
The possibility of my being able to leave the business of
Congress, and make a visit to New-York, diminishes daily.
I wish much to see you, and, if you are equally sincere,
we can accomplish it by meeting at Trenton. I can be
there on Friday night, but with much greater convenience on

Saturday noon or forenoon, and stay till Monday morning at least. Congress adjourns every week from three o'clock on Friday until eleven o'clock on Monday following. If, therefore, you write me that you will be at Trenton at the times above mentioned, you may rely on seeing me there: I mean at Mrs. Hooper's. This, though very practicable at present, will not long be so, by reason of the roads, which at present are good. If you make this trip, your footman must be on horseback; the burden will be otherwise too great, and I must have timely notice by letter. Mr. and Mrs. Paterson have invited you to make their house your home at Brunswick.

Mat. laughs at your compliments, as you know he does at every thing. I expect Theodosia's messages to be written by herself. I inquire about your health, but you do not answer me.

Yours affectionately,

A. BURR.

TO MRS. BURR.

Philadelphia, December 13th, 1791.

I regret the disappointment of the Trenton visit, but still more the occasion of it. Are you afflicted with any of your old, or with what new complaint?

Tell Bartow that I have this evening received his letter by Vining, who arrived in town last Monday. Beg him never again to write by a private hand about business when there is a post. After the lapse of five or six days without an answer, he should have sent a duplicate. You have herewith the note for 4500 dollars.

I was charmed with your reflections on the books of two of our eminent characters. You have, in a few words, given a lively portrait of the men and their works. I could not repress the vanity of showing it to a friend of *one* of the authors.

The melancholy news of the disasters of our western

army has engrossed my thoughts for some days past. No public event since the war has given me equal anxiety. Official accounts were received from General Sinclair on Sunday. The reports which preceded, and which have doubtless reached you before this time, had not exaggerated the loss or the disgrace. No authentic estimate of the number of the killed has yet been received; I fear it will not be less than eight or nine hundred. The retreat was marked with precipitation and terror. The men disencumbered themselves even of their arms and accoutrements. It is some small consolation to have learned that the troops which fled to Fort Jefferson have received a supply of provisions, and are secure from any attack of the savages.

I approve, and hope at some time to execute, your plan of literary repose. Tell Bartow to send a deed for me to execute to Carpenter, pursuant to our contract. Pray attend to this; you will see that it may be a little interesting to me.

Yours truly,

A. BURR.

· TO MRS. BURR.

Philadelphia, 15th December, 1791.

The post which arrived this afternoon (Thursday) brought the mail which left New-York on Tuesday, and with it your sprightly and engaging letter of the 12th. I thank you for your attention to my friend, and still more for the pleasure you express at his visit. Your "nonsense" about Voltaire contains more good sense than all the strictures I have seen upon his works put together.

Next to your own ideas, those you gave ·me from Mr. J. were most acceptable. I wish you would continue to give me any fugitive ideas or remarks which may occur to you in the course of your reading; and what you call your rattling way is that of all others which pleases me the most.

In short, let the way be your own, and it cannot fail to be acceptable, to please, and to amuse.

I enclose this evening's paper. It contains *Strictures on Publicola*, which you, perhaps, may find worth reading.

From an attentive perusal of the French Constitution, and a careful examination of their proceedings, I am a warm admirer of the essential parts of the plan of government which they have instituted, and of the talents and disinterestedness of the members of the National Assembly. Adieu.

                                        A. BURR.

                    TO MRS. BURR.

                            Philadelphia, 18th December, 1791.

Mr. Learned arrived yesterday with your letter of the 15th. He appeared pleased with your attentions, which you know gratified me.

I cannot recollect what hint I gave to Major P. which could have intimated an expectation of seeing you in New-York during the *current year ;* unless, indeed, some of those wishes which I too often cherish should have escaped me. We shall have no intermission of business during the holydays. If I should find it at any time practicable to absent myself for a few days, it will most probably be about the middle of next month. You have indeed, in your last letter, placed yourself before me in the most amiable light ; and, without soliciting, have much more strongly enticed me to a visit. But for the present I must resist. Will it not be possible for you to meet me at Trenton, that we may travel together to New-York? If you assent to this, I will name a day. Yet do not expose your health. On this subject you leave me still to apprehension and conjecture. .

Your account of Madame Genlis surprises me, and is a new evidence of the necessity of reading books before we put them into the hands of children. Reputation is indeed a precarious test. I can think at present of nothing better than what you have chosen.

I am much in want of my maps of the different parts of North America. It will, I believe, be best to send them all, carefully put up in a box which must be made for the purpose. You may omit the map of New-Jersey. The packing will require much care, as many are in sheets. Ask Major P. for the survey he gave me of the St. Lawrence, of different parts of Canada, and of other provinces, and send them also forward. They may be sent by the Amboy stage, taking a receipt, which transmit to me.

You would excuse the slovenliness, and admire the length of this scrawl, if you could look into my study, and see the file of unanswered, and even *un*perused letters ; bundles of papers on public and on private business; all soliciting that preference of attention which Theodosia knows how to command from her

AARON ·

TO MRS. BURR.

Philadelphia, 27th December, 1791. ·

What can have exhausted or disturbed you so much? You might surely have given some hint of the cause. It is an additional reason for wishing you here. If I had, before I left New-York, sufficiently reflected on the subject, I would never have consented to this absurd and irrational mode of life. If you will come with Mr. Monroe, I will see you to New-York again ; and if you have a particular aversion to the city of Philadelphia, you shall stay a day or two at Dr. Edwards's, ten miles from town, where I can spend the greater part of every day.

You will perhaps admire that I cannot leave Congress as well as others. This, if a problem, can only be solved at a personal interview.

You perceive that I have received your letter of the 18th. It was truly acceptable, and needed no apology. I do not always expect letters of wit or science ; and I beg you will write wholly without restraint, both as to quantity and manner. If you write little, I shall be glad to receive it; and if you write more, I shall be still more glad; but when you find it a troublesome or laborious occupation, which I have the vanity to hope will never happen, omit it. I take, and shall continue to use, this freedom on my part; but I am for ever obliged to put some restraint on myself, for I often sacrifice the calls of business to the pleasure of writing to you.

27th December, at night.

This evening I am suffering under a severe paroxysm of the headache. Your letters, received to-night, have tended to beguile the time, and were at least a temporary relief. I am now sitting with my feet in warm water, my head wrapped in vinegar, and drinking chamomile tea, and all hitherto to little purpose. I have no doubt, however, but I shall be well to-morrow. As I shall not probably sleep till morning, and shall not rise in season to acknowledge your kind letters, I have attempted this line. I am charmed with your account of Theodosia. Kiss her a hundred times for me.

The reports of my style of life are, I should have thought, too improbable to be related, and much too absurd to gain belief, or even attention.

I have been these three weeks procuring two trifles to send you; but am at length out of all patience with the stupidity and procrastination of those employed; especially as the principal article is a piece of furniture, a personal convenience, which, when done, will not cost five dollars. The other is something between a map and a picture. Though they will not arrive at the season I wished, they will at any season be tokens of the affection of

A. BURR.

TO MRS. BURR.

Philadelphia, 2d January, 1792.

MY DEAR THEODOSIA, .

Mr. Trumbull is good enough to engage to deliver this. You have long known and admired the brilliancy of his genius and wit; I wish you also to know the amiable qualities of his heart.

A. BURR.

TO MRS. BURR.

Philadelphia, 19th February, 1792.

Yesterday I received your truly affectionate letters; one dated Thursday evening, the other without date.

You may expect a host of such falsehoods as that about the Indian war. I have not been offered any command. When the part I take in the bill on that subject shall be fully known, I am sure it will give entire satisfaction to my friends.

It will not do for me at present to leave this place. I shall therefore expect you here; and if you cannot spare the time to come here, I will meet you either at Princeton or Trenton (preferring the latter) any evening you shall name. Saturdays and Sundays, you know, are our holy-days. I can with ease be at Trenton at breakfast on Saturday morning, or even on Friday evening, if thought more eligible. But I expect this letter will pass you on your way here. My rooms at No. 130 South Second-street are ready to receive you and Mrs. A., if she chooses to be of the party. But the tenour of your last induces me to think that you intend a very short visit, or rather, that you will come express. Arrange it as you please, provided I see you somewhere and soon.

I have a letter from Witbeck of a later date than that by Strong, and of much more satisfactory tenour. I believe he will not disappoint the expectations of my friends. He requests that some persons in New-York may write to him and others in and about Albany, giving an account of the expectations in Ulster, Dutchess, and the Southern District, and naming persons who may be corresponded with.

My lodgings are on the right hand as you come. Drive directly up a white gate between two lamps, and take possession. If I should be out, the servant will know where, and will find me in a few minutes. Do not travel with any election partisan (unless an opponent).

Yours,

A. BURR.

TO MISS THEODOSIA BURR.

Albany, 5th August, 1792.

MY DEAR THEO.,

I have received your letter, which is very short, and says not one word of your mamma's health. You talk of going to Westchester, but do not say when or how.

Mr. and Mrs. Witbeck and their daughter talk very much about you, and would be very glad to see you.

See what a letter I have got from little Burr,* and all his own work too. Before I left home I wrote him a letter requesting him to tell me what I should bring him; and in answer, he begs me to bring mamma and you. A pretty present, indeed, that would be!

Your father,

A. BURR.

FROM DR. BENJAMIN RUSH.

Philadelphia, 24th September, 1792.

DEAR SIR,

This letter will be handed to you by Mr. Beckley. He possesses a fund of information about men and things. The republican ferment continues to work in our state; and the time, I think, is approaching very fast when we shall uni-

---

* Nephew of Colonel Burr.

versally reprobate the maxim of sacrificing public justice and national gratitude to the interested ideas of stock-jobbers and brokers, whether in or out of the legislature of the United States.

Your friends everywhere look to you to take an active part in removing the monarchical rubbish of our government. It is time to speak out, or we are undone. The association in Boston augurs well. Do feed it by a letter to Mr. Samuel Adams. My letter will serve to introduce you to him, if enclosed in one from yourself. Mrs. Rush joins me in best compliments to Mrs. Burr, with

Yours sincerely,

BENJAMIN RUSH.

TO MISS THEODOSIA BURR.

Westchester, 8th October, 1792.

– I rose up suddenly from the sofa, and rubbing my head—" What book shall I buy for her ?" said I to myself. " She reads so much and so rapidly that it is not easy to find proper and amusing French books for her ; and yet I am so flattered with her progress in that language, that I am resolved that she shall, at all events, be gratified. Indeed, I owe it to her." So, after walking once or twice briskly across the floor, I took my hat and sallied out, determined not to return till I had purchased something. It was not my first attempt. I went into one bookseller's shop after another. I found plenty of fairy tales and such nonsense, fit for the generality of children of nine or ten years old. " These," said I, " will never do. Her understanding begins to be above such things ;" but I could see nothing that I would offer with pleasure to an *intelligent, well-informed girl of nine years old.* I began to be discouraged. The hour of dining was come. " But I will search a little longer." I persevered. At last I found it. I found the very thing I sought. It is contained in two volumes octavo, handsomely bound, and with prints and registers. It is a

work of fancy, but replete with instruction and amusement.
I must present it with my own hand.

Your affectionate

A. BURR

CHAPTER XVI.

THE correspondence in the last chapter between Mr.
and Mrs. Burr has been selected and published that the
world may judge him as husband and parent, so far as his
letters afford a criterion. As literary productions they cannot fail to interest and amuse.

On the 8th day of March, 1790, the legislature passed an
act appointing Gerard Bancker, treasurer, Peter Curtenius,
auditor, and Aaron Burr, attorney-general, a board of commissioners to report on the subject of the various claims
against the state for services rendered, or injuries sustained,
during the war of the revolution. The task was one of
great delicacy, and surrounded with difficulties. On Colonel
Burr devolved the duty of making that report. It was performed in a masterly manner. When presented to the
house, notwithstanding its magnitude, involving claims of
every description to an immense amount, it met with no
opposition from any quarter. On the 5th of April, 1792,
the report was ordered to be entered at length on the journals of the assembly, and formed the basis of all future settlements with public creditors on account of the war. In
it the various claimants are classified; legal and equitable
principles are established, and applied to each particular
class. The report occupies eighteen folio pages of the
journals of the assembly. An extract from it is made, as
justly meriting a place in this work.

The said report is in the words and figures following :—

"The treasurer, the auditor, and the attorney-general, pur
suant to the act entitled *An act to receive and state accounts
against this state*, did forthwith, after the passing of the said
act, give such notice of their appointment and duties, and of
the times and places for the execution thereof, and of the
period by the said act limited for receiving and auditing
claims, as is directed by the said act. And do herewith
transmit to the legislature their report upon the accounts
and claims against the state, which have been thereupon
exhibited.

"The anxiety of the commissioners to render the execution of this trust useful and acceptable has occasioned a
delay of some weeks; if their success in this attempt has
been in any degree proportioned to their attention to the
subject, it will furnish their excuse; indeed, when the legislature shall have seen the number, the variety, and intri-
cacy of the matters which have been submitted to the consideration of the commissioners, it is hoped that a further
apology will be thought unnecessary.

"The commissioners have endeavoured to reduce these
various demands into classes, in such manner as to present
to the legislature, in one view, all which have appeared to
depend on similar principles. Notwithstanding their utmost attention to this object, they have found it necessary
to report on a considerable number of single cases. As the
authority under which they have acted required of them a
state of facts, together with their opinion thereupon, whenever there was a want of uniformity either in the facts
submitted or in the principles to be applied in the determination, they have thought that strict justice could not
be done to the merit of the claim without a separate discussion; though this has tended to lengthen the report be
yond what could have been wished, and to a degree which
perhaps may in some instances be thought prolix, yet the
commissioners supposed it of moment that their investigation should be not only satisfactory to themselves, but that

it should be apparent to the citizens upon whose claims they have pronounced, that each hath received a distinct attention, and that demands substantially different from each other have not been inconsiderately blended. If the perusal of the proceedings now submitted shall give an impression of this kind, it will, in the opinion of the commissioners, tend to produce a more cheerful acquiescence in the determination of the legislature, when that determination shall reject the demand, and prevent a revival of claims which shall now be extinguished. The commissioners have thought that these were desirable objects, and have therefore been cautious of generalizing, so as to destroy real distinctions, or suppress a fact even of the lightest importance.

" In order to preserve uniformity in their opinions, the commissioners have adopted certain principles, from which the hardship of any particular case hath not induced them to depart. The most general and important of these are,

" *First.* Where any species of claims is barred by an act of the legislature, they have considered the act as a bar to their investigation, farther than to ascertain it to be unquestionably within the meaning of the law. This principle will be found to extend to all claims for pay and rations alleged to be due for militia service; to most of the demands against forfeited estates; to all claims for property sequestered, when the sequestration was warranted by the resolutions of the convention and the authority of the commissioners; to all claims of payment of state agents' notes, and to some other particular cases, which will appear in the report. In support of this principle the commissioners have considered, that to sanction by their opinion the admission of claims against the spirit and letter of the statute would be an impeachment of the wisdom of those laws; would be arrogating an authority not exercised by, or permitted to, any court of law or equity, and would open a door to the importunate and perhaps least deserving class

of citizens, while others, having similar demands, had withdrawn them from a spirit of submission to the laws, by
which these demands were precluded. The commission
ers have been confirmed in the propriety of their ideas by
a reflection that, if it shall for any reasons seem expedient
to the legislature to repeal or suspend the limitation of
those or any of those statutes, the avenues to redress will
at once be open through the ordinary officers of the state,
without farther legislative interposition ; and that the opportunities of recompense would then be notorious and equal ;
but that the redress, if any should be obtained through the
medium of the commissioners, would be partial in its operation, and to the exclusion of those who with equal merits
had acquiesced in the known laws.

"*Second.* In the cases of claims for services done and
supplies furnished during the war, when the demand, though
originating under the authority of this state, is properly
against the United States, the opinion of the commissioners
is against the allowance of any recompense, because those
claims should more properly be preferred to Congress ; and
for that this state can have no credit with the United States
for payment or assumptions after the 1st day of October,
1788.

" And that, therefore, the claimants having neglected to
exhibit their demands within the period during which this
state could without loss have assumed them, cannot complain if they are now referred to the proper tribunal. Payments by the state were in such cases, at all times, of
favour, and not of right.

" *Third.* All claims for the subsistence and services of
the levies and militia, or other troops, composing a part of
the continental army, or destined to join the army, and
moving to such places of destination, or under the command
or orders of a continental officer, and all claims for supplies and services beforehand for such troops, are considered as proper against the United States only, and are

classed accordingly; the commissioners have been led to a
more strict attention to this distinction by the reasons just
before mentioned, and are warranted by the practice of the
continental commissioners for settling accounts, in declaring that such accounts and demands were proper against
the United States.

"Principles of more limited operation, and other remarks, will appear in those parts of the report to which
they apply.

"Explanatory of particular parts, and of the general form
of the report, it may be proper to observe,

"That where the claim or account appears, upon the face
of it, to be evidently against the United States only, or for
other reasons palpably inadmissible, the commissioners have
thought it would have been superfluous to state the proof,
and have therefore, in those cases only, given such abstracts
of the claim or account as suffice to render the exception
apparent.

"In giving their opinion, the commissioners have not detailed all the reasons which led to it, but have given a summary of such as appeared to them most conclusive; and, as
well in this as in stating the facts, have aimed at as much
brevity as appeared to them to consist with perspicuity. If
they shall be found in any instances obscure, a reference to
the claim and proofs will probably elucidate them. When
the claim is provided for by existing laws, the opinion of
the commissioners refers the claimant to the mode pointed
out by such law.

"Demands of different natures by the same person are
placed under the head which comprises the greater demand.
The claim and vouchers being in such cases usually contained in the same paper or annexed together, it was necessary so to place them in the report that there might be no
confusion in the references.

"To produce facility in the review of these proceedings,
the documents referred to are all herewith delivered, and

are in bundles, marked agreeably to the heads under which they are classed.

" *Claims for Militia Pay.*

[In the report a number of cases are here inserted.]

" By an act passed the 27th of April, 1784, entitled *An act for the settlement of the pay of the levies and militia for their services in the late war, and for other purposes therein mentioned*, the mode in which the rolls and abstracts for pay and subsistence are to be made out and settled is particularly pointed out, and competent powers and directions for the liquidation of those accounts are thereby given to the treasurer and auditor.

" By the 14th section of an act passed the 21st of April, 1787, entitled *An act for the relief of persons who paid money into the treasury*, &c., the aforesaid act of the 27th of April, 1784, is repealed. The commissioners consider this repeal as an exclusion of all further claims for pay and subsistence of the militia and levies. They are constrained to adopt this opinion, not only from the obvious intention of the act, but because, by the absolute repeal of the act of the 27th of April, 1784, there remains no prescribed mode of authenticating these demands ; that any rules which the discretion of the commissioners should lead them to adopt would have been unknown to the claimants, who could therefore have had no opportunity of adapting their demands to such rules ; and because, if the legislature shall be disposed to direct compensations for such services, it will, in the opinion of the commissioners, be most properly effected by a revival of the said act of the 27th of April, 1784, with such further provisions and checks as may be thought necessary ; or by some other general statute, to be passed for those purposes, and which may give equal opportunities to the claimants, and place the liquidation and settlement of such demands in the hands of the ordinary officers of the state.

"*Claims for services, supplies, and losses, which, if admissible, can be made against the United States only.*

[In the report details follow, and the commissioners remark]—.

"The foregoing claims and accounts the commissioners conceive to be proper against the United States only. This is, in their opinion, sufficiently evident in most of the cases from a bare statement of the demands. Some few appear to require a more special report. The resolutions of Congress of the 7th of May, 1787, and 24th of June, 1788, relative to the settlement of accounts between· the United States and individual states, will show the extent of the powers of the Continental Commissioners, and will serve to explain the opinions in such of the preceding cases as may appear to require farther illustration.

"*Claims for payment of State Agents' Certificates.*·

"By the 25th section of the act passed the 5th of May, 1786, entitled *An act for the payment of certain sums of money, and for other purposes therein mentioned,* all persons holding or possessing certificates of Udny Hay or any of his assistants, or of Jacob Cuyler, Morgan Lewis, or Andrew Bostwick, were required to present them, in the manner therein prescribed, to the treasurer, before the 1st of September, 1786; and those who failed therein are thereby declared *to be barred and for ever precluded* from any compensation, of which the treasurer was directed to give public notice by advertisement, which was accordingly done.

"By another act, passed the 31st of March, 1787, the time for presenting the certificates of Udny Hay and his assistants was extended until the first of May then next, which time has not been further extended by any law of this state : so that all certificates of those denominations which were not presented within the times and in the manner specified in those laws, are expressly barred and for ever precluded from compensation.

"The commissioners have therefore, for the reasons contained in the observations prefixed to this report, conceived that a reference to the aforesaid acts was the most proper discharge of their duty with respect to all claims of compensation for such certificates.

"*Claims for grain impressed for the use of the army by virtue of warrants issued by his excellency the governor, pursuant to an act passed 23d June, 1780.*

"The law authorizing these impresses declares the articles impressed to be for the *use and service of the army,* and that the owner shall be entitled to receive from the public officer authorized to pay the same the current price for the articles impressed, but does not say by whom that public officer is to be appointed. The commissioners have, however, no doubt but these were proper claims against the United States, and would have been allowed by the Conti nental Commissioner if exhibited in proper season; therefore, and for the reasons contained in the second preliminary observation, the commissioners are of the opinion that these claimants cannot of right demand payment of this state.

"The claims of Van Rensselaer and Dumond, the commissioners are of opinion are reasonable; that, having been employed under the governor, the claimants could have no demand against the United States, and that the charges are proper against this state.

"*Claims for services in assisting H. I. Van Rensselaer and Egbert Dumond in making the said impresses.*

"The commissioners consider the reasons just before stated in favour of the claims of Van Rensselaer and Du mond to apply to the eleven preceding, and that they are therefore proper charges against this state.

" *Claims for payment of debts due from persons whose property hath been forfeited or sequestered.*

" The several foregoing demands against forfeited es tates arose after the 9th day of July, 1776, and are expressly precluded by the 42d section of an act passed the 12th of May, 1784, entitled *An act for the speedy sale of the confiscated and forfeited estates within this state, and for other purposes therein mentioned.*

" The next twenty-five claims are for satisfaction of debts out of the proceeds of property sequestered. The estates of the several debtors have become forfeited, but in some instances no property hath come to the hands of the com missioners of forfeitures; and in others, the property which has come to their hands hath been insufficient for the discharge of debts which have been certified.

" The succeeding twenty-six claims are to have debts satisfied out of the proceeds of property sequestered, though there had been no conviction of adherence or other forfeiture of the estate of the debtors.

" The commissioners are of opinion that a law should be passed authorizing the treasurer to pay demands against forfeited estates, in all cases where there still remains in his hands a surplus from the proceeds of such estates, notwithstanding the limitation contained in the act of 12th May, 1784. But the commissioners would recommend that some mode different from that prescribed in the said act be directed for the ascertaining the amount of those demands. The several claimants and such others as have neglected to avail themselves of the benefit of the said act, may, in the opinion of the commissioners, be with propriety holden to strict legal proof of their respective demands, in due course of law, in some court of record, where the interest of the state may be defended by some officer to be for that purpose appointed.

" The commissioners are further of opinion, that where

there has been a sequestration of any part of the property of a person *whose estate hath become forfeited*, the avails of the property so sequestered, as far as the same *can be distinguished*, should be subject to the payment of his debts, in like manner as may be provided with respect to other demands against forfeited estates ; but it would not, in the opinion of the commissioners, be at this time advisable to assume the payment of the debts of persons whose property hath been sequestered, and where there hath been no other forfeiture or confiscation.

" *Claims relative to sequestration, and property taken by orders of the Convention.*

" These persons were voluntarily within the British lines, and their property was therefore liable to sequestration under the acts of the Convention.   They produce a certificate of their attachment to the American cause, signed by some respectable characters.   But being within the resolutions of the Convention, the commissioners cannot advise a recompense.

> " GERARD BANCKER, *Treasurer.*
> " PETER T. CURTENIUS, *State Auditor*
> " AARON BURR, *Attorney-general.*"

On the 19th of January, 1791, Colonel Burr was appointed a senator of the United States, in the place of General Schuyler, whose term of service would expire on the 4th of March following.   Until about this period he was but little known as a partisan politician.   After the organization of the federal government under the new constitution, he appears to have felt a great interest in its operations.   In the French revolution also, his feelings were embarked ; and he was among the number of those who condemned the cold and repulsive neutrality which characterized the administration of that day.   That he was now about to launch into the troubled ocean of politics was evident to Mrs. Burr, and therefore in a letter to him under date of the 23d of July, 1791, she says, " It is of serious consequence to you to establish your health *before you commence politician*," &c.

In the autumn of 1791 Congress convened at Philadelphia, and Colonel Burr took his seat in the Senate of the United States. It has often been remarked of him, and truly, that no man was ever more cautious or more guarded in his correspondence. A disposition, from the earliest period of his life, to write in cipher, has already been noticed. To this may be added an unwillingness, on all important questions, to commit himself in writing. As soon as he entered the political arena, this characteristic was visible even in his letters to Mrs. Burr. On the 14th of November, 1791, he writes her—" To the subject of politics I can at present make no reply. The *mode of communication would not permit*, did no other reason oppose." And again, December 21st, he says—" You will perhaps admire that I cannot leave Congress as well as others. This, if a problem, *can only be solved at a personal interview*."

At the commencement of the revolutionary war, the State of New-York held an extensive tract of wild and unimproved lands. Sundry laws were passed in the years 1779, 1780, 1784, 1785, and 1786, providing for their sale and settlement. A board was created, entitled " the Commissioners of the Land Office." It was composed of the governor, the secretary of state, the attorney-general, the treasurer, and the auditor. The powers conferred by the several acts above referred to having been found inadequate to the proposed object, the legislature, on the 22d of March, 1791, have unlimited powers to the commissioners, authorizing them to " dispose of any of the waste and unappropriated lands in the state, in such parcels, and on such terms, and in such manner as they shall judge most conducive to the interests of the state." In pursuance of this authority, the commissioners sold during the year 1791, by estimate, five millions five hundred and forty-two thousand one hundred and seventy acres of waste land, for the sum of one million and thirty thousand four hundred and thirty-three dollars; leaving in the possession of the state, yet to be disposed of, about two millions of acres. Among the sales was one to Alexander Macomb, for three millions six hundred and thirty-five thousand two hundred acres. The magnitude of this sale, and the price at which it was sold, created a great excitement throughout the state, and at the session of the legislature which commenced on the 4th of January, 1792, the subject was brought before the assembly.

The price at which Mr. Macomb made his purchase was eight pence per acre, payable in five annual instalments, without interest, with permission to discount for prompt payment at six per cent. per annum, which made the price about equal to seven cents per acre cash. Colonel Burr, as attorney-general, was a member of the board. On the 9th of April, 1792, the report of the commissioners being the order of the day, the subject was taken up in the house. Mr. Talbot, from Montgomery county, moved sundry resolutions. They were intended as the foundation for an impeachment of a part of the commissioners of the land office. They assumed to contain a statement of facts, evidencing on the part of the commissioners great indiscretion and want of judgment, if not corruption, in the sale of the public lands, and they charged the commissioners with a wilful violation of the law. These resolutions, however, excepted Colonel Burr from any participation in the maleconduct complained of, inasmuch as the minutes of the board proved that he was not present at the meetings (being absent on official duty as attorney-general) when these contracts, so ruinous, as they alleged, to the interests of the state, were made: nor did it appear that he (Colonel Burr) was ever consulted in relation to them. These resolutions elicited a heated debate; in the progress of which all the commissioners, except the attorney-general, were assailed with great bitterness; and charges of corruption by innuendo

VOL. I.—T t

were unceremoniously made. At a late hour the house adjourned without decision until the next day.

On the 10th of April, 1792, Mr. Melancton Smith moved the following resolution, with a preamble as a substitute :—

" Resolved, That this house do highly approve of the conduct of the commissioners of the land office in the judicious sales by them, as aforesaid, which have been productive of the before mentioned beneficial effects."

This resolution was adopted by a vote of ays 35— noes 20.

Of Melancton Smith it is proper to remark here that he was a plain, unsophisticated man. A purer patriot never lived. Of the powers of his mind some opinion may be formed by the following anecdote. Dr. Ledyard, who was afterwards health officer of the port of New-York, was a warm federalist. He was at Poughkeepsie while the federal constitution was under discussion in the state convention. Smith was an anti-federal member of that body. Some time after the adoption of the constitution, Ledyard stated to a friend of his, that to Colonel Alexander Hamilton had been assigned, in a special manner, the duty of defending that portion of the constitution which related to the judiciary of the United States. That an outdoor conversation between Colonel Hamilton and Mr. Smith took place in relation to the judiciary, in the course of which Smith urged some of his objections to the proposed system. In the evening a federal caucus was held ; at that caucus Mr. Hamilton referred to the conversation, and requested that some gentleman might be designated to aid in the discussion of this question. Robert R. Livingston, chancellor of the state, was accordingly named. Mr. Livingston was at that time a distinguished leader in the ranks of the federal party. Whoever will take the trouble to read the debates in the Convention, in which will be found the reply of Smith to Livingston, will perceive in that reply the efforts of a mighty mind. It was a high but merited compliment to the talents of Melancton Smith, that such a man as Colonel Hamilton should have wished aid in opposing him.

During the winter of 1791–92, being Colonel Burr's first session in the Senate of the United States, he spent much of his leisure time in the state department. For several sessions after the organization of the federal government, all the business of the Senate was transacted with closed doors. At that period the correspondence of existing ministers was kept secret, even from the senators. With every thing connected with the foreign affairs of the country, Colonel Burr was exceedingly anxious to make himself intimately acquainted. He considered it necessary to the faithful and useful performance of his duty as a senator. He obtained permission from Mr. Jefferson, then secretary of state, to have access to the records of the department before the hour for opening the office arrived. He employed one of the messengers to make a fire at five o'clock in the morning, and occasionally an intelligent and confidential clerk to assist him in searching for papers. Here he was engaged until near ten o'clock every day. It was his constant practice to have his breakfast sent to him. He continued this employment the greater part of the session, making notes on, or extracts from, the records of the department, until he was interrupted by a peremptory order from the president (Washington) prohibiting his farther examination.

Wishing some information that he had not obtained in relation to a surrender of the western posts by the British, he addressed a note to the secretary of state, asking permission to make that particular examination; to which he received the following answer:—

"Thomas Jefferson presents his respectful compliments to Colonel Burr, and is sorry to inform him it has been concluded to be improper to communicate the correspondence of existing ministers. He hopes this will, with Colonel Burr, be his sufficient apology."

In April, 1792, there was an election for governor of the

State of New-York. By some it was supposed that Governor Clinton would decline being again considered a candidate. It was known that John Jay would be the candidate of the federal party. At that period Colonel Burr had warm personal friends in both parties, who were urging his pretensions. Among the most ardent was Judge Yates. In the latter part of February, 1792, he authorized his friends to state that he declined a nomination. He was placed, however, in an unpleasant dilemma. The connexions, and many of the personal friends of Governor Clinton, were jealous of Colonel Burr's talents and growing influence. Between the governor and himself there was very little intercourse. On the other hand, the kindest feelings towards him were evinced by Chief-justice Jay, who was a most amiable man. It was his wish, therefore, as far as practicable, consistent with his principles, to remain neuter. He had never been an electioneering character, and with the people he wished to leave the pending question, without the exercise of any influence he might be supposed to possess.

By the then existing laws of New-York, the ballots that were taken in the several counties were, immediately after the election, transmitted to the office of the secretary of state, and there kept until the second Tuesday in May, when the board of canvassers were, by law, to convene and canvass them. The election for governor was warmly contested; the federal party supporting Judge Jay, the anti-federal party George Clinton. When the canvassers met, difficulties arose as to the legality of the returns from certain counties, particularly of Otsego, Tioga, and Clinton. The canvassers differing in opinion on the question whether the ballots should be counted or destroyed, they agreed to ask the advice of Rufus King and Colonel Burr. These gentlemen conferred, and, like the canvassers, differed: whereupon Mr. Burr proposed that they should decline giving advice. To this Mr. King objected, and expressed a determination to give his own opinion separate. This rendered it necessary for Colonel Burr to adopt a like procedure. He thus became a partisan, and a most efficient partisan, in that controversy.

Seven of the canvassers determined to reject and destroy the ballots alleged to have been illegally returned. To this decision *four* objected. The ballots were accordingly destroyed, and George Clinton declared to be duly elected governor. The excitement produced was without a parallel in the state. The friends of Judge Jay contended that he had been chosen by the people, but was cheated out of his election by the corruption of the canvassers. Great asperity and virulence were exhibited by both political parties on the occasion.

From the moment that Colonel Burr was driven to interfere in the controversy, he took upon himself, almost exclusively, the management of the whole case on the side of the anti-federal party. His accustomed acumen, vigilance, and zeal, were promptly put in requisition. Full scope was allowed for the display of those great legal talents for which he was so pre-eminently distinguished. It has been known to only a very few individuals that on Colonel Burr rested nearly the whole labour; and that nothing was done, even by the canvassers, but under his advice and direction. It has therefore been deemed proper to insert here some of the official details of the case. They are worthy record, as an interesting part of the political history of the State of New-York.

" *Statement of the case by the Canvassers, for the advice of Rufus King and Aaron Burr.*

"OTSEGO.—By the 26th section of the constitution of the State of New-York, it is ordained that sheriffs and coroners be annually appointed, and that no person shall be capable of holding either of the said offices for more than four years successively, nor the sheriff of holding any other office at

the same time. By the ninth section of the act for regulating elections, it is enacted that one of the inspectors shall
deliver the ballots and poll-lists, sealed up, to the sheriff of
the county ; and, by the tenth section of the said act, it is
further enacted, that each and every sheriff of the respective counties in this state shall, upon receiving the said enclosures, directed to be delivered to him as aforesaid, with
out opening or inspecting the same, or any or either of
them, put the said enclosures, and every one of them, into
one box, which shall be well closed and sealed up by him,
under his hand and seal, with the name of his county written on the box, and be delivered by him into the office of
the secretary of this state, where the same shall be safely
kept by the secretary or his deputy. By the eleventh sec
tion of the said act, all questions arising on the canvass
and estimate of the votes, or on any of the proceedings
therein,' shall be determined by a majority of the members
of the joint committee attending; and their judgment shall
be final, and the oath of the canvassers requires them faithfully, honestly, and impartially to canvass and estimate
the votes contained in the boxes delivered into the office of
the secretary of this state by the sheriffs of the several
counties.

"On the 17th of February, 1791, Richard R. Smith was
appointed sheriff of the county of Otsego, and his commission gives him the custody of that county until the 18th of
February, 1792. On the 13th of January, 1792, he writes
a letter to the Council of Appointment, informing them that,
as the year for which he was appointed had nearly elapsed,
he should decline a reappointment.

"On the 30th of March, 1792, the Council of Appointment appointed Benjamin Gilbert to the office of sheriff of
the said county, with a commission, in the usual form, to
keep the county until the 17th of February next. His
commission was delivered to Stephen Van Rensselaer, Esq.,
on the 13th of April last, to be forwarded by him to the

said Benjamin Gilbert.   By the affidavit of the said Benjamin Gilbert, herewith delivered, it appears that he qualified into the office of sheriff on the 11th day of May, 1792. On the first Tuesday in April, 1792, Richard R. Smith was elected supervisor of the town of Otsego, in said county, and on the first Tuesday in May took his seat at the board of supervisors, and assisted in the appointment of loan officers for the county of Otsego.   By the affidavit of Richard R. Smith, herewith delivered, it appears that the ballots taken in the county of Otsego were delivered to him as sheriff, and by him enclosed in a sufficient box, on or about the 3d of May, which box he then delivered into the hands of Leonard Goes, a person specially deputed by him for the purpose of delivering the said box into the hands of the secretary of this state, which was accordingly done, as appears by information from the secretary.

"A small bundle of papers, enclosed and sealed, was delivered to the secretary with the box, on which is written, 'The votes of the town of Cherry Valley, in the county of Otsego.   Richard R. Smith, Sheriff.'   Several affidavits, herewith delivered, state certain facts respecting this separate bundle, said to be the votes of Cherry Valley.

"On this case arise the following questions :—

"1. Was Richard R. Smith the sheriff of the county of Otsego when he received and forwarded the ballots by his special deputy ?

"2. If he was not sheriff, can the votes sent by him be legally canvassed ?

"3. Can the joint committee canvass the votes when sent to them in two parcels, the one contained in a box, and the other contained in a paper, or separate bundle ?   Or,

"4. Ought they to canvass those sealed in the box, and reject the others?

"TIOGA.—It appears that the sheriff of Tioga delivered the box containing the ballots to B. Hovey, his special deputy, who set out, was taken sick on his journey, and delivered the box to H. Thompson, his clerk, who delivered it into the secretary's office.

" *Question.* Ought the votes of Tioga to be canvassed ?

" CLINTON.—It appears that the sheriff of Clinton delivered the box containing the ballots to Theodorus Platt, Esq., who had no deputation, but who delivered them into the secretary's office, as appears by his affidavit.

" *Question.* Ought the votes of Clinton to be canvassed ?"

Mr. King's opinion to the Canvassers.

" OTSEGO.—It may be inferred, from the constitution and laws of the state, that the office of sheriff is held during the pleasure of the Council of Appointment, subject to the limitation contained in the 26th section of the constitution. The sheriff may therefore hold his office for four years, unless within that period a successor shall have been appointed, and shall have entered upon the execution of the office. The term of four years from the appointment of R. R. Smith not having expired, and B. Gilbert not having entered upon the execution of the office before the receipt and delivery of the votes by R. R. Smith to his deputy. I am of opinion that R. R. Smith was then lawful sheriff of Otsego.

" This opinion is strengthened by what is understood to be practice, namely, that the office of sheriff is frequently held for more than a year under one appointment.

" R. R. Smith's giving notice to the Council of Appointment of his disinclination to be reappointed, or his acting as supervisor, cannot, in my opinion, be deemed a resignation or surrender of his office. ·

" Should doubts, however, be entertained whether R. R. Smith was *lawfully* sheriff when he received and delivered the votes to his deputy, the case contains facts which in another view of the subject are important. It appears that R. R. Smith was appointed sheriff of Otsego on the 17th of February, 1791, and afterwards entered upon the exe-

cution of his office : that no other person was in the execution of or claimed the office after the date of his appointment, and before the time when he received and delivered
the votes of the county to his deputy ; that during that interval R. R. Smith was sheriff, or the county was without a
sheriff; that R. R. Smith, during the election, and when he
received and delivered the votes to his deputy, continued in
the actual exercise of the shrievalty, and that under colour of
a regular appointment.   From this statement it may be inferred, that if R. R. Smith, when he received and delivered
the votes to his deputy, was not *de jure*, he was *de facto*,
sheriff of Otsego.

" Though all the acts of an officer *de facto* may not be
valid, and such of them as are merely voluntary and exclusively beneficial to himself are void ; yet such acts as tend
to the public utility, and such as he would be compellable
to perform, such as are essential to preserve the rights of
third persons, and without which they might be lost or
destroyed, when done by an officer *de facto*, are valid.

" I am therefore of opinion, that admitting R. R. Smith,
when he received and delivered the votes to his deputy, was
not *de jure* sheriff, yet that he was *de facto* sheriff ; and that
his receiving and delivering the votes being acts done under
colour of authority, tending to the public utility, and *necessary* to the carrying into effect the rights of suffrage of the
citizens of that county, they are and ought to be deemed
valid ; and consequently the votes of that county may lawfully be canvassed.

" 2d Question.   The preceding answer to the first question renders an answer to the second unnecessary.

" 3d and 4th Questions.   The sheriff is required to put
into one box every enclosure delivered to him by an inspector appointed for that purpose by the inspectors of any
town or district ; and for omitting to put any such enclosure
into the box, he is liable to prosecution ; but in case of such
omission, the votes put into the box, and seasonably deliv

ered into the secretary's office, may, notwithstanding such omission, be lawfully canvassed; and equally so whether the omitted enclosure be kept back or sent forward with the box to the secretary's office. I am therefore of opinion that the votes contained in the box may lawfully be canvassed; that those contained in a separate packet, from considerations explained in the depositions, and distinct from the objection of not being included within the box, cannot be law fully canvassed.

" CLINTON.—The deputy having no interest in the office of sheriff, but being merely the sheriff's servant, it does not seem to be necessary that the evidence of his being employed or made a deputy should be a deed or an instrument in writing, though the latter would be proper; yet a deputy may be made by *parole:* I am therefore inclined to the opinion that the votes of Clinton may be canvassed.

"TIOGA.—The sheriff is one who executes an office in person or by deputy, so far at least as the office is ministerial; when a deputy is required of the sheriff conomine, he may execute it in person or by deputy ; but if the deputy appoints a deputy, it may be doubtful whether ordinarily the acts of the last deputy are the acts of the sheriff. The present instance is an extreme case ; had the duty been capable of being performed within the county, the sheriff or another deputy could have performed. Here the deputy, being in the execution of his duty, and without the county, is prevented by the act of God from completing it; the sheriff could not appoint, and the deputy undertakes to appoint a deputy to finish his duty, who accordingly does so. The election law is intended to render effectual the constitutional right of suffrage ; it should therefore be construed liberally, and the means should be in subordination to the end.

" In this case it may be reasonably doubted whether the canvassers are obliged to reject the votes of Tioga.

"RUFUS KING."

Mr. Burr's opinion to the Canvassers.

" OTSEGO.—The duration of the office of sheriff in England having been limited by statute to one year, great inconveniences were experienced, as well by suiters as by the public. To remove which it was thought necessary to pass an act of parliament. The statute of 12 Ed. IV., ch. 1, recites at large these inconveniences, and authorizes the sheriff to execute and return writs in the term of St. Michael, before the delivery of a writ of discharge, notwithstanding the expiration of the year. The authority given by this statute being to execute only certain specified duties, the remedy was not complete, and another statute* was soon after passed, permitting sheriffs to do every act pertaining to the office, during the term of St. Michael and St. Hilary, after the expiration of the year, if not sooner discharged. The practice in England appears to have been conformable to these statutes,† though the king did pretend to dispense with them by force of the royal prerogative ; and this claim and exercise of a power in the crown to dispense with and control the operation of statutes, has been long and universally condemned as odious and unconstitutional ; yet the form of the commission is said still to be during pleasure.

" These considerations tend to show the principles of several opinions and adjudications, which are found in English law-books, relative to the holding over of the office of sheriff.

" None of the statutes of England or Great Britain continued to be laws of this state after the first of May, 1778. So that at present there remains no pretence for adopting any other than the obvious meaning of the constitution, which limits the duration of the office to one year, beyond which the authority to hold cannot be derived from the constitution,

---

* 17 Ed., ch. 7, more general.

† 2 Hawks., 5, 51, Irish oct. edit., 2 mod. 261 statute 1 Wm. and Mary, sess. 2, ch. 2. See also sec. 12 of the same statute.

the appointment, or the commission. If inconveniences arise, remedies can be provided by *law only*, as has in sim ilar cases been done in England, deciding on legal princi ples ; therefore, the appointment and commission, and with them the authority of Mr. Smith, must be deemed to have expired on the 18th of February.

" Yet there are instances of offices being exercised by persons holding under an authority apparently good, but which, on strict legal examination, proves defective ; whose acts, nevertheless, are, with *some limitations*, considered as valid. This authority is called *colourable*, and the officer in such cases is said to be an officer *de facto ;* which intends an intermediate state between an exercise strictly lawful and one without such colour of right. Mr. Smith does not ap- pear to me to have holden the office of sheriff on the 3d of May under such colour or pretence of right. The term of his office had expired, and he had formally expressed his determination not to accept a reappointment ; after the ex- piration of the year he accepted, and even two days before the receipt of the ballots, openly exercised an office incom- patible with that of sheriff ; and it is to be inferred, from the tenour of the affidavits, that he then knew of the appoint- ment of Mr. Gilbert. The assumption of this authority by Mr. Smith does not even appear to have been produced by any urgent public necessity or imminent public inconve- nience. Mr. Gilbert was qualified in season to have dis- charged the duty, and, for aught that is shown, his attend- ance, if really desired, might have been procured still earlier

" Upon all the circumstances of this case, I am of opin- ion,

" 1. That Mr. Smith was not sheriff of Otsego when he received and forwarded the ballots.

" 2d. That the ballots delivered by the deputy of Mr. Smith cannot be legally canvassed

" The direction of the law is positive, that the sheriff shall put all the enclosures into one box. How far his inattention or misconduct in this particular shall be deemed to vitiate the ballots of a county, appears to be left to the judgment of the canvassers. Were the ballots of this county subject to no other exception than that stated in the third and fourth questions, I should incline to think it one of those cases in which the discretion of the canvassers might be safely exercised, and that the ballots contained in the boxes might be legally canvassed; those in the separate package do not appear to be subject to such discretionary power; the law does not *permit* them to be estimated. But the extent to which this power might be exercised in cases similar in kind, but varying in degree, cannot be precisely defined. Instances may doubtless be supposed, in which sound discretion would require that the whole should be rejected.'

"CLINTON.—To the question relative to the ballots of this county, it may suffice to say, that verbal and written deputation by a sheriff are, in law, considered as of equal validity, particularly when it is to perform a single ministerial act.

"TIOGA.—It is said that a deputy may make a deputy to discharge certain duties merely ministerial; but, considering the importance of the trust in regard of the care of the ballots, and the extreme circumspection which is indicated in the law relative to elections, I think that the ballots of this county cannot, by any fiction or construction, be said to have been delivered *by the sheriff;* and am of opinion that they ought not to be canvassed.

"AARON BURR."

The opinion of Rufus King in this case was concurred in by Stephen Lush, T. V. W. Graham, and Abraham Van Vechten, of Albany; Richard Harrison, John Lawrence, John Cozine, Cornelius J. Bogart, Robert Troup, James M. Hughes, and Thomas Cooper, of New-York.

The opinion of Colonel Burr was sustained by Pierpont Edwards of Connecticut, Jonathan D. Sergeant, of Phila-

delphia, Edmund Randolph, of Virginia, United States attorney-general, Zephaniah Swift, Moses Cleaveland, Asher Miller, David Daggett, Nathaniel Smith, and Dudley Baldwin.
These opinions were procured by Colonel Burr, as appears
from the private correspondence on the subject.

FROM JONATHAN D. SERGEANT.

Philadelphia, 4th May, 1792.

DEAR SIR,

You will perceive by the date of the enclosed that it has
been ready some time, but I have waited in hopes that I
should have the pleasure of sending forward Mr. Randolph's
opinion in company with mine. As he is not yet quite
ready, and I am going out of town, I send forward my own
singly. He is very solicitous to collect all possible information on the subject before he gives his opinion, and would
willingly excuse himself from the task, were it not, as he
says, that it would look like a want of that independence
and firmness which dispose a man to meet any question,
however important or strongly contended.

His opinion hitherto has been conformable to yours, and
I expect will continue so. When it is ready I will forward
it without the delay of sending it round to Dr. Edwards's
in the country. The doctor had spoken to me some time
before your letter came to me, so that I was nearly prepared
when I received yours.

Your obedient servant,

JONATHAN D. SERGEANT.

On the 6th of November, 1792, the legislature met. On
the 13th, petitions, memorials, &c. were presented to the
House of Assembly, demanding an inquiry into the conduct
of the board appointed to canvass the votes given for governor, &c. at the preceding election, held in the month of
April. On the 21st the house, in committee of the whole,
took up the subject. Witnesses were examined at the bar ;

various resolutions and modifications were offered and rejected. The debate was continued at intervals from the
21st of November, 1792, until the 18th of July, 1793. The
minority of the canvassers entered a protest against the
proceedings of the majority, which it is due to them to insert here.

" *The Protest of Messrs. Jones, Roosevelt, and Gansevoort.*

" We, the subscribers, members of the joint committee
appointed to canvass and estimate the votes taken at the last
election in this state for governor, lieutenant-governor, and
senators, do dissent from, and protest against, the determination of the major part of said committee respecting the
votes taken at the said election in the county of Otsego.

" I. Because these votes having been given by the freeholders of Otsego, and the packages containing the same having
been received and transmitted in season to the secretary's
office by the person acting as sheriff of the county, the committee have no right to reject them under the pretence of
judging of the legality, validity, operation, or extent of the
sheriff's authority or commission ; these commissions being
foreign to the duty of their appointment, and capable of a
decision only in the ordinary courts of law.

" II. Because, if the committee were by law authorized to
examine and determine the legality and extent of the sheriff's
authority and commission, we are of opinion that Richard
R. Smith, at the time he received and transmitted the ballots, was the lawful sheriff of Otsego. By the constitution,
the sheriff, whatever may be the form of his commission,
must hold his office during the pleasure of the Council of
Appointment; and, by the law of the land, he must continue
therein until another is appointed and takes upon himself the
office. Richard R. Smith, having been appointed on the
27th of February, 1791, and Benjamin Gilbert having been
appointed on the 30th of March, 1792, but not having qualified or taken upon himself the office until Richard R.

Smith had received and forwarded the same, must be deemed the lawful sheriff of the county. The uniform practice which has prevailed since the establishment of the constitution, precludes all doubt respecting its true construction on this point. For although the commissions of the sheriffs are for one year, they have nevertheless continued to exercise the office until others were appointed and entered upon the execution thereof, which has often been long after the expiration of the year, and sometimes after the same person has remained in office more than four years successively. And such sheriffs, sometimes after the expiration of their year, at others after having held the office for four successive years, have received and transmitted ballots for governor, lieutenant-governor, and senators, which ballots have on former elections been received and canvassed; and even upon the present canvass, the committee have canvassed the ballots taken in the counties of Kings, Orange, and Washington, notwithstanding the year had expired for which the sheriffs of these counties were commissioned, and no new commissions had been issued. Hence the sheriffs of those counties, in receiving and transmitting the ballots, must have acted under their former commissions, since a mere appointment without a commission, and a compliance with the requisites prescribed by law, could not, in our opinion, give any authority as sheriff to the person so appointed.

"III. Because, if Richard R. Smith, at the time he received and forwarded the ballots, was not sheriff, the county was without a sheriff, a position too mischievous to be established by a doubtful construction of law.

"IV. Because, if Richard R. Smith was not of right sheriff of the county at the time he received and forwarded the ballots, he was then sheriff in fact of that county; and all the acts of such an officer which tend to the public utility, or to preserve and render effectual the rights of third persons, are valid in law.

"V. Because, in all doubtful cases, the committee ought,

in our opinion, to decide in favour of the votes given by the citizens, lest by too nice and critical an exposition of the law the rights of suffrage be rendered nugatory.

"We also dissent from, and protest against, the determination of the major part of the said committee respecting the votes taken at the said election in the county of Clinton:

"Because it appears that the sheriff of the said county deputed a person by parole to deliver the box containing the ballots of the said county into the secretary's office. Such deputation we deem to be sufficient; and as there is satisfactory evidence that the box was delivered in the same state in which it was received from the sheriff, the votes, in our opinion, ought to be canvassed.

"We also dissent from, and protest against, the determination of the major part of the said committee, by which they declare that George Clinton was, by the greatest number of votes taken at the last election for governor, lieutenant-governor, and senators, chosen governor of this state; and that Pierre Van Courtlandt was, by the greatest number of votes at the said election, chosen lieutenant-governor; and that John Livingston was, by the greatest number of votes at the said election, in the eastern district of this state, chosen a senator in the said eastern district.

"Because it cannot be ascertained whether George Clinton was chosen governor, or Pierre Van Courtlandt lieutenant-governor of this state, by the greatest number of votes at the last election, without examining the ballots contained in the boxes delivered into the secretary's office by the sheriffs of the counties of Otsego and Clinton—there being a sufficient number of freeholders in these counties, with the votes given in the other parts of the state for John Jay as governor and Stephen Van Rensselaer as lieutenant-governor, to give them a majority of votes for those offices. Nor can it be ascertained whether John Livingston was chosen a senator in the eastern district by the greatest number of votes in that district, without examining the votes taken in the county of Clinton—there being a sufficient number of freeholders in that county, with the votes given in other parts of the district for Thomas Jenkins as a senator, to give him a greater number of votes for a senator than the number given for the said John Livingston.

" SAMUEL JONES,
" ISAAC ROOSEVELT,
" LEONARD GANSEVOORT."

Joshua Sands, another member of the board of canvassers, entered separately a protest, but substantially the same as the preceding.

The majority of the canvassers presented a document to the legislature, in which they assigned their reasons for the course they had pursued. That document was drawn by Colonel Burr. The original draught, with his emendations, has been preserved among his papers. On the motion of a member, it was read in the house the 28th day of December, 1792, and is entered at large on their journals as follows :—

" *The reasons assigned by the majority of the Canvassers in vindication of their conduct.*

" The joint committee appointed to canvass and estimate the votes for governor, lieutenant-governor, and senators at the last election, having been constrained, by a sense of their duty in the discharge of the trust reposed in them, to reject the ballots returned from the counties of Clinton, Otsego, and Tioga ; and perceiving that attempts are made to misrepresent as well the principles of their determination as the facts on which they are founded, feel it incumbent on them to state the grounds of their decision.

" CLINTON AND TIOGA.—A box, said to contain the ballots of the county of Clinton, was deposited in the secretary's office by a Theodore Platt, without any deputation or other authority, accompanied only by his own affidavit, that he had received the said box from the sheriff of Clinton.

Another box, said to contain the ballots of the county of
Tioga, was delivered by the sheriff of the county of Tioga
to his deputy, Benjamin Hovey, who, being detained by illness on the road, delivered the said box to one James H.
Thompson, by whom it was deposited in the secretary's office.

" The joint committee, pursuant to the law, are sworn to
canvass the votes ' contained in the boxes delivered into the
office of the secretary of the state by the sheriffs of the
several counties.' .Hence arose a question, whether this
was not a *personal trust*, which could not be legally performed by deputy ?   Upon this point we entertained different opinions ; but agreed that, if the discretion of the committee was to be in any degree controlled by the directions
of the law, there appeared no room to doubt of the illegality
of canvassing boxes which were not delivered by a sheriff
or the deputy of a sheriff.   The ballots contained in these
boxes were therefore rejected; not, however, without sensible regret, as no suspicion was entertained of the fairness
of those elections

" OTSEGO.—It appears that Richard R. Smith, on the
17th of February, 1791, was appointed sheriff of the county
of Otsego, to hold that office until the 18th of February,
1792 ; that a commission was issued agreeably to that appointment; that on the 13th of January, 1792, he wrote to
the governor and council that he should decline a reappointment ; that on the 30th of March, 1792, Benjamin Gilbert
was appointed sheriff of the said county ; that the commission to the said Benjamin Gilbert was, on the 13th of April,
1792, delivered to Stephen Van Rensselaer, one of the
Council of Appointment, to be by him forwarded ; that the
said commission was in the hands of William Cooper, Esq.,
first judge of the said county, on or before the 3d of May ;
that the said Richard R. Smith, on the first Tuesday in
April, was elected supervisor of the town of Otsego, accepted that office, and on the 1st day of May took his seat

at the board of supervisors, assisted in the appointment of loan officers, and *then* declared that he was no longer sheriff of the county, but that Benjamin Gilbert was appointed in his place. It also appeared that Benjamin Gilbert had no notice of his said appointment, or of the receiving of the ballots by the said Richard R. Smith, until the 9th day of May, and that he was sworn to the execution of the office on the 11th; that, on the 3d of May, the said Richard R. Smith put up the ballots of the said county in the store of the said William Cooper, Esq., in whose hands the commission of Benjamin Gilbert then was; that the box said to contain the votes of the said county was delivered into the secretary's office by Leonard Goes previous to the last Tuesday in May, under a deputation from the said Richard R. Smith; together with the said box, and at the same time, the said Leonard Goes delivered a separate packet or enclosure, which, by an endorsement thereon, purported to contain ' the ballots received from the town of Cherry Valley, in the county of Otsego.'

" The manner of the delivery of the said box and enclosure, and the authority of the said Leonard Goes, were reported to the committee by the secretary of the state.

" These votes were not canvassed for the following reasons :—

" 1. The committee found themselves bound, by their oath and by the directions of the law before mentioned, to canvass only the votes contained in the boxes which may have been delivered into the secretary's office by the *sheriffs* of the several counties. It appeared to them absurd to suppose this duty should be so expressly enjoined, and that they should nevertheless be prohibited from inquiring whether the boxes were or were not delivered by such officers; or that they should be restrained from ascertaining a fact, without the knowledge of which it was impossible that they could discharge the duty with certainty to the public or with confidence to themselves. They could not persuade them-

selves that they were, under *that* law and *that* oath, com
pelled to canvass and estimate votes, however fraudulently
obtained, which should be delivered into the secretary's office by *any person styling* himself sheriff, though it should
at the same time be evident to them that he was *not the
sheriff.* If such was to be their conduct, a provision intended as a security against impositions would be an engine
to promote them. They conceived, therefore, that the objection to an inquiry so important, and in a case where the
question was raised and the inquiry imposed upon them by
the suggestions of the secretary, must have arisen from
gross misrepresentation or wilful error.

"Upon investigating the right of the said Richard R.
Smith to exercise that office, the facts appeared as herein-
before stated.

"2. The constitution requires that sheriffs shall *be annu
ally appointed;* which, to our apprehension, implies that nc
person shall exercise the office by virtue of any other than
an *annual* appointment. And should it even be admitted
that the council may, at *their pleasure,* remove a sheriff
within the year, yet we do not see on what ground it can
be denied that the duration of the office is limited to one
year, unless a new appointment should take place. It would
otherwise be true that the council could indirectly, or by a
criminal omission, accomplish what is not within their direct
or legal authority. It will be readily admitted that an appointment and commission for three years would be void;
and surely the pretence of one thus claiming should be preferred to a usurpation without even such appearance of
right, and against the known right of another. To assert,
therefore, that 'by the constitution the sheriff, whatever may
be the form of his commission, must hold his office during
the pleasure of the Council of Appointment; and that, by the
law of the land, he must continue therein until another is
appointed and has taken upon himself the office,' is an as-
sertion accompanied with no proof or reason, and is repug-

nant to the letter and spirit of the constitution, which is eminently *the law of the land.* The practice which has prevailed since the revolution, as far as hath come to our
knowledge, does not warrant the position; neither could
mere practice, if such had prevailed, justify the adoption of
a principle contrary to the obvious meaning of the constitution. Upon the present occasion we have not canvassed the
votes of any county which were not returned by a sheriff
holding his office under an appointment unexpired. The
sheriffs of Kings, Orange, and Washington had all been reappointed within the present year, which satisfied the words
of the constitution, and was the *known* and avowed reason
which influenced the committee to estimate the ballots of
those counties. The doctrine concerning the constitutional
pleasure of the council in the appointment of the office of
sheriffs *had not then been invented.*

"3. But even admitting the visionary idea that the office
of sheriff (*whose duration is limited by the constitution*)
can nevertheless be holden *during the pleasure* of the
Council of Appointment, yet that appears to have been de
termined by the letter of the appointment and commission,
by the appointment of Benjamin Gilbert, by the declaration
of Richard R. Smith, and by his acceptance and exercise
of another office, which is, by the constitution, declared to
be incompatible with the office of sheriff.

"It was evident, therefore, that Richard R. Smith had
no authority by appointment, by commission, by the constitution, or by any law, to hold or exercise the office of
sheriff on the third of May.

"4. As Richard R. Smith was not legally or constitu-
tionally sheriff on the third of May, neither, under the circumstances of the case, can he be said to have been sheriff
in fact, so as to render his acts valid in contemplation of
law: the assumption of power by Mr. Smith appears to
have been warranted by no pretence or colour of right.
The time limited for the duration of his office had expired

by the express tenure of his commission and appointment, and he had formally declared his determination not to accept a reappointment. He had, two days previous to his receiving the ballots, openly exercised an office incompatible with that of sheriff; then declared that he had resigned the office of sheriff, and that Benjamin Gilbert was appointed in his place; and by an affidavit which was produced to the committee, it appeared that, upon the day upon which he had put up the ballots in the house of the said William Cooper, he, the said Richard R. Smith, declared that he had resigned the office of sheriff. The business might with equal care and certainty have been executed by Benjamin Gilbert. The single act of receiving ballots could of itself continue *no man* a sheriff—least of all *a man disavowing that office, and then in the exercise of another.* It was foreign to the duty of the committee to provide against evils which may possibly arise from casual vacancies in the office of sheriff by death and otherwise. Vacancies will sometimes unavoidably happen, without further legislative provision.

" There is not, therefore, in our opinion, any application to the subject, or force in the objection, ' that if Richard R. Smith was not sheriff, the county was without a sheriff;' neither is the position true in fact, for it appears that the county was not then without a sheriff. At the time the ballots were received, it was well known that Benjamin Gilbert was appointed sheriff, and that his commission was in the hands of *William Cooper, in whose store Richard R. Smith put up the ballots.* It is also to be fairly inferred that, had proper measures been taken to give notice to Mr. Gilbert, he would forthwith have qualified and undertaken the execution of the office. It cannot, therefore, consistent with truth or candour, be asserted that there was the remotest probability that ' mischiefs' could in any parallel case ensue from the principles adopted by the committee.

" It did not seem possible, therefore, by any principle of

law, by any latitude of construction, to canvass and estimate the ballots contained in the box thus circumstanced.

"But, had the question been doubtful, it was attended
by other circumstances, which would have determined the
committee against canvassing those ballots. '

"5. Because the notice of the appointment of Benjamin
Gilbert was received by Richard R. Smith on or before
the first of May, and his commission was received by William Cooper on or before the third of May. Mr. Gilbert
might therefore have been notified, qualified, and executed the duty. He did actually qualify on the eleventh,
which gave ample time to have forwarded the ballots before the last Tuesday in May. These facts, with other
suggestions of unfair practices, rendered the conduct of the
Otsego election justly liable to suspicion; and the committee were constrained to conclude that the usurpation of
authority by Richard R. Smith was wanton and unnecessary, and proceeded from no motive connected with the preservation of the rights of the people or the freedom and
purity of elections.

"6. Because, having in several instances, by _unanimous
vote,_ rejected ballots of whole towns, free from any suspicion of unfairness, by reason of a defect in _form only_ of
the return, the committee conceived themselves the more
strongly bound to reject ballots where the defect was substantial, and the conduct at least questionable; especially
as the law regards the custody of enclosures containing the
ballots as a trust of high importance, and contemplates but
three persons in whose hands they are to be confided until
they come to the possession of the canvassers, to wit, the
inspector, the sheriff, and the secretary; all officers of
great responsibility and confidence.

"7. Because the return, upon the face of it, appeared to
be illegal. The law requires the sheriff, 'upon receiving
the said enclosure, directed to be delivered to him as aforesaid, without opening or inspecting the same, or any or

either of them, to put the said enclosures, and *every one of them, into one box*, which shall be well closed, &c., and be delivered by him, without opening the same, or the enclosures therein contained, into the office of the secretary of this state before the last Tuesday in May in every year.'

"By recurring to the preceding state of facts it will be evident that this direction of the law had been disregarded. If irregularities of this kind should be permitted and countenanced, it would be in the power of the sheriff, by excluding a part of the votes, to confer a majority on any candidate, in counties where there were divisions of interests. Affidavits were indeed produced tending to show that there had been, in that town, disputes respecting the election of town officers; that two enclosures, purporting to contain the votes of the town, were delivered to Mr. Smith, and that he had put into the box that enclosure which contained the votes taken by the persons whom *he judged* to be the legal inspectors : a matter proper to have been submitted to the opinion of the committee.

" The committee have considered this subject with deliberate attention, and in every light in which it could be placed; and whether they regarded the channels of conveyance, the mode of the return, or the general principles which ought to govern their decisions touching the freedom of elections and security against frauds, they found undeniable reasons which compelled them to reject the votes.

" David Gelston,
" Thomas Tillotson
" Daniel Graham,
" Melancton Smith,
" David M'Carty,
" P. V. Courtlandt, jun.,
" Jonathan N. Havens."

On the 18th of January, 1793, the House of Assembly passed the following resolutions on the subject. " Thereupon, *Re-*

solved, That the mode of prosecuting any joint committee of
the Senate and Assembly, appointed for the purpose of can
vassing and estimating the votes taken in this state for governor, lieutenant-governor, and senators, and the penalties to
be inflicted on such committee, or any of them, for any improper conduct in the execution of the trust reposed in them
by law, are clearly pointed out in the twentieth and twenty-
first sections of the act for regulating elections, passed the
13th day of February, one thousand seven hundred and
eighty-seven ; and that, therefore, any person or persons who
may suppose that any such joint committee, or any of them
have conducted themselves improperly in the execution of
the trust reposed in them, may prosecute the same to effect
in the ordinary course of law.

" *Resolved,* That notwithstanding this provision in the act
for regulating elections, this house hath gone into an inquiry with respect to the conduct of the late committee appointed to canvass and estimate the votes for governor,
lieutenant-governor, and senators, taken at the last general
election held in this state, *to the intent* that satisfaction may
be given those citizens of the state who have been dissatisfied with the decision of the major part of the said committee, with respect to the votes taken in the counties of Otsego, Tioga, and Clinton.

" *Resolved,* That after a full and fair examination into the
conduct of the major part of the said canvassing committee,
it does not appear to this house that the said major part
of the committee, to wit : David Gelston, Thomas Tillotson,
Daniel Graham, Melancton Smith, David M'Carty, Pierre
Van Courtlandt, junior, and Jonathan N. Havens, have been
guilty of any mal or corrupt conduct in the execution of the
trust reposed in them by law.

" And whereas, by the eleventh section of the act for regulating elections, it is enacted that all questions which shall
arise upon any canvass and estimate, or upon any of the
proceedings therein, shall be determined according to the

opinion of the major part of the said canvassing committee, and that their judgment and determination shall in all cases be binding and conclusive; therefore,

" *Resolved*, As the sense of this house, that the legislature cannot annul or make void any of the determinations of the said committee."

The question was taken on the preceding resolutions together, by yeas and nays, and passed in the affirmative. Ays 35.   Nays 22.

Among the individuals for whom Colonel Burr entertained a high degree of respect, was Jacob De Lamater, Esq., of Marbletown.   Between these gentlemen, for several years, a friendly, and, in some instances, a confidential correspondence existed.   Mr. De Lamater was a federalist, but personally attached to Colonel Burr.   In 1792 he was among those who wished him to become a candidate for the office of governor.   After the death of De Lamater, the letters addressed to him by Colonel Burr were returned.   They were written under the sacred seal of friendship; but they contain not a sentence, not a word, that is not alike honourable to his head and his heart.   One is selected and here published as explanatory of his *feelings* and his *conduct* in the contested election (which so much agitated the State of New-York) between George Clinton and John Jay.   It requires no comment.

TO MR. DE LAMATER.

New-York, 15th June, 1792.

MY DEAR SIR,

You will, before this can reach you, have heard of the event of the late election.   Some questions having arisen among the canvassers respecting the returns from Clinton, Otsego, and Tioga, they requested the advice of Mr. King and myself.   We conferred, and, unfortunately, differed; particularly as to the questions upon the Otsego return.   I therefore proposed that we should decline giving any opinion, being for my own part much averse to interfere in the business. Mr. King, however, determined to give his separate opinion, from what motives you may judge. This laid me under the necessity of giving mine also, which I did. If I can procure copies of both opinions, and of the protest of the minority, and the reasons assigned by the majority of the canvassers, I will send them herewith. They will enable you to form a competent judgment of the law question, and of the fairness of the Otsego return.

I do not see how any unbiased man can doubt, but still I do not pretend to control the opinion of others, much less to take offence at any man for differing from me. The reasons contained in my opinion, and assigned by the majority of the canvassers, have never been answered except by abuse. I can, in a personal interview, inform you of some circumstances relative to the opinions which have been procured in favour of the Otsego votes.

I have heard with much pride and pleasure of the warm and disinterested manner in which I was espoused by some respectable characters in your county. I shall never fail to recollect it with sensibility and gratitude. It would therefore give me real pain to believe that any part of my conduct had tended to thwart their wishes. If it has had any such effect, it should at least be remembered that I did not seek to gratify any wish or interest of my own. I took no part in the election. I never gave to any person the most distant intimation that I supposed you engaged to support Mr. Clinton, or to take any other part than that which your inclinations and judgment should direct. I felt no disposition to influence your conduct on that occasion. Had I been so inclined, I have no doubt but I could, in various parts of the state, have essentially injured Mr. Jay's interest; but I made no attempt of the kind. Yet I shall never yield up the right of expressing my opinions. I have never exacted that tribute from another.

. Upon the late occasion, indeed, I earnestly wished and

sought to be relieved from the necessity of giving any opinion, particularly from a knowledge that it would be disagreeable to you and a few others whom I respect and wish always to gratify. But the conduct of Mr. King left me no alternative. I was obliged to give an opinion, and I have not yet learned to give any other than which my judgment directs.

It would, indeed, be the extreme of weakness in me to expect friendship from Mr. Clinton. I have too many reasons to believe that he regards me with jealousy and malevolence. Still, this alone ought not to have induced me to refuse my advice to the canvassers. Some pretend, indeed, but none can believe, that I am prejudiced in his favour. I have not even seen or spoken to him since January last.

I wish to merit the flattering things you say of my talents; but your expressions of esteem and regard are still more flattering, and these, I am sure, I shall never fail to merit, if the warmest friendship and unalterable attachment can give me a claim.

Will you be abroad any, and what part of the summer? I ask, because I propose to make you a visit on my way to, or return from, Albany, and wish to be certain of finding you at home. No political changes can ever diminish the pleasure with which I subscribe myself

Your affectionate friend,
A. BURR.

The following letter is evidence of Colonel Burr's propensity to correspond in cipher with his most intimate friends, even on unimportant topics. Hundreds of the same character might be given.

TO JACOB DE LAMATER.

New-York, October 30th, 1792

DEAR SIR,

Your letter by Mr. Addison was particularly kind, after my long *supposed* silence. We may make use of *both keys or ciphers*, and if some of the persons or things are designated by different characters, no inconvenience will arise ; if there should, we will correct it..

V is to be the candidate, as my former letter will have told you. He has the wishes of 9 for his success, for reasons which will be obvious to you. Do you think that 8 would be induced from any motive to vote for him ?

Yours affectionately,

A. BURR.

CHAPTER XVII.

ON the 2d of October, 1792, Governor Clinton nominated Colonel Burr to the Council of Appointment as Judge of the Supreme Court of the state, which nomination was immediately confirmed. Thus, within the short space of about three years, he was appointed by the democratic party to the several important stations of Attorney-General, Senator of the United States, and Judge of the Supreme Court. The last appointment was made without consulting Mr. Burr. As soon as he was notified of the fact, he informed the governor of his non-acceptance ; yet so anxious was his excellency, and so strong were his hopes that Colonel Burr might be induced to withdraw his resignation, that he refused to lay it before the council until the legislature, on the 7th of December, adopted the following resolution —

" Whereas it appears to the legislature, by the records of

the Council of Appointment, that Aaron Burr, Esq., one of the senators for this state in the Senate of the United States, was, on the 2d day of October last, appointed one of the puisne justices of the Supreme Court of Judicature of this state: Thereupon,

"*Resolved* (if the honourable the Senate concur herein), That his excellency the governor be and hereby is requested to inform the legislature whether the said Aaron Burr hath accepted or refused the said office."

On the 24th of October, 1791, Congress convened, and Colonel Burr took his seat in the Senate of the United States. In those days it was the practice of the president, accompanied by the heads of departments, to proceed to Congress Hall for the purpose of meeting the two branches of the national legislature, and opening the session with a speech, to which a response was made by each body separately. On the 25th the president made his annual communication; whereupon the Senate "*Ordered*, That Messrs. Burr, Cabot, and Johnston be a committee to prepare and report the draught of an address to the President of the United States, in answer to his speech, delivered this day to both houses of Congress in the Senate Chamber."

The next day Colonel Burr, as chairman of the committee, draughted and reported an answer, which was adopted by the Senate without alteration or amendment: an occurrence, it is believed, that happened in only two other instances during the period that speeches were delivered by the executive. After the election of Mr. Jefferson the system of sending messages was substituted.

The journals of the Senate afford ample evidence that Colonel Burr was an industrious and efficient member of that body. During the first session of his term of service he was placed on numerous committees, some of them important, and generally as chairman. His business habits soon became evident, and were called into operation. His character for firmness was well established before he took his seat in the Senate ; but on the 9th of January, 1794, it was displayed with effect. In consequence of a difference between the two houses, a bill to increase the standing army was lost.

Mr. King, of New-York, by consent, introduced a new bill ; it was entitled " An act for the more effectual protection of the southwestern frontier settlers." Unsuccessful efforts were made by Colonel Burr and others to amend it, by striking out some of its most odious features; but there was a decided majority, as it was known to be an administration measure, determined on carrying it through. The bill was ordered to be engrossed for a third reading, and the question on its passage was to be taken on the last day of the session. By the rules of the Senate, the question could not be put if any member objected. Colonel Burr objected, and the bill was thus defeated.

Notwithstanding his public engagements, Colonel Burr's mind was constantly employed with the education of his daughter. Mrs. Burr's health was gradually declining, insomuch that she was unable, at times, to attend to her domestic concerns. This to him was a source of unceasing care and apprehension. His letters to his daughter are numerous. They are frequently playful, always interesting, displaying the solicitude of an affectionate father anxious for the improvement of his child.

TO MRS. BURR.

Philadelphia, 18th January, 1793.

By the enclosed to Mr. Gurney,* I have requested him to write me a letter respecting the health of the family, and Theo.'s improvement. Request him to enclose, on a separate sheet, some columns of figures, pounds, shillings, and pence. I shall show the letter and enclosure as a specimen of his talents to some persons to whom I wish to

---

* Theodosia's preceptor.

recommend him. Beg him to use no uncommon word or expression. He will pardon this piece of advice when he recollects that I know so much better than he does what will suit the persons to whom it is to be shown. If he should offer his letter for your perusal before he sends it, remark freely ; it will be a kindness of which no one is so capable.

Should this come to hand after he has given his lesson on Saturday, send him his letter, and request him to call on you, if you should be able to bear five minutes conversation with him.

I wrote you yesterday, and have nothing to add respecting myself ; and only a repetition of my prayers for you, with my most affectionate and anxious wishes.

A. Burr.

TO MRS. BURR.

Philadelphia, 8th February, 1793.

You may recollect that I left a memorandum of what Theo. was to learn. I hope it has been strictly attended to. Desire Gurney not to attempt to teach her any thing about the " concords." I will show him how I choose that should be done when I return, which, I thank God, is but three weeks distant.

It is eight days since I left home, and I have not a word from any one of the family, nor even about any one of them. I have been out but once, half an hour at Mrs. P.'s, a concert ; but I call often at Mrs. L.'s. I am more and more struck with the native good sense of one of that family, and more and more disgusted with the manner in which it is obscured and perverted : cursed effects of fashionable education ! of which both sexes are the advocates, and yours eminently the victims. If I could foresee that Theo. would become a *mere* fashionable woman, with all the attendant frivolity and vacuity of mind, adorned with whatever grace and allurement, I would earnestly pray God to

take her forthwith hence. But I yet hope, by her, to convince the world what neither sex appear to believe—that
women have souls!

Most affectionately yours,

A. Burr.

TO MRS. BURR.

Philadelphia, 15th February, 1793.

I received with joy and astonishment, on entering the
Senate this minute, your two elegant and affectionate letters. The mail closes in a few minutes, and will scarce
allow me to acknowledge your goodness. The roads and
ferries have been for some days almost impassable, so that
till now no post has arrived since Monday.

It was a knowledge of your mind which first inspired me
with a respect for that of your sex, and with some regret, I
confess, that the ideas which you have often heard me express in favour of female intellectual powers are founded
on what I have imagined, more than what I have seen; except in you. I have endeavoured to trace the causes of this
rare display of genius in women, and find them in the errors
of education, of prejudice, and of habit. I admit that men
are equally, nay more, much more to blame than women.
Boys and girls are generally educated much in the same
way till they are eight or nine years of age, and it is admitted that girls make at least equal progress with the boys ;
generally, indeed, they make better. Why, then, has it
never been thought worth the attempt to discover, by fair
experiment, the particular age at which the male superiority
becomes so evident ? But this is not in answer to your letter ; neither is it possible now to answer it. Some parts
of it I shall never answer. Your allusions to departed angels I think in bad taste.

I do not like Theo.'s indolence, or the apologies which
are made for it. Have my directions been pursued with
regard to her Latin and geography ?

Your plan and embellishment of my mode of life are fanciful, are flattering, and inviting. We will endeavour to realize some of it. Pray continue to write, if you can do it with impunity. I bless Sir J., who, with the assistance of Heaven, has thus far restored you.

In the course of this scrawl I have been several times called to vote, which must apologize to you for its incoherence. Adieu.   A. BURR.

TO MRS. BURR.

Philadelphia, 16th February, 1793.

A line of recollection will, I am sure, be more acceptable than silence. I consider myself as largely in your debt, and shall of necessity remain so.

You have heard me speak of a Miss·Woolstonecraft, who has written something on the French revolution; she has also written a book entitled " Vindication of the rights of Woman." I had heard it spoken of with a coldness little calculated to excite attention; but as I read with avidity and prepossession every thing written by a lady, I made haste to procure it, and spent the last night, almost the whole of it, in reading it. Be assured that your sex has in *her* an able advocate. It is, in my opinion, a work of genius. She has successfully adopted the style of Rousseau's Emilius; and her comment on that work, especially what relates to female education, contains more good sense than all the other criticisms upon him which I have seen put together. I promise myself much pleasure in reading it to you.

Is it owing to ignorance or prejudice that I have not yet met a single person who had discovered or would allow the merit of this work?

Three mails are in arrear; that of Tuesday is the last which has arrived. I am impatient to know how writing agrees with you. Pray let me hear, from day to day, the progress of your cure.

Most affectionately yours,

A. BURR.

Philadelphia, 18th February, 1793.

Just what I apprehended, I find, has taken place. Three
sheets were too much for a first attempt. It will, I fear,
discourage you, if not disable you from more moderate experiments. Yet I will hope to receive by this day's mail at
least one line, announcing your progressive recovery, under
your own hand.

Be assured that, after what you have written, I shall not
send for Gurney. Deliver him the enclosed. I hope it
may animate his attention; and tell him, if you think proper,
that I shall be much dissatisfied if Theo.'s progress in Latin
be not very considerable at my return. Geography has, I
hope, been abandoned, for he has no talent at teaching it.

The close of a session being always crowded with business, keeps me much engaged. You must expect short letters—mere notes. Adieu.

A. BURR.

TO HIS DAUGHTER THEODOSIA.
Philadelphia, 20th February, 1793.

At length, my dear Theo., I have received your letter of
the 20th of January—written, you see, a month ago. But
I observe that it was not put into the postoffice until the
day before yesterday. I suppose Frederick or Bartow had
carelessly put it in some place where it had lain forgotten.
It would indeed have been a pity that such a letter should
have been lost. There is something in the style and arrangement of the words which would have done honour to a
girl of sixteen.

All three of the Miss A.s will visit New-York next summer, and pass some weeks there. I hope to be at home in
ten or twelve days from this time. Let me receive one or
two more letters from you, even if you are obliged to neglect a lesson to find time to write them.

Alexis* often bids me to send you some polite and respectful message on his part, which I have heretofore omitted. He is a faithful, good boy. Upon our return home he
hopes you will teach him to read.

I am, my dear Theo.,

Your affectionate papa,

A. BURR.

TO HIS DAUGHTER THEODOSIA.

Philadelphia, 24th February, 1793.

MY DEAR THEO.,

In looking over a list made yesterday (and now before
me), of letters of consequence to be answered immediately,
I find the name of T. B. Burr. At the time I made the
memorandum I did not advert to the compliment I paid you
by putting your name in a list with some of the most eminent persons in the United States. So true is it that your
letters are really of consequence to *me*. I now allude to
that of the 19th instant, covering a fable and riddle. If the
whole performance was your own, which I am inclined to
hope and believe, it indicates an improvement in style, in
knowledge of the French, and in your handwriting. I have
therefore not only read it several times, but shown it to several persons with pride and pleasure.

I confess myself unable to solve your riddle, unless the
teeth or the *alphabet* (generally supposed to be twenty-four
in each) will give the solution. But I have not yet had an
opportunity to consult Miss P. A. To-morrow I shall call
on her for the purpose, and will not fail to inform you of her
conjectures on the subject.

Your affectionate papa,

A. BURR.

* A coloured boy.

Philadelphia, 16th December, 1793.

I have a thousand questions to ask, my dear Theo., but nothing to communicate; and thus I fear it will be throughout the winter, for my time is consumed in the dull uniformity of study and attendance in Senate; but every hour of *your* day is interesting to *me*. I would give, what would I not give to see or know even your most trifling actions and amusements? This, however, is more than I can ask or expect. But I do expect with impatience your journal. Ten minutes every evening I demand; if you should choose to make it twenty, I shall be the better pleased. You are to note the occurrences of the day as concisely as you can; and, at your pleasure, to add any short reflections or remarks that may arise. On the other leaf I give you a sample of the manner of your journal for one day.

18th December.

I began this letter at the date which you see, being Monday last—was interrupted, and the mail closed. Yesterday I was confined with a severe headache, owing, I believe, to a change from an active to a sedentary life without a corresponding change in diet.

A week and more has elapsed since I left home, and not a line from you; not even the Sunday letter. Observe, that the journal is to be sent to me enclosed in a letter every Monday morning.

Plan of the Journal.

16th December, 1793.

Learned 230 lines, which finished Horace. Heigh-ho for Terence and the Greek grammar to-morrow.

Practised two hours less thirty-five minutes, which I begged off.

Hewlett (dancing-master) did not come.

Began Gibbon last evening. I find he requires as much study and attention as Horace; so I shall not rank the reading of *him* among amusements.

Skated an hour; fell twenty times, and find the advantage of a hard head and .

Ma better—dined with us at table, and is still sitting up and free from pain.

Your affectionate papa,
A. BURR.

TO MRS. BURR.

Philadelphia, 24th December, 1793.

Since being at this place I have had several conversations with Dr. Rush respecting your distressing illness, and I have reason to believe that he has given the subject some reflection. He has this evening called on me, and given me as his advice that you should take hemlock. He says that, in the way in which it is usually prepared, you should commence with a dose of one tenth of a grain, and increase as you may find you can bear it; that it has the narcotic powers of opium, superadded to other qualities. When the dose is too great, it may be discovered by a vertigo or giddiness; and that he has known it to work wonderful cures. I was the more pleased with this advice, as I had not told him that you had been in the use of this medicine; the concurrence of his opinion gives me great faith in it. God grant that it may restore your health, and to your affectionate

A. BURR.

TO HIS DAUGHTER THEODOSIA.

Philadelphia, 25th December, 1793.

The letter, my dear Theo., which (I have no doubt) you wrote me last Sunday, has not yet come to hand. Am I to blame Strong? or the postmaster? or whom?

When you have finished a letter, read it carefully over, and correct all the errors you can discover. In your last there were some which could not, upon an attentive perusal, have escaped your notice, as you shall see when we meet.

I have asked you a great many questions, to which I have as yet no answers. When you *sit* down to write to me, or when you *set* about it, be it sitting or standing, peruse a'' my letters, and leave nothing unanswered. Adieu.

. A. BURR.

TO HIS DAUGHTER THEODOSIA.

Philadelphia, 31st December, 1793.

I received your letter and journal yesterday in the Senate Chamber, just before the closing of the mail, so that I had only time to acknowledge it by a hasty line. You see I never let your letters remain a day unanswered, in which I wish you would imitate me. Your last had no date ; from the last date in the journal, and your writing about Christmas holydays as yet at some distance, I suppose you wrote about Sunday the 22d. Nine days ago! I beg you again to read over all my letters, and to let me see by your answers that you attend to them. I suspect your last journal was not written from day to day ; but all on one, or at most two days, from memory. How is this ? Ten or fifteen minutes every evening would not be an unreasonable sacrifice from *you* to *me*. If you took the Christmas holydays, I assent : if you did not, we cannot recall the time. This is all the answer which that part of your letter now admits of.

It is said that some few yet die of the yellow fever which lately raged here ; but the disorder does not appear to be, *at present*, in any degree contagious; what *may* be the case upon the return of warm weather, is a subject of anxious conjecture and apprehension. It is probable that the session of Congress will continue into the summer.

Give a place to your mamma's health in your journal. Omit the formal conclusion of your letters, and write your name in a larger hand. I am just going to Senate, where I hope to meet a letter from you, with a continuation of your journal down to the 29th inclusive, which, if it gives a good account of you and mamma, will gladden the heart of

A BURR.

TO HIS DAUGHTER THEODOSIA.

Philadelphia, 31st December, 1793.

This day's mail has brought me nothing from you. I have but two letters in three, almost four weeks, and the journal is ten days in arrear. What—can neither affection nor civility induce you to devote to me the small portion of time which I have required? Are authority and compulsion then the only engines by which you can be moved? For shame, Theo.! Do not give me reason to think so ill of you.

I wrote you this morning, and have nothing to add but the repetition of my warmest affection. ·

A. BURR.

TO HIS DAUGHTER THEODOSIA.

Philadelphia, 4th January, 1794.

At the moment of closing the mail yesterday, I received your letter enclosing the pills. I cannot refer to it by date, as it has none. Tell me truly, did you write it without assistance? Is the language and spelling your own? If so, it does you much honour. The subject of it obliged me to show it to Dr. Rush, which I did with great pride. He inquired your age half a dozen times, and paid some handsome compliments to the handwriting, the style, and the correctness of your letter.

The account of your mamma's health distresses me extremely. If she does not get better soon, I will quit Congress altogether and go home. Doctor Rush says that the pills contain two grains each of pure and fresh extract of hemlock; that the dose is not too large if the stomach and head can bear it; that he has known twenty grains given at a dose with good effect. To determine, however, whether this medicine has any agency in causing the sick stomach, he thinks it would be well to take an occasion of omitting it for a day or two, if Doctor Bard should approve of such an experiment, and entertains any doubts about the effects of the pills on the stomach.   Some further conversation which I have had with Doctor Rush will be contained in a letter which I shall write by this post to Doctor Bard.

My last letter to you was almost an angry one, at which you cannot be much surprised when you recollect the length of time of your silence, and that you are my only corre- spondent respecting the concerns of the family.   I expect, on Monday or Tuesday next, to receive the continuation of your journal for *the fortnight past.*

Mr. Leshlie will tell you that I have given directions for your commencing Greek.   One half hour faithfully applied by yourself at study, and another at recitation with Mr. Leshlie, will suffice to advance you rapidly.

Your affectionate,

A. BURR.

TO HIS DAUGHTER THEODOSIA.

Philadelphia, 7th January, 1794.

When your letters are written with tolerable spirit and correctness, I read them two or three times before I per- ceive any fault in them, being wholly engaged with the pleasure they afford me ; but, for your sake, it is necessary that I should also peruse them with an eye of criticism.   The following are the only mispelled words.   You write *acurate* for *accurate ; laudnam* for *laudanum; intirely* for *entirely ;* this last word, indeed, is spelled both ways, but *entirely* is the most usual and the most proper.

Continue to use all these words in your next letter, that I may see that you know the true spelling.   And tell me what is laudanum ? Where and how made ? And what are its effects ?

——" It was what she had long wished for, and was at a loss how to procure *it.*"

Don't you see that this sentence would have been perfect and much more elegant without the last *it?* Mr. Leshlie will explain to you why. By-the-by, I took the liberty to erase the redundant *it* before I showed the letter.

I am extremely impatient for your farther account of mamma's health. The necessity of laudanum twice a day is a very disagreeable and alarming circumstance. Your letter was written a week ago, since which I have no account. I am just going to the Senate Chamber, where I hope to meet a journal and letter. Affectionately,

A. BURR.

TO HIS DAUGHTER THEODOSIA.

Philadelphia, 8th January, 1794

Your two letters of Friday and Saturday came together by yesterday's mail, which did not arrive till near sunset. Your letter of Friday was not put into the postoffice until Saturday afternoon. You might have as well kept it in your own hands till Monday eleven o'clock. Since the receipt of these letters I have been three times to Doctor Rush to consult him about a drink for your mamma; but not having had the good fortune to find him, have written to him on the subject. I shall undoubtedly procure an answer in the course of this day, and will forward it by to-morrow's post.

I beg, Miss Prissy, that you will be pleased to name a single "*unsuccessful effort*" which you have made to please me. As to the letters and journals which you *did* write, surely you have reason abundant to believe that they gave me pleasure; and how the deuse I am to be pleased with those you *did not* write, and how an omission to write can be called an " *effort,*" remains for your ingenuity to disclose.

You improve much in journalizing. Your last is far more sprightly than any of the preceding. Fifty-six lines sola was, I admit, *an effort* worthy of yourself, and which I hope will be often repeated. But pray, when you have got up to two hundred lines a lesson, why do you go back again to one hundred and twenty, and one hundred and twenty-five? You should strive never to diminish; but I suppose that *vis inertiæ*, which is often so troublesome to you, does sometimes preponderate. So it is now and then even with your

A. BURR.

Learn the difference between *then* and *than*. You will soonest perceive it by translating them into Latin.

Let me see how handsomely you can subscribe your name to your next letter, about this size,

A. BURR.

TO HIS DAUGHTER THEODOSIA.

Philadelphia, 10th of January, 1794.

I fear that you will imagine that I have been inattentive to your last request about Dr. Rush; but the truth is, I can get nothing satisfactory out of him. He enumerates over to me all the articles which have been repeatedly tried, and some of which did never agree with your mamma. He is, however, particularly desirous that she should again try milk —a spoonful only at a time: another attempt, he thinks, should be made with porter, in some shape or other. Sweet oil, molasses, and milk, in equal proportions, he has known to agree with stomachs which had rejected every thing else. Yet he says, and with show of reason, that these things depend so much on the taste, the habits of life, the peculiarity of constitution, that she and her attending physician can be the best, if not the only advisers. It gives me very great pleasure to learn that she is now better. I shall write you again on Sunday, having always much to say to you. Adieu.

A. BURR.

Philadelphia, 13th January, 1794.

Your letter of the 9th, my dear Theo., was a most agreeable surprise to me. I had not dared even to hope for one until to-morrow. In one instance, at least, an attempt to please me has not been " unsuccessful." You see I do not forget that piece of impudence.

Doctor Rush says that he cannot conceive animal food to be particularly necessary ; nourishment is the great object. He approves much of the milk punch and chocolate. The stomach must on no account be offended. The intermission of the pills for a few days (not however for a whole week) he thinks not amiss to aid in determining its effects. The quantity may yet be increased without danger, but the present dose is in his opinion sufficient; but after some days continual use, a small increase might be useful.

I was yesterday thronged with company from eight in the morning till eleven at night. The Greek signature, though a little mistaken, was not lost upon me. I have a letter from Mr. Leshlie, which pays you many compliments. He has also ventured to promise that you will every day get a lesson in Terence by yourself. You know how grateful this will be to

A. BURR.

TO THEODOSIA.

Philadelphia, 14th January, 1794.

. I really think, my dear Theo., that you will be very soon beyond all verbal criticism, and that my whole attention will be presently directed to the improvement of your style. Your letter of the 9th is remarkably correct in point of spelling. That word recieved still escapes your attention. Try again. The words *wold* and *shold* are mere carelessness ; necessery instead of necessary, belongs, I suspect to the same class.

"Dr. B. called here, but did not speak of his having recieved a letter from you, but desired," &c.

When I copied the foregoing, I intended to have shown you how to improve it; but, upon second thought, determine to leave it to yourself. Do me the favour to *endorse* it on, or *subjoin* it to, your next letter, corrected and *varied* according to the best of your skill.

"Ma begs you will omit the thoughts of leaving Congress," &c.; "omit" is improperly used here. You mean "*abandon, relinquish, renounce,* or *abjure* the thoughts," &c. Your mamma, Mr. Leshlie, or your dictionary (Johnson's folio), will teach you the force of this observation. The last of these words would have been too strong for the occasion.

You have used with *propriety* the words "encomium" and "adopted." I hope you may have frequent occasion for the former, with the like application.

"Cannot be committed to paper," is well expressed.

A. BURR.

TO THEODOSIA.

Philadelphia, 16th January, 1794.

I hope the mercury, if tried, will be used with the most vigilant caution and the most attentive observation of its first effects. I am extremely anxious and apprehensive about the event of such an experiment.

I fear, my dear little girl, that my letter of the 13th imposed too much upon you; if so, dispense with what you may find too troublesome. You perceive by this license the entire confidence which I place in your discretion. .

Your journal still advances towards perfection. But the letter which accompanied it is, I remark with regret, rather a falling off. I have received none more carelessly written, or with more numerous omissions of words. I am sensible that many apologies are at hand; but you, perhaps, would not be sensible that any were necessary, if I should omit to remind you.

On Sunday se'nnight (I think the 26th) I shall, unless baffled or delayed by ice or weather, be with you at Richmond Hill. I will not bid you adieu till the Friday preceding. In the interim, we shall often in this way converse.

I continue the practice of scoring words for our mutual improvement. The use, as applicable to you, was indicated in a former letter.

I am sure you will be charmed with the Greek language above all others. Adieu.

A. BURR.

TO THEODOSIA.

Philadelphia, 23d January, 1794.

Io, triumphe! There is not a word mispelled either in your journal or letter, which cannot be said of a single page you ever before wrote. The fable is quite classical, and, if not very much corrected by Mr. Leshlie, is truly a surprising performance, and written most beautifully. But what has become of poor Alpha Beta? Discouraged? That is impossible. Laid aside for the present? That, indeed, is possible, but by no means probable. Shall I guess again? Yes; you mean to surprise me with some astonishing progress. And yet, to confess the truth, your lessons in Terence, Exercises, and "music" (without a k, observe) seem to leave little time for any other study. I must remain in suspense for four days longer.

Doctor Rush thinks that bark would not be amiss, but may be beneficial if the stomach does not rebuke it, which must be constantly the first object of attention. He recommends either the cold infusion or substance as least likely to offend the stomach.

Be able, upon my arrival, to tell me the difference between an *infusion* and *decoction;* and the history, the virtues, and the *botanical* or medical name of the bark. Chambers will tell you more perhaps than you will wish to read of it. Your little mercurial disquisition is ingenious, and prettily told.

I have a most dreary prospect of weather and roads for my journey. I set off on Saturday morning, and much fear that it will take two or three days to get to New-York.

              A. BURR.

TO THEODOSIA.

           Philadelphia, 13th February, 1794.

I received your letter and enclosures yesterday in Senate. I stopped reading the letter, and took up the story in the place you directed; was really affected by the interesting little tale, faithfully believing it to have been taken from the Mag. D'Enf., and was astonished and delighted when I recurred to the letter and found the little deception you had played upon me. It is concisely and handsomely told, and is indeed a performance above your years.

Mr. Leshlie is not, I am afraid, a competent judge of what you are capable of learning; you must convince him that you can, when you set in earnest about it, accomplish wonders. ·

Do you mean that the forty lines which you construed in Virgil were in a part you had not before learned?

I despair of getting genuine Tent wine in this city. There never was a bottle of real unadulterated Tent imported here for sale. Mr. Jefferson, who had some for his own use, has left town. Good Burgundy and Muscat, mixed in equal parts, make a better Tent than can be bought. But by Bartow's return you shall have what I can get— sooner if I find a conveyance.

Bartow is the most perfect gossip I ever knew: though, I must say, it is the kind of life I have advised him to while he stays here. Adieu.

              A. BURR.

TO THEODOSIA.

Philadelphia, 7th March, 1794.

Your letter of the 4th was three days on the road. I am certain that I have answered punctually all which have come to hand. True, I have not written to you as frequently as during the first few weeks of my residence here. For the last month I have been very much occupied by public business. You will need no other proof of it when I tell you that near twenty unanswered letters are now on my desk, not one of yours among them, however, except that received last evening. I have not even been to the theatre except about an hour, and then it was more an errand of business than amusement.

Poor Tom,* I hope you take good care of him. If he is confined by his leg, &c., he must pay the greater attention to his reading and writing.·

I shall run off to see you about Sunday or Monday; but the roads are so extremely bad that I expect to be three days getting through. I will bring with me the cherry sweetmeats, and something for *Augusta Louisa Matilda Theodosia Van Horne.* I believe I have not recollected all her names.

Affectionately,

A. BURR.

TO THEODOSIA.

Philadelphia, 31st March, 1794.

I am distressed at your loss of time. I do not, indeed, wholly blame you for it, but this does not diminish my regret. When you want punctuality in your letters, I am sure you want it in every thing; for you will constantly observe that you have the most leisure when you do the most business. Negligence of one's duty produces a self-

---

* A coloured man, the slave of Colonel Burr.

dissatisfaction which unfits the mind for every thing, and
ennui and peevishness are the never-failing consequences.
You will readily discover the truth of these remarks by
reflecting on your own conduct, and the different feelings
which have flowed from a persevering attention to study,
or a restless neglect of it.

I shall in a few days (this week) send you a most beautiful assortment of flower-seeds and flowering shrubs.

If I do not receive a letter from you to-morrow, I shall
be out of all patience. Every day's journal will, I hope,
say something of mamma.

A. BURR.

TO THEODOSIA.

Philadelphia, 7th June, 1794.

I have received my dear Theo.'s two little, very little,
French letters. The last left you tormented with headache
and toothache, too much for one poor little girl to suffer at
one time, I am sure : you had doubtless taken some sudden cold. You must fight them as well as you can till I
come, and then I will engage to keep them at bay.

I remark that you do not acknowledge the receipt of a
long letter which I wrote you on the road the night after
I left New-York. I hope it has not missed you ; but it is
needless now to ask about it, for I shall certainly see you
before I could receive your answer to this.

Whatever you shall translate of Terence, I beg you to
have copied in a book in a very fair handwriting.

A. BURR.

TO THEODOSIA.

Albany, 4th August, 1794.

MY DEAR THEO.,

We arrived here yesterday, after a hot, tedious passage
of *seven days*. We were delayed as well by accidents as
by calms and contrary winds. The first evening, being

under full sail, we ran ashore at Tappan, and lay there
aground, in a very uncomfortable situation, twenty-four
hours. With great labour and fatigue we got off on the
following night, and had scarce got under sail before we
missed our longboat. We lost the whole tide in hunting
for it, and so lay till the morning of Wednesday. Having
then made sail again, with a pretty strong head wind, at the
very first tack the Dutch horse fell overboard. The poor
devil was at the time tied about the neck with a rope, so
that he seemed to have only the alternatives of hanging or
drowning (for the river is here about four miles wide, and
the water was very rough); fortunately for him, the rope
broke, and he went souse into the water. His weight
sunk him so deep that we were at least fifty yards from
him before he came up. He snorted off the water, and
turning round once or twice, as if to see where he was,
then recollecting the way to New-York, he immediately
swam off down the river with all force. We fitted out our
longboat in pursuit of him, and at length drove him on
shore on the Westchester side, where I hired a man to
take him to Frederick's. All this delayed us nearly a
whole tide more. The residue of the voyage was without accident, except such as you may picture to yourself in
a small cabin, with seven men, seven women, and two cry-
ing children—two of the women being the most splenetic,
ill-humoured animals you can imagine.

On my arrival here I was delighted to receive your letter of the 30th, with the journal of that and the preceding
days. Your history of those three days is very full and
satisfactory, and has induced me, by way of return, to enlarge
on the particulars of my journey. I am quite gratified that
you have secured Mrs. Penn's (observe how it is spelled)
good opinion, and content with your reasons for not saying
the civil things you intended. In case you should dine in
company with her, I will apprize you of one circumstance,
by a trifling attention to which you may elevate yourself in

her esteem. She is a great advocate for a very plain, rather abstemious diet in children, as you may see by her conduct with Miss Elizabeth. Be careful, therefore, to eat of but one dish; that a plain roast or boiled: little or no gravy or butter, and *very sparingly* of dessert or fruit: not more than half a glass of wine; and if more of any thing to eat or drink is offered, decline it. If they ask a reason—*Papa thinks it not good for me*, is the best that can be given.

It was with great pain and reluctance that I made this journey without you. But your manners are not yet quite sufficiently formed to enable you to do justice to your own character,* and the expectations which are formed of you, or to my wishes. Improve, therefore, to the utmost the present opportunity; inquire of every point of behaviour about which you are embarrassed; imitate as much as you can the manners of Madame De S., and observe also every thing which Mrs. Penn says and does.

You should direct your own breakfast. Send Cesar every morning for a pint of milk for you; and, to save trouble to Madame De S., let her know that you eat at breakfast only bread and butter.

I wish you would read over your letters after you have written them; for so many words are omitted, that in some places I cannot make out the sense, *if any they contain*. Make your figures or ciphers in your letters, but write out the numbers at length, except dates.

. Adieu, affectionately adieu,

A. BURR.

TO THEODOSIA.
Albany, 14th August, 1794.

My dear Theo.,

Last evening's mail brought me your letter and journal from the 1st to the 11th of August, according to your dates, which, however, are wrong.

* Theodosia had now entered her *twelfth* year.

The account of your time is very satisfactory. You really get along much better than I expected, which is infinitely to the credit of your good sense, that being your only guide. From the attentions you receive from Mrs. Penn and her family, I judge you have been so fortunate as to gain her esteem, and that her prejudices are turned into prepossessions, which I assure you gratified me not a little.

Your invitation to the Z.'s was, I confess, a very embarrassing dilemma, and one from which it was not easy to extricate yourself. For the future, take it as your rule to visit only the families which you have known me to visit; and if Madame De S. should propose to you to visit any other, you may tell her what are my instructions on the subject. To the young ladies, you may pretend business or engagements : avoid, however, giving any offence to your companions. It is the manner of a refusal, much more than the refusal, which gives offence. This direction about your visits applies only to the citizens or English families. You may, indeed it is my wish, that you should visit with Madame De S. all her French acquaintance.

I go this afternoon to attend a court at Ballston, and shall, on Monday, attend one at Troy, which will probably last about three days; after which I shall take passage for New-York, proposing, however, to pass a day at Kingston, and another at Poughkeepsie, with citizen Hauterieve, so that I may be expected home some time in the week after next; but you will hear often from me before that time. You must not send me any letter after those which will come by the mail leaving New-York on Monday next; yet you must continue your letters and journal as usual, for my amusement on my return.

In future, write no more on the little paper, but let the letters and journal be together on paper of this size, or common letter-paper. Set apart every day half an hour or an hour to write to me, and I must again entreat you to write at least legibly: after great pains, I am wholly unable to decipher some of the hieroglyphics contained in your last.

Four pages in Lucian was a great lesson; and whv, my dear Theo., can't this be done a little oftener? You must, by this time, I think, have gone through Lucian. I wish you to begin and go through it again; for it would be shameful to pretend to have read a book of which you could not construe a page. At the second reading you will, I suppose, be able to double your lessons; so that you may go through it in three weeks. You say nothing of writing or learning Greek verbs;—is this practice discontinued? and why?

I wish you to go oftener to the house. You may, if you like, go any morning, to take an early breakfast there, giving notice the day before to Mr. Leshlie, that he may attend at the hour of your return, when I know you can readily make up the lost time.

Do you continue to preserve Madame De S.'s good opinion of your talents for the harp? And do you find that you converse with more facility in the French? These are interesting questions, and your answer to this will, I hope, answer fully all the questions it contains. Vale, vale.

A. BURR

TO THEODOSIA.

Albany, 16th August, 1794.

Another post has arrived, and brought me no letter from you. It is the last omission which I shall readily pardon, and this only in consideration of your not having then received my last. I returned this day from Ballston, and my principal business to this city was to receive and answer your letters. Judge, therefore, of my disappointment.

Mr. and Mrs. Witbeck made many inquiries about you, and appeared much mortified that you did not accompany me.

I hope you will, before this can reach you, have answer-

ed J. Yates's letter.   Once more I place my expectations on
the arrival of the next post.

Let me know whether Mrs. Penn has left town, how often
you have been with her, and what passed.   I need not repeat my anxiety to know how you and Madame de S. agree,
and what progress you make in music, dancing, and speaking French.   She promised to give you now and then a lesson on the forte-piano ; is she as good as her word ?

Having failed in your promise to write by every post, you
cannot expect me to return within the month—one promise
being founded on the other.

Your affectionate papa, .

.   A. BURR.

TO THEODOSIA.

Albany, 18th August, 1794.

Yesterday I received your letter and journal to the 13th
inclusive.   On the 13th you say you got nine pages in Lucian.   It was, to be sure, a most surprising lesson.   I suspect it must have been the second time going over ; and
even then it would have been great, and at the same rate
you will be through a second time before my month is up.
I should be delighted to find it so.   I have not told you directly that I should stay longer than a month, but I was angry enough with you to stay three months when you neglected to write to me for two successive posts.

I am very sorry to see so many blank days with Mr.
Leshlie.   If he is not at your room within a quarter of an
hour of his time, Cesar should be forthwith sent off express
for him.   Let Cesar, therefore, call on you every morning
at the hour Mr. Leshlie ought to come.

I left New-York on the 28th of July.   My month, there
fore, will expire on the 28th of August, so that you cannot
complain until that day is past.   The court at Troy will
probably detain me the whole of this week, which is three
days longer than I expected.

I long to hear what you contributed towards Madame de S.'s *jour de fete.* No letter yet for John Yates. Why do you delay it so long? You have had several leisure days; for this delay there should be some apology in your letter.

Affectionately your papa,

A. BURR.

TO THEODOSIA.

Troy, 21st August, 1794.

MY DEAR THEO., . . .

I sent Alexis in the rain to Albany for your letter of the 18th and journal, which he has just brought me. Your letters are my only consolation during this afflicting absence— for it is to me a real affliction. I have forborne to express to you my impatience, lest it should increase yours.

The business I have undertaken here will, contrary to all expectation, detain me till Saturday night. I hope to be on my return on Monday, when you must begin to pray for northerly winds; or, if you have learned, to say mass, that the French Roman Catholics rely on to procure them all earthly and spiritual blessings. By-the-by, if you have not been to the Roman chapel, I insist that you go next Sunday, if you are not engaged in some other party.

I am very happy to receive a letter for John Yates. I shall send it to him to-day; it is very handsome, and will please him much. I will indeed return with all possible speed. Continue your journal. Adieu.

A. BURR.

TO THEODOSIA.

Philadelphia, 21st December, 1794.

I obeyed faithfully the command in your letter which bade me read the journal first, and I read it with great eagerness, hoping to find what I did find in the last sentence. That 16th was really a surprising day. Three hundred and ninety-five lines, all your exercises, and all your music. Go on, my dear girl, and you will become all that I wish.

I keep carefully your letters and journals, and when we meet you shall read them again, which I am sure you will do with pleasure. It is always delightful to see and correct our own errors.

· Monsieur Maupertuis is highly mortified that you should suppose him so ignorant as to have lost himself on the road. It seems he only went a little off the highway *from curiosity to see the country.*

I hope you like Terence. Can't you lug a scrap from him now and then, apropos, into your letters? It will please

Your affectionate papa,

A. BURR.

TO THEODOSIA IN PHILADELPHIA.

New-York, 5th January, 1795.

You see me safe arrived in New-York. I have passed but one hour at Richmond Hill. It seems solitary and undesirable without you. They are all well, and much, very much disappointed that you did not come with me.

Pray write to Mrs. A., if but one line; she expects and deserves it. I was there last evening for the first time. Your picture is really like you ; still it does not quite please me. It has a *pensive, sentimental* air ; that of a love-sick maid! Stewart has probably meant to anticipate what you may be at sixteen; but even in that I think he has missed it.

Bartow has grown immensely fat. Mrs. A. has recovered and walks about. There has been a serious attempt to institute masquerade. It has not succeeded, nor is it yet abandoned.

We (you and I) have both neglected one duty of civility. Some weeks ago Mrs. Jackson was polite enough to call on you, with Miss Jackson and Miss Brown, who left you cards. You have never returned the visit. I beg you to do it without delay. Doctor Edwards will probably make time to go with you for a few minutes. It is at Doctor Jackson's in Third-street, between High and Arch.

Our house in Partition-street is very neatly finished, and pleases me much; so much that I propose to inhabit it upon our return from Philadelphia, at least until the hot weather.

You are now in the arms of Somnus, or ought to be; for though I date my letter the 5th, it is in truth about half past eleven at night of the 4th. So wants half an hour of the 5th. Dream on. *Salutem.*

.   A. BURR.

.

.   .

TO THEODOSIA.
Bristol, 14th September, 1795.

Saturday night I lodged at Elizabethtown, and, after two wettings, dined on Sunday with General Freelinghuysen. Madame (late Miss Yard) asked much after you, as did Maria, the general's daughter. The family is a picture of cheerfulness and happiness. At Princeton (to-day) I met Le Mercier, who is well, except a broken scull, a face disfigured, and some bruises about the ribs—considerable deductions, you will say, from the "corpore sano." They are the effects of a very huge beating bestowed on him (gratis) by two gentlemen of the town. He had some difference with one of them, who had challenged him, which Le Mercier refused, not being a Christian-like and clerical way of settling differences. So the challenger, with a friend (for L. M. could have thrashed him singly), took an opportunity to catch poor Le Mercier alone, and discussed the subject with him in the manner above stated. .   .

Your friends Miss Stockton and Miss Smith said some civil things about you, and send abundance of love, which I promised them I would forget to deliver.

My journey thus far has been wonderfully fortunate, having only overset once and broken down once, which, considering that I am seventy miles on my route, is, for me, a very small list of grievances;· but I shall count it full measure if

I am prevented from entering Philadelphia to-morrow, which is a little to be apprehended.

You must pay off Meance and Hewlet for their attendance on you and Natalie.* They must be paid regularly at the end of each month. I forgôt it. Get their accounts, and give them an order on Strong for the amount. When either of you want money, Roger Strong will furnish it. Pray settle also your account with Madame Senat, and write me that these things are done.

Tell Mr. Martel that I request that all the time he can spare you be devoted to Latin; that I have provided you with a teacher of French, that no part of his attention might be taken off. I will send from Philadelphia the certificate he requested, which escaped my memory while at New-York.

I fear it will puzzle you all to decipher this. You may show to Mr. Martel the clause which relates to him. Salutem, chère Theodosia.

A. BURR.

TO THEODOSIA.

Philadelphia, 17th September, 1795.

By this post I received a letter from Colonel Ward, requesting leave to remove his family into my house, Richmond Hill. He lives, you may recollect, in the part of the town which is said to be sickly. I could not therefore refuse. He will call on you to go out with him. You had better, immediately on receipt of this, go out yourself, and apprize Anthony and Peggy.

Your letter to Kersaint is much to the purpose. It came by this day's mail, though put in the postoffice on Tuesday, but after the closing of the mail. With it I have also re-

* Natalie De Lage was the daughter of a French lady, who was once a member of the family of the Princess L'Arnbaul. Natalie was adopted and educated by Colonel Burr as his child. She married the son of General Sumter, of South Carolina.

ceived your letter, written, I suppose, on Tuesday evening, because it speaks of the circus; but, as usual, without date. I beg that, when you sit down to write a letter, you will be gin by putting a date at the top; this will then presently become a habit, and will never be omitted.

I am sorry, very sorry that you are obliged to submit to some reproof. Indeed, I fear that your want of attention and politeness, and your awkward postures, require it. As you appear desirous to get rid of these bad habits, I hope you will soon afford no room for ill-nature itself to find fault with you—I mean in these particulars; for as to what regards your heart and your motives of action, I know them to be good, amiable, and pure. But to return to the subject of manners, &c. I have often seen Madame at table, and other situations, pay you the utmost attention; offer you twenty civilities, while you appeared scarcely sensible that she was speaking to you; or, at the most, replied with a cold *remercie*, without even a look of satisfaction or complacency. A moment's reflection will convince you that this conduct will be naturally construed into arrogance; as if you thought that all attention was *due* to you, and as if you felt above showing the least to anybody. I know that you abhor such sentiments, and that you are incapable of being actuated by them. Yet you expose yourself to the censure without intending or knowing it. I believe you will in future avoid it. Observe how Natalie replies to the smallest civility which is offered to her.

Your habit of stooping and bringing your shoulders forward on to your breast not only disfigures you, but is alarming on account of the injury to your health. The continuance in this vile habit will certainly produce a consumption: then farewell papa; farewell pleasure; farewell life! This is no exaggeration; no fiction to excite your apprehensions. But, setting aside this distressing consideration, I am astonished that you have no more pride in your appearance. You will certainly stint your growth and disfigure your person.

Receive with calmness every reproof, whether made kindly or unkindly; whether just or unjust. Consider within yourself whether there has been no cause for it. If it has been groundless and unjust, nevertheless bear it with composure, and even with complacency. Remember that one in the situation of Madame has a thousand things to fret the temper; and you know that one out of humour, for any cause whatever, is apt to vent it on every person that happens to be in the way. We must learn to bear these things; and, let me tell you, that you will always feel much better, much happier, for having borne with serenity the spleen of any one, than if you had returned spleen for spleen.

You will, I am sure, my dear Theodosia, pardon two such grave pages from one who loves you, and whose happiness depends very much on yours. Read it over twice Make me no promises on the subject. On my return, I shall see in half an hour whether what I have written has been well or ill received. If well, it will have produced an effect.

I have sent Alexis with your letter to Kersaint while I write this. After closing of the mail I shall present myself. To-morrow morning I take stage for Baltimore; thence to Washington, &c. You shall certainly hear often from me. You have not yet acknowledged the receipt of my letter from Bristol. R. Strong has received his, written at the same time. Having many letters to answer by this mail, I cannot add any thing sprightly to this dull letter. One dull thing you will hear me repeat without disgust, that

I am your affectionate friend,

A. BURR

TO THEODOSIA.

City of Washington, 23d September, 1795.

I write from the house of our friends, Law and Duncanson, where I make my home. Miss Duncanson, who is mistress of the house, is a very sprightly, sensible, ladylike woman. My remarks on this city are reserved till we meet.

Your letter of the 17th, and one without date (I suppose the 18th), came in this evening. They contain more wit and sprightliness than you ever wrote in the same compass, and have amused me exceedingly. But why do you diminish their value by carelessness? There is an omission of one or more words in almost every sentence. At least I entreat you to read over your letters before you seal them : some clauses are absolutely unintelligible, though in several I can guess what word you intended.·

Why are you still in town? I am very much dissatisfied with it; for Mr. Strong writes me that the fever is in Parti tion-street. I beg you to go off with a good parcel of books to Frederick's.

I told Madame Senat that I should want the two front rooms in Partition-street, and the very small room which adjoins the smallest of the front rooms; and surely she will have room enough without it. Try to arrange this so; that is, by asking her if she cannot spare that room (the large front). Mr. Strong writes me that she is taking possession of it. In that case my papers will be moved, which will be very disagreeable to me.

I fix the 24th of October for my return; if any very extraordinary thing should detain me, you shall be advised of it seasonably. Direct to me at the city of Washington until the 10th of October. Tell R. Strong the same. I forgot to write it to him.

When you go on any party from Pelham, to Brown's Mrs. Cox's, &c., your studies may be intermitted. At least as much of them as may be necessary. I am tired, and half sick; a great cold, for which I shall lie by here to-morrow.   Thine,

                                        A. BURR.

TO THEODOSIA.

City of Washington, 26th September, 1795.

Since Tuesday last I have been here much against my will; arrested by high command; performing quarantine by authority not to be questioned or controverted. In plain English, I am sick. On Wednesday I found one side of my face as large as your uncle F.'s; red swollen eyes; ears buzzing and almost stopped; throat so closed as to refuse a passage to words out or food in; and a stupid mazy-headedness, well adapted to the brilliancy of my figure. Being the guest of my friends Law and Duncanson, I receive from them the most distressing attentions, but especially from Miss Duncanson, a well-bred, sprightly, and agreeable woman. My person had not, however, till this morning, received its last embellishment. Alexis came in at his usual hour, and presenting himself at my bedside, after staring at me for half a minute, exclaimed, with an air of great astonishment—*Diable!* and not a word more. *Qu' a-t-il*, Alexis? To which he made not a word of reply, but fell to drawing up the curtains; and having also very deliberately opened the window-shutters, he returned again to his examination. After gazing for some time (which I found it useless to interrupt), he *diabled* two or three times at intervals of some seconds, and then pronounced that I had *ou la petite vérole ou la rougeole;* and to convince me, brought a glass. In truth he did not *diable* without reason, for my whole face, neck, hands, and arms are most bountifully covered with something like the measles or rash. All these pleasant appearances seem to be the effects of a great cold, taken I know not when or how—

" *Nil illi larva aut tragicis upus esse cothurnis.*"

My throat is something better, notwithstanding I went abroad yesterday.

I am so much better to-day, that, if the weather was
good, I should prosecute my journey if I could find the
means of getting on ; but the rain, which is continual and
very heavy, keeps well and sick within doors.

It is now ten days since I have heard from you; a very
long time, considering the situation in which you was left
at the date of your last : in a city infected with a mortal
and contagious fever. I hope, nay, I persuade myself that
you obeyed my wishes by escaping from it to Pelham
The next mail will tell me, and, I trust, relieve me from an
anxiety which pursues me day and night.

Your letter of the 21st, written, I suppose, at Dr. Brown's,
is just come in, and relieves me from a weight of anxiety
about your health. I am sorry, however (very sorry), that
you are not at Frederick's, and am not absolutely either
pleased or satisfied with the change.

Of attention and tenderness you will receive not only
enough, but a great deal too much ; and an indulgence to
every inattention, awkward habit, and expression, which
may lead you to imagine them to be so many ornaments :
as to your language, I shall expect to find it perfectly
infantine. As to studies or lessons, I do not know which
of them you allude to, as you do not say what books you
have taken up. If Mr. Leshlie is your *only* master, as I
suppose, your lesson must be larger than ever heretofore.
Your translation of the comedy into French, if not finished,
must go on ; and if finished, something similar must be
taken up. Some English or French history must employ
a little of every day. I hope you will ride on horseback
daily if the weather should permit—Sam* always with
you. Visit your neighbours B. B. as often as you please,

---

* A slave of Colonel Burr's.

taking very great care not to surfeit the family with your charming company, which may happen much sooner than you would be inclined to believe.

You ought to be out of the Odyssey before this will reach you, counting only two hundred lines a day since we parted. You may begin the Iliad, if you please. Since you are at uncle B.'s, I will not now pretend to inquire into the motives, much less to censure. I have no doubt but you meant to do the best, and I now hope you will endeavour to make the best *of* it, and bad enough that will be, with respect to all improvement, if I am not disappointed.

Pray allot an hour for your journal, and never let it be a day in arrear I shall consider this as occupying usefully the hour which used to be Hewlet's or Meance's. At any rate, let me not, on my return, have occasion to apply to you the motto,

"Strenua me exercet inertia,"

nor that other of

" Operose nihil agit."

But so improve your time that you may with pleasure review and commit it to journal.

————" Hoc est,
Vivere bis, vita priori frui."

And let it, at no very distant period, be said of you,

" Tot, tibi, sunt, ergo dotes, quot sidera cœlo."

If you should never deserve this, it shall not be the fault of

A. BURR.

TO THEODOSIA IN PHILADELPHIA.
New-York, 8th February, 1796.

What will you think of the taste of New-York when I shall tell you that Miss Broadhurst is not very generally admired here ? Such is the fact. I have contributed my feeble efforts to correct this opinion.

Mat's* child will not be christened until you shall be pleased to indicate the time, place, manner, and name.

I have promised Tom that he shall take me to Philadelphia if there be sleighing. The poor fellow is almost crazy about it. He is importuning all the gods for snow, but as yet they don't appear to listen to him.

Your being in the ballette charms me. If you are to practise on Wednesday evening, do not stay away for the expectation of receiving me. If you should be at the ballette, I will go forthwith to see you. Adieu, chère fille.

A. BURR.

TO THEODOSIA.

Philadelphia, 16th January, 1797.

When I write to you oftener than your turn, you must not let it be known, or there will be jealousy. Your two letters of the 11th and 13th have so much wit, sprightliness, and good sense, that I cannot delay to tell you how much they pleased me. Go on, and you will write better than Cynthia herself. To aid your advances towards perfection, I shall often point out such errors as shall appear to me more particularly to claim your attention.

At present you fail most in punctuation. A very little thought will teach where the sense is complete and a full period is proper. The lesser pauses may be found by reading over two or three times what you may have written. You will naturally make small pauses where the sense shall require it. In spelling you are very well. Always write your name with great care. Adieu.

A BURR.

* A servant of Colonel Burr.

Philadelphia, 23d January, 1797.

You must not "puzzle all day," my dear little girl, at one hard lesson. After puzzling faithfully one hour, apply to your arithmetic, and do enough to convince the doctor that you have not been idle. Neither must you be discouraged by one unlucky day. The doctor is a very reasonable man, and makes all due allowance for the levities as well as for the stupidity of children. I think you will not often challenge his indulgence on either score.

And do you regret that you are not also a woman? That you are not numbered in that galaxy of beauty which adorns an assembly-room? Coquetting for admiration and attracting flattery? No. I answer with confidence. You feel that you are maturing for solid friendship. The friends you gain you will never lose; and no one, I think, will dare to insult your understanding by such compliments as are most graciously received by too many of your sex.

How unpardonably you neglect C. and N. B. Where are the promised letters? I see with delight that you improve in diction, and in the combination and arrangement of your little ideas. With a view to farther improvement, your letters to me are a most useful exercise. I feel persuaded that all my hopes and wishes concerning you will be accomplished.

Never use a word which does not fully express your thoughts, or which, for any other reason, does not please you. Hunt your dictionary till you find one. Arrange a whole sentence in your mind before you write a word of it; and, whatever may be your "hurry" (never be in a *hurry*), read over your letter slowly and carefully before you seal it. Interline and erase lightly with your pen what may appear to you to require amendment or correction. I dispense with your copying unless the letter should be much defaced, in which case keep it till the next mail. Copy and improve it.

Your play on " Light" is pretty and witty, and the turn
on the *dear little* letter does not dishonour the metempsy-
chosis of Madame Dacier.

I shall probably see you very soon; we will then rear-
range your hours, and endeavour to remove the present and
forestall all future troubles. I should be mortified—I should
be almost offended—if I should find that you passed over
any word in my letters without becoming perfectly acquainted with its meaning, use, and *etymology*.

Since I commenced this letter, yours of the 21st has come
in. It speaks of another which has not come, and of Martel's paper, neither of which have come. This arises from
" hurry." The note to Mr. Livingston is middling. Affectionately—no, you hate that word; perhaps every thing is
implied in plain

                                        A. BURR.

TO THEODOSIA.

Albany, 4th January, 1799.

On Tuesday I arrived here, and yesterday received your
two letters of the 29th and 30th of December. Your despondency distresses me extremely. It is indeed unfortunate, my dear Theodosia, that we are constrained to be separated. I had never so much need of your society and
friendship, nor you, perhaps, of mine. It is a misfortune
which I sincerely regret every hour of the day. It is one,
however, which you must aid me to support, by testifying
that you can support your share of it with firmness and activity. An effort made with decision will convince you that
you are able to accomplish all I wish and all you desire.
Determination and perseverance in every laudable undertaking is the great point of difference between the silly and
the wise. It is essentially a part of your character, and requires but an effort to bring it into action. The happiness
of my life depends on your exertions; for what else, for
whom else do I live? Not that the acquisition of the lan-

guages alone can decide your happiness or mine; but if you
should abandon the attempt, or despair of success, or relax
your endeavours, it would indicate a feebleness of character
which would dishearten me exceedingly. It is for my sake
that you now labour. I shall acknowledge your advancement with gratitude and with the most lively pleasure. Let
me entreat you not to be discouraged. I know you to be
capable of much greater efforts than this will require. If
your young teacher, after a week's trial, should not suit you,
dismiss him on any pretence without wounding his pride,
and take the old Scotchman. Resolve to succeed, and you
cannot fail.

I parted with you amid so much hurry and confusion, and
so many vexations, that, when I had time to reflect, I seemed to have said none of the things which I had wished and
intended. I reproached myself perpetually that I had not
urged you to attend me. Your letters almost confirmed me
in the design of returning to fetch you; and yet more sober
reason seems to tell me that these things were rather the
effusions of sentiment than of a deliberate estimate of your
real interests. In six weeks, however, we shall meet.

I intended to have recommended to you the ancient and
modern history of Millot. Natalie has some of the volumes
—some are in the library at Mrs. D.'s, of which I hope you
keep the key. Millot is concise, perspicuous, and well selected. Rollin is full of tedious details and superstitious
nonsense.

There is nothing more certain than that you may form
what countenance you please. An open, serene, intelligent
countenance, a little brightened by cheerfulness, not wrought
into smiles or simpers, will presently become familiar and
grow into habit. A year will with certainty accomplish it.
Your physiognomy has naturally much of benevolence, and
it will cost you some labour (which you may well spare) to
eradicate it. Avoid, for ever avoid, a smile or sneer of contempt; never even mimic them. A frown of sullenness or

discontent is but one degree less hateful. You seem to require these things of me, or I should have thought them unnecessary. I see, with pleasure I see, that you have engaged in this matter. We shall both be gratified by the result, which cannot fail to accord with our wishes.

R. has a deal of godly coquetry. It makes a strange
medley. I was most hospitably received, and full opportunity given with pretty apparent design. R. has promised
to be in Albany in a month. Things are in *statu quo.*

I am unsettled, and at present at Witbeck's. One would
think that the town was going into mourning for your ab
sence. I am perpetually stopped in the streets by little and
big girls. Where is Miss Burr? Won't she come up this
winter? Oh, why didn't you bring her? &c.

J. B. P. arrived yesterday; he has not given me a letter,
or any other thing from you. He suspects, however, that he
has at least a letter; a fact which he will endeavour to ascertain in the course of this week. I wrote you two letters
on my way up, addressed to 135 Greenwich-street. Is that
right? Adieu, chere amie,

A. BURR.

TO THEODOSIA.

Albany, 11th February, 1799.

On Saturday, the 9th, I received your two letters, from
the 1st to the 6th inclusive; the last of which is the only
one that has come in due season, or in what is termed
the course of post. You now see that a letter can come
from New-York in three days; a truth which has been frequently verified by the receipt of my letters, but never be
fore by the despatch of your own.

How very perverse and provoking you are about your
correspondence with Mr. Martin. I told you expressly that
he was not angry, but, on the contrary, that he sent it laugh-
ingly and as a good joke. Pray, from whom did you learn
that he was angry?

You charge me with not noticing two of your letters, and that I have not given you any directions about heedlessness. With submission, miss, you are mistaken. It is true that I have not repeated the word, but I have intimated several things intended to this point. You expected, I presume, that I should treat the subject scientifically, as Duport does his art, and begin by explanation of terms, and then proceed to divide and subdivide the matter, as a priest does a sermon. Such a dose would, I am sure, have sickened you. I have therefore thought it best to give you very little at a time, and watch, as physicians do with potent medicines, the effect produced. When we meet, which I verily believe will be in five or six days after the receipt of this, you shall have as much as I shall find your stomach will bear.

What the deuse can have got into Madame S. and N., I am utterly at a loss to conjecture, and beg you not to give the remotest hint, but meet them as usual.

My overtures to B. Livingston and Mr. and Mrs. R. were mere volunteers, not produced by any thing you said or wrote; but I thought it might tend to produce a certain effect in your favour. So you have no apologies to make or pardons to ask on this subject. As this, however, is much the best composed part of your letter, I am particularly obliged to you for it, even if you did it to display your eloquence. It is, indeed, very happily expressed.

You seem to have emerged from your lethargy, which, I must confess, was obvious to an alarming degree in several preceding letters. I congratulate you upon it, and hope you will never suffer it again to invade your faculties.

We will talk of houses, &c. about the 19th inst. Henry Walton has gone to New-York by the last stage. He is one of those whose good opinion and esteem I wish you to acquire. He has delicacy, taste, and refinement—very, very rare qualities in this country at this day. He will be often at your house; receive him with courtesy.

I go to bed between 12 and 1, and rise between 7 and 8.

For some reasons to me unknown, I cannot drink a single glass of wine without serious injury; still less can I bear ardent spirits; of course, I am pretty much in the bread and water line; this is the more provoking, as I dine out almost every day, and the dinners are really excellent and well-dressed, not exceeded in New-York. I have dined at home but four days since my arrival in this city. Think of that Miss B., and be hush about hospitality, &c.

Your name to one letter is beautifully written; to the other, *la la*. The handwriting of the letters various; very good, very bad, and middling; emblematic, shall I say, of the fair authoress? Please to resolve me whether author is not of both genders, for I hate the appendix of *ess*?

What novel of Miss Burney or D'Arblay is that in which the heroine begins by an interesting account of little details on her debut in London, and particularly of a ball where she met Lord Somebody and did twenty ridiculous things? I want such a description of a ball from you. Be pleased to read those first letters of the novel referred to, and take them for a model.

You don't say half enough about the long letter which I wrote you on Sunday of the last week. Adieu, chere amie.

A. BURR

TO THEODOSIA.

Albany, 26th January, 1800.

We arrived yesterday without accident. To-day I expected Alexis and John; but the stage has arrived without them, and without a line explanatory of the cause of their delay.

On alighting from the stage yesterday, I found at the door of my intended lodgings a number of persons who were impatiently expecting my arrival. I perceive that I shall be day and night engrossed by business. If I should write to you less or less often than usual, you will know the cause.

The ideas, of which you are the object, that daily pass through my mind, would, if committed to writing, fill an octavo volume ; invent, then, and teach me some mode of writing with the facility and rapidity that we think, and you shall receive by every mail some hundred pages. But to select from a thousand thoughts that which is best and most seasonable ; of the variety of attitudes of which every object is susceptible, to determine on that which is most suitable for the thing and the occasion ; of all possible modes of expression and language, to discern the most appropriate, *hic labor, hoc opus est.* Yet have we both known persons of a moderate grade of intellect who could write whenever you would put a pen in their hands, and for any length of time you might please, without one moment of reflection or embarrassment. Pray explain to me this phenomenon. All this I confess is not very applicable to you or to my present occupation, for I generally write you what first offers, without considering whether it be the best; and if many obtrude themselves at once, I write you, as at present, of—*nothing.*

Indeed, my dear Theodosia, I have many, many moments of solicitude about you. Remember that occupation will infallibly expel the fiend ennui, and that solitude is the bugbear of fools. God bless and aid thee.

A. Burr

TO THEODOSIA.

Albany, 30th January, 1800.

At length John and Alexis have arrived ; but what gratified me more, and what I looked for with much more impatience was, a letter. I selected yours from the number which they brought me. I was not disappointed. It merits all the eagerness with which I had expected it.

You reflect, and that is a security for your conduct. Our most humiliating errors proceed usually from inattention, and from that mental dissipation which we call heedlessness. You estimate your situation with great truth. Many are surprised that I could repose in you so great a trust as that of yourself; but I knew that you were equa₁ to it, and I am not deceived.

You do right to stay much at home. It will scarcely be worth while to go to V. P.'s. C. is excluded from all rule. I am quite oppressed with the kindness and friendship of *b. b.* towards you. How fortunate you are in such a friend. If their invitations should be so frequent as to interrupt your lessons, you will do well to refuse even them. There is a measure to be observed in the acceptance of the good offices even of our best friends; and at your age, to prefer duty to pleasure when they are in collision, is a degree of firmness rarely exhibited, and, therefore, the more calculated to inspire respect. I perceive that I am not very explicit; but you will *reflect* and discern my meaning. Montesquieu said he wrote to make people think, and not to make them read—and why may not A. Br. Perhaps, however, there may be no collisions; and then your good sense will teach you not to wear out good-will. ·

.You indicate a very pleasant mode in which you suppose I may make you happy; but you do not estimate things rightly. What you imagine to be symptoms of love are the mere effusions of politeness, added to respect and esteem.

I forget the plan we projected, but there can be no better one than that of your last letter, to which, therefore, you may adhere, unless indeed you can invent a better.

You may tell C. that as she and I *are on ceremony,* I shall expect the first letter. She knows well that the bare sight of her handwriting would drive Le Guen and the parchments to the antipodes. I do thank you for your constancy about the French ball. Do not be alarmed lest I expect too much. I know your force, and now feel assured that I shall have reason to be more than satisfied both with your discretion and your attainments.

I shall not again find time to write you two pages; so do

not expect it. Nevertheless, you will engross much, very much of the thoughts and affections of

A. BURR

Previous to the year 1800, slavery existed in the State of New-York. Colonel Burr, at different periods, was the owner of slaves. All those that remained in his family for any length of time were taught to read and write. During his absence from home it was his practice to correspond with one or more of them. As a master, he was beloved. A few letters are here given as specimens of this correspondence. They are copied *literally*.

TO COLONEL BURR.

New-York, 3d December.

HONOURED MASTER,

I received your letter December 1st, and we are all happy to hear that you are well. Harry has taken the chair to the coachmaker's, and has gave him directions according to your orders. I have asked James to write to you to know how the venison was to be done ; but I will now have it cured as you have ordered. The sashes of the windows were nailed down the day that you went away, and the ladder that you mention belongs to Mr. Halsey, and he has taken it away. All the papers that have any writing on is put into the drawers, and I will take care of the ink that it does not freeze. Colonel Platt was here, and has taken the four red cases that was in the wine-room; and he asked me for a square box, and as you had not told me of it, I said that I had never seen it. There is nothing in the stable; but don't know what is in Sam's room, as he has locked the door. We are happy to hear that Sam, and George, and the horses are in good order, and all the family gives their love to them.

PEGGY GARTIN.

TO COLONEL BURR.

New-York, 17th December.

HONOURED MASTER,

I received your letter, and am happy to hear that you are in a good state of health. Harry went to Mr. Alston's farm the day after I received the letter, and the man had gone away the 11th day of December. Stephen was not at home when he went there, and by what he could understand there was a great difference between Daniel and Stephen; and Harry says that for the time that he has been there he had not neglected his work. But, master, I wish to beg a favour of you; please to grant it. I have found there is a day-school, kept by an elderly man and his wife, near to our house, and if master is willing that I should go to it for two months, I think it would be of great service to me, and at the same time I will not neglect my work in the house, if you please, sir.

PEGGY.

TO COLONEL BURR.

New-York, 29th December.

HONOURED MASTER,

I received your letter, which has given me no satisfaction concerning your health ; and as there has been a report in the paper that you was wounded, it has made us very uneasy, supposing it to be true; but I hope that it is not so, as I hear that people gives no credit to it. I go to the school, since master is willing, and I like the teacher very much. He pays great attention to my learning, and I have teached Nancy her letters ever since you have been gone, which I think will be of as much service to her as if she went to school. We are all well at present, and I hope that you are the same.

PEGGY

New-York, 12th January.

HONOURED MASTER,

I have received your letter of the 4th inst., and it gives us great happiness to hear that you are in good health, as all the family are except myself. I was taken sick on the 30th of last month, so that I have not been able to go to school; and as I am better than I have been, to write these few lines; I am too weak to write Mrs. Alston, but Elenora's child is well. The woman came here the 7th of this month for the money, and Harry went to Mrs. Van Ness the 9th, and she said that Mr. Van Ness did not tell her any thing of it, and she could not give it.

PEGGY.

CHAPTER XVIII.

THE preceding correspondence not only introduces the reader into the social circle of Colonel Burr, but into the bosom of his family. It develops his character, so far as the most sacred and confidential communications can develop it—as a friend—a husband—a parent—and a master. We are approaching a period, however, in his history when the scene is to be changed. In the spring of 1794 Mrs. Burr died; and in 1801 his daughter was married, and removed to South Carolina. Thus terminated, in a great measure, all those domestic relations and enjoyments which had afforded him so much pleasure, and connected with which he had indulged the best feelings of his heart.

Colonel Burr was a member of the Senate of the United States from the 4th of March, 1791, until the 4th of March,

1797.   During this period he continued to practise the law.
He was in that class of his profession to which belonged a
Hamilton, a Harrison, and a Livingston.   The partiality
of some of his friends may have placed him at the head of
the bar.   His opponents ranked him second *only* to their
particular favourite.   As a speaker, Colonel Burr was calm
and persuasive.   He was most remarkable for the power
which he possessed of condensation.   His appeals, whether
to a court or a jury, were sententious and lucid.   His
speeches, generally, were argumentative, short, and pithy.
No flights of fancy, no metaphors, no parade of impassioned
sentences, are to be found in them.   When employed on
the same side of a cause with General Hamilton, it was
his uniform practice to permit that gentleman to select his
own place in the cause.

It has often been remarked that Colonel Burr's character
could not be better drawn than it is in a short sketch of
his father, by Governor Livingston.   " Though a person"
(says the governor) " of a slender and delicate make, to
encounter fatigue he has a heart of steel ; and, for the despatch of business, the most amazing talents, joined to a
constancy of mind that ensures success in spite of every obstacle.   As long as an enterprise appears not absolutely impossible, he knows no discouragement ; but, in proportion to
its difficulty, augments his diligence ; and, by an insuperable
fortitude, frequently accomplishes what his friends and acquaintance conceive utterly impracticable."

In the year 1793 Albert Gallatin was appointed a senator of the United States by the State of Pennsylvania.   On
claiming his seat in January, 1794, a petition was presented
against his admission into that body, on the ground that he
had not been a citizen the requisite number of years.   The
subject was referred to a committee of seven.   Their report elicited a warm debate, which continued for several
days.   Colonel Burr took an active part, and greatly distinguished himself in support of Mr. Gallatin's claim.   His

colleague, Mr. King, had taken the lead against the right of Mr. Gallatin to a seat. John Taylor, of Caroline, Virginia, addressed a note to Colonel Burr, in which he says— "We shall leave you to reply to King: *first*, because you desired it; *second*, all depends upon it; no one else *can* do it, and the audience will expect it."

On the 28th of February, 1794, the Senate " *Resolved*, That the election of Albert Gallatin to be a senator of the United States was void, he not having been a citizen of the United States the term of years required as a qualification to be a senator of the United States."—Ays 14, nays 12.

On the 20th of February, 1794, the Senate adopted a resolution, declaring that their galleries, at the commencement of the next session, should be opened while the Senate were " engaged in their legislative capacity." For this, or a similar resolution, Colonel Burr had voted at every previous session since he had been a member.

His personal respect for John Jay has been heretofore mentioned; but on no occasion did he permit such feelings to interfere with his political acts, when called upon to perform a public duty. On the 16th of April, 1794, the president nominated John Jay, then chief-justice of the United States, as envoy extraordinary to Great Britain. On the 19th, when the nomination was called up for consideration, Mr. Burr offered the following resolutions :—

" *Resolved*, That any communications to be made to the court of Great Britain may be made through our minister now at that court with equal facility and effect, and at much less expense, than by an envoy extraordinary ; and that such an appointment is at present inexpedient and unnecessary :

" That to permit judges of the Supreme Court to hold, at the same time, any other office or employment emanating from, and holden at the pleasure of, the executive, is contrary to the spirit of the constitution; and, as tending to ex-

pose them to the influence of the executive, is mischievous
and impolitic." Ays 10, nays 17.

The nomination was then confirmed by a vote of 18 to
8, Mr. Burr voting in the negative. This vote, it was understood at the time, gave pain to Mr. Jay. In a letter to
his lady, dated the 20th of April, the judge says—" Yester
day the Senate approved of the nomination by a great majority. · *Mr. Burr was among the few who opposed it.*"

About this period the democratic party were highly in-
censed against the president for continuing Gouverneur Morris as a minister to the French Republic. The Executive
Provisory Council had requested his recall. He was considered a monarchist, and hostile to the revolution. Many
of the opposition senators had spoken with great freedom
of the policy of General Washington in this particular.
These remarks having been communicated to the president,
he expressed, informally, a willingness to recall Mr. Morris,
and to nominate a member of the opposition, if they would
designate a suitable person. In consequence of this sug-
gestion, the democratic members of the Senate, and some of
the most distinguished members of the House, had a conference, and resolved on recommending Colonel Burr. Mr.
Madison, Mr. Monroe, and another member of Congress
whose name is not recollected, were delegated to wait on
the president and communicate the wishes of the party.

General Washington paused for a few moments, and then
remarked, that he had made it a rule of life never to recommend or nominate any person for a high and responsible situation in whose integrity he had not confidence ; that, wanting confidence in Colonel Burr, he could not nominate him ;
but that it would give him great pleasure to meet their
wishes if they would designate an individual in whom he
could confide. The committee returned and reported the
result of their conference. The senators adhered unanimously to their first nomination, and the same delegates
waited upon the president and reiterated the adherence of

their friends to Colonel Burr. Whereupon General Washington, with some warmth, remarked that his decision was
irrevocable; but immediately added, " I will nominate you,
Mr. Madison, or you, Mr. Monroe." The former replied
that he had long since made up his mind never to leave his
country, and respectfully declined the offer. They retired,
and reported the result of their second interview. The
democratic gentlemen were not less inflexible, and instruct-
ed their delegates to say to the president that they would
make no other recommendation. On the third visit they
were received by Mr. Randolph, secretary of state, to whom
they made the communication, but who considered it inde
corous, knowing the president's feelings, to repeat the message.

This incident demonstrates, on the one hand, the strong
and unchangeable prejudices of General Washington against
Colonel Burr; and on the other, the firm and unbounded
confidence reposed in him by the democracy of those days.
The anecdote is not related on the authority exclusively of
Colonel Burr. It is confirmed by the written statement of
a gentleman of high standing, to whom Mr. Monroe repeated all the details. No other selection was made by the opposition senators; but, on the 27th of May, 1794, James
Monroe was nominated as Minister Plenipotentiary to the
French Republic.

On the 8th of June, 1795, the president submitted to the
Senate of the United States the treaty negotiated with Great
Britain by John Jay. This question called into operation
all the powers of Mr. Burr's mind. He was opposed to it
in the form it had been negotiated. His views and opinions
may be distinctly understood by comparing the amendments
which he proposed with the original treaty. On the 22d
June the Senate resumed the consideration of it, whereupon
he offered the following resolutions :—

" That the further consideration of the treaty concluded
at London the 19th of November, 1794, be postponed, and

that it be recommended to the President of the United States to proceed without delay to further friendly negotiation with his Britannic Majesty, in order to effect alterations in the said treaty in the following particulars :—.

" That the 9th, 10th, and 24th articles, and so much of the 25th as relates to the shelter or refuge to be given to the armed vessels of states or sovereigns at war with either party, be expunged.

" 2d Art. That no privilege or right be allowed to the settlers or traders mentioned in the 2d article, other than those which are secured to them by the treaty of 1783 and existing laws.

" 3d. Art. That the 3d article be expunged, or be so modified that the citizens of the United States may have the use of *all* rivers, ports, and places within the territories of his Britannic Majesty in North America, in the same manner as his subjects may have of those of the United States.

" 6th Art. That the value of the negroes and other property carried away contrary to the 7th article of the treaty of 1783, *and the loss and damage sustained by the United States by the detention of the posts*, be paid for by the British government—the amount to be ascertained by the commissioners who may be appointed to liquidate the claims of the British creditors.

" 12th Art. That what relates to the West India trade, and the provisos and conditions thereof in the 12th article, be expunged, or be rendered much more favourable to the United States, and without any restraint on the exportation, in vessels of the United States, of any articles not the growth, produce, or manufacture of the said islands of his Britannic Majesty.

" 15th Art. That no clause be admitted which may restrain the United States from reciprocating benefits by discriminating between foreign nations in their commercial arrangements, or prevent them from increasing the tonnage or other duties on British vessels on terms of reciprocity, or in a stipulated ratio.

"21st Art. That the subjects or citizens of either party be not restrained from accepting commissions in the army or navy of any foreign power."

In 1797, while Colonel Burr was yet a member of the United States Senate, his mind was occupied with the project of a bank, and he conferred with several of his personal friends on the subject. Among others, he wrote the honourable Thomas Morris, who was at the time a member of the state Senate.

TO THOMAS MORRIS.

New-York, 1st February, 1797.

SIR,

I have been informed that the present sheriff of Dutchess either has resigned or will decline a reappointment, and that Platt Smith is among the candidates. I have very little personal acquaintance with Mr. Smith—am not, indeed, certain that I should recognise him if I should meet him ; but I have long known him by reputation, and can assure you that he is a man of irreproachable character, of independent property, and much above ordinary in point of intelligence His connexions are very influential (perhaps the most so) in that county. He is, in short, a man, in my opinion, every way qualified to fill the office. Has always been of your party, and supported Jay's election. He is withal a generous, manly, independent fellow, of that cast which you like; one who will feel sensibly any favours or civilities which may be done him. If you should not be otherwise pledged, you will oblige several of your personal friends by supporting his pretensions.

. I have drawn out a plan for a bank, but find that it will require so many explanations that I forbear to send it. I perceive that you are about selling our stock in the funds of the United States. We have already talked over this mat ter. The more I reflect, the stronger appear the objections. It will doubtless be urged in favour of an immediate sale, that our funds are in danger of seizure by the United States. This is a mere bugbear. Such a thing will never again be even proposed, and, if proposed, will never receive three votes in the Senate. I hope, therefore, our legislature will not suffer themselves to be precipitated into this sale from any such unfounded apprehensions.

Mr. Belasies, a gentleman, a man of education and fortune, by birth an Englishman, has come out with his family to reside in this country. If he should apply for leave to hold lands in this state, I hope he may be gratified; from the little I have seen, and the much I have heard of him, I am persuaded that he will be a valuable acquisition to any state and to any society. He is no politician.

I return to-morrow to Philadelphia, where I shall remain for this month. May I expect to see you here in the spring? Present me most respectfully to Williamson, and be assured of my esteem and attachment.

                                        A. BURR.

In April, 1798, Colonel Burr was elected a member of Assembly for the city and county of New-York by the democratic party. This year was marked with more political virulence than any other year since the independence of the country. It was during the year 1798 that the alien and sedition laws were passed. In the autumn of 1798, Matthew Lyon, then a representative in Congress from Vermont, was endicted for harbouring an intention " to stir up sedition, and to bring the president and government of the United States into contempt," &c. He was convicted, and the sentence was—" Matthew Lyon, it is the pleasure of this court that you be imprisoned four months, pay costs, and a fine of one thousand dollars, and stand committed until the judgment be complied with." This year the celebrated mission to France, consisting of Messrs. Marshall, Pinckney, and Gerry, excited the attention not only of the American people, but of the civilized world. In short, this year the foundation was laid for the overthrow of federal power in the United States.

In no section of the country was there more political excitement than in New-York. Parties were nearly balanced. There were only two banks in the city ; the Bank of New-York, and the branch of the United States Bank. They were charged with being influenced in their discounts by political considerations. At all events, they were under the management and control of federalists ; and to counteract their alleged influence, Colonel Burr was anxious for the establishment of a democratic institution. With this view he proposed to obtain a charter for supplying the city with water ; and as it was certain that if confined to that particular object the stock would not be subscribed, he caused the application to be made for two millions of dollars, and inserted a clause in that charter, that the "surplus capital might be employed in any way not inconsistent with the laws and constitution of the United States or of the State of New-York." It is under this clause that the Manhattan Company use and exercise all the privileges of a bank. The directors were named in the charter, and a majority of them were of the democratic party.

It has been said that the charter was obtained by trick and management ; and that, if suspicion had been entertained by any of the federal members, Colonel Burr could not have got the bill through the legislature. It is due to him, so far as it can be justly done, to rescue his memory from the imputation of having *misrepresented* or *misstated* to any member the object he had in view. The facts in reference to the passage of the charter of the Manhattan Company through the Senate will now be given. The statement is upon authority that cannot be contradicted.

When the bill had passed the Assembly and was sent to the Senate, Colonel Burr, during the hours of business, went into the Senate Chamber, and requested a federal senator (now living) from the western district to move a reference

of that bill to a select committee, to report complete, which
would supersede the necessity of its going to a committee
of the whole. The senator replied, that though he had no
objection to make the experiment, yet that he was persuaded
the motion would not prevail, because the Senate, not having
a press of business before them, uniformly refused thus committing bills to select committees instead of a committee of
the whole. Colonel Burr then suggested, that perhaps if
the mover would intimate, while on the floor, that the honourable Samuel Jones was contemplated as chairman of that
committee, the confidence which the Senate was known to
repose in him, and in his uniform attention to every thing
relating to the city of New-York, would perhaps induce
the Senate on this occasion to depart from its accustomed
mode of proceeding. Accordingly the motion was made,
and passed without opposition.

The committee named by the honourable Stephen Van
Rensselaer, then lieutenant-governor, were Samuel Jones,
Ambrose Spencer, and Thomas Morris. It was suggested
to one of these gentlemen that the part of the bill authorizing the employment of the surplus capital had better be
stricken out of it; in consequence of which that gentleman
applied to Colonel Burr for an explanation on this point.
Mr. Burr promptly and frankly informed the honourable
member, that it not only did authorize, but that it was in
tended the directors should use the surplus capital in any
way they thought expedient and proper. That they might
have a bank, an East India Company, or any thing else that
they deemed profitable. That the mere supplying the city
with water would not, of itself, remunerate the stockhold-
ers. Colonel Burr added, that the senator was at liberty to
communicate this explanation to other members, and that
he had no secrecy on the subject. The bill was subsequently reported by Mr. Jones and passed.

This view of the proceedings of the legislature is sus

tained by what occurred in the Council of Revision, from the minutes of which an extract has been made.

"*At a meeting of the Council of Revision, held at the City Hall of the City of Albany, on Monday, the 1st of April, 1799.*

"PRESENT—His Excellency the Governor, the Honourable the Chancellor, the Chief Justice, and Judge Benson.

" Mr. Reynolds and Mr. Robbins, from the honourable the Assembly, delivered to the council the bill entitled *An act for the relief of John Lansing*, the bill entitled *An act for supplying the city of New-York with pure and wholesome water*, and the bill entitled *An act to amend the statute of limitation*, and the bill entitled *An act making provision to keep in repair the bridge over Schoharie Creek, at Fort Hunter, in the county of Montgomery.*

" The council proceeded to take the said bills into consideration, and thereupon   .

"*Resolved,* That the bill entitled *An act for supplying the city of New-York with pure and wholesome water* be committed to the honourable the Chief Justice ; that the bill entitled *An act to amend the statute of limitation* be committed to the honourable the Chancellor."

"*At a meeting of the Council of Revision, held at the City Hall of the City of Albany, on Tuesday, the 2d of April, 1799.*

" PRESENT—His Excellency the Governor, the Honourable the Chancellor, the Chief Justice, and Judge Benson.

" The honourable the Chief Justice, to whom was committed the bill entitled *An act for supplying the city of New-York with pure and wholesome water*, reported the following objections, to wit :

" *Because* the bill creates a corporation, with a capital of two millions of dollars, vested with the unusual power to divert its surplus capital to the purchase of public or other stock, *or any other moneyed transactions or operations not inconsistent with the constitution and laws of this state or of the United States*, and which surplus may be applied to the purposes of trade, or any other purpose which the very comprehensive terms in which the clause is conceived may warrant; this, in the opinion of the council as a novel experiment, the result whereof as to its influence on the community must be merely speculative and uncertain, peculiarly requires the application of the policy which has heretofore uniformly obtained, that the powers of corporations relative to their money operations should be of limited instead of perpetual duration."

" The council proceeded to take the preceding objections into consideration, which were overruled; it was thereupon

" *Resolved*, That it does not appear improper to the council that the said bill, entitled *An act for supplying the city of New-York with pure and wholesome water*, should become a law of this state.

" *Ordered*, That the honourable the Chancellor deliver a copy of the preceding resolution, signed by his excellency the Governor, to the honourable the Assembly."

" *State of New-York, Secretary's Office.*

" I certify the preceding to be true extracts from the minutes of the Council of Revision of this state.

(Signed)   " Archd. Campbell,

" *Deputy Secretary.*

" *Albany, April 29th, 1836.*"

Of the correctness of the above statement, and the fairness of Mr. Burr's conduct in relation to the Manhattan Company, there cannot be the shadow of a doubt; but it is probable that a large portion of the members never attempted to examine into the extent of the powers granted to the Manhattan Company; while another portion considered the project of Colonel Burr, in reference to an East India Company or a bank, as chimerical and visionary. It is, however, evident that no trick or misrepresentation was practised to procure the passage of the bill; unless, indeed, his silence on the floor of the house as to his ulterior views may be so construed. His object was a bank; and when appealed to on this particular point, he admitted the fact. At all other times he remained silent on the subject. When the bill had passed he was lauded by the democratic party for his address, and they rejoiced in his success. Its political effect was considered highly important, as it tended to break down a system of pecuniary favouritism, which was made to operate in support of the party in power.

During the summer of 1799 vague rumours were privately circulated respecting certain transactions of Colonel Burr with the Holland Land Company. It was whispered that a bond, which the company held against him for twenty thousand dollars, had been given up for secret services rendered them. In other circles it was hinted that the compensation was for procuring the passage of a bill through the legislature authorizing aliens to hold lands, &c. Connected with these rumours, John B. Church, Esq. had spoken with so much freedom as to produce a challenge from Colonel Burr. On the 2d of September, 1799, the parties met at Hoboken, and having exchanged a shot without effect, Mr. Church made the *amende honorable*, and the affair was so satisfactorily adjusted as to restore the social intercourse of these gentlemen. Mr. Church was attended by Abijah Hammond, Esq., and Colonel Burr by Judge Edanus Burke, of South Carolina.

On the ground a most ludicrous incident occurred. Previous to leaving the city of New-York, Colonel Burr presented to Judge Burke his pistol-case. He explained to the judge that the balls were cast intentionally too small; that chamois leather was cut to the proper size to put round them, but that the leather must be greased (for which purpose grease was placed in the case), or that

Vol. I.—G g g   18*

there would be a difficulty in getting the ball home. After the parties had taken their stand, Colonel Burr noticed the judge hammering the ramrod with a stone, and immediately suspected the cause. When the pistol was handed him by his friend, he drew the ramrod, and ascertained that the ball was not home, and so informed the judge; to which Mr. Burke replied, "I forgot to grease the leather; but you see he is ready, don't keep him waiting; *just take a crack as it is, and I'll grease the next!*" Colonel· Burr bowed courteously, but made no reply, and discharged his pistol in the state it had been given to him. The anecdote for some time after was the subject of merriment among those who had heard it.

No explanation was ever given, it is believed, of the transactions between Colonel Burr and the Holland Land Company. It was his practice to let his actions speak for themselves, and to let the world construe them as they pleased. This was a great error, and was the source in after life of much trouble and suffering to him, yet he would not depart from it. A few weeks subsequent to this duel, however, he received from a friend a kind letter, asking confidentially an explanation of these transactions, to which he replied.

COLONEL BURR TO ——.

New-York, 6th October, 1799.

Dear Sir,

I cannot refuse to the manner of your request, nor to the friendly motives which have produced it, to satisfy your inquiries with regard to Witbeck's bond and the Holland Company.

In December, 1795 or 1796, I forget which, I entered into a covenant with the Holland Company for the purchase of one hundred thousand acres of land, at twelve shillings per acre, payable by instalments. The covenant contained a penalty of twenty thousand dollars; as security on my part for this penalty, in case it should become due, I mortgaged to Cazenove, or the Holland Company, twenty thousand acres of land in Presque Isle, being one hundred shares of two hundred acres each in the Population Company, and I assigned to him Thomas L. Witbeck's bond, payable to me, for twenty thousand dollars, as further collateral security.

In the fall of 1797 Cazenove joined with me in a power of attorney to James Wadsworth, then in Europe, for the sale of one hundred thousand acres, and, until the summer or fall of the year following, we had reason to believe that they were or would be sold, which of course would have terminated all questions about the penalty. Some time in the year 1797 or 1798, it was noised in Albany that Thomas L. Witbeck had given a bond for twenty thousand dollars, and his credit at the bank and elsewhere became affected by it. He wrote me often on the subject. In reply, I begged him to explain that the bond was not for the payment of money, and that, even if it should become forfeited, the twenty thousand acres of Presque Isle lands were alone a sufficient security. Witbeck, however, continued to be uneasy for his credit, and teased me to take up his bond by giving other security. I thought this rather unkind, and did not trouble myself about it. Indeed, I was in hopes that the sale of the land in Europe would have closed the transaction. Not long after this, I think in November last, Cazenove informed me that he had been applied to by Witbeck to change that security, and added that· he was willing to change it for one of equal solidity, provided it would not impair his rights.

Witbeck's importunities continued, and he became so very urgent and repeated that I was finally (November last), long after the passing of the alien bill, induced to offer A. I. Frederick Prevost's bond in the place of Witbeck's. Cazenove took time to consider and inquire ; and finding, in fact, that Prevost's bond was a much better one than Wit-

beck's, agreed to take it. Prevost accordingly executed *to
me* a bond for twenty thousand dollars, of which Harrison
drew a special assignment to the Holland Company. We
made a memorandum that this exchange should not vary
the rights of the parties (viz., the Holland Company and
Aaron Burr), and Thomas L. Witbeck's bond was given
up. In this transaction I never suspected that Cazenove
imagined that *he* was doing a favour either to me or Thomas L. Witbeck, and I am confident that he never entertained so absurd a belief. It was with great reluctance
that I gave Prevost's bond. I had claims on Witbeck
which justified me in exposing him to some hazard. Prevost had a family, a clear, independent estate, and did not
owe a cent in the world; but he had better nerves than Witbeck, and would not tease me.

About this time we learned that all prospect of selling
the land in Europe had failed, and as I never had an expectation of paying except from the land itself, it became necessary to close the transaction. It should be observed, that
soon after my contract with Cazenove he received orders, as
he informed me, to sell no more under sixteen shillings (two
dollars), and afterward I understood that he had raised the
price to twenty shillings. In December last we had several
conferences for the purpose of settling this business. I offered to give back the land and cancel the covenants. He
talked of the penalty. I replied that he would only recover
the damages sustained, which, by his own account, were
nothing; for, as the price of the land was raised to twenty
shillings, the Holland Company would, by their own estimation, gain one hundred thousand dollars by taking back
the land. He appeared to feel the unreasonableness of his
demand, and finally evaded my proposal by questioning his
own authority. This I considered as a pretence; some ir-
ritation ensued, and we parted without concluding any thing.

Thus the matter remained until May last (1799), when
our negotiations were renewed. After various overtures

and propositions on either side, it was at length agreed that I should convey to the Holland Company, absolutely, the twenty thousand acres Presque Isle lands. That this should be received in discharge of the advances that Cazenove had made thereon, and in full satisfaction of all damages claim ed on the covenants; and that thereupon the covenants should be cancelled, the bond of I. A. Frederick Prevost be given up, and the Holland Company take back their lands. This was accordingly done a few days before Cazenove sailed for Europe, which was, I think, in June last.

I should have noted, that about the year 1792 or 1793, I became jointly concerned with the Holland Company and sundry individuals in the purchase from the State of Pennsylvania of the whole Presque Isle angle, and of other lands adjoining to the amount of a million of acres. The association was called the Population Company, and was under the management of directors, who had a right to assess on the proprietors or associates any sums they might think proper to promote the settlements required by the patents. My interest was one hundred shares, or twenty thousand acres, for which I had paid, at the time I mortgaged to Caz enove, upwards of seven thousand five hundred dollars. The thing was considered as extremely valuable, and I have no doubt but my interest would, if I could have retained it five years, have been worth to me more than one hundred thousand dollars. Lands within the angle were last year sold at twenty dollars per acre.

Though it be obvious that no damages were due or could have been recovered by the Holland Company on the penalty contained in the covenants, yet I had several motives to urge me to some sacrifice in order to get rid of the business. *First:* I could not repay the advances made by Cazenove, which amounted to several thousand dollars. *Second.* I could not bear to give any uneasiness to Frederick Prevost, which might have been the consequence of a legal proceeding. *Third.* I was a little apprehensive of being sued

on the covenants for payment of the purchase money. Cazenove, on his part, had but a single motive, to wit—he found
that these lands were all I had to give, and that a suit would
have produced only expense.

The aforegoing facts are substantially known to Le Roy,
Bayard, and McEvers, and to Harrison and Ogden. The
two last were consulted on the closing of the business in
May and June last (1799). The former of them, Harrison,
several times on the exchange of the bonds. I have not
spoken to either of those gentlemen on the subject since the
transactions took place; but any person is at liberty to do it
who may choose to take the trouble.

I have given you a summary of my whole concern with
Cazenove and the Holland Company, not knowing what part
of it might tend to elucidate your inquiries.

By those who know me, it will never be credited that any
man on earth would have the hardiness even to propose to
me dishonourable compensations ; but this apart, the absurdity of the calumny you allude to is obvious from the following data, resulting from the deeds and known facts :

That at the time the Alien Bill was under consideration,
and long after, the bond, the covenant, and the penalty were
objects of no concern, as we had reason to believe that the
lands were or would be sold in Europe, so as to leave me a
profit :

That Witbeck's bond was *never given up*, but exchanged
for one more safe and valuable:

That I had not, nor by possibility could have, any inter
est in this exchange, as it was relieving one friend to involve
another still more dear to me :

That, so far from any understanding between Cazenove
and me, we had controversies about the very bond and penalty for more than a year after the passing of the Alien
Bill :

That no part of the penalty was ever due from me to the
Holland Company; and that of course, they could never

have demanded the bond, which was expressly a security
for the penalty, and not for the payments:

That nevertheless I did finally give Cazenove a valuable
and exorbitant compensation to induce him to cancel the
covenants and discharge the penalty.

This, sir, is the first time in my life that I have conde-
scended (pardon the expression) to refute a calumny. I
leave to my actions to speak for themselves, and to my character to confound the fictions of slander. And on this very
subject I have not up to this hour given one word of explanation to any human being. All the explanation that can be
given amounts to no more than this—*That the thing is an
absolute and abominable lie.* I feel that the present detail
is useless and trifling; but you have asked with good-nature, and I could not, with the appearance of good-nature,
refuse. I pardon you the labour I have had in writing, and
for that which you will have in reading no apology can be
due from

Your friend and obedient servant,

A. BURR.

In January, 1801, Colonel Burr's daughter Theodosia
was married to Joseph Alston, Esq., of South Carolina. Mr.
Alston was in his twenty-second, Miss Burr in her eigh-
teenth year. He was a gentleman of talents and fortune, and
a few years after his marriage was chosen governor. Some
opinion of his style of writing may be formed by his defence of early marriages; while that portion of his letter
which relates to his native state cannot be uninteresting to
South Carolinians.

THEODOSIA BURR TO JOSEPH ALSTON.

New-York, January 13th, 1801.

I have already written to you by the post to tell you that
I shall be happy to see you *whenever you choose;* that I
suppose is equivalent to *very soon;* and that you may no

longer feel doubts or suspicions on my account, I repeat
the invitation by a packet as less dilatory than the mail; but
for all these doubts and suspicions I will take ample re-
venge when we meet.

I yesterday received your letter of the 26th of December,
and am expecting your defence of early marriages to-day.
My father laughs at my impatience to hear from you, and
says I am in love; but I do not believe that to be a fair de
duction, for the post is really very irregular and slow—enough
so to provoke anybody.

We leave this for Albany on the 26th inst., and shall remain there till the 10th February. My movements will after that depend upon my father and *you*. I had intended
not to marry this twelvemonth, and in that case thought it
wrong to divert you from your present engagements in Carolina; but to your solicitations I yield my judgment. Adieu.
I wish you many returns of the century.

14th January.

I have not yet received your promised letter; but I hope
it may be long in proportion to the time I have been expecting it. The packet has been delayed by head-winds, but
now that they are fair she will have a quick passage; at
least such I wish it. Adieu, encore.

THEODOSIA.

JOSEPH ALSTON TO THEODOSIA BURR.

Charleston, S. C. December 28th, 1800.

Aristotle says "that a man should not marry before he is
six-and-thirty:" pray, Mr. Alston, what arguments have you
to oppose to such authority? Hear me, Miss Burr.

It has always been my practice, whether from a natural
independence of mind, from pride, or what other cause I
will not pretend to say, never to adopt the opinion of any
one, however respectable his authority, unless thoroughly
convinced by his arguments; the "ipse dixit," as logicians

term it, even of Cicero, who stands higher in my estimation than any other author, would not have the least weight with me ; you must therefore, till you offer better reasons in support of his opinion than the Grecian sage himself has done, excuse my differing from him.

Objections to early marriages can rationally only arise from want of discretion or want of fortune in the parties ; now, as you very well observe, the age of discretion is wholly uncertain, some men reaching it at twenty, others at thirty, some again not till fifty, and many not at all ; of course, to fix such or such a period as the proper one for marrying, is ridiculous. Even the want of fortune is to be considered differently, according to the country where the marriage is to take place ; for though in some places a fortune is absolutely necessary to a man before he marries, there are others, as in the eastern states for example, where he marries expressly for the purpose of making a fortune. :

But, allowing both these objections their full force, may there not be a single case that they do not reach ? Suppose (*for instance, merely*) a young man nearly two-and-twenty, already of the *greatest* discretion, with an ample fortune, were to be passionately in love with a young lady almost eighteen, equally discreet with himself, and who had a " sincere friendship" for him, do you think it would be necessary to make him wait till thirty ? particularly where the friends on both sides were pleased with the match.

Were I to consider the question personally, since you allow that " individual character" ought to be consulted,.no objection clearly could be made to my marrying early.

From my father's plan of education for me, I may properly be called a hot-bed plant. Introduced from my infancy into the society of men, while yet a boy I was accustomed to think and act like a man. On every occasion, however important, I was left to decide for myself ; I do not recollect a single instance where I was controlled even by advice ; for it was my father's invariable maxim, that the

Vol. I.—H h h

best way of strengthening the judgment was to suffer it to be constantly exercised. Before seventeen I finished my college education; before twenty I was admitted to the bar. Since that time I have been constantly travelling through different parts of the United States; to what purpose I leave you to determine.

From this short account of myself you may judge whether my manners and sentiments are not, by this time, in some degree formed.

But let us treat the subject abstractedly; and, as we have shown that under particular circumstances no disadvantages result from early marriages, let us see if any positive advantages attend them.

Happiness in the marriage state, you will agree with me, can only be obtained from the most complete congeniality of mind and disposition, and the most exact similarity of habits and pursuits; now, though their natures may generally resemble, no two persons can be entirely of the same mind and disposition, the same habits and pursuits, unless after the most intimate and early association; I say *early*, for it is in youth only the mind and disposition receive the complexion we would give them; it is then only that our habits are moulded or our pursuits directed as we please; as we advance in life they become fixed and unchangeable, and instead of our governing them, govern us. Is it not *therefore* better, upon every principle of happiness, that persons should marry young, when, directed by mutual friendship, each might assimilate to the other, than wait till a period when their passions, their prejudices, their habits, &c. become so rooted that there neither exists an inclination nor power to correct them? Dr. Franklin, a very strong advocate for my system, and, I think, at least as good authority as Aristotle, very aptly compares those who marry early to two young trees joined together by the hand of the gardener;

"Trunk knit with trunk, and branch with branch intwined,
Advancing still, more closely they are join'd;

At length, full grown, no difference we see,
But, 'stead of two, behold a single tree !"*

Those, on the other hand, who do not marry till late, say " thirty," for example, he likens to two ancient oaks ;

" Use all your force, they yield not to your hand,
But firmly in their usual stations stand ;
While each, regardless of the other's views,
Stubborn and fix'd, it's natural bent pursues !"†

But this is not all ; it is in youth that we are best fitted to enjoy that exquisite happiness which the marriage state is capable of affording, and the remembrance of which forms so pleasing a link in that chain of friendship that binds to each other two persons who have lived together any number of years. ⋅ Our ideas are then more refined ; every generous and disinterested sentiment beats higher ; and our sensibility is far more alive to every emotion our associate may feel. Depend upon it, the man who does not love till " thirty" will never, never love ; long before that period, he will become too much enamoured of his own dear self to think of transferring his affections to any other object. He may marry, but interest alone will direct him in the choice of his wife ; far from regarding her as the sweetest friend and companion of his life, he will consider her but as an unavoidable encumbrance upon the estate she brings him. And can you really hope, my Theodosia, with all your ingenuity, to convince me that such a being will enjoy equal happiness in marriage with me ? with me, about to enter into it with such rapture ; who anticipate so perfect a *heaven* from our uniting in every study, improving our minds together, and informing each other by our mutual assistance and observations ? No—I give you full credit for your talents, but there are some causes so bad that even you cannot support them.

Enough, however, of this topic till we meet ; I have already given you a volume of nonsense upon it.

* Manuscript poem of my own.   † From the same.

Now for the fable, I cannot call it description, your
"dear friends" have given you of this state. "The country," they say, because of the marshy grounds, "is rendered
continually unhealthy with fever and agues." One would
really conclude from this that we were a good representation of a meeting of *Shaking Quakers.* Alas! beautiful
and romantic hills of Carolina, which the delighted traveller
so often stops to admire; fair and fertile plains interspersed
with groves of the orange, the lemon, and the myrtle, which
fling such healthful fragrance to the air, where are ye fled?
Has some earthquake, some sudden and dreadful concus-
sion of nature, ingulfed you? No! You still remain for
the delight and ornament of our country; you have lost
existence only in the imagination of some beau or belle of
New-York; who, ignorant of the geography and appearance of the most celebrated states, believes every other
place except the Park and the Battery a desert or a marsh.
But let us proceed:—"As to Charleston, an annual epidemic, joined to the yells of whipped negroes, which assail
your ears from every house, and the extreme heat, make it
a perfect purgatory!" What! is Charleston, the most de-
lightfully situated city in America, which, entirely open to
the ocean, twice in every twenty-four hours is cooled by
the refreshing seabreeze, the Montpelier of the south, which
annually affords an asylum to the planter and the West-
Indian from every disease, accused of heat and unhealthi-
ness?—Island of Calypso, where reigned perpetual spring!
may we not, after this, expect thy flower-enamelled fields
to be metamorphosed into dreary wastes of snow, and the
sweet concerts of the feathered choir, which elysionized
thy woods, converted into the howling of the tiger, or the
horrid bark of the wolf? But this is not all, unfortunate
citizens of Charleston; your disposition has been even still
more outraged than your climate. Your mildness, humanity, and benevolence, are no more; cruelty, barbarity, a
sanguinary love of torture, are now your distinguishing

characteristics; the scream, the yell of the miserable, un
resisting African, bleeding under the scourge of relentless
power, affords music to your ears! Ah! from what un
friendly cause does this arise? Has the God of heaven, in
anger, here changed the order of nature? In every other
region, without exception, in a similar degree of latitude,
the same sun which ripens the tamarind and the anana,
ameliorates the temper, and disposes it to gentleness and
kindness. In India and other countries not very different
in climate from the southern parts of the United States, the
inhabitants are distinguished for a softness and inoffensive-
ness of manners, degenerating almost to effeminacy; it is
here then, only, that we are exempt from the general influence of climate : here only that, in spite of it, we are cruel
and ferocious! Poor Carolina!

" The state of society, too, is equally inviting. The men
and women associate very little; the former employ themselves either in the business of life, or in hunting, horse-
racing, and gaming; while the latter meet in large parties,
composed entirely of themselves, to sip tea and look prim !"
Would a stranger who had been among us, who had witnessed the polished state of our society, the elegance of
our parties, the ease and sociability of manners which prevail there, the constant and agreeable intercourse between
the sexes, the accomplishments of our ladies, that proud
and elevated spirit among the men which would feel " a
stain like a wound," believe the account you have written
meant as a picture of South Carolina? Would he believe,
still further, that it was drawn by an American? No. He
would suppose it the production of some jaundiced foreign-
er, who had never visited us, and who set down every
thing out of his own country as rude and Gothic. Now I
recollect Morse gives a description something like this of
North Carolina; and I suspect your " friends" stole their
account, with a little exaggeration, from him, but mistook
the state.

I have now replied to the fable of your "dear friends" in a *veritable* style; but, setting aside rhapsody, if you have time to read it, I will give you a proper and impartial account of our country in a few words. Possibly it may serve to amuse you, if still confined by your ankle.

For about sixty or seventy miles from the seacoast, the land is, perhaps, more uninterruptedly level than any equal tract of territory in the United States; from that distance it gradually becomes more hilly, till, as you advance into the interior, you become entangled in that chain of mountains which, rising in the back parts of Pennsylvania, runs through that state, touches a corner of Maryland, and, extending through North Carolina, South Carolina, and Georgia, forms a line between the Atlantic and transatlantic states. In upper Carolina it is as healthy as anywhere on the continent. The people are robust, active, and have a colour as fine as those of Rhode Island. In the low country, it is true, we are visited by "the fevers and agues" you mention, but it is only at a particular season, and near the banks of the rivers. In this we are by no means singular; those who reside on the borders of the lakes, the Connecticut, the Delaware, and the Potomac, are equally exposed. On the seacoast we again find health; Charleston, till within a few years past, was remarkably healthy. Since '93 it has been afflicted, at different times, during the summer, with an epidemic, which has certainly proved extremely fatal; but ought it to be called an "annual visitant" here any more than at Boston, New-York, Philadelphia, Baltimore, &c., all of which places have been equally, and some of them more, afflicted by it?

With regard to our manners; if there is any state which has a claim to superior refinement, it is certainly South Carolina. Generally speaking, we are divided into but two classes, very rich and very poor; which, if no advantage in a political view, is undoubtedly favourable to a polished state of society. Our gentlemen having large fortunes, and being very little disposed by the climate to the drudgery of business or professions, have full leisure for the attainment of polite literature, and what are usually called accomplishments; you therefore meet with few of them who are not tolerably well informed, agreeable companions, and completely well bred. The possession of slaves renders them proud, impatient of restraint, and gives them a haughtiness of manner which, to those unaccustomed to them, is disagreeable; but we find among them a high sense of honour, a delicacy of sentiment, and a liberality of mind, which we look for in vain in the more commercial citizens of the northern states. The genius of the Carolinian, like the inhabitants of all southern countries, is quick, lively, and acute; in steadiness and perseverance he is naturally inferior to the native of the north; but this defect of climate is often overcome by his ambition or necessity; and, whenever this happens, he seldom fails to distinguish himself. In his temper he is gay and fond of company, open, generous, and unsuspicious; easily irritated, and quick to resent even the appearance of insult; but his passion, like the fire of the flint, is lighted up and extinguished in the same moment. I do not mention his hospitality and kindness to strangers, for they are so common they are no longer esteemed virtues; like common honesty, they are noticed only when not possessed. Nor is it for the elegance of their manners only that the South Carolinians are distinguished; sound morality is equally conspicuous among them. Gaming, so far from being a fashionable vice, is confined entirely to the lower class of people; among gentlemen it is deemed disgraceful. Many of them, it is true, are fond of the turf; but they pursue the sports of it merely as an amusement and recreation, not a business. As to hunting, the country gentlemen occasionally engage in it, but surely there is nothing criminal in this! From my education and other pursuits I have seldom participated in it myself; but I consider it, above all exercises, the most manly and healthful.

But come, let us dismiss the gentlemen and their amusements, and take up the female part of the community.

The ladies of Carolina, I confess, are not generally as handsome as those of the northern states; they want that bloom which, in the opinion of some, is so indispensable an ingredient in beauty; but their paleness gives them an appearance of delicacy and languor which is highly interesting. Their education is perhaps more attended to than anywhere else in the United States; many of them are well informed, all of them accomplished. For it would be far more unpardonable in a girl to enter a room or go through a congo ungracefully, than to be ignorant of the most common event in history or the first principles of arithmetic. They are perfectly easy and agreeable in their manners, and remarkably fond of company; no Charleston belle ever felt " ennui" in her life. In the richness of their dress and the splendour of their equipages they are unrivalled. From their early introduction into company, and their constant and unreserved intercourse with the other sex, they generally marry young; and if their husbands want only companions for the theatre or the concert-room, or some one to talk over the scandal of the day with when at home, they make tolerable wives. As we have now brought them to the " ne plus ultra" of human happiness, marriage, we will leave them there, and so finish our description.

The reason of your not hearing from me so long after your return to New-York was this: not knowing till you wrote me from Ballston how my letters would be received, I was really afraid to venture writing.

You ask how Miss P. walks? If it is your object, as you say, from knowing how you stand with her in point of forces, to preserve better what you have won, receive a general lesson. " Continue in every respect exactly as you are, and you please me most."

You wish me to acquire French. I already understand something of it, and, with a little practice, would soon speak it. I promise you, therefore, if you become my instructress, in less than two months after our marriage to converse with you entirely in that language. I fix the period *after* our marriage, for I cannot think of being corrected in the mistakes I may make by any other person than my wife. Suppose, till then, you return to your Latin, and prepare to use that tongue with me, since you are averse to one understood by all the canaille. Adieu. I have literally given you a folio volume.

Yours, my dear Theodosia,

Jos. Alston.

P. S. The arrangement you speak of proposing in your letter for an interview has determined me. I shall therefore sail certainly in a few days. Winds be propitious!
Miss Burr.

In April, 1799, the federal party were triumphant in the State of New-York. The city was entitled to thirteen members of Assembly. They were federalists, and were elected by an average majority of 944 ; the whole number of votes being about 6000. Colonel Burr during this year was not in public life, but he was not an idle spectator of passing events. The year following a President of the United States was to be elected. It was now certain, that unless the vote of the State of New-York could be obtained for Mr. Jefferson, he could not be elected. It was equally certain, that unless the city could be carried by the democratic party, the state would remain in the hands of the federalists.

During the winter of 1799 and the spring of 1800, Colonel Burr commenced a system of party organization for the approaching contest. The presidential electors were at that time chosen by the legislature, meeting in joint ballot. His first object was to secure such a committee of nomination for the city and county of New-York as, in the selection of candidates for the assembly, would be influenced by his recommendation. His opinion, often expressed to his confidential friends during the winter of 1800, was, that without a most powerful ticket there was no prospect of success; with such a ticket and proper exertions it could be elected. He entertained no doubt (and the result proved that he was correct), that on the city and county of New-York were suspended the destinies of the country, whether for good or whether for ill. These views and these opinions were presented and enforced by him for days, and weeks, and months previous to the election upon all the young and ardent politicians of the city with whom he had any intercourse. The effect of which was, that when the crisis arrived, every member of the party seemed to feel the great responsibility which rested upon him.

The next object with Colonel Burr was to inculcate harmony in the party and concert in action. It was known that a most unconquerable jealousy existed between the Clinton and Livingston families and the adherents of those factions. The Clintons and their supporters were anti-federalists. The Livingstons were not less distinguished as federalists, until some time after the organization of the general government under the new constitution. Colonel Burr enforced, in mild and persuasive terms, the necessity of sacrificing all prejudices and partialities; of surrendering all personal and ambitious considerations; of standing shoulder to shoulder, and uniting in one great effort to rescue the country from misrule. By the most unceasing perseverance he succeeded in both these objects.

Every section of the democratic party felt the necessity of Colonel Burr's being a member of the legislature that was to choose the electors; but a difficulty arose. It was understood that General Hamilton would personally attend the several polls during the three days of election; that he would counsel and advise with his political friends, and that he would address the people. Here again all seemed to feel that Colonel Burr was the man, and perhaps the only man, to meet General Hamilton on such an occasion. But if his name was on the Assembly ticket as a candidate, his personal exertions during the election would be lost to the party. To place him in that situation appeared to many like abandoning the field without a struggle to the federalists. In this dilemma, the county of Orange patriotically came forward and nominated him as a candidate on their Assembly ticket, thus leaving him free to act in the city of New-York; and by the people of Orange Colonel Burr was elected a member of the legislature.

All the details connected with the formation of the Assembly ticket in April, 1800, for the city and county of New-York, will be given hereafter. The result is known. It succeeded. The legislature was democratic. Presidential electors of the democratic party were appointed. Colonel Burr's services were appreciated by the democracy in every section of the country, and he was nominated on the ticket with Mr. Jefferson for the offices of President and Vice President of the United States. By the constitution, as it was originally adopted, the person who had the greatest number of votes, provided they were a majority of the whole number given, was president; and the person having the next highest number, with the like proviso, was vice-president. When the ballots were examined, it appeared that Mr. Jefferson and Colonel Burr were the two highest candidates, and that their votes were equal. By the provisions of the constitution, it devolved upon the House of Representatives of the United States, voting by states, to designate which of these gentlemen should be president, and which vice-president.

On proceeding to the ballot a contest ensued, which lasted for several days, producing the most implacable and bitter animosities; a contest which terminated in the election of Mr Jefferson and the ruin of Colonel Burr. Until within a few years that scene has been completely enveloped in mystery. A part of the incidents connected with it, however, in a fugitive form, are before the world. But the period has arrived when the question should be met with manly firmness ; when the voice of history should announce to posterity the truth, the whole truth, and nothing but the truth, so far as it can be ascertained. The generation which were the actors in those scenes have passed away. The parties immediately interested are sleeping the sleep of death. Few, very few indeed now living, understand the nature of that contest. The curtain shall be drawn aside. The documents which develop its character, and which are scattered in fragments, will be brought together, and recorded (it is hoped) in a permanent and tangible form.

It will be seen that the immediate friends and advisers of Mr. Jefferson, until within a few hours of the balloting, had no confidence in certain leading and distinguished members of Congress, whose names shall be given, but who, on his coming into power, promptly received the most substantial evidence of his kind feelings by appointments to office. The clearest evidence will be presented that Mr. Jefferson entered into terms and conditions with the federal party or some of their leaders ; that the honourable James A. Bayard, of Delaware, acted on the part of the federalists, and the honourable Samuel Smith, of Maryland, at present mayor of Baltimore, on the part of Mr. Jefferson ; and that terms and conditions were agreed upon between them before Mr. Jefferson could be elected ; while, on the other hand, it will be demonstrated that the charges which have been made against Colonel Burr of having intrigued and negotiated with the federal party to obtain the office of president were as unjust as they were groundless. But " *I come to bury Cesar, not to praise him.*"

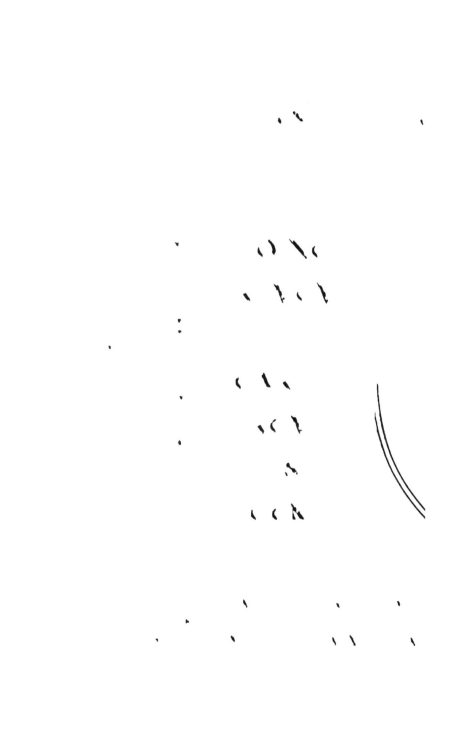